Foreign Business in China and Opportunities for Technological Innovation and Sustainable Economics

Anna Visvizi
Deree – The American College of Greece, Greece

Miltiadis Lytras
Deree – The American College of Greece, Greece

Xi Zhang
Tianjin University, China

Jie Zhao
Anhui University, China

A volume in the Advances in Finance, Accounting, and Economics (AFAE) Book Series

IGI Global
DISSEMINATOR OF KNOWLEDGE

Published in the United States of America by
IGI Global
Business Science Reference (an imprint of IGI Global)
701 E. Chocolate Avenue
Hershey PA, USA 17033
Tel: 717-533-8845
Fax: 717-533-8661
E-mail: cust@igi-global.com
Web site: http://www.igi-global.com

Library of Congress Cataloging-in-Publication Data

Names: Visvizi, Anna, 1976- editor. | Lytras, Miltiadis D., 1973- editor. | Zhang, Xi, 1982 December 28- editor.
Title: Foreign business in China and opportunities for technological innovation and sustainable economics / Anna Visvizi, Miltiadis Lytras, Xi Zhang, and Jie Zhao, editors.
Description: Hershey, PA : Business Science Reference, [2019]
Identifiers: LCCN 2018058913| ISBN 9781522589808 (hardcover) | ISBN 9781522589822 (ebook) | ISBN 9781522589815 (softcover)
Subjects: LCSH: International business enterprises--China. | Information technology--Economic aspects--China. | Sustainable development--China.
Classification: LCC HD2910 .F67 2019 | DDC 658/.0490951--dc23 LC record available at https://lccn.loc.gov/2018058913

This book is published in the IGI Global book series Advances in Finance, Accounting, and Economics (AFAE) (ISSN: 2327-5677; eISSN: 2327-5685)

British Cataloguing in Publication Data
A Cataloguing in Publication record for this book is available from the British Library.

For electronic access to this publication, please contact: eresources@igi-global.com.

Advances in Finance, Accounting, and Economics (AFAE) Book Series

ISSN:2327-5677
EISSN:2327-5685

Editor-in-Chief: Ahmed Driouchi, Al Akhawayn University, Morocco

MISSION

In our changing economic and business environment, it is important to consider the financial changes occurring internationally as well as within individual organizations and business environments. Understanding these changes as well as the factors that influence them is crucial in preparing for our financial future and ensuring economic sustainability and growth.

The **Advances in Finance, Accounting, and Economics (AFAE)** book series aims to publish comprehensive and informative titles in all areas of economics and economic theory, finance, and accounting to assist in advancing the available knowledge and providing for further research development in these dynamic fields.

COVERAGE

- Microeconomics
- Economic Downturn
- Statistical Analysis
- Public Finance
- Auditing
- Interest Rates and Annuities
- Investments and Derivatives
- Economics of Innovation and Knowledge
- Economics of Intellectual Property Rights
- Applied Finance

IGI Global is currently accepting manuscripts for publication within this series. To submit a proposal for a volume in this series, please contact our Acquisition Editors at Acquisitions@igi-global.com or visit: http://www.igi-global.com/publish/.

The Advances in Finance, Accounting, and Economics (AFAE) Book Series (ISSN 2327-5677) is published by IGI Global, 701 E. Chocolate Avenue, Hershey, PA 17033-1240, USA, www.igi-global.com. This series is composed of titles available for purchase individually; each title is edited to be contextually exclusive from any other title within the series. For pricing and ordering information please visit http://www.igi-global.com/book-series/advances-finance-accounting-economics/73685. Postmaster: Send all address changes to above address.

Titles in this Series

For a list of additional titles in this series, please visit:
https://www.igi-global.com/book-series/advances-finance-accounting-economics/73685

Organizational Auditing and Assurance in the Digital Age
Rui Pedro Marques (University of Aveiro, Portugal) Carlos Santos (University of Aveiro, Portugal) and Helena Inácio (University of Aveiro, Portugal)
Business Science Reference • ©2019 • 404pp • H/C (ISBN: 9781522573562) • US $225.00

International Firms' Economic Nationalism and Trade Policies in the Globalization Era
Harish C. Chandan (Argosy University, USA) and Bryan Christiansen (Global Research Society, LLC, USA)
Business Science Reference • ©2019 • 299pp • H/C (ISBN: 9781522575610) • US $215.00

FinTech as a Disruptive Technology for Financial Institutions
Abdul Rafay (University of Management and Technology, Pakistan)
Business Science Reference • ©2019 • 302pp • H/C (ISBN: 9781522578055) • US $195.00

The Circular Economy and Its Implications on Sustainability and the Green Supply Chain
Ulas Akkucuk (Bogazici University, Turkey)
Business Science Reference • ©2019 • 327pp • H/C (ISBN: 9781522581093) • US $215.00

Planning and Analyzing Foreign Direct Investment Projects Emerging Research ...
Halil Sarıaslan (Başkent University, Turkey)
Business Science Reference • ©2019 • 338pp • H/C (ISBN: 9781522576969) • US $215.00

Maintaining Financial Stability in Times of Risk and Uncertainty
Abhishek Behl (Indian Institute of Technology Bombay, India) and Sushma Nayak (Symbiosis International University (Deemed), India)
Business Science Reference • ©2019 • 377pp • H/C (ISBN: 9781522572084) • US $265.00

Global Trends of Modernization in Budgeting and Finance
Denis Ushakov (Suan Sunandha Rajabhat University, Thailand)
Business Science Reference • ©2019 • 354pp • H/C (ISBN: 9781522577607) • US $215.00

For an entire list of titles in this series, please visit:
https://www.igi-global.com/book-series/advances-finance-accounting-economics/73685

IGI Global
DISSEMINATOR OF KNOWLEDGE

701 East Chocolate Avenue, Hershey, PA 17033, USA
Tel: 717-533-8845 x100 • Fax: 717-533-8661
E-Mail: cust@igi-global.com • www.igi-global.com

We dedicate our work, a depiction of our commitment to enhancing collaboration among European and Chinese scholars in the spirit of trust, respect and friendship, to all academics, researchers, policy makers and industry leaders that envision social inclusive sustainable economic growth for all countries and build bridges of peace and collaboration.

Table of Contents

Section 2
Belt and Road Initiative and International Collaboration

Section 3
Technology-Driven Innovation in Belt and Road Initiative (BRI)

Detailed Table of Contents

The chapter also highlights the current state of infrastructure investment levels of participating countries. The evidence shows that most member countries lack quality infrastructure levels. The concluding part of the chapter explores economic integration among member countries. Through network analysis, it is evident that though member countries are gradually being integrated, such integration is at a slower rate than expected. Massive investment in infrastructure in China and by extension the countries along the Belt and Road would not only provide financial gains to business partners but would as well lead to an improved wellbeing of countries in the initiative. This provides an opportunity for both domestic and foreign businesses to consider massive investment in infrastructure in China, which is at the center of the initiative.

The criteria used in measuring the competition the country level, determined by the International Management Development Center in the World Competitiveness Report, are economic performance, government efficiency, business efficiency, and infrastructure. The international competitiveness of China, which is claimed to be some position with the United States in the world market in 2050, has been evaluated in this study, based on IMD competitiveness criteria. China has great progress in development through major changing strategies, methods, and reforms over the last 70 years. According to the international competition report, its rank is 13th in the international competition. The reason for China's capability on international competitiveness and its impact on the world economy is based on the fact that it combines cheap labor with the liberalization in foreign trade and foreign direct investment.

This chapter examines how the intersection of economy, politics, law, and culture in contemporary China influences the choices and alternatives of EU businesses seeking to invest in China. Although China recorded a tremendous growth of its trade volume with other countries, the institutional and regulatory frameworks of the Chinese economy have proven to be at least challenging to EU businesses. In fact, several disputes have arisen and many of them have been dealt with in the WTO Dispute Settlement Body. The chapter elaborates on one of them to explain in which ways China may not be the easiest place to conduct business.

One Belt One Road (OBOR) first declared by the China's President is believed by some to be a new hope and a new horizon for a number of developing countries. OBOR has been viewed as a new challenging proposal and as an ice breaking for the decades-long stagnant infrastructure in Indonesia, the largest economic region in Association Southeast Asian Nations (ASEAN). This chapter is an update on OBOR's recent development in Indonesian which also coincidentally was declared as a new maritime-axis when new reform government has taken into power since 2014. Many views have been released, pro-contra has been severely dispatched into two separate blocks of Indonesian experts in two standpoints, one to support and the other to challenge involving Indonesia in the OBOR. This chapter has been thoroughly analyzed by mining information and data from big data sources, combined with semi-structured interviews of various executives and contractors.

This chapter per the authors examines the feasibility of a learning analytics tool in the Chinese Higher Institutions educational environment. At first, the general definition of learning analytics is examined. Additionally, the authors shed light on case studies of universities that have already implemented learning analytics. Moreover, the Chinese educational environment is examined through a thorough analysis of the learning analytics necessity. Based on the literature review, a learning analytics tool is proposed. In a technical basis, the tool is a combination of ELLI or Effective Lifelong Learning Inventory, a dispositional learning analytics tool and a recommender system. The ultimate function of the tool is that it links students with a specific educational profile with successful students with similar profiles. Finally, the author identified the key limitations of the prototype and performed a general analysis on the tools goals and expectations in the Chinese Higher Education Institutions.

Preface

The economic growth in China is tremendous. A thorough examination of Chinese economy, business, innovation and technology seems to be more timely than ever. The Belt and Road Initiative (BRI) provides a new context for economic development, expansion and impact of the Chinese economy globally.

The subject area of this book is related to the integration of four complimentary areas:

- International Business
- Innovation and Technology Management
- Sustainability Research
- Economic Development

The overall context provides a fascinating perspective to the study of the Chinese economy through the lens of the new generation of entrepreneurship and global expansion. Moreover, this edited volume adopts and promotes an interactive exploratory strategy that aims at facilitating the processes of teaching, learning and acquisition of skills necessary to engage with business in or with China. The objective of this edited volume is two-fold:

- To serve as a leading, innovative reference edition on Chinese Business, Technology, Economy and Innovation
- To serve as a reference edition for all those interested in understanding the key aspects of the new generation of business and innovation in China

Ideally, contributions exploring diverse issues delineated by the above-mentioned research-areas, will seek to present the outcomes of the scientific inquiry in a manner conducive to their use for active learning. In this manner, this edited volume will turn into a very much sought-after reference edition for postgraduate studies and executive seminars.

SUBJECT AREAS

Sustainable economic growth, international business, collaboration and innovation are the key concepts that define the topics discussed in this volume.

This edited volume promotes a 4-tier integrative approach:

- A detailed overview of the latest developments of International Business and Innovation Management Domain
- A detailed analysis of Key Competitive Advantages and Value propositions of Chinese Economy
- A thorough discussion of Technological Innovation and Key Pillars of Economic Development in China
- Discussion of key cases studies of successful companies and lessons learnt in China

The purpose of the *Foreign Business in China and Opportunities for Technological Innovation and Sustainable Economics* is to demonstrate state-of-the art approaches of International Business and Innovation Management in China and to show how new, advanced, international business and innovation models and adoptive strategies can expand the sustainability frontiers for China. Consequently, chapters are sought that touch on these aspects and extend technical and domain knowledge in the global economy. In fact we intend to initiate a dialog between the educational, computing, business, human, and technical views of the field that effect the International Business and Innovation Domains through the adoption of novel teaching strategies.

TARGET AUDIENCE

The audience of this edited volume consists of students, educators, international business experts, innovation experts, computer engineers, scientists, and non-technical readers who are interested for innovation and entrepreneurship and international business in China and worldwide. It can be used as a reference editions for all those interested in Innovation, Emerging Technologies and International Business as well as for textbook for advanced and focused Innovation and International Business courses.

TOPICS

Topics of interest include, but are not limited to, the following scope:

Strategic Objective 1: The Emerging Agenda of Innovation Management and International Business Domain

- Technology Driven Innovation
- Business Models
- New Markets Expansion
- International Collaboration
- Distributed Production Schemas
- Multinational Companies Strategies
- Innovation Strategies
- Sustainability Research
- Smart Cities Research
- High Tech Industries Innovation
- Business Models for e-innovation
- Electronic Marketplaces
- Global Innovation Networks

Strategic Objective 2: A Detailed Analysis of Key Competitive Advantages and Value Propositions of Chinese Economy

- Mass production management in China
- Value Adding workflow integration
- Logistics and Distribution Centers
- Robotics and Industrial Automation
- Shipping Industry in China
- High Tech Industry
- Entertainment Parks in China
- Smart Cities in China

Strategic Objective 3: A Thorough Discussion of Technological Innovation and Key Pillars of Economic Development in China

- Sectoral Studies in Education, Industry, Bioinformatics, Tourism, Services Industry, Logistics, Commerce, Retailing, E-services and Applications, Mobile Systems
- Sectoral Studies in Healthcare and Biotechnology,
- Sectoral Studies in Robotics, Nanotechnology, Green Energy, Green Computing
- Sectoral Studies on Public Administration and E-Government

Strategic Objective 4: Discussion of Key Case Studies of Successful Companies and Lessons Learnt in China – Emerging Technologies Focus

- The Internet of Everything (IoE)
- E-research
- Innovations for emerging services and Systems
- Cloud Computing: SaaS, PaaS, IaaS
- Data Science and Artificial Intelligence
- Cognitive Computing
- Virtual Reality and 3D modeling
- Medical Informatics
- Smart City innovations
- Predictive Analytics Reporting (PAR) Framework, Learning, and Transfer
- Integration of Semantic Web Approaches in Educational Learning Systems
- Case Studies

Strategic Objective 5: Policy Making for Technology-Driven Innovation

- Strategic Studies
- Roadmaps
- Actions and Guidelines
- Best Practices and Lessons Learnt

ORGANIZATION OF THE BOOK

The book is the first in a series of three books planned in order to cover the five strategic objectives analyzed in the previous section. It is organized into nine chapters. In this book, authors discuss different aspects of international business, innovation management, and technology-driven innovation in the context of China's Belt and Road Initiative.

A brief overview of each of the chapters follows:

Section 1: Foundations of China's Growth, Innovation, Competitiveness, and Belt and Road Initiative Strategies

- Chapter 1. China's Economic Growth and Innovation in Globalization
- Chapter 2. One Belt One Road: Capital Investments, Economic Integration, and Growth of Participating Countries

- Chapter 3. An Analysis of China's International Competitiveness Capability
- Chapter 4. Doing Business in China: An EU Firm Perspective
- Chapter 5. Literature Survey on the "Belt and Road" Initiative: A Bibliometric Analysis

Section 2: Belt and Road Initiative and International Collaboration

- Chapter 6. China's Belt and Road Initiatives: Prospects and Challenges in the Islamic World
- Chapter 7. OBOR: A New Hope for Future Indonesian or a New Trap? Case Study in Indonesia

Section 3: Technology-Driven Innovation in Belt and Road Initiative (BRI)

- Chapter 8. Use of Learning Analytics in China: A Benchmarking model for Higher Education
- Chapter 9. Connecting One Belt One Road Countries via Wireless Sensor Network

Chapter 1 discusses China's Economic Growth and Innovation in Globalization. The purpose of this chapter is to investigate the potential long-term effects of contemporary globalization on the Chinese economy and innovation in an era of global hypercompetition. Globalization today is basically accepted as the process that removes geographical boundaries and enables the economic integration and interdependence of national economies into the international economy through trade, foreign direct investment, migration, and capital flows. Since productivity remains the critical determinant of long-term national growth and prosperity, the effects of today's globalism on productivity demands the need for business organizations in particular to sustain a competitive advantage and to remain profitable over time. Based on an integrative literature review, this chapter explores why China must continue to develop its innovation capabilities as well as to provide opportunities for foreign businesses over the long-term via responsible economic development that also benefits the nation's domestic population.

Chapter 2 discusses the Belt and Road Initiative in in the context of Capital Investments, Economic Integration and Growth of Participating Countries. This chapter starts with the need for infrastructure investment in One Belt One Road (OBOR) countries. By employing a simple linear regression analysis, it is evident that massive infrastructure could lead to an improved well-being of member countries. The chapter also highlights the current state of infrastructure investment levels of participating countries. The evidence shows that most member countries lack quality infrastructure levels. The concluding part of the chapter explores economic integration among member countries. Through network analysis, it is evident that though member countries are gradually being integrated, such integration is at a slower rate than expected. Massive investment in infrastructure in China and by extension the countries along the Belt and Road would not only provide financial gains to business partners but would as well lead to an improved well-being of countries in the Initiative. This provides an opportunity for both domestic and foreign businesses to consider massive investment in infrastructure in China which is at the center of the Initiative.

Chapter 3 is devoted to the Analysis of The China's International Competitiveness Capability. The criteria used in measuring the competition at the country level, determined by the International Management Development Center in the World Competitiveness Report are economic performance, government efficiency, business efficiency, infrastructure. The international competitiveness of China, which is claimed to be same position with the United States in the world market in 2050, has been evaluated in this study, based on IMD competitiveness criteria. China has great progress in development through major changing strategies, methods, and reforms over the last seventy years. According to the international competition report, its rank is 13th in the international competition. The reason for China's capability on international competitiveness and its impact on the world economy is based on the fact that it combines cheap labor with the liberalization in foreign trade and foreign direct investment.

Chapter 4 delivers a study on Doing Business in China from an EU firm perspective. This chapter examines how the intersection of economy, politics, laws and culture in contemporary China influences the choices and alternatives EU businesses seeking to invest in China. Although China recorded a tremendous growth of its trade volume with other countries, the institutional and regulatory frameworks of the Chinese economy have proven to be at least challenging to the EU businesses. In fact, several disputes have arisen and many of them have been discussed in the WTO Dispute Settlement Body. The chapter elaborates on one of them to explain in which ways China is not the easiest place to conduct business.

Chapter 5 summarizes authors' contribution related to a Literature Survey on the 'Belt & Road' Initiative: A Bibliometric Analysis. The purpose of this chapter is to analyze some peer-reviewed publications to find out the key research journals, contents and emerging issues of the 'B&R' Initiative led by China. Based on the tools and techniques of bibliometric approach, a total of 210 research papers were extracted systematically from the Science Direct and the Web of Science database. The research methods integrated in this chapters are: systematic literature review, bibliometric citation, authorships and affiliations, and contents analyses. This paper argues that there are growing academic interests and attentions in the B&R research across the world. The principal reasons for the increase in research in the B&R Initiative are the appearance of publications in prestigious journals, the global economic rise of China and its model of development, and the policy priorities of the government of China. The results show that a total of 32 peer-reviewed research papers were published in 10 prestigious journals.

Chapter 6 tries to determine how China's Belt and Road Initiatives will interact and integrate with Prospects and Challenges in the Islamic World. China's multi-billion dollars Belt and Road Initiative (BRI) has become a talk of the town due to the huge financial investment and economic opportunities for poor Eurasian states. BRI promises fast-track infrastructure development, transnational connectivity, unimpeded trades and calibrates economic growth in developing countries through shared development model. However, BRI has also engendered sensitive economic and security challenges. The Islamic world has warmly welcomed the BRI but China's engagement in the Islamic world also poses serious challenges to its foreign policy. This chapter aims to highlight the potential prospects and challenges related to BRI projects in the Islamic world and its implication for China's foreign policy. It also provides useful policy guideline for better execution of BRI-related projects and to evade China's possible debilitating conflict with regional and global powers.

Chapter 7 addresses the impact of BRI in the surrounding countries: OBOR, Is a New Hope for Future Indonesian or a New Trap? Study case in Indonesia. One Belt One Road (OBOR) first declared by the China's President is believed by part of people as a new hope and a new horizon for a number of developing countries. OBOR has been viewed as a new challenging proposal and as an ice breaking for the long decades of infrastructure's stagnant in Indonesia, the largest economic region in Association Southeast Asian Nations (ASEAN). This study is an update OBOR recent development in Indonesian which also coincidentally declared as a new maritime-axis when new reform government has taken in to power since 2014. Many views had been released, pro-contra had been severely dispatched into two separate blocks of Indonesian's experts in two standpoints; one to support and the other to challenge involving Indonesia in the OBOR. This study has been thoroughly analyzed by mining information and data from big data sources, combined with semi-structured interviews of various executives and contractors.

Chapter 8 provides a study about the Use of Learning Analytics in China - A Benchmarking model for Higher Education. This chapter per the authors examines the feasibility of a learning analytics tool in the Chinese Higher Institutions educational environment. At first, the general definition of learning analytics is examined. Additionally, the authors shed light on case studies of universities that have already implemented learning analytics. Moreover, the Chinese educational environment is examined through a thorough analysis of the learning analytics necessity. Based on the literature review, a learning analytics tool is proposed. In a technical basis, the tool is a combination of ELLI or Effective Lifelong Learning Inventory, a dispositional learning analytics tool, and a recommender system. The ultimate function of the tool is that it links students with a specific educational profile with successful students with similar profiles. Finally, the author identified the key limitations of the prototype and performed a general analysis on the tools goals and expectations in the Chinese Higher Education Institutions.

Chapter 9 discusses the challenge of Connecting One Belt One Road Countries via Wireless Sensor Network. The economy of China grows rapidly attributable to the advent of wireless networks. The networks provide connection between nodes (sensors, gateways, systems, people, etc.) for data transmission and communication seamlessly. This is crucial element to achieve sustainable economics. It is worth mentioning that wireless communication is the optimal solution compared with wired communication given the fact that China has huge land area and largest number of population in the world. Traditional wireless technologies like 4G, Bluetooth, ZigBee, ISA 100.11a and WirelessHART have been well addressed in literature. In this chapter, the focus is moved to 5G, Lora, IEEE 802.11 af, ah, ax and ay. Selected applications health monitoring, toxic gas monitoring, connected target coverage Problem and mobile crowd sensing are discussed in detail. Geographic routing, wireless charging and wireless coexistence are challenging issues that need to be addressed in the near future.

Miltiadis Lytras
Deree – The American College of Greece, Greece

Anna Visvizi
Deree – The American College of Greece, Greece

Xi Zhang
Tianjin University, China

Jie Zhao
Anhui University, China

Section 1

Foundations of China's Growth, Innovation, Competitiveness, and Belt and Road Initiative Strategies

Chapter 1
China's Economic Growth and Innovation in Globalization

Bryan Christiansen
https://orcid.org/0000-0001-7282-8497
Global Research Society, LLC, USA

ABSTRACT

The purpose of this chapter is to investigate the potential long-term effects of contemporary globalization on the Chinese economy and innovation in an era of global hypercompetition. Globalization today is basically accepted as the process that removes geographical boundaries and enables the economic integration and interdependence of national economies into the international economy through trade, foreign direct investment, migration, and capital flows. Since productivity remains the critical determinant of long-term national growth and prosperity, the effects of today's globalism on productivity demands the need for business organizations in particular to sustain a competitive advantage and to remain profitable over time. Based on an integrative literature review, this chapter explores why China must continue to develop its innovation capabilities as well as to provide opportunities for foreign businesses over the long-term via responsible economic development that also benefits the nation's domestic population.

DOI: 10.4018/978-1-5225-8980-8.ch001

INTRODUCTION

The nation with a global blue-water navy is the master of today's economy - Capt. Earle G. Gardner, Jr. (USN)

The purpose of this chapter is to investigate the potential long-term effects of contemporary globalization on Chinese economic growth and innovation in an era of worldwide hypercompetition. Globalization today is basically accepted as the process that removes geographical boundaries and enables the economic integration and interdependence of national economies into the international economy through trade, foreign direct investment (FDI), migration, and capital flows (Cooper, 2008). Since productivity remains the critical determinant of long-term national economic growth and prosperity in an aging world (McKinsey Global Institute, 2015; Drucker, 2002), the effects of globalism today on productivity demands the need for business organizations to sustain a competitive advantage and to remain *profitable* over time (Chatterji & Patro, 2014; Teece, 2014; Campbell, Coff, & Kryscynski, 2012; Porter, 1998). Based on an integrative literature review and personal business experience in China during various periods since 1986, this chapter explores why the country should continue to develop its innovation capabilities as well as to provide opportunities for foreign businesses over the long-term for responsible economic development that also benefits the nation's *domestic* population – a concern which should not be overlooked in any serious discussion on China (Ren, 2016; Shellekens, 2013).

This chapter is based on a key question: "Can China continue its economic growth and innovativeness developed over the past 30 years for the remainder of this century within the context of global hypercompetition?". China has undoubtedly made serious strides in its economic development since Deng Xiaoping's market-economy reforms that started in the late 1970s. However, recent events such as the current trade war with the USA or China's chronic debt problems which have developed over the years, in an attempt to maintain economic growth, underscore structural issues that could collectively inhibit future development in the world's second largest economy (CIA Factbook, 2018; Bradsher, 2018).

Anderson and Wong (2013) state that competitive advantage in the digital economy of the 21st century focuses on *intangible factors* including firm strategy and positioning, radical innovation and first mover advantages, organizational ambidexterity, network effects and externalities, transaction cost efficiency, intangible resources and competencies, and relational optimality. Global competition today is an entirely new game compared to the last century, and the future of national economies, consumers, and workers are tied to the success of regional, national, and corporate activity based largely on productivity and competitive advantage. Despite its impressive economic development since the 1980s, China is no exception in the 21st century.

Each year the World Economic Forum (WEF) ranks 144 countries in terms of a Global Competitiveness Index (GCI) which captures the fundamentals of an economy on a scale that ranges from 1 to 7. The GCI uses statistical data such as government debt and life expectancy obtained from a variety of internationally recognized agencies such as the International Monetary Fund (IMF) and the World Bank to rank nations in terms of ability to compete on a global scale. The most recent GCI ranking (2017) for China (not including Hong Kong or Taiwan) places the country at 27th in the world behind the Republic of Korea. However, it is important at this juncture to also examine China's current innovativeness standing in the world. According to a recent WEF report via data from the National Science Foundation, China is the world's second-largest spender on Research & Development (R&D) after the USA and states the former will overtake the latter in the next 5-10 years (Harris, 2018).

However, does this fact on its own really matter or is there much more involved in the long-term? Productivity, R&D expenditures, profits, debt concerns, innovativeness, trade wars, environmental problems, corruption, economic blocs (e.g., BRIC, MENA), geopolitical and military realities, sustainability, a growing global skills gap, and other issues are all a collective and sometimes contradictory mix in today's globalization. It is from a *holistic perspective* that includes these facts from which one must view the current situation in China (and elsewhere) with regards to overall economic growth (and prosperity) in this century, despite some recent writings of a new world order (Muggah & Tiberghien, 2018; World Bank, 2018a; Global Firepower, 2018; Christiansen & Kasarci, 2016; Transparency International, 2016; De Vaal & Ebben, 2011).

This chapter is organized below in the following manner. First is an integrative Literature Review covering subjects deemed most critical, within the scope of this chapter, for that holistic perspective mentioned above as it pertains specifically to China as follows (Yue, 2018; Maswood, 2018; Stiglitz, 2015):

- The Chinese economy today
- Productivity
- The growing global skills gap

- Open innovation and diversification
- Profitability and national debt
- Geopolitics and naval power
- Corruption
- Employment and poverty
- Pollution/environment

Second is an Analysis and Conclusion section followed finally by a section on Future Research Directions. The reader should note this work is to be considered as a *scholar-practitioner* effort and not solely as an academic endeavor; research demonstrates that practitioner knowledge often complements that of academics (Bartunek, 2007, p. 1327; Mohrman & Lawler, 2012). Therefore, the content (and style) of this chapter will not necessarily follow a familiar pattern common in strictly academic work. The contribution this chapter makes to the extant literature on China's economy and innovation is one of managerial applicability in the digital age.

INTEGRATIVE LITERATURE REVIEW

The International Monetary Fund (2018) ranks the Chinese economy as the second largest in the world with a value of US$14 trillion behind the USA with a value of US$20.4 trillion, which the WEF (2018) states currently amounts to more than 25% of the global economy. However, the World Bank (2018a) estimates that China will represent 35.2% of global growth in terms of real Gross Domestic Product (GDP) by 2020. Furthermore, it has been reported that China has already overtaken the size of the US economy in terms of Purchasing Power Parity (PPP) dollars (PwC, 2017).

Clearly, China is a fast-growing economic entity that cannot be dismissed on the global stage. Nonetheless, there are other issues to consider against these facts that could affect the overall long-term outcome in terms of timing and value as mentioned in the latter part of the Introduction. Jaffe (2014) states that although scientific knowledge and technical expertise promote the wealth of nations in general, the scientific productivity of a country correlates more strongly with gross national income (GNI) per capita for advanced economies than does technological sophistication, which is fundamentally more critical for currently developing nations such as China (United Nations, 2018).

However, as China transitions from a current Stage 2 (Efficiency-driven) to a Stage 3 (Innovation-driven) economy such as Australia or the European Union (EU), the country will need to become more competitive and productive than in the past;

in addition, along with this stage change normally comes higher wages associated with a higher standard of living, the need for the most efficient production processes, and – of course – superior innovation capabilities (Schwab, 2017). Can China achieve *and* sustain all of these over time, especially with regards to achieving higher and sustainable living standards for the entire country?

Productivity is not always an easy concept to define, but it is basically measured by the efficiency with which nations and organizations turn inputs into outputs via new technologies and business models, a capable workforce, and efficient management (Drucker, 2002; Bartelsman, Haltiwanger, & Scarpetta, 2013). While mainstream academia stresses that productivity is highly critical to national economic growth and corporate stability over time, recently there has actually been a global productivity slowdown recently for many of the world's largest economies (Andrews, Criscuolo, & Gal, 2016; OECD, 2016). Eichengreen (2015) highlights that Total Factor Productivity (TFP), which measures the combined productivity of capital and labor, has been basically zero for three consecutive years, thus meaning the living standards of today's young adults could possibly rise much more slowly than those of their parents if there is no major change in TFP over time. This would extend to all regions of the world, including China, and any increase would depend entirely on improvements in education and training as well as investment in equipment and structures (Eichengreen, 2015).

Linked to productivity is the growing global skills gap which is reshaping the world economy (Association for Talent Development, 2018; McKinsey Global Institute, 2012). Strains on the global labor force have become increasingly obvious over the past decade. The demand for higher-skilled workers will increase as the working age population decreases worldwide, and approximately 70% of all immigrants educated to the university level head to only four nations: Australia, New Zealand, the United Kingdom, and the USA (Hays Global Skills Index, 2017). It should be noted that 20% of all migrants in the world live in the USA (approximately 50 million people as of 2017), and until recently only one in every seven Chinese students returned to China from the USA following higher education; however, this trend has reversed substantially due to Chinese investments in higher education (especially science and engineering) and general salary levels (Pew Research Center, 2018; Pells, 2018). It should be added that global growth will be increasingly driven by investment in skills and innovation (OECD, 2016).

Open innovation is a strategy by which organizations allow a flow of knowledge across their boundaries as they seek ways to enhance their innovation capability (University of Cambridge Institute for Manufacturing, 2009). Chesbrough (2003) first introduced the concept to emphasize that firms generate, develop, build, market, and finance their ideas on their own volition. Wang et al. (2012) studied how Chinese firms have successfully used open innovation to strengthen their innovative performance, based on empirical research of 91 native Chinese firms in high-technology industries. Their research showed the innovative performance of these companies is improved by internal R&D and licensing agreements with foreign firms to obtain new technology. Furthermore, Zhang et al. (2018) examined how human capital can affect the relationship between open innovation and the financial performance of firms using evidence from the Chinese mechanical manufacturing industry. Their efforts demonstrate there is an inversed U-shape relationship between open innovation and firm performance; in addition, they generally found that the higher the education level of employees, the better the financial performance will be of the firm.

Diversification within the scope of this chapter comes in two forms: industry and international. These two aspects of diversification were chosen because they are related to ***profitability*** which is a key factor in this chapter. Wan (1998) empirically explored the relationship between industrial and international diversification of Hong Kong multinational corporations (MNCs) and found that international diversification has a positive impact on profitability stability and sales growth, but not on profitability itself. Additionally, the study determined that industrial diversification also enhances profitability stability but reduces profitability significantly. The empirical results from a study on China's Listed Energy Companies by Li et al. (2016) indicated that industrial diversification hinders corporate performance while international diversification improves the performance of renewable energy firms but hinders the performance of conventional energy firms. These studies suggest that any diversification activities should be carefully considered by Chinese organizations and the government in general.

In China profits and the growing national debt have an inverse connection. While there is good news for Chinese banks and industry regarding their net profits as of 2018, the Chinese government debt-to-GDP rose to an all-time high in 2017 of 47.60 percent (Trading Economics, 2018; McKinsey & Company, 2017). It is expected that China's national debt shall rise to a value of US$12.1 trillion by 2022 or approximately a 63% ratio of debt-to-GDP (Statista, 2018b; IMF, 2018). It should be noted here that general consensus states an optimal debt-to-GDP ratio for developing nations such as China is 40% while the same ratio for developed countries is 60% of GDP. Therefore, China will need to rein in its government (and corporate credit) debt to remain in balance in this century. Continuing its current debt ratio to the level of a developed nation could place China's debt management strategy and even the global financial system into jeopardy.

Geopolitics today is a very complex issue and usually does not follow what might best be labeled as "logical" (Christiansen & Kasarci, 2017). The Washington, DC-based international affairs organization, The Brookings Institution, recently developed a research series titled, "Order from Chaos: The New Geopolitics", which contains material related to Asia, Europe and Russia, and the Middle East. The series on Asia "analyzes the major dynamics at play in the region and and provides ideas and strategies to guide critical countries and key leaders on how they should act to preserve and renovate the established international order to secure peace and prosperity for another generation" (Brookings Institution, 2018).

Recent coverage includes issues such as the potential end of US engagement with China, North Korea's nuclear program, and the general geopolitical situation in Central Asia. What is important to highlight now is that the entire world has entered into a completely new phase of international relationships which is quite volatile, depending highly on fast-changing global events such as the first-ever meeting in 2018 between the leaders of North Korea and the USA in Singapore to discuss nuclear disarmament. In order to maintain a stable flow of goods throughout the world in such global uncertainty, it is necessary to develop and sustain a strong naval power since approximately 90% of all world trade is carried at some point by the international shipping industry with over 70% as containerized cargo (International Maritime Organization, 2018; UNCTAD, 2017).

While literature can vary somewhat with regards to global naval force strength, the current undisputed naval power in the world remains the United States Navy in that it is a *global* blue-water navy and is considered the only one in the world to date (IISS, 2018; RAND, 2018). This means the country can effectively project its naval power anywhere in the world for a continuously sustained period of time, although the US Navy has not had a direct and major confrontation since World War II with the Japanese Imperial Navy at the time. China has launched an extensive buildup of its navy for two primary reasons: 1) to challenge US maritime dominance in East Asia; and 2) to obtain great-power maritime capabilities since the country understands the value of a *global* blue-water navy (Ross, 2018). Whether or not this massive effort actually materializes over the remainder of this century is probably anybody's guess; however, it is important to understand that simply building ships for a *global* blue-water navy is not enough as it requires more than a generation to train capable admirals and commanders to lead such task forces around the world (Thomassen, 2016).

Corruption generally reduces economic development and creates inefficiencies (WEF, 2015; Blackburn, Bose, & Haque, 2006; Shleifer & Vishny, 1993; Mauro, 1995), although some literature suggests corruption helps to overcome bureaucratic constraints, rigid laws, and inefficient public services in nations with weak institutions (De Vaal & Ebben, 2011; Luo & Han, 2008; Lein, 1990). Nonetheless, while corruption is found throughout the globe at different levels, it is in the developing world such as China that the effects are the most destructive (UN, 2004); however, its effects can also be seen in developed economies (Acemoglu & Verdier, 2000). Transparency International (TI), an international non-governmental organization based in Berlin, Germany, each year produces its Corruption Perception Index (CPI) in which it ranks individual nations. Its CPI for 2016 shows that the least corrupt nations include Denmark, New Zealand, Finland, Sweden, and Switzerland (in order), while the most corrupt countries at the bottom of the index include Yemen, Syria, North Korea, and Somalia (TI, 2017). In 2017, China ranked 77 out of 180 countries listed in the CPI. Clearly, the country needs to improve its standing in the world with regards to corruption or risk its capability for sustainable development (Otusanya, 2011).

Employment and poverty have an inverse relationship, and with regards to the latter China has apparently done exceptionally well by lifting over 700 million from its grips since the 1980s (World Bank, 2016). However, it is necessary to investigate further into China's situation regarding both issues before concluding that the country is "free and clear" both economically and politically. For example, Chow (2018) states that China's war on poverty is actually in danger of turning into a war on the poor by pushing them into urban dependence outside of the already capped cities such as Beijing and Shanghai and into second- and third-tier areas like Liaocheng and Zhengzhou which often lack basic infrastructure. In addition, we must examine the meaning of poverty as it relates to today's global economy in general and in China specifically.

According to the United Nations Educational, Scientific, and Cultural Organization (UNESCO, 2018), poverty can be defined as either absolute or relative with the former referring to basic needs such as food, clothing, and shelter while the latter referring to economic status compared to other members of society. Absolute poverty has been largely eradicated in China; however, relative poverty (or economic inequality) remains an issue in the country (Asian Development Bank, 2016, 2018; Holcombe, 2017; Li, Su, & Liu, 2016; Stuart, 2015). Exactly how this is eventually achieved in a nation of over 1.4 billion people remains to be seen, but there is some mounting evidence that it can be done (Zhuang & Shi, 2016).

Within this context it is important to consider two issues: *i*) the Gini coefficient that is the most commonly used measure of inequality by economists in which a higher Gini score equates to higher inequality; and *ii*) the Kuznets Inverted U-Curve which graphs economic inequality against income per capita over the course of economic development, and is considered one of the most influential statements ever made regarding inequality and development (Catalano, Leise, & Pfaff, 2009; Melikhova & Čížek, 2014; Kuznets, 1955). The Chinese Government would be well-advised to pay close attention to these two indicators as time passes during this century.

The employment rate in China as of 2018 appears solid with a labor participation rate of 69 percent and an unemployment rate of only 3.9 percent (Statista, 2018a; Trading Economics, 2018). However, some underlying facts tell more of the story such as 8.2 million college graduates seeking suitable jobs, labor disputes, and rising wages as they relate to high employee turnover (Scheltema, 2017; Nie & Sousa-Poza, 2017; Zhai et al., 2013). The Chinese government has long been concerned about job creation and satisfaction, higher living standards, and wage levels as it should given the population of the country. As such, it is imperative for the government to monitor employment rates in the country so as not to foment civil unrest in the long-term.

The environment as it relates to pollution in China is a critical concern to the Chinese government and industry as incomes rise in the country. Evidence shows the country is starting to win its overall war on pollution, although China still lags behind international standards in air quality despite significant gains following its National Action Plan of 2013 (Greenstone & Schwarz, 2018). In addition, Currell and Han (2016) state that China's water pollution is of major concern to the world as well as the country; for example, it is reported that over 80% of the shallow groundwater in large parts of northern China is affected by pollution, thus making it undrinkable without treatment. Jiao, Xu, and Liu (2018) found in a nationwide multilevel data study that there is a nonlinear relationship between community socioeconomic status and community air pollution; in addition, the study emphasized that air pollution had the greatest impact on the lower socioeconomic groups that exist mostly outside the major cities.

It comes as no surprise there is an economic as well as a human cost to increasing worldwide air and water pollution; furthermore, the extant literature tends to show that socioeconomic status can vary the extent of the human cost by means of health care and living location among other factors. The cost to China varied among the different literature on the subject; therefore, no specific numbers will be given here.

ANALYSIS AND CONCLUSION

The globalization of today is very different from that of the past due in no small part to the speed of technological advancement and use that drives world markets

(Gates & Hemingway, 1999; Ritzer & Dean, 2015; Roberts, Hite, & Chorev, 2015), in addition to the facts and issues covered in the integrative literature review. In fact, it is not common knowledge that globalization has actually long existed (Nye, 2003). One pertinent example can include China's "Silk Road" which has existed for centuries and was developed to link China with the West at the time. World trade has increased one thousandfold since the end of World War II when modern economic globalization began (Lechner & Boli, 2015), and it is expected to continue rising during this century despite the potential effects of *de*globalization which has numerous sources such as threats to tradition and corporate lay-offs (Kobrin, 2017).

In fact, it is a somewhat ironic twist of fate that the primary source of any deglobalization is actually be the very group of nations which created the construction of an international order thus leading to globalization during the second half of the 20th century (e.g., the original G-7). Essentially, the world now has two options: 1) a backlash against globalization with economic nationalism and market segmentation; or 2) transition to a new type of globalization also referred to as "Globalization 2.0" (James, 2017). Whichever way the world turns regarding the two options above, China will most likely continue largely on its own path given the country's growing economic, military, and political strengths. However, there are consequences to "going against the global grain" in the form of economic sanctions, financial market fallout, and so forth.

It is important to realize here that China remains largely a "Middle-Income nation" despite its many billionaires and, given the characteristics of today's globalization, there is no guarantee any such country can necessarily or eventually escape the "Middle-Income Trap", which is the phenomenon of otherwise rapidly growing economies stagnating at middle-income levels and failing to eventually graduate into the ranks of high-income countries – an occurrence that is particularly common during economic growth slowdowns which China is now facing (World Bank Group, 2018; Yiping, Qin, & Xun, 2014; Aiyar et al., 2013).

One of the issues intentionally not covered in the integrative literature review due mainly to its enormous complexity is the rapidly aging global population which includes China. Chand and Tung (2014) state that aging is already very apparent in developed nations such as Japan or the USA, and is also expected to accelerate even in the developing world (e.g., Africa, parts of Asia). They also highlight that for much of world history, the elderly (those over age 65) have never exceeded 4% of a country's population. However, the Washington, DC-based Center for Strategic and International Studies estimates this percentage could reach an average of 25% by 2050. The result will be much additional pressure on national and local governments such as those in China which are already experiencing serious shortfalls to implement public policies such as pensions and unemployment benefits (WEF, 2017a). In fact, China's pension gap through 2050 is expected to grow by seven percent each year (WEF, 2017b); the social ramifications are self-evident.

It is noteworthy at this point to highlight that most nation states have failed to contend with major global challenges today, and that the 200 inter-city networks worldwide may very well be the signal of the future since half of humanity today lives in cities which power over two-thirds of global GDP. In the Future Research Directions section, we will briefly examine the major cities of the world which are taking the lead in one of the most critical aspects of economic development today: innovation.

When considering all of the factors presented in this chapter, China has numerous challenges to rise beyond a middle-income nation to join the ranks of the advanced economies such as those found in North America and the EU. Systemic and global geopolitical conflict during the first half of the 21st century will undoubtedly shape the remainder of this century (Friedman, 2009). This fact will eventually affect nearly all countries, especially those which are in transition such as China towards becoming Stage 3 innovation-driven or developed economies such as Australia, Canada, Japan, South Korea, the United Arab Emirates, and the United Kingdom (Schwab, 2016, p. 38).

The WEF classifies *Factor-driven* nations as those which compete based largely on unskilled labor and natural resources; *Efficiency-driven* countries are those which have developed efficient production processes leading to higher quality products due to increased education and training; *Innovation-driven* economies are those which are able to sustain higher living standards due to sophisticated production processes and innovation (Schwab, 2017). The critical message here is that for a national economy to develop to the point of providing a sustainable and high standard-of-living in this century, it is imperative over time to become an *Innovative-driven* entity (Aghion & Howitt, 2009).

To achieve this goal requires a regional / national economy to be diversified and to encourage creativity that translates into products and services that are desired on a global scale. China certainly has at least most of the means to achieve this goal, but it must be remembered that economic growth is beginning to slow as the working-age population shrinks and the scope for catch-up diminishes. As demand rebalances in favor of more household consumption, China must successfully implement the latest round of reforms if the country is to avoid the middle-income trap and ensure shared prosperity for all its citizens over time (OECD, 2015).

The question now is if China can effectively direct her vast resources to obtain *long-term profitability and sustainability* in order to overcome the various challenges and issues covered in this chapter? We must remember the purpose of this chapter is to explore why China must continue to develop its innovation capabilities as well as to provide opportunities for foreign businesses over the long-term via responsible economic development that also benefits the nation's domestic population.

Today's globalization has created, among other issues, at least seven major challenges the Chinese Government fundamentally must overcome in the long-term (CIA Factbook, 2018; Morrison, 2018): 1) raise productivity growth rates via efficient allocation of capital and innovation; 2) manage the country's high corporate debt burden to maintain financial stability; 3) maintain competitiveness while facilitating higher-wage job opportunities for the middle class including rural migrants and college graduates; 4) reduce a high domestic savings rate and correspondingly low domestic household consumption; 5) lower speculative investment in the real estate sector without sharply slowing the economy; 6) reduce industrial overcapacity; and 7) keep unemployment under control or risk huge civil unrest. Following are some suggestions to address at least some of the items on this list.

RECOMMENDATIONS

Below are some suggestions for China's consideration with regards to its long-term economic (and political) viability during the 21st century. The following are key long-term efforts based on a synthesis of the points outlined in this chapter.

- **Raise National Productivity:** Despite the recent global slowdown of productivity growth, it remains important for China to further develop its respective productivity levels. How this is achieved involves numerous tenets such as improved human resource management practices. Professor Michael Porter of Harvard University in the USA has long stated since publishing his book, *The Competitive Advantage of Nations*, in 1990 that prosperity is earned, not inherited. The same premise stands for productivity.
- **Address Corruption:** This chapter has addressed the issue of corruption including its long-term negative effects which is adequate mention here with regards to China.
- **Select Diversification With a Focus on Profitability and Innovation:** In general, national economies must be diversified to remain sustainable today. This is an effort which also includes moving from risk averse to higher risk

with higher reward industries such as pharmaceuticals or medical equipment for sustainable profitability. Since transitional markets such as China's are considered the most likely to lead global growth during this century, it would be advisable to develop so-called "disruptive industries" requiring innovation like smart manufacturing, cloud-to-edge computing, and 3D metal printing. The Chinese government must streamline its various bureaucracies, especially with regards to the establishment of new firms, scientific development, and international collaboration that provides opportunities for foreign companies. Essentially, China must walk something of a "fine line" between industrial and international diversification since some empirical evidence demonstrates the former can enhance profitability stability but not necessarily profitability itself, while the latter has a positive impact on profitability stability and sales growth, but not necessarily on profitability itself.

- **Increase Domestic Consumption:** The Chinese economy has long been export-oriented with relatively little attention paid to raising domestic consumption of its own products. While wages have increased significantly over the years, many of China's own products remain outside the reach of the average person due to price, especially in rural areas.
- **Continue to Develop a Global "Blue Water" Navy:** It has long been established that a strong naval presence is a foundation of economic growth and security; this is particularly true today. In his August, 2018 report to the United States Congress, Ronald O'Rourke, who is a specialist in naval affairs, stated that China has been steadily building a modern and powerful navy since the early to mid-1990s. China's navy has become a formidable military force within China's near-seas region, and it is conducting a growing number of operations in more-distant waters, including the broader waters of the Western Pacific, the Indian Ocean, and waters around Europe. China's naval modernization effort encompasses a wide array of platform and weapon acquisition programs such as anti-ship ballistic missiles (ASBMs), anti-ship cruise missiles (ASCMs), and submarines.
- **Continue to Lower Both Air and Water Pollution:** This is self-evident based on the Literature Review as well as any cursory examination of this topic in the extant literature or via qualified search on the Internet. As mentioned above, the country has made good strides towards these goals but much more remains to be done to meet international standards.
- **Decrease or at Least Limit the National Debt While Refraining From Continuing the Country's "Debt Trap" With Other Nations:** Statista (2018) reports that China's national debt will amount to over US$7 trillion

> in 2018 increasing to over US$12 trillion by the end of 2022. Prudent macroeconomic policies combined with productivity-enhancing structural reforms should allow the country to manage its fiscal issues while concurrently addressing growth-related reforms. Additionally, one of the related issues is China's "debt trap diplomacy" with other nations otherwise referred to as China's "Belt and Road Initiative". This entails China supporting large infrastructure projects in strategically located developing countries by extending enormous loans to their governments with the ulterior motive of gaining long-term influence over their economies and politics. Djibouti, Sri Lanka, Kyrgyzstan, Laos, Pakistan, Mongolia, and Tajikistan are some of the prime examples of this initiative. However, the plan could very well backfire for China in the wake of the country's own sovereign indebtedness leading to unrest at home.

What must be understood above all is that the global geopolitical and economic situation the world faces in 2018 has not been seen since before World War II (Krugman, 2009; SIC, 2017). Worldwide destabilizing events are currently impacting the entire globe far beyond simple economics and politics (e.g., the globalization of society). Examples of such events can include the growing militarization of foreign policy, continued conflict in the Middle East and the Ukraine, erosion of multilateral trading agreements, and even international cybersecurity attacks. The main message here is that the ever-changing global landscape creates a cascade of unexpected outcomes on national fortunes, including China's, which can easily disrupt even the best laid and well-intentioned plans.

Of special note for the reader to consider is the potential partnership between China and Russia over the coming years despite their long-standing mutual suspicion of each other. These two nations collectively possess great strength in the combined form of human and natural resources, innovation, technological development, and exporting power. It is possible these two nations working together could diminish many of the negative effects of contemporary globalization which is fast approaching its next natural stage of development (Sheffield, Korotayev, & Grinin, 2013). One poignant example regarding their collaboration can be found in the Chinese protest with the USA in September, 2018 over the former's purchase of Russian Sukhoi Su-35 fighter jets and S-400 surface-to-air missile systems. If history has taught humanity anything over time, it is that strange bedfellows can often create unusual circumstances in an unsuspecting world. As mentioned earlier in this chapter, geopolitics normally does not follow logical paths.

FUTURE RESEARCH DIRECTIONS

There are several suggested research directions based on this chapter that would be useful for future benefit by academics and practitioners alike. First is the development of an algorithm or related mathematical formula to quantify the combination of issues raised in this chapter. The purpose of this chapter has largely been to investigate the potential effects of contemporary globalism on China; however, this effort requires further exploration to include a *quantifiable* outcome. Therefore, enlisting the assistance of mathematical experts would enhance the work covered in this chapter and provide new insights for future research.

Examining the development of innovative cities today would help national and local governments in China to further develop their own. To date no Chinese city ranks in the Top 10 of the "Innovative Cities Index 2018"; in fact, Hong Kong ranks 27 while Shanghai ranks 35 on this list (Innovation Cities Program, 2018). Other cities such as London, New York, Tokyo, Los Angeles, and Singapore should be investigated to see why these have made the top of the list and implement a plan for China.

Investigating the "Middle-income Trap" as it relates to China would be very helpful to prevent the region's major cities from falling into, and remaining in, this conundrum that has afflicted numerous other areas of the world in the past and present. The growth rates of transition economies such as China's typically slow down substantially at GDP per capita incomes in current prices of US$10,000 - $15,000 after which future development becomes exceedingly difficult to achieve. China today has a GDP per capita income in current prices of approximately US$10,000 at the end of 2018 and is expected to reach just over US$15,000 by 2023 (Statista, 2018b).

Since innovation is one of the key components of sustainability in the 21st century, it would be of significant interest to further investigate the influence of language structure on innovation. Berman, Mudambi, and Shoham (2017) have conducted some studies on language structure and its effects on innovation, but they state more research should be done to support their findings. The Chinese language is considered one of the most difficult in the world and does not as easily integrate foreign concepts as some other languages like Japanese via its *kana* syllabary, which is largely believed to have allowed Japan to rapidly develop its massive military power before World War II because of long-term incorporation of foreign scientific and technological concepts from Europe and the USA at the time.

Finally, it would be worthwhile to analyze why global productivity has dropped in recent years and apply the observations or results to the Chinese economy via simulation of different scenarios. While there is argument among academicians and practitioners as to why this phenomenon has occurred, it is known that productivity-enhancing reform will be a key driver of long-term growth and jobs on a global scale as has been mentioned throughout this chapter.

REFERENCES

Acemoglu, D., & Verdier, T. (2000, March). The Choice between Market Failures and Corruption. *The American Economic Review*, *90*(1), 194–211. doi:10.1257/aer.90.1.194

Aghion, P., & Howitt, P. (2009). *The economics of growth*. Cambridge, MA: The MIT Press.

Aiyar, S., Duval, R., Puy, D., Wu, Y., & Zhang, L. (2013). *Growth Slowdowns and the Middle-Income Trap*. International Monetary Fund Working Paper, WP/13/71, Asia and Pacific Department.

Andersen, B., & Wong, D. (2013, February). *The new normal: Competitive advantage in the digital economy*. London: Big Innovation Centre. Retrieved on June 2, 2018, from: http://www.biginnovationcentre.com/Assets/Docs/The%20New%20Normal.pdf

Andrews, D., Criscuolo, C., & Gal, P. N. (2016, September). *The Global Productivity Slowdown, Technology Divergence and Public Policy: A Firm Level Pespective*. Hutchins Center Working Paper #24, Brookings Institution.

Asian Development Bank. (2016). *Reducing Income Inequality in the People's Republic of China*. Retrieved on September 15, 2018, from: https://www.adb.org/publications/reducing-income-inequality-prc

Asian Development Bank. (2018). *Poverty in the People's Republic of China*. Retrieved on September 15, 2018, from: https://www.adb.org/countries/prc/poverty

Association for Talent Development. (2018). *2018 Workplace Learning Report*. Retrieved on August 14, 2018, from: https://www.cornerstoneondemand.com/sites/default/files/partner/asset/files/linkedin-learning-workplace-learning-report-2018.pdf

Bartelsman, E., Haltiwanger, J., & Scarpetta, S. (2013). Cross-country Differences in Productivity: The Role of Allocation and Selection. *The American Economic Review*, *103*(1), 305–334. doi:10.1257/aer.103.1.305

Bartunek, J. M. (2007). Academic-practitioner collaboration need not require joint or relevant research: Toward a relational scholarship of integration. *Academy of Management Journal*, *50*(6), 1323–1333. doi:10.5465/amj.2007.28165912

Berman, A., Mudambi, R., & Shoham, A. (2017). Language Structure and Its Effects on Innovation. *Academy of International Business Insights, 17*(4), 14–17.

Blackburn, K., Bose, N., & Haque, M. E. (2006). The incidence and persistence of corruption in economic development. *Journal of Economic Dynamics & Control, 30*(12), 2447–2467. doi:10.1016/j.jedc.2005.07.007

Bradsher, K. (2018, August 23). As Trade War Intensifies, China Moves to Bolster Its Economy. *New York Times*. Retrieved on September 2, 2018, from: https://www.nytimes.com/2018/08/23/business/china-economy-trade.html

Brookings Institution. (2018). *The New Geopolitics of Asia*. Retrieved on September 3, 2018, from: https://www.brookings.edu/series/the-new-geopolitics-of-asia/

Campbell, B. A., Coff, R., & Kryscynski, D. (2012). Rethinking Sustained Competitive Advantage from Human Capital. *Academy of Management Review, 37*(3), 376–395. doi:10.5465/amr.2010.0276

Catalano, M. T., Leise, T. L., & Pfaff, T. J. (2009). Measuring Resource Inequality: The Gini Coefficient. *Numeracy, 2*(2), 1–22. doi:10.5038/1936-4660.2.2.4

Chand, M., & Tung, R. L. (2014). The Aging of the World's Population and Its Effects on Global Business. *The Academy of Management Perspectives, 28*(4), 409–429. doi:10.5465/amp.2012.0070

Chatterji, A., & Patro, A. (2014). Dynamic Capabilities and Managing Human Capital. *The Academy of Management Perspectives, 28*(4), 395–408. doi:10.5465/amp.2013.0111

Chesbrough, H. W. (2003). *Open Innovation: The New Imperative for Creating and Profiting from Technology*. Cambridge, MA: Harvard Business School Press.

Chow, E. K. (2018, January 8). China's War on Poverty Could Hurt the Poor Most. *Foreign Policy*. Retrieved on September 17, 2018, from: https://foreignpolicy.com/2018/01/08/chinas-war-on-poverty-could-hurt-the-poor-most/

Christiansen, B., & Kasarci, F. (2016). *Corporate Espionage, Geopolitics, and Diplomacy Issues in International Business*. Hershey, PA: IGI Global.

CIA Factbook. (2018). *China*. Retrieved on August 31, 2018, from: https://www.cia.gov/library/publications/the-world-factbook/geos/ch.html

Cooper, R. N. (2008, Summer). Global Imbalances: Globalization, Demography, and Sustainability. *The Journal of Economic Perspectives*, *22*(3), 93–112. doi:10.1257/jep.22.3.93

Currell, M. J., & Han, D. (2016). The Global Drain: Why China's Water Pollution Problems Should Matter to the Rest of the World. *Environment*, *59*(1), 16–29. doi:10.1080/00139157.2017.1252605

De Vaal, A., & Ebben, W. (2011). Institutions and the Relation Between Corruption and Economic Growth. *Review of Development Economics*, *15*(1), 108–123. doi:10.1111/j.1467-9361.2010.00596.x

Drucker, P. (2002). *Management Challenges for the 21st Century*. New York: Butterworth-Heinemann.

Eichengreen, B. (2015). Secular Stagnation: The Long View. *The American Economic Review*, *105*(5), 66–70. doi:10.1257/aer.p20151104

Friedman, G. (2009). *The Next 100 Years: A Forecast for the 21st Century*. New York: Anchor.

Gates, B., & Hemingway, C. (1999). *Business at the speed of thought*. New York: Warner Books. doi:10.1111/1467-8616.00097

Global Firepower. (2018). *2018 Military Strength Ranking*. Retrieved on June 2, 2018, from: https://www.globalfirepower.com/countries-listing.asp

Greenstone, M., & Schwarz, P. (2018, March). *Is China Winning its War on Pollution*? Chicago: Energy Policy Institute at the University of Chicago.

Harris, B. (2018, February 7). *China is an innovation superpower. This is why*. Retrieved on September 2, 2018, from: https://www.weforum.org/agenda/2018/02/these-charts-show-how-china-is-becoming-an-innovation-superpower/

Hays Global Skills Index. (2017). *Regional Dynamics of the Global Labour Market: Skills in Demand and Tomorrow's Workforce*. London: Hays PLC.

Holcombe, A.N. (2017, June). *Can China Reduce Entrenched Poverty in Remote Ethnic Minority Regions? Lessons from Successful Poverty Alleviation in Tibetan Areas of China During 1998-2016*. Cambridge, MA: Harvard Kennedy School.

Innovation Cities Program. (2018). *Innovation Cities Index*. Retrieved on September 25, 2018, from: https://www.innovation-cities.com/innovation-cities-index-2018-global/13935/

International Institute of Strategic Studies (IISS). (2018). *The Military Balance 2018*. Retrieved on September 1, 2018, from: https://www.iiss.org/publications/the-military-balance/the-military-balance-2018

International Maritime Organization. (2018). *IMO Profile*. Retrieved on September 17, 2018, from: https://business.un.org/en/entities/13

International Monetary Fund (IMF). (2018). *IMF DataMapper.* Retrieved on September 10, 2018, from: https://www.imf.org/external/datamapper/NGDP_RPCH@WEO/OEMDC/ADVEC/WEOWORLD

Jaffe, K. (2014). The Relevance of Science in Development: Scientific Development Favors Economic Prosperity, But Not Necessarily through its Effect on Technological Knowledge in Middle Income Countries. In B. Christiansen & M. Basilgan (Eds.), *Economic Behavior, Game Theory, and Technology in Emerging Markets* (pp. 1–17). Hershey, PA: IGI Global. doi:10.4018/978-1-4666-4745-9.ch001

James, H. (2017, June). *Deglobalization as a Global Challenge*. Ontario, Canada: Center for International Governance Innovation.

Jiao, K., Xu, M., & Liu, M. (2018). Health status and air pollution-related socioeconomic concerns in urban China. *International Journal for Equity in Health, 17*(18), 1–11. PMID:29402280

Kobrin, S. J. (2017). Bricks and Mortar in a Borderless World: Globalization, the Backlash, and the Multinational Enterprise. *Global Strategy Journal*, *7*(2), 159–171. doi:10.1002/gsj.1158

Krugman, P. (2009). *The Return of Depression Economics and the Crisis of 2008*. New York: W.W. Norton & Company.

Kuznets, S. (1955). Economic Growth and Income Inequality. *The American Economic Review*, *45*(1), 1–28.

Lechner, F. J., & Boli, J. (2015). *The Globalization Reader* (5th ed.). New York: Wiley-Blackwell.

Lein, D.-H. D. (1990). Corruption and allocation efficiency. *Journal of Development Economics*, *33*(1), 153–164. doi:10.1016/0304-3878(90)90013-2

Li, Y., Su, B., & Liu, Y. (2016). Realizing targeted poverty alleviation in China. *China Agricultural Economic Review*, *8*(3), 443–454. doi:10.1108/CAER-11-2015-0157

Luo, Y., & Han, B. (2008). Graft and businesses in emerging economies: An ecological perspective. *Journal of World Business*, *44*(3), 225–237. doi:10.1016/j.jwb.2008.08.006

Maswood, S. J. (2018). *Revisiting Globalization and the Rise of Global Production Networks*. New York: Palgrave Macmillan. doi:10.1007/978-3-319-60294-3

Mauro, P. (1995). Corruption and growth. *The Quarterly Journal of Economics*, *110*(3), 681–712. doi:10.2307/2946696

McKinsey & Company. (2017, December). *What can we expect in China in 2018?* Retrieved on September 15, 2018, from: https://www.mckinsey.com/featured-insights/china/what-can-we-expect-in-china-in-2018

McKinsey Global Institute. (2012, March). *Help wanted: The future of work in advanced economies*. Retrieved on June 1, 2017, from: https://www.mckinsey.com/~/media/McKinsey/Featured%20Insights/Employment%20an d%20Growth/Future%20of%20work%20in%20advanced%20economies/Help_wanted_future_of_work_full_report.ashx

McKinsey Global Institute (2015, January). *Global Growth: Can Productivity Save the Day in An Aging World?* New York: McKinsey & Company.

Melikhova, O., & Čížek, J. (2014). Kuznets Inverted U-Curve Hypothesis Examined on Up-to-Date Observations for 145 Countries. *Prague Economic Papers*, *3*(3), 388–410. doi:10.18267/j.pep.490

Mohrman, S. A., & Lawler, E. E. III. (2012, February). Generating Knowledge that Drives Change. *The Academy of Management Perspectives*, *26*(1), 41–51. doi:10.5465/amp.2011.0141

Morrison, W.M. (2018, February 5). *China's Economic Rise: History, Trends, Challenges, and Implications for the United States*. Washington, DC: Congressional Research Service.

Muggah, R., & Tiberghien, Y. (2018, January 30). *5 facts you need to understand the new global order*. Retrieved on August 19, 2018, from: https://www.weforum.org/agenda/2018/01/five-facts-you-need-to-understand-the-new-global-order

Nie, P., & Sousa-Poza, A. (2017, August). *What Chinese Workers Value: An Analysis of Job Satisfaction, Job Expectations, and Labor Turnover in China*. IZA Institute of Labor Economics, Discussion Paper Series No. 10963, Bonn, Germany.

Nye, J. S. (2003). *The Paradox of American Power: Why the World's Only Superpower Can't Go It Alone*. Oxford, UK: Oxford University Press. doi:10.1093/0195161106.001.0001

O'Rourke, R. (2018, August 1). *China Naval Modernization: Implications for U.S. Navy Capabilities—Background and Issues for Congress*. Washington, DC: Congressional Research Service.

OECD (2015, March). *China in a changing global environment*. Paris: OECD.

OECD. (2016). *OECD Science, Technology, and Innovation Outlook 2016*. Paris: OECD.

Otusanya, O. J. (2011). Corruption as an obstacle to development in developing countries: A review of literature. *Journal of Money Laundering Control*, *4*(4), 387–422. doi:10.1108/13685201111173857

Pells, R. (2018, March 1). *China's Brain Drain is Ending*. Retrieved on September 14, 2018, from: https://www.insidehighered.com/news/2018/03/01/experts-see-end-sight-chinas-brain-drain

Pew Research Center. (2018, February 28). *Origins and Destinations of the World's Migrants, 1990-2017*. Retrieved on September 14, 2018, from: http://www.pewglobal.org/2018/02/28/global-migrant-stocks/?country=US&date=2017

Porter, M. E. (1998). *Competitive Advantage: Creating and Sustaining Superior Performance*. New York: Free Press. doi:10.1007/978-1-349-14865-3

PriceWaterhouseCoopers (PwC). (2017, February). *The Long View: How will the global economic order change by 2050?* Retrieved on June 21, 2018, from: https://www.pwc.com/gx/en/world-2050/assets/pwc-world-in-2050-summary-report-feb-2017.pdf

RAND Corporation. (2018). *Corporate Website*. Retrieved on August 2, 2017, from: https://www.rand.org/

Ren, H. (2016). *Narratives of Worker's Resistance*. Chicago: Haymarket Books.

Ritzer, G., & Dean, P. (2015). *Globalization: A Basic Text* (2nd ed.). Malden, MA: Wiley Blackwell.

Roberts, J. T., Hite, A. B., & Chorev, N. (2015). *The Globalization and Development Reader: Perspectives on Development and Global Change* (2nd ed.). Chicester, UK: John Wiley & Sons.

Ross, R. S. (2018). Nationalism, Geopolitics, and Naval Expansionism: From the Nineteenth Century to the Rise of China. *Naval War College Review*, *71*(4), 17–50.

Scheltema, C. (2017, September 18). China Employment and Labor Disputes: Anticipate the Unexpected, Act to Prevent Disruption. *China Briefing*. Retrieved on September 17, 2018, from: http://www.china-briefing.com/news/2017/09/18/china-employment-and-labor-disputes-anticipate-the-unexpected-act-to-prevent-disruption.html

Schwab, K. (2017). *The Global Competitiveness Report 2017-2018*. Geneva: World Economic Forum.

Sheffield, J., Korotayev, A., & Grinin, L. (2013). *Globalization: Yesterday, Today, and Tomorrow*. Litchfield Park, AZ: Emergent Publications.

Shellekens, P. (2013, May). *A Changing China: Implications for Developing Countries*. New York: The World Bank.

Shliefer, A., & Vishny, R. W. (1993). Corruption. *The Quarterly Journal of Economics*, *108*(3), 599–617. doi:10.2307/2118402

Statista. (2018a). *Employment in China – Statistics and Facts*. Retrieved on September 8, 2018, from: https://www.statista.com/topics/1317/employment-in-china/

Statista. (2018b). *China: Gross domestic product (GDP) per capita in current prices from 2013 to 2023 (in US dollars)*. Retrieved on September 23, 2018, from: https://www.statista.com/statistics/263775/gross-domestic-product-gdp-per-capita-in-china/

Stiglitz, J. E. (2015). *Globalization and its discontents*. New York: Penguin.

Strategic Investment Conference (SIC). (2017). *Paradigm Shift: A Destabilizing World*. Omni Orlando Resort.

Stuart, E. (2015, August 19). China has almost wiped out urban poverty. Now it must tackle inequality. *The Guardian*. Retrieved on September 3, 2018, from: https://www.theguardian.com/business/economics-blog/2015/aug/19/china-poverty-inequality-development-goals

Teece, D. J. (2014). The Foundations of Enterprise Performance: Dynamic and Ordinary Capabilities in an (Economic) Theory of Firms. *The Academy of Management Perspectives*, *28*(4), 328–352. doi:10.5465/amp.2013.0116

Thomassen, D. (2016, November). Russian Blue-Water Navy is a Pipe Dream. *U.S. Naval Institute Proceedings*, *142*(11). Retrieved on September 17, 2018, from: https://www.usni.org/magazines/proceedings/2016-11/russian-blue-water-navy-pipe-dream

Trading Economics. (2018). *China Employed Persons*. Retrieved on September 10, 2018, from: https://tradingeconomics.com/china/employed-persons

Transparency International (TI). (2017). *Corruption Perceptions Index 2016*. Retrieved on July 27, 2018, from: https://www.transparency.org/news/feature/corruption_perceptions_index_2017

UNESCO. (2018). *Poverty*. Retrieved on September 17, 2018, from: http://www.unesco.org/new/en/social-and-human-sciences/themes/international-migration/glossary/poverty/

United Nations Conference on Trade and Development (UNCTAD). (2017). *Review of Maritime Transport, 2017*. Geneva: United Nations. Retrieved on August 13, 2018, from: http://unctad.org/en/pages/PublicationWebflyer.aspx?publicationid=1890

United Nations (UN). (2018). *World Economic Situation and Prospects*. Retrieved on September 11, 2018, from: https://www.un.org/development/desa/dpad/wp-content/uploads/sites/45/publication/WESP2018_Full_Web-1.pdf

University of Cambridge Institute for Manufacturing. (2009). *How to implement open innovation. Lessons from studying large multinational companies*. Cambridge, UK: Institute for Manufacturing.

Wan, C.-C. (1998). International Diversification, Industrial Diversification and Firm Performance of Hong Kong MNCs. *Asia Pacific Journal of Management, 15*(2), 205–217. doi:10.1023/A:1015489514744

Wang, Y., Roijakkers, N., Vanhaverbeke, W., & Chen, J. (2012). How Chinese firms employ open innovation to strengthen their innovative performance. *International Journal of Technology Management, 59*(3/4), 235–354. doi:10.1504/IJTM.2012.047245

World Bank. (2018a). *Where is global growth happening*? Retrieved on September 4, 2018, from: http://www.visualcapitalist.com/chart-global-growth-happening/

World Bank Group. (2018). *The World Bank in China*. Retrieved on September 22, 2018, from: http://www.worldbank.org/en/country/china/overview

World Economic Forum (WEF). (2015). *How does corruption affect economic growth*? Retrieved on June 18, 2017, from: https://www.weforum.org/agenda/2015/05/how-does-corruption-affect-economic-growth/

World Economic Forum (WEF). (2017a). *Global Competitive Index 2017-2018*. Retrieved on July 3, 2018, from: http://www3.weforum.org/docs/GCR2017-2018/04Backmatter/TheGlobalCompetitivenessReport2017%E2%80%932018AppendixB.pdf

World Economic Forum (WEF). (2017b). *5 things you need to know about the global pension crisis*. Retrieved on August 3, 2018, from: https://www.weforum.org/agenda/2017/05/5-things-you-need-to-know-about-the-global-pension-crisis/

World Economic Forum (WEF). (2017c). *Global Pension Timebomb: Funding Gap Set to Dwarf World GDP*. Retrieved on August 31, 2018, from: https://www.weforum.org/press/2017/05/global-pension-timebomb-funding-gap-set-to-dwarf-world-gdp/

World Economic Forum (WEF). (2018). *The World's Biggest Economies in 2018*. Retrieved on July 30, 2018, from: https://www.weforum.org/agenda/2018/04/the-worlds-biggest-economies-in-2018/

Yiping, H., Qin, G., & Xun, W. (2014). Financial liberalization and the middle-income trap: What can China learn from the cross-country experience? *China Economic Review, 31*, 426–440. doi:10.1016/j.chieco.2014.04.009

Yue, J. (2018). *China's Rise in the Age of Globalization*. New York: Palgrave Macmillan. doi:10.1007/978-3-319-63997-0

Zhai, Q., Willis, M., O'Shea, B., Zhai, Y., & Yang, Y. (2013). Big Five personality traits, job satisfaction and subjective wellbeing in China. *International Journal of Psychology*, *48*(6), 1099–1108. doi:10.1080/00207594.2012.732700 PMID:23075216

Zhang, S., Yang, D., Qiu, S., Bao, X., & Li, J. (2018). Open innovation and firm performance: Evidence from the Chinese mechanical manufacturing industry. *Journal of Engineering and Technology Management*, *48*, 76–86. doi:10.1016/j.jengtecman.2018.04.004

Zhuang, J., & Shi, L. (2016, July). *Understanding recent trends in income inequality in the People's Republic of China* (ADB Economics Working Paper Series No. 489). Mandaluyong City, Philippines: Asian Development Bank.

ADDITIONAL READING

Chatzoglou, P., & Chatzoudes, D. (2018). The role of innovation in building competitive advantages: An empirical investigation. *European Journal of Innovation Management*, *21*(1), 44–69. doi:10.1108/EJIM-02-2017-0015

De Jong, M., Marston, N., & Roth, E. (2015). The eight essentials of innovation. *The McKinsey Quarterly*, (April): 1–12.

Denktas, S., Karatas-Cetin, C., & Saatgioğlu, O. Y. (2014). Discovering the Nexus Between Market Orientation and Open Innovation: A Grounded Theory Approach. In B. Christiansen, S. Yildiz, & E. Yildiz (Eds.), *Transcultural Marketing for Radical and Incremental Innovation* (pp. 1–43). Hershey, PA: IGI Global. doi:10.4018/978-1-4666-4749-7.ch001

Godart, F. C., Maddux, W. W., Shipilov, A. V., & Galinsky, A. D. (2015). Fashion With a Foreign Flair: Professional Experiences Abroad Facilitate The Creative Innovations of Organizations. *Academy of Management Journal*, *58*(1), 195–220. doi:10.5465/amj.2012.0575

KEY TERMS AND DEFINITIONS

Disruptive Technologies: Technologies which significantly alter the manner in which businesses or entire industries operate.

Gini Coefficient: A measure of statistical dispersion intended to represent the income or wealth distribution of a nation's residents, and is the most commonly used measurement of inequality.

Globalization: The process that removes geographical boundaries and enables the economic integration and interdependence of national economies into the international economy through trade, foreign direct investment, migration, and capital flows.

Innovative Cities Index: A benchmark of the world's top cities with regards to innovation.

Kuznets Curve: The hypothesis that as an economy develops, market forces first increase and then decrease economic inequality.

Productivity: The effectiveness of productive effort, especially in industry, as measured in terms of the rate of output per unit of input.

Chapter 2
One Belt One Road:
Capital Investments, Economic Integration, and Growth of Participating Countries

John Boamah
https://orcid.org/0000-0003-4586-9896
Xiamen University, China

Michael Appiah-Kubi
https://orcid.org/0000-0001-5243-1847
Xiamen University, China

ABSTRACT

This chapter starts with the need for infrastructure investment in One Belt One Road (OBOR) countries. By employing a simple linear regression analysis, it is evident that massive infrastructure could lead to an improved wellbeing of member countries. The chapter also highlights the current state of infrastructure investment levels of participating countries. The evidence shows that most member countries lack quality infrastructure levels. The concluding part of the chapter explores economic integration among member countries. Through network analysis, it is evident that though member countries are gradually being integrated, such integration is at a slower rate than expected. Massive investment in infrastructure in China and by extension the countries along the Belt and Road would not only provide financial gains to business partners but would as well lead to an improved wellbeing of countries in the initiative. This provides an opportunity for both domestic and foreign businesses to consider massive investment in infrastructure in China, which is at the center of the initiative.

DOI: 10.4018/978-1-5225-8980-8.ch002

INTRODUCTION

In a capital-intensive project like One Belt One Road (OBOR) Initiative – also referred to as the Initiative, the benefits and risks involved are quite huge. This Initiative brings together China Central Asia, Russia, Central, Eastern and Western Europe, Southeast Asia, South Asia and East Africa. Estimates suggest that the Initiative seeks to encompass more than 60% of emerging market economies with a total population of over 4 billion (Swaine, 2015). It is a grand plan for China's economic integration with various parts of the world (Du & Zhang, 2017). Becoming part of such an Initiative is expected to lead to massive infrastructure investment inflows into the joining country. The welfare of such a country is expected to improve. Countries which hitherto had little link with China will subsequent to joining the Initiative experience expansion of trade as a result of the expected improvement of transportation infrastructure as a result of the Initiative (Herrero & Xu, 2016).

After almost five years of it coming into force, it is important to highlight the impact the Belt and Road Initiative has had on member countries and the potentials for future developments. Villafuerte et al. (2016) in a simulated analysis of the Initiative after assuming reductions in international road and sea transport margins, as well as iceberg trading costs in the Initiative's member countries, find that the Initiative brought large but uneven benefits to its members. Zhai (2018) suggests that the countries within the Initiative would gain significantly from the expansion of regional infrastructure in transport and communication. Countries within the Initiative with an expected investment of $1.4 trillion in regional infrastructure during the period of 2015-2030 are likely to enjoy welfare gains of 2.9% of GDP with a spillover effect of a boost in global trade of about 5.6% expansion in 2030.

In this chapter, capital and bilateral investments among participating countries and how the economies of participating firms have fared since the inception of the Initiative are empirically discussed. Findings suggest that this integration, with regards to bilateral investments, is being achieved but rather at a slower pace than expected. This chapter would, among other things, highlight the trends in capital investments, explain the level of economic integration among member countries and explain the trends in the growth rate of participating countries.

ECONOMIC GROWTH OF OBOR COUNTRIES

The study of growth of member countries is important as it will help to understand how member countries have fared since joining the Initiative. Though the Initiative is still at its infant state (about five years old), the findings would suggest the possible effect and suggest strength that demands attention to help in the mutual benefit of participating countries (Huang, 2016).

In classical growth models, the GDP growth of countries is modeled as being dependent on other growth determinants. Not only is it important to understand the growth potentials of member countries, it is equally important to understand the well-being of citizens of member countries. In basic economic sense, one single measure of the well-being of people is GDP per capita. Scaled by the population level, we are able to understand, in terms of per person, how the citizens of nationals compare to each other.

To understand relationship between growth and capital investment, we model GDP per capita as being dependent on two determinants; infrastructure score and Gross Fixed Capital Formation (GFCF). These measures are meant to highlight the possible effect of capital investments on the growth of OBOR countries. An Initiative like OBOR has at its core infrastructure investments (Du and Zhang 2017). One best way to understand the impact of the project and to also highlight the possible impact of the policy is to understand the possible impact of infrastructure on member countries. Table 1 presents average of three key variables, GDP growth levels, GDP per capita and Gross Fixed Capital Formation.

The minimum level of gross fixed capital formation is about $109 billion while the average growth level of member countries is about 3.8% (see note 1 for list of member countries). This highlight high levels income inequality among participating countries.

Model and Estimation Strategy

The relationship between growth of nations and the level of infrastructure is very important. To understand how infrastructure levels impact growth, the authors proxy

Table 1. Average GDP growth, per capita and gross fixed capital formation

Variable	Mean	Std. Dev.	Minimum	Maximum
GDP growth rate (%)	3.769838	7.070986	-62.07592	123.139
GDP per capita ($)	11236.4	13844.12	341.3099	88564.82
Gross Fixed Capital Formation ($m)	109,000	506,000	310	5,130,000

growth by GDP per capita and measure infrastructure levels by two indicators. First, infrastructure score of member countries is used. This score highlights the performance of countries in terms of infrastructure levels. Second, GFCF replaces infrastructure score and the relationship is reinvestigated. Subsequently, in sections 3 and 4, scatter diagram and network structure analysis are respectively used to shed more light on the discussion.

In a simple model, the above discussed relationship is modeled as:

$$Y = f(C, X) \tag{1}$$

where Y represents per capita levels, C represents infrastructure which is proxied by infrastructure score and GFCF and X denotes covariates. In equation (1), the growth (Y) is dependent on Infrastructure/GFCF (C) and a vector of control variables (X).

Assuming a linear relationship between the variables, equation (1) could be expanded to be:

$$Y_{it} = \alpha + \beta C_{it} + X'_{it}\gamma + \varepsilon_{it} \tag{2}$$

where the variables Y, C and X have their definitions as per that of equation (1) with ε representing error term and i t represent country i in year t. The variables are based on annual data from the World Bank database. It is an annual panel data from 2013 to 2017 based on 78 countries (HKTDC, n.d.). We collect data on GDP per capita (Y), infrastructure score, Gross Fixed Capital Formation and other covariates. The control variables include log transformed net foreign direct investment (FDI), trade openness, inflation levels and exchange rate. The variables have their definitions as per the World Bank's. Equation (2) is estimated using OLS regression with β being the coefficient of interest to highlight the effect of infrastructure levels on growth. The regression accounts for both country and year fixed effects. A positive(negative) sign of β would mean that, keeping other factors constant, a unit increase in infrastructure levels would improve(hinder) the growth levels and by extension the well-being of member countries.

Empirical Results

In simple terms, the regression is meant to highlight the potential effect of massive investment in infrastructure on the growth and well-being of member countries. Columns (1) and (2) are obtained by regressing log (GDP per capita) on infrastructure score with (2) accounting for control variables. In (3) and (4) the infrastructure score is replaced with log (GFCF). In all the equations, infrastructure is found to significantly (positive) affect the well-being of people (GDP per capita). Trade openness also exerts a positive and significant impact on per capita. Summary statistics and regression results are presented in Tables 2 and 3.

Table 2. Summary statistics

Variable	Observation	Mean	Std. Dev.	Min	Max
Log (per capita)	668	8.667	1.214	5.832	11.391
Infrastructure score	303	2.698	.579	1.500	4.278
Log (GFCF)	584	23.448	1.763	19.551	29.265
Trade openness	631	.929	.500	.001	3.796
Log (net FDI flow)	630	21.107	1.849	15.516	26.396
Inflation rate	634	4.750	6.064	-3.749	59.219
Exchange rate	600	1042.424	3874.444	.275	33226.3

Note: The infrastructure variable is from the World Bank's logistic performance index. The other variables are from WDI and have their definitions as per World Bank's.

Table 3. OLS regression results – dependent variables = log (GDP per capita)

Independent variables	(1) log(per capita)	(2) log(per capita)	(3) log(per capita)	(4) log(per capita)
Infrastructure	1.331***	1.057***		
	(0.143)	(0.173)		
log(net FDI inflow)	0.0341	0.0947	-0.0631	0.0199
	(0.0440)	(0.0497)	(0.0452)	(0.0476)
Trade openness	0.399**	0.430***	1.134***	0.947***
	(0.125)	(0.129)	(0.0901)	(0.0851)
Exchange rate		-0.0000512**		-0.0000547***
		(0.0000188)		(0.0000130)
Inflation rate		-0.0127		-0.0160***
		(0.00754)		(0.00439)
log(GFCF)			0.349***	0.277***
			(0.0446)	(0.0469)
Constant	3.908***	3.412***	0.667	0.860
	(0.739)	(0.777)	(0.562)	(0.557)
Country Fixed Effects	Yes	Yes	Yes	Yes
Year Fixed Effects	Yes	Yes	Yes	Yes
Observations	285	258	558	500
R^2	0.517	0.512	0.384	0.418

Note: Robust standard errors are presented in parentheses with the respective number of observations reported. Columns 1 to 4 account for country and year fixed effects.

The results suggest that the investment in capital (infrastructure) will indeed have positive impact on the well-being of member countries. Though the Initiative is still in its infant stage, this evidence suggests that the Initiative could be a step closer to realizing its aim of improving economic prosperity of member countries. Measured in USD thousands, the average GDP per capita of member countries in 2010 was 10.28 while the minimum and maximum values were 0.34 and 70.31 respectively. In 2014 and 2016, the average was respectively 12.04 and 10.32, while the maximum for the same respective periods were 86.85 and 59.32.

In column 2 it is observed that a unit increase in infrastructure score would lead to 1.06 increase in log (GDP per capita) while a unit increase trade openness would increase log (GDP per capita) by about 0.43. In column 4, when infrastructure measure is proxied by GFCF, a 1% increase in GFCF would lead to a 0.28% improvement in GDP per capita while a unit increase in trade openness would increase log (GDP per capita) by 0.95. These results have quite interesting implications for foreign business in China and perhaps other OBOR countries. The impact of infrastructure on GDP per capita is not only positive but statistically significant. This means that efforts to increase infrastructure levels in OBOR countries would not only reap financial gains for investors, such an investment would have a positive and significant impact on the well-being of the people. Countries that are close to each other are expected to have more advantage in terms of trade. Fu et al. (2018) show that when geographical distance coupled with factor endowment and cultural distance is smaller, flow of trade between economies will be larger. In an Initiative as OBOR, trade openness is important and will play a significant role in determining the flow of trade among member countries. The results in columns 2 and 4 highlight a significant and positive impact of trade openness. Member countries are expected to open their borders to each other to fully utilize the benefits of the initiative.

The success of the Belt and Road Initiative is expected to increase the growth of China's economy (Xiayan, 2015). The above findings suggest that successful investment of capital in the OBOR countries may not only lead to a tremendous growth of participating economies but may also transcend into an improved well-being of member countries. Analyzing overseas direct investment by China, Du and Zhang (2018) report that China's overseas direct investment (ODI) in the Belt and Road countries increased significantly. With China as the leader in the OBOR project, such tremendous increase in infrastructure investment is expected to lead to an increased growth of member countries. One other important issue is equity. In such a project, it is possible for some economies to enjoy the benefits more than others. It is not surprising that some economies see the Initiative as a threat to sovereignty. As the Initiative passes through the test of time, one interesting area to be looked at by researchers is the sharing of the Initiative's benefits. The findings are consistent with literature and makes a case for massive investment in member countries. Technological enhancements and increased levels of infrastructure would surely improve the growth and well-being of member countries. OBOR is expected to improve foreign trade and improved infrastructure levels and the progress of this project would undoubtedly be keenly monitored by researchers.

INFRASTRUCTURE NEEDS OF OBOR COUNTRIES

The investment needs of participating countries in the area of infrastructure is quite high. The Initiative is expected to raise the infrastructure levels in member countries in the near future. The Asia Development Bank (ADB) has estimated the infrastructure needs of the Asia and Pacific to be about $1.7 trillion annually. Such huge investment is necessary to raise the investment level of many OBOR countries which at the moment is very low. Based on data from the World Bank Indicators, in 2010 and right before the coming into force of the Initiative, a handful of the countries had an infrastructure score less than 2.5. More than thirty countries had a score less than 2.5. The number reduced to twenty-seven in 2014.

Though this is difficult to be attributed to the coming into force of the Initiative, what is clear is that most member countries need a lot more investment in infrastructure. It is however evident that the member countries have improved in terms of infrastructure. The performance did not get any better as about thirty-four countries had a score less than 2.5 in 2016. This highlights that more countries need more infrastructure investment.

As different phases of the Initiative are implemented, we expect that the Initiative would produce a win-win outcome for participating countries. The effect of infrastructure gap could be damaging. The effects of these gaps have the tendencies to have massive tolls especially on venerable households, aside the obvious toll on the region's growth. Only two in five people in South Asia have access to improved sanitation. Seventy one percent of people in South Asia have access to electricity versus ninety-two percent in East Asia (The World Bank, 2014). The dynamics of the gap and its effects are interwoven such that an inadequate power supply, poor transportation system, lack of adequate health facilities, have all contributed to the slow growth of the industrial and manufacturing sectors of the region below the anticipated levels. The report on South Asia emphasizes how the women, the poor, and marginalized social groups are particularly affected by the region's infrastructure gap. It is possible to build infrastructure in a way that targets inequality and poverty alleviation while enhancing economic growth.

Alternatively, countries could just keep providing infrastructure services to the rich in society, threatening the environment and social stability. Ironically, those are exactly the ones who can often afford many of these services from private provision. Countries should aim at building infrastructure in a way that reduces inequality not enhances it. Like the Chinese adage goes "If you want to reduce poverty, construct a road". The following graphs show the infrastructure level (needs) of member countries. Compared to the GDP per capita of member countries, the infrastructure level is measured in terms of quality. The point is that, while massive investment in infrastructure is necessary, the distribution of such infrastructure is as well important. Quite less privileged countries should be given attention in order to create a win-win OBOR.

Section 2 highlights the relative importance of infrastructure on the growth of participating countries. To reiterate, the findings suggest a significantly positive effect of infrastructure on the growth of OBOR countries. However, Figures 1 and 2 highlight the shortfall in infrastructure investment in many OBOR countries. Many OBOR countries still need heavy investments in infrastructure. With the likes of Singapore, China and South Africa showing signs of having quite high-quality infrastructure, more efforts should be put in lifting the infrastructure levels of other participating countries. As stated earlier, OBOR is still at its genesis state and we expect massive infrastructure investment in the coming years.

Figure 1. 2014 infrastructure score of OBOR countries

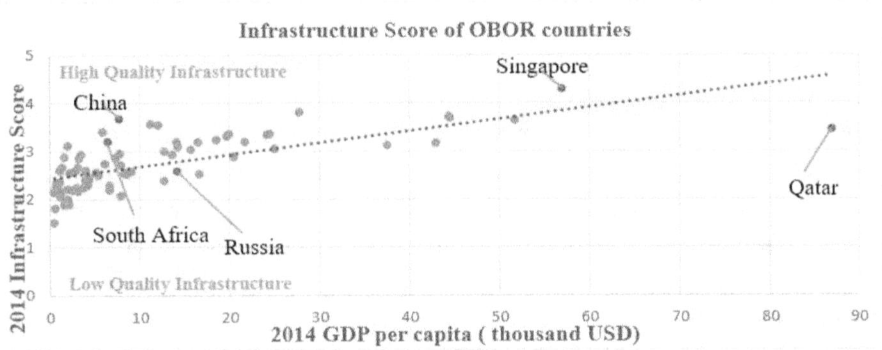

Figure 2. 2016 infrastructure score of OBOR countries

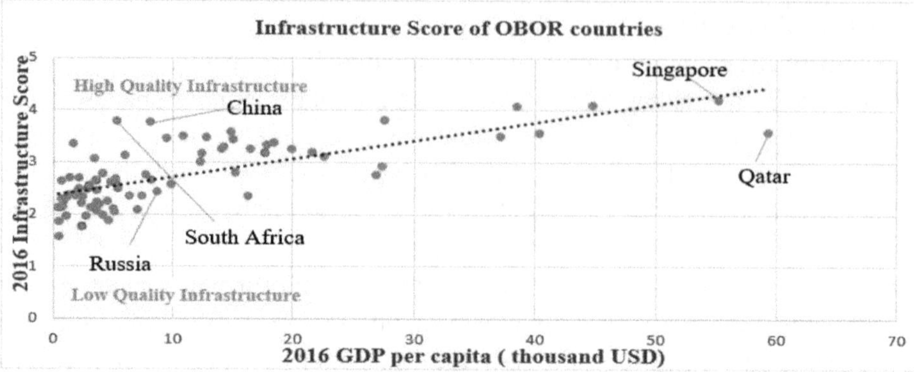

BILATERAL INVESTMENTS (FDI FLOWS) AND ECONOMIC INTEGRATION OF MEMBER COUNTRIES

Network analysis helps to understand how countries trade with each other (Nguyen, Pham & Vallee, 2016). The nodes in the network over time helps to highlight how member countries open-up to each other in terms of trade and other relations. By focusing on Foreign Direct Investment (FDI), we are able to analyze how member countries get integrated over time.

Many economics scholars and especially international economists have taken a glimpse at international trade and investment as a flow of a network relationship (Boamah et al., 2018; Moussa & Varsakelis, 2017; Chaney, 2014; Tajoli & Vicarelli, 2013). The movement of goods and services and investments between and among countries can be described as a link connecting two vertices representing the two countries (Andrade & Rêgo, 2018). This understanding thus makes it possible to evaluate the relationship between countries in the network and or the overall network structure.

This structure of network continues to evolve over time and is based on four types of international networks of trade flows, military interventions, diplomatic relations, and conjoint treaty memberships with international trade as a core-semi-periphery network structure. These findings have made it possible to focus on the relations and how these relations evolve over time in both a regional and world trade and investment structures characterized by an enlargement of the core countries, reduction of within-core distance and the progressive marginalization of peripheral countries.

More importantly in the context of international investments, network analysis helps in assessing the attractiveness of a country's position within a regional and world trade structure (Roth & Dakhli, 2015). It is important to note that in the hierarchical structure of global trade and investment, countries at the periphery of the structure which mostly are smaller in size over time integrate considerably into the network.

The position of a country in the network has substantial implications for economic growth, and the network position of a country is not a substitute for its physical capital but a complement to its human capital (Kali and Reyes 2007). In the event of an entrance into the network of world trading system by an important player, the structure and characteristics of the network change considerably with further implications for the countries on the peripheral (Benedictis & Tajoli, 2011). The dilemma here is whether trade and investment liberalization should be made the stay of globalization or if there should be some level of protectionism. The analysis of regional trade and investment has recently been in focus. This has helped understand the features of regional trade and investments and more importantly the role of the dominant players in the network structure. For instance, China plays the role of an export hub in South East Asia; Brazil, Russia, and India being the dominant local suppliers in their regions (Iapadre & Tajoli, 2014).

Network analysis, rather than analyzing country attributes such as economic, legal, political and social indicators in isolation, does so in conjunction with the resulting network structures for a complete assessment (Roth & Dakhli, 2015). Irrespective of the increased use network analysis in the international management research, such analysis has not been applied to the study of country attractiveness and the possible implication for foreign direct investment. By analyzing the position each country occupies in the flow of goods, services, and capital, a complete picture of the relative attractiveness of specific countries can be ascertained and would thus lead to better foreign direct investment decisions (Roth & Dakhli, 2015).

The existing literature reveals that using network analysis to analyze international trade and investment bring to fore very interesting revelations beyond results of the econometric analysis. Notwithstanding, this analysis has mainly been done at the world level. In the light of that, we apply network analysis to shed light on the changes in the trade and investment network structure at the regional level with emphasis on the countries in the Belt, Road Initiative with a concentration on FDI flows.

The findings of Boamah et al. (2018) show that the countries involved in the Belt and Road Initiative appear to have integrated in 2015. Using the convergence correlation, the writers document common subgroup characteristics for the four subgroups. China, Kazakhstan, Japan and the Koreas Republic have been identified to the central point of the Initiative. The distribution of nodes have become stronger as year on year, suggesting that the countries have gradually become more integrated than before. As the Initiative proceeds we expect these ties to be even stronger.

Figure 3 shows that the group level of connectivity is growing among countries in the Initiative, moving from 0.136 in 2005 to 0.147 in 2010, indicating an increasingly close connection between countries. It declined however in 2015 to 0.142. This shows that the Initiative may not be having an impact as might have been anticipated after the implementation of the Initiative as the rate of aggregation is slower than before the execution of the Initiative. In the same light, the overall centrality also saw continuous increment in 2015. This indicates that the network status of the countries in the center is strengthening and the control in the Initiative is becoming centralized, a trend which is expected to continue with the increased Chinese influence through investments.

Figure 4 shows an improved level of centralization in the network with less number of countries in the peripheral indicating the increase in the degree of common links. The number of contact lines to a country indicates its strength in network connectivity which defines the weight of the country in the Initiative. China, Russia, Japan, Korea, India, and Turkey were the most central countries in the network. Figure 4 shows that China has assumed the core position in the network. This position suggests increasing level of influence with the implementation of various investment agreements between China and countries in the Initiative.

One of the main objects of the Belt and Road Initiative is trade integration or facilitation. Network analysis serves as a good means of analyzing the integration

Figure 3. Density measurement
Source: Boamah et al. (2018)

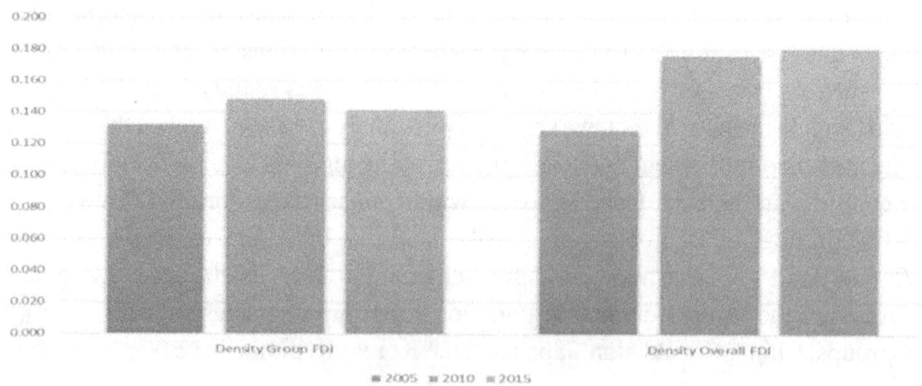

Figure 4. Network map (2015)
Source: Boamah et al. (2018)

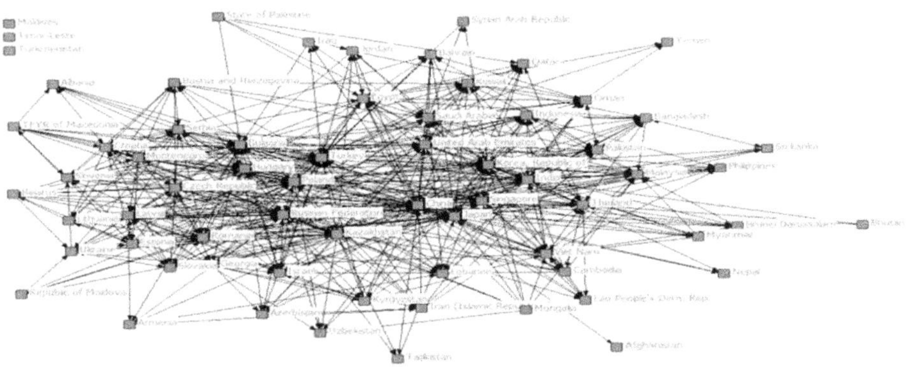

of trade among countries. The countries along the Belt and Road have attained some level of trade integration but rather at a slower pace than expected. The countries experience leadership shift from one country to the other, disappearance or reemergence (Chen et al., 2018). With China at the center of the Initiative, we expect capital investment among member countries and trade integration to attain greater heights.

SUMMARY

So far in this chapter, we have discussed and made a strong case for the need for massive investment in infrastructure to aid growth and well-being of member countries. The simple regression output suggests that improved infrastructure levels would produce a tremendous advancement in welfare of OBOR countries. That notwithstanding, the evidence also highlights massive shortfall of infrastructure levels in member countries. In the near future, the quality and quantity of trade, transport and other infrastructure levels of member countries is expected to rise. Though trade integration among member countries seems to be on the rise, network analysis highlights that this integration is rather at a slower pace than anticipated. In the era of trade and other macroeconomic shocks, the level of trade openness and economic integration demands critical attention. Specifically, the results show that the level of infrastructure in most member countries is still low. While the Initiative seems to integrate member countries in terms of trade, such integration is at a slower pace. This provides an opportunity for both domestic and foreign investors to consider massive investment in infrastructure in the member countries. Using both regression analysis and network structure study, we provide insight on capital/infrastructure and growth levels and economic integration of OBOR countries. As noted earlier, future studies may consider looking at the equity aspect of the initiative. That is, the distribution of the Initiative's benefits and how this affects foreign business in China.

The network analysis highlights that China has assumed core or central position and this speaks a lot in so far as doing business in China is concerned. As member countries integrate, doing business in China would offer one a wider market as business partners may have access to markets of countries along the Initiative. The Belt and Road Initiative is a mini-global project on it own and its future prospects would be of interest to us all.

REFERENCES

Boamah, J., Appiah-Kubi, M., & Osei, M. (2018). Network Structure Analysis of Bilateral Investments of One Belt, One Road Initiative countries. *Scholars Bulletin*, 689-699.

Chaney, T. (2014). The Network Structure of International Trade. *The American Economic Review*, *104*(11), 3600–3634. doi:10.1257/aer.104.11.3600

Chen, W., Liu, Z., Wang, T., & Jung, W. S. (2018). The structure and evolution of trade relations between countries along the Belt and Road. *Journal of Geographical Sciences*, 1233–1248.

De Benedictis, L. & Tajoli, L. (2011). The World Trade Network. *The World Economy*, *34*(8), 1417–1454.

Du, J., & Zhang, Y. (2018). Does One Belt One Road Initiative promote Chinese overseas direct investment? *China Economic Review*, *47*, 189–205. doi:10.1016/j.chieco.2017.05.010

Fagiolo, G., Reyes, J., & Schiavo, S. (2007). *International trade and financial integration: a weighted network analysis. Documents de Travail de l'OFCE. 2007-11*. Observatoire Français des Conjonctures Economiques.

Fu, X.-M., Chen, H.-X., & Xue, Z.-K. (2018). Construction of the Belt and RoadTrade Cooperation Network from the Multi-Distances Perspective. *Sustainability*, *10*(5), 1439. doi:10.3390u10051439

Herrero, A. G., & Xu, J. (2016). *China's Belt and Road Initiative: Can Europe expect trade gain?* Bruegel working paper series. Issue 5.

HKTDC. (n.d.). *The belt and road initiative: Country profiles*. HKTDC. Retrieved from: http://china-trade-research.hktdc.com/business-news/article/The-Belt-and-Road-Initiative/The-Belt-and-Road-Initiative-Country-Profiles/obor/en/1/1X000000/1X0A36I0.htm

Huang, Y. (2016). Understanding China's Belt and RoadInitiative: Motivation, framework and assessment. *China Economic Review*, *40*, 314–321. doi:10.1016/j.chieco.2016.07.007

Iapadre, P. L., & Tajoli, L. (2014). Emerging countries and trade regionalization. A network analysis. *Journal of Policy Modeling*, *36*, 89–110. doi:10.1016/j.jpolmod.2013.10.010

Kali, R., & Reyes, J. (2007). The architecture of globalization: A network approach to international economic integration. *Journal of International Business Studies*, *38*(4), 595–620. doi:10.1057/palgrave.jibs.8400286

Lopes de Andrade, R., & Rêgo, L. C. (2018). The use of nodes attributes in social network analysis with an application to an international trade network. *Physica A*.

Moussa, B. & Varsakelis, N. C. (2017). International patenting: An application of network analysis. *The Journal of Economic Assymetries.*

Nguyen, T., Pham, T., & Vallee, T. (2016). Economic Integration in ASEAN+3: A Network Analysis. *Journal of Economic Integration.*, *31*(2), 275–325. doi:10.11130/jei.2016.31.2.275

Roth, M. S., & Dakhli, M. (2000). Regional trade agreements as structural networks: Implications for foreign direct investment decisions. *Connections*, *23*(1), 60–71.

Roth, M. S., & Dakhli, M. (2015). *Regional Trade Agreements as Structural Networks:Implications for Foreign Direct Investment Decisions*. The Dana Moore School of Business.

Schiavo, S., Reyes, J., & Fagiolo, G. (2010). International trade and financial integration: A weighted network analysis. *Quantitative Finance*, *10*(4), 389–399. doi:10.1080/14697680902882420

Swaine, M. D. (2015). Chinese views and commentary on the "One Belt One Road" Initiative. *China Leadership Monitor, no. 47.* United nations Conference on Trade and Development. Bilateral FDI Statistics. Retrieved from http://unctad.org/en/Pages/DIAE/FDI%20Statistics/FDI-Statistics-Bilateral.aspx

The World Bank. (2014). *South Asia's $2.5 trillion infrastructure gap*. The World Bank. Retrieved from: http://www.worldbank.org/en/news/feature/2014/04/02/south-asia-trillion-infrastructure-gap

Villafuerte, J., Corong, E., & Zhuang, J. (2016). *The one belt, one road Initiative: Impact on trade and growth.* Paper presented at the 19th annual conference on global economic analysis.

Xiaoyan, Y. (2015). One belt, one road" can boost China's GDP growth by 0.25 percentage points in 2015. *Jieman*. Retrieved from: http://china-trade-research.hktdc.com/business-news/article/The-Belt-and-Road-Initiative/The-Belt-and-Road-Initiative-Country-Profiles/obor/en/1/1X000000/1X0A36I0.htm

Zhai, F. (2018). China's Belt and Road Initiative: A preliminary quantitative assessment. *Journal of Asian Economics*, *55*, 84–92. doi:10.1016/j.asieco.2017.12.006

Chapter 3
An Analysis of China's International Competitiveness

Ahu Coşkun Özer
Marmara University, Turkey

ABSTRACT

The criteria used in measuring the competition the country level, determined by the International Management Development Center in the World Competitiveness Report, are economic performance, government efficiency, business efficiency, and infrastructure. The international competitiveness of China, which is claimed to be some position with the United States in the world market in 2050, has been evaluated in this study, based on IMD competitiveness criteria. China has great progress in development through major changing strategies, methods, and reforms over the last 70 years. According to the international competition report, its rank is 13th in the international competition. The reason for China's capability on international competitiveness and its impact on the world economy is based on the fact that it combines cheap labor with the liberalization in foreign trade and foreign direct investment.

DOI: 10.4018/978-1-5225-8980-8.ch003

INTRODUCTION

China has great progress in development through major changing strategies, methods, and reforms over the last seventy years. According to the international competition report, its rank is 13th in the international competition. China's economic success is based on significantly more stable governments, trade supported by state, industry and investment policies, and the implementation of macroeconomic policies which mainly control inflation and public account deficits. The reason for China's capability of international competitiveness and its impact on the world economy is based on the fact that it combines cheap labor with the liberalization in foreign trade and foreign direct investment.

Although China is not at the first rank of international competitiveness, it has become one of the most competitive countries in the world with its economy. The breakthroughs are noteworthy in China, which is expected to have greater economy than the U.S. economy, which ranks first in international competition (Sachs, 2004., as cited in Fishmen 2006). According to the 2018 Competition Report of the International Institute of Management Development (IMD), China ranks 13th among 63 economies in competition.

The international competitiveness of China, which is claimed to be some position of the United States in the world market in 2050, has been evaluated in this study, based on IMD competitiveness criteria.

Background

International competitiveness depends on some basic factors. According to the Porter (1990), "A nation's competitiveness depends on the capacity of its industry to innovate and upgrade. Upgrading an economy is the result of broadening and upgrading the competitive advantages of a nation's firms" (as cited in Bhatt, 2008).

International competitiveness has been explained by the theoretical approach based on the comparative advantage, and depends on factor price in production(Ricardo and Heckscher-Ohlin). Ricardo focused on one production factor and technological differences. Heckscher and Ohlin facous on labor and capital inputs, comparative advantage depends on the relative factor prices differences and differences in factor endowments(Adams, Gangnes & Shachmurove, 2006). Also, IMD's world competitiveness ranking based on economic performance, business efficiencey, government efficiency, and infrastructure.

Analyses on China's international competitiveness in the literature are limited. According to the Adams, Gagnes and Shachmoure (2006) China's export competitiveness depends on several factors: low wages with supply of unskilled labour, low cost of transportation and communication, favourable exchange rate, foreign direct investments, foreign management and its implications for China's productive abilities, foreign trade policy, the opening of the world markets and the large scale of the potential Chinese domestic market. Bei, Gang, and Zhi (2006) state that the international competitiveness of China manufacturing has been improved greatly and that development is mainly due to the sustaining promotion of competitive advantage. Many factors give the advantage to China on international competitiveness.

MAIN FOCUS OF THE CHAPTER

The IMD World Competitiveness Index is comprised of four sub-indices which are divided into 20 pillars made up of 323 variables. The sub-indices are economic performance, government efficiency, business efficiency, infrastructure. In this research, China's international competitiveness analyzed with IMD's four sub-indices. The factors that provide the international competitive advantage to China is analyzed based on the IMD criteria. According to the IMD World Competitiveness Ranking 2018, the U.S.A was the 1st ranking, Hong Kong was the 2nd ranking, Singapore was in 3rd ranking. According to the IMD Competitiveness ranking China ranked 23rd in 2014, China raised to 13th position in 2018.

Figure 1. Competitiveness ranking of China
Source: IMD World Competitiveness Online, Country Profile, Retrieved from: https://worldcompetitiveness.imd.org/countryprofile/CN/wcy

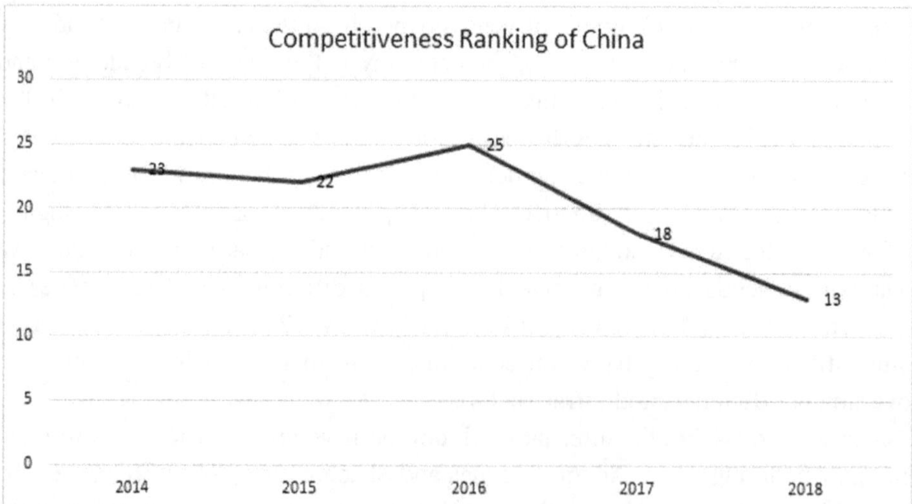

ECONOMIC PERFORMANCE OF CHINA

Although China is not at the first rank of international competitiveness, it has become one of the most competitive countries in the world with its economy.

If there is a country in the world market which can take over the place of the United States it will be China. Jeffrey Sachs, economist and government consultant of Columbia University suggests that Americans should be ready for a world where the economy of China will be 75 percent greater than the US by 2050 (Fishmen, 2006). China ranks 13th in the competition.

The breakthroughs are noteworthy in China, which is expected to have a 75 percent greater economy than the U.S. economy, which ranks first in international competition. According to the 2018 Competition Report of the International Institute of Management Development (IMD), China ranks 13th among 63 economies in competition.

Economic Performance of China

When the People's Republic of China was founded from 1949 until today, the economy of China has grown rapidly. The welfare of the people increases day by day. According to World Bank data, China's gross domestic product (GDP) was 11.2 trillion dollars in 2016. GDP of the US, the world's largest economy was 18.57 trillion dollars. China, which had a GDP of $ 92.6 billion in 1970, is the second largest economy in the world after the US. China's GDP grew 6.9 percent in 2017. In 2008, when the global crisis experienced, there was a contraction in the economies in Europe and the US. China was least affected by this crisis, grew 9.7 percent in GDP in 2008. When assessed historically, the GDP of China, only declined by 1.57 percent in 1976, has grown steadily since 1976. (GDP Growth Annual (%), World Bank National Accounts Data,2018).

When the statistical data the beginning of the 2000s are evaluated, China's GNP is increasing yearly. When the economy of China is evaluated from the perspective of total GNP and real growth rate, it has a steady upward trend between 2001 and 2004. The ratio of gross national product per capita is also increasing.

China was the first country in the world in export, with 2.263 trillion dollars in 2017. It is respectively followed by the US, Germany, and Japan (Top 20 export countries worldwide in 2017, Statista).

China population is 1.379 billion, and it is the world's second-largest economy. It is expected that the economic size of China will outpace the Eurozone and the U.S.

Table 1. Economic indicators of China

	2001	2002	2003	2004	2005
GNP	1.175,70	1.270,70	1.448,00	1.681,30	2224.9
Growth Rates of GNP		8	9,3	9,5	
Inflation Rates	0,7	-0,8			
Export (fob) $ billion	266,1	325,7	438,3	593,4	762,0
Imports (fob) $ billion	232,1	281,5	393,6		660,12
Foreign debts billion $	170,1	168,3	193,6	227,2	252,8

Source: Economic İntelligence Unit

According to a report of Organization for Economic Cooperation and Development (OECD) an overview of the 2060s economy, is based on the 2005 purchasing power parity, China's GDP will outpace the Eurozone in a year and the U.S. economy in just a few years.

The most striking finding is related with the share of the economy of China in global over the next 17 years. It is expected that China's share of the production in total production of the world's 42 largest economies will be 28 percent by 2030. The share of the U.S., which is now at the peak of the biggest economy league, will fall to 18 percent, the share of the Euro area will be 12 percent, and Japan's share will be 4 percent. China will maintain its share with 28 percent during the next 30 years(New Age: China, the world leader in 2030 with the economy,2013).

Internationalization of China

International Trade

In the process of globalization, countries have opened their economies to international areas and increased their international economic relations. Countries are trying to integrate into the world economy with the opening of the economies to the international area. Trade of goods and services between the international borders and territories constitutes a significant part of the gross domestic product in many countries.

National economies can integrate into the globalization process by carrying out various activities; national economies can take a place in the international area with the trade of goods and services, capital and service flows, production and transfer of technology, and the like. While such economic relations are not new, the intensity and diversity of these relationships have increased significantly over the last decade (The Union of Chambers and Commodity Exchanges of Turkey, 2005).

The most important indicator in comparing the size of international trade and domestic trade is the percentage of trade to GDP, means the arithmetic average of goods and services exports and imports that make up GDP. International trade is important for countries that are small and populated, open to the market economy and surrounded by self-sufficient countries, or geographically isolated, have high transportation costs (The Union of Chambers and Commodity Exchanges of Turkey, 2005).

According to the international trade statistics of China, in the 1960's the share of the foreign trade in GDP was between the % 6-8, in 1970s, when reforms began, the share of foreign trade in GDP in China was 10 percent. The ratio of China's foreign trade to GDP rose to 12 percent in 1980 and 1990.It was %39 in 2000. The economy of China is based on more foreign trade than the U.S., EU, and Japan (Worldbank National Accounts Data).

In 2016, China exported $ 2.27 trillion and imported $ 1.23 trillion. The most exported regions are the United States with 436 billion dollars in the first place, Hong Kong with 250 billion dollars in the second place, and Japan with 148 billion dollars in the third place. This is followed by Germany, South Korea respectively. The region where the China highest imports is the US with 122 billion dollars. This is followed by South Korea with $ 121 billion, followed by Japan and Germany (China, Observation of Economic Complexity, 2016). China is mainly in trade relations with the closed regional countries, Japan, South Korea, Indonesia, and Malaysia. Trade with these countries has also increased over the years.

The last reform is the project of the OBOR, it is One Belt One Road Project, the word of Belt refers to the routes for overland road and rail transportation, it is called 'the Silk Road Economic Belt'; and also "road" refers to the sea routes, or the 21st Century Maritime Silk Road (Lily, n.d). The project aims at international integration through transport networks, energy networks and telecommunications. OBOR project comprises the 69 member states, 42% of the world's GDP, 64% of the world's population, 40% of the land, and 75% of the known energy. China has aimed to completed the project in 30-35 years and has been trying to complete the project in its foundation to the 100th year (Güner, 2018). China aims to increase its trade volume with OBOR project.

GOVERNMENT EFFICIENCY

After the establishment of the People's Republic of China, a number of state-initiated reforms have led to planned growth in the country's economy. Regulation in taxes, creating incentive zones and investment incentives have played a major role in China's economic growth. Policies that particularly encourage investments based on high technology are supported by the government. The economy of China has developed with the planned economic policies.

Reforms in China

Reforms Made in the Rural Area

Agriculture is important for the economy of China economy because the majority of the population in China lives in rural areas. Land reform provided land for the landless villagers and a number of radical measures were taken in the agriculture after the establishment of the People's Republic of China in 1949. The government of China saw the development of agriculture as one of the most important subject and increased investment in agriculture. As a result of the reforms implemented, the income of the villagers has been increased in line with the productivity and there has been a parallel development between the villagers and the urban people. In the process of the first five-year development plan between 1953 and 1957, successful policies were implemented in agriculture and an annual average growth was 4.5 percent. In the period between the 1958 and 1978, as a result of the communal production and sharing policies, the production efficiency decreased and the famine started. In 1978, the communal production system was changed and policies promoting production started to be implemented (DEİK, Çin Halk Cumhuriyeti Ekonomisi ve Türkiye İlişkileri, 2003).

The farmers, who had to process the inefficient lands of the state, which had previously been of no benefit to them, have prosperity with the reforms in agriculture. After the Mao-era reforms, the villagers could process land as a result of the contract they signed, but they could not have it. A constitutional amendment in 1988, it has been possible for the villagers to buy and sell the land they used. Taxes and the minimum amount of crops the farmers had to raise was decreased, control over the crop and price was loosened, and purchase prices of agriculture for the state were increased with the reforms implemented. The farmers were allowed to work in other sectors. A new reform in 1985 also aimed to bring market-based production conditions. Agricultural production has grown by an average of 6.5 percent over the past two decades. (DEİK,2003).

According to 2003 data, the agricultural sector contributed 14.6% to the economy of China; employed 313 million workers, 42.6 percent of the workforce. In 2004, agricultural production was directly subsidized and it is estimated that the production target of 455 million tons is exceeded. This allowed to decrease of the increased grain prices from the second half of 2004 and reduce inflationary pressures (China Report, Center for Economic Policy and Strategic Studies,2018).

Reforms in Urban Area

The Economic System Restructuring Decision, adopted at the 12th Central Committee Meeting of the Communist Party of China, in October 1984, became the reporter of China's reform of the economic system gets into an urban-centric phase. This reform includes mainly the following objectives: (Qin Shi, 1997).

- Making changes in ownership structure,
- Encouraging the development of various property systems in the general socialist economy in China, where public ownership dominates
- Increase and strengthen the decision-making power of state-owned enterprises,
- Promotion of horizontal links between the enterprises and establishment of business groups,
- Implementation of price reform and the development of a market system,
- Implementing reforms in planning public finance and banking systems, and making functional of macroeconomic management. The narrowing of the scope of government on direct planning-based, the strengthening of the determinative role of the market,
- Reforms in China's foreign trade are the removal of import taxes, reduction of quotas and licensing requirements for commercial goods and termination of mandatory import and export planning,
- Improvement of the income distribution system, use of a wide variety of income distribution patterns, based on the principle that 'income according to everyone's work'

Based on the structural reforms described above, the 14th National Congress of the Communist Party of China in October 1992 marked the historic change in the development of the national economy of China, setting the formation of a socialist market economy as the goal of China's economic reform.

The constitutional amendment adopted at the first meeting of the 8th National People's Congress gathered in March 1993 and the constitutional guarantee for the implementation of the "Chinese Variant of Socialist Market Economy" was adopted in November 1993. Chinese Variant of Socialist Market Economy established at the 3rd meeting of the 14th Central Committee of the Communist Party of China, based on the idea that "Chinese Socialist Market Economy is closely linked to the basic socialist system, in other words, the market controlled by the state at macro level will function as the basic instrument for the allocation of resources", the general plan for economic structural reform of China and action program. The main elements of this program can be summarized as follows (Qin Shi, 1997).

- While various forms of ownership are developed together, public ownership will continue to be in the form of substantive ownership. Changes shall be made in state-owned enterprises in the operating mechanism in accordance with market economy conditions; the ownership rights and responsibilities of the enterprises shall be clearly defined and the duties of the state shall be separated from the duties of these enterprises.
- A clear and unified national market system that combines urban and rural markets and optimizes resource allocation will be established.
- A distribution system will be established according to the work that prioritizes productivity and is considered fairness in distribution;
- Some regions and some people will enrich themselves before others, but this process will be encouraged because the country is on the path of common welfare;
- For those living in urban and rural areas, a multilayered social security system that guarantees social security that supports economic development and social stability in line with China's national characteristics will be established.

In addition to these program, there have been developments in 1999 and 2005 on private sector. In 1999, the private sector was recognized with an important constitutional amendment. The private sector is accepted with its importance in creating the business in the slowing economy. In 2005, regulations that prevented private companies from entering certain areas such as public services, financial services were abandoned.

Regulations in Economics

The economic reform process in China demonstrates the typical transition economy characteristic. In the transition process from the planned economy to market-driven economy shows the characteristic features of the privatization (The Chinese Economy, Hung-Gay Fung, 2006).

Shortly after Mao's death, Deng Xiaoping took over in 1978, and he began to market reform in China. Until his death in 1997, Deng made the pioneering change in China. During this time, Deng aimed to modernize in the fields of industry, agriculture, science and technology, and national defense. As a result of the reform movements, China has become enormously enriched (Arısoy, Bayar & Soranlar, 2005).

The economy of China has had a growth performance which is difficult for economies since the beginning of economic reforms in 1978. Between 1978 and 2005, China's GNP grew at an annual average rate of 9.5 percent, depending on the stable environment created for economic development and efforts to make integration with the global economy. This is more than three times of the average figure of the US economy (Yılmaz, Koyuncu,2005).

According to World Bank data, per capita national income in China was 1949, 9 dollars in 2006, 2415.9 dollars in 2008, 2891 dollars in 2010, 3377 dollars in 2012, 2014 was 3,865 dollars. In 2015, it is stated that per capita gross domestic product in China is about 7,800 dollars(National Income in China came to $ 7800, 3 November 2015).

However, regional disparities and imbalances in the distribution of industrialization and GNP in China are also striking. When China's economic structure and basic economic indicators are analyzed in some provinces, the per capita income is low in some states but high in others. The reasons for this difference depend on the reforms. The reason for the low per capita income in some states is the application of economic reforms. As a result of these applications, special economic areas, coastal cities, and regions have been created. In these regions, production is supported by legal regulations and incentive policies are implemented (Unay,2005).

The industrialization of the country does not develop at the same level in the western and inner parts. Because the policies only implemented to develop the western part of China. As a result of launching free market applications, the external interaction was easier and infrastructure developed, but inner regions are not developed in the same level with coastal areas.

In the 1960s and early 1970s, while the economy of China was performing poorly, the performance of the economy of China has increased since the start of

Figure 2. Map of China
Source: http://geography.about.com/library/cia/blcchina.htm, Temmuz, 2005

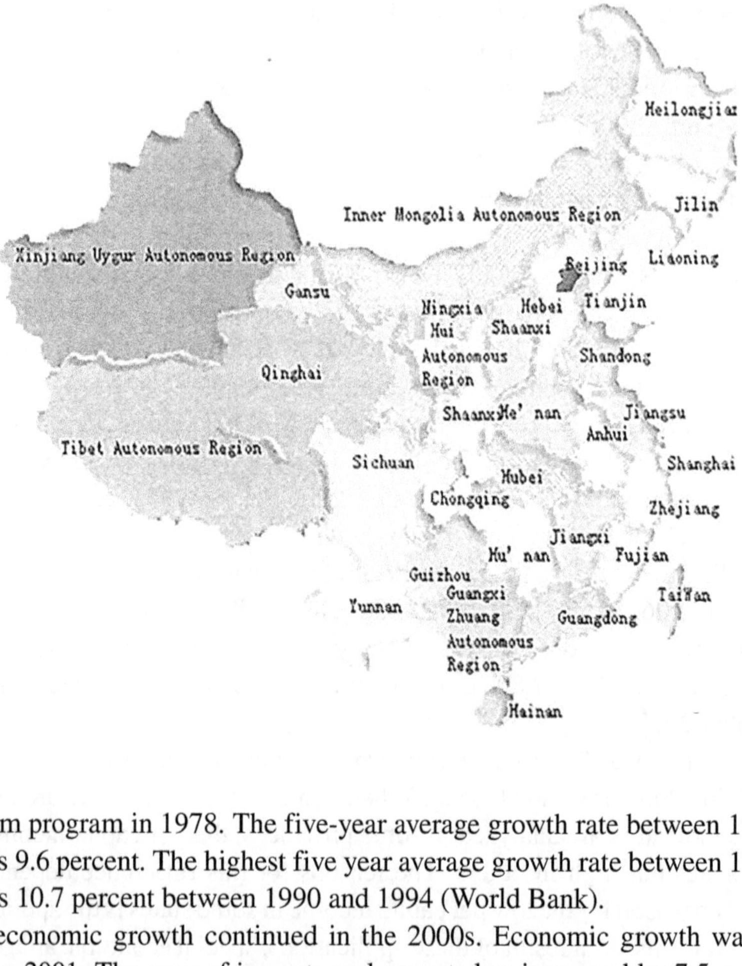

the reform program in 1978. The five-year average growth rate between 1975 and 1979 was 9.6 percent. The highest five year average growth rate between 1960 and 2002 was 10.7 percent between 1990 and 1994 (World Bank).

The economic growth continued in the 2000s. Economic growth was at 7.3 percent in 2001. The sum of imports and exports has increased by 7.5 percent to 509, 8 billion dollars. By the end of 2001, foreign exchange reserves reached $ 212.2 billion. The registered unemployment rate in the cities was 3.6 percent. At the end of 2001, the People's Republic of China became a member of WTO. Economic growth was %6.9, unemployment rate was %3.9 in 2017 (World Bank, Statista).

According to the 2002 International Economic Indicators of the State Planning Organization, China was the sixth largest economy in the world with 1.4 trillion dollars of GDP in the GDP rankings after the USA, Japan, Germany, England, and France.

China's share of GDP in goods trade doubled from 1997 to 2002, higher than the U.S., EU, and Japan. This growth was achieved through the production of high-tech goods. China was the first country to attract foreign investment with the US $ 50 billion in 2002 (The Union of Chambers and Commodity Exchanges of Turkey, 2005).

The reason why China increases its weight in world trade is the policy of internalization and reform initiated by China's former leader Deng Xiaoping in 1978. Reforms initiated in agriculture, foreign capital investments, reforms in the economy and the preparation of their legal subdivisions, reform in state enterprises, the transition from a strictly planned economic perspective to a controlled planned economy and market economy are causes of the epochal development in China in the last quarter of the century (Çin Gerçeği, 2004).

BUSINESS EFFICIENCY

Human Resource and Cost of Labor

The rapidly growing economy of China over the last twenty-five years based on the population. The number of the population makes it possible for almost every field in the country to be an incredible workforce. China's population is likely to approach 1.5 billion, but official sources give it 1.3 billion. If this unprecedented population of China was considered the only country in the world, China could be the fifth largest country in the world (Fishman, 2006).

According to the information in the 2004 Bulletin of China's Statistical Institute of Population, China is the world's fourth largest country with 9.6 million square kilometers and the world's most populous country with 1.3 billion people. Population increases by 6 per year on average so eight million people are added to China's population each year. 23.6 percent of the population is between the ages of 0 and 14, 69.1 percent is between the ages of 14 and 65, and 7.2 percent is over 65. The unemployment rate is 4.3 percent in urban and the literacy rate is 91 percent.

However, although the population is an advantage for the country, the rate of literacy is high, but in the international competitiveness, report states that the enrollment rates of higher education in China are below international standards and it is problem for the competitiveness of China. Although the reforms of the last 20 years have helped to develop in the Chinese higher education system, China's higher education system has not progressed internationally in parallel with modernization in Chinese society.

In China, the proportion of graduates of the population from faculty, aged 25 to 64 years was only 5 percent in 2000. It seems to be a low standard compared with developed and industrial countries. The education system does not meet the demands of China in line with its national strategic development (Ministry of Education of the People's Republic of China, 2007)

The steady increase in the amount of labor force puts pressure on the government to follow a strategy of high economic growth. In the year 1960, 52.6 percent of the total population was in the workforce, but this rate increased to 60.1 percent in 2002 (Yılmaz, Koyuncu,2005).

Nowadays, the hourly workers' wages in the manufacturing industry in China are 3.60 dollars. This figure is higher than in some Latin American countries. China has started to lose its attractiveness in terms of low wages. In the meantime, the minimum wage has started to increase in China in recent years. The minimum wage in Shanghai has been 318 dollars and 283 dollars in Tianjin. The figures are higher than some European countries. For example, the minimum wage in Bulgaria is 248 dollars (China is losing 'labor' advantage, Evrim Küçük,2017).

Finance in China

In recent years, the government of China has pursued reformist policies in finance and banking sectors as well as in many other areas. Through reforms in China, banks and financial institutions have been restructured. These reforms bring positive results in terms of the growth of the country.

The great majority of the banking sector in China is state-owned and lending has political priorities (China Country Profile, The Economist, 2006). Although reforms in the field of finance and banking are a positive influence for the growth of the country, one of the issues that have lost strength to China in the international competitive capability is the problems in finance and banking.

An intensive reform program should be implemented in China's financial system to avoid the devastating effects of the past surge. Private investors should be allowed in the financial sector and the limits of foreign bank partnerships should be increased to stimulate competition in the financial system(China's Financial Need an Overhaul, Farrel Diana,2006). In China, while the fixed exchange rate system was applied with the pressure of US, this application was softened in 2005 and the floating exchange rate has been applied. Until August 2015, China used a modified version of a traditional fixed exchange rate. Today China use controlled floating exchange rate. China has a strictly controlled currency policy. China's exchange rate compared the yuan's value to a basket of currencies reflecting its trading partners (Amadeo, 2018). The value of yuan is determined by the prices in the currencies.

INFRASTRUCTURE IN CHINA

Natural Resources and Energy

The need for natural energy resources is also increasing with the economic growth of China. China's internal resources are not at a level that meets the country's needs. The main source of energy consumption in China is coal with 69 percent. This is followed by oil with 22 percent. Natural gas is negligible at 2 percent. As of 2004, China's proven oil reserves amounted to 18 billion barrels, daily oil production amounted to 3.5 million barrels, and daily petroleum consumption amounted to 6.7 million (Pamir, 2005).

China has been a country importing petroleum from a petroleum exporting country. It imports 8.4 million barrels of oil per day and is expected to reach 10 million by 2025. These numbers have exceeded 7.9 million barrels per day of US daily oil imports (Tuncay, 2003).

China imports 20 percent of its petroleum needs and 65 percent of the imported petroleum is taken from in the Middle East. The proven natural gas reserves of the country are 2.2 trillion cubic meters. 41 billion cubic meters of natural gas are consumed annually. China has 13% of the world total coal reserves with 114 billion tons of coal reserves. It produces 990 million tons of coal and consumes 960 million tons of coal per year (Pamir, 2005).

Transportation

The infrastructure in China is inadequate and undeveloped, especially in western and rural areas. Large investments are being made to solve the transportation problem of these regions. In China, rail systems are the most used transportation among the transportation types. While there are no highways connecting the Chinese provinces up to ten years ago, major steps are being taken in highway construction.

In recent years, the ports of the country are showing great development. The number of ports are 200, ports are on the coastline which length is 14,500 kilometers, cargoes discharged to these ports was 483 million tons in 1990 and 2 billion tons in 2003. China's air transport is also a huge sector with a volume of 9.5 billion dollars (Çin Ülke Bülteni, Deik, 2006). China is also building smart cities in terms of infrastructure. Smart technologies are used in everything from resource and environmental management to welfare of the citizens.

Within this context, technology utilization contributes welfare of the people. The quality of the people lives and their happiness, human rights and justice, innovative strategies, human centric policymaking must be integral propositions of any smart approach for competitiveness (Visvizi, 2018).

Science and Technology in China

The incentives and supports for China's economic development are also being realized in the field of science and technology. In 1985, a reform of the science and technology management system was implemented in China. This reform provided links between science and technology to the economy.

There are now over 2,000 scientific research institutions in China, 500 of its state-owned. Independent scientific research institutions are financed by the government. Researches are carried out in new and advanced technology fields in scientific research institutions (China Towards the Year 2000, 1989, as cited in Varaprasad, 2015)

SOLUTIONS AND RECOMMENDATIONS

As it is in the theories, specialization and exports of goods produced by countries cheaply have provided international competitiveness capability for the countries. Qualified labor, natural resources, demands, and competitors are important factors that determine the international competitiveness.

When China's international competition capability analyzed it is explained with the reforms have a great influence on China's international competition capability. China has made great strides in development through major change strategies, methods and reforms over the last seventy years and has gained great international strength.

However, low rates of higher education enrollment is a disadvantage for China's international competition capability. Education does not in the same level with international standards so educational reforms should be done in China. While the population is an advantage for China, the productivity of the workforce is the basic problem so qualified personnel is needed.

China's international competitiveness and the great impact on the world economy is due to the fact that China combines a large open economy with a cheap labor force, foreign trade and foreign direct investment.

There are a number of factors affecting the international competitiveness of the countries. Particularly, the importance of qualified labor and specialization in production, the reforms and the development of foreign trade policies by the state, the promotion of foreign investments with taxes provide the increase of international competitiveness.

FUTURE RESEARCH DIRECTIONS

China will be the factory of the world in the future. It has the important place in the world economy so it can be evaluated from the production aspect. International competitiveness factors determined by the Porter can be used to analyze China's international competitiveness. Innovation capacity of the industries in China should be a research subject to determine the place of China in the future. Also, the effect of the OBOR project to China development and competitiveness can be analyzed

CONCLUSION

As it is in the theories, specialization and exports of goods produced by countries cheaply have provided international competitiveness. Qualified labor, natural resources, demands, and competitors are also factors that determine the international competitiveness.

Reforms have a great influence on China's international competition capability. China has made great strides in development through major change strategies, methods and reforms over the last seventy years and has gained great international strength.

In the Mao period in China, the Soviet Union model was adopted and the planned economic structure was implemented, but the planned economy failed due to waste of resources and insufficient technological development. It has shown great growth thanks to the radical reforms that began in 1978 by the reformist wing of the Communist Party of China. These reforms have been the most important factor in China's international competitiveness. As a result of implementing reforms in accordance with their own structures, the countries can take place in the international area.

In addition, the economic policies implemented in China, China's economic success can be based on stable governments, government-supported trade, industry and investment policies, and macroeconomic policies that control inflation and public account deficits.

In addition to the implemented economic policies and reforms, a population of 1.379 billion population, living on a surface area of 9.6 million square kilometers, is a great advantage for China. The cheapest labor force in China, the world's most populous country, has been the cause for investments in the country. For this reason, China is seen as the world's factory in the future. However, the greatest disadvantage for China is the low rates of higher education enrollment and the fact that the quality of higher education does not at the same level as international standards. The crowded population has an advantage in international competitiveness by causing the cheapness of the labor force of the countries, but it is important that countries should employ with qualified personnel.

China's international competitiveness and the great impact on the world economy is due to the fact that China combines a large open economy with a cheap labor force, foreign trade and foreign direct investment.

According to the research result, China is a sampling country, there are a number of factors affecting international competitiveness. Particularly, the importance of qualified labor and specialization in production, the reforms and the development of foreign trade policies by the state, the promotion of foreign investments with taxes provide the increase of international competitiveness.

REFERENCES

Adams, F. G., Gangnes, B., & Shachmurove, Y. (2006). Why is China so Competitive? Measuring and Explaining China's Competitiveness. *World Economy, 29*(2), 95–122. doi:10.1111/j.1467-9701.2006.00773.x

Amadeo, K. (2018). *How China Influences the U.S. Dollar.* Retrieved from https://www.thebalance.com/how-does-china-influence-the-u-s-dollar-3970466

Arısoy, E., Bayar, G., & Soranlar, B. (2005). *Asya'nın Devi: Çin Halk Cumhuriyeti*. Retrieved from http://www.dtm.gov.tr/ead/DTDERGl/temmuz2004/asyaI.htm

Atlas Media, M. I. T. (2016). *China*. Observation of Economic Complexity. Retrieved from https://atlas.media.mit.edu/en/profile/country/chn/

Bei, J., Gang, L., & Zhi, C. (2006). *An Empirical Analysis on International Competitiveness of China Manufacturing since WTO Accession*. China Industrial Economy. Retrieved from http://en.cnki.com.cn/Article_en/CJFDTOTAL-GGYY200610000.htm

Bhatt, P. R. (2008). *Trade Competitiveness in ASEAN. Anveshak, 38(2).*

Bilim Kültür Yönetim Platformu. (2004). *Çin Gerçeği*. Ankara: Author.

Business Dictionary. (n.d.). Labor. *Business Dictionary.* Retrieved from: http://www.businessdictionary.com/definition/labor.html

Center for Economic Policy and Strategic Studies. (2018). *Report on China*. Retrieved from http://tesam.org.tr/cin-raporu/

Economics Help. (2012). Factors that determine international competitiveness. *Economics Help.* Retrieved from: https://econ.economicshelp.org/2007/06/what-determines-international.html

Farrel, D. (2006). China's Financial Need an Overhaul. *Business Week Online*.

Fishman, T. C. (2006). *Çin Inc*. İstanbul: Klan Publication.

Foreign Economic Relations Board of Turkey. (2003). *China Economy and Turkey Relations*. İstanbul: Author.

Foreign Economic Relations Board of Turkey. (2006). *China.* Retrieved from ww.deik.org.tr/buıtenıer/20061 128 1854 ICin_kasim2006.pdf

Güner, B. (2018). *OBOR Girşimininin Coğrafyası*. Marmara Coğrafya Dergisi. Retrieved from: https://tr.wikipedia.org/wiki/Bir_Kuşak,_Bir_Yol

Hung-Gay Fung. (2006). *The Chinese Economy* (Vol. 39). ME Sharpe.

Investopedia. (2018). Infrastructure. *Investopedia*. Retrieved from: https://www.investopedia.com/terms/i/infrastructure.asp

Küçük, E. (2017). *China is losing the 'labor' advantage*. Retrieved from https://www.dunya.com/dunya/cin-iscilik-avantajini-kaptiriyor-haberi-351690

Lily, K. (n.d.). *What is China's Belt and Road Initiative?* Retrieved from: https://www.theguardian.com/cities/ng-interactive/2018/jul/30/what-china-belt-road-initiative-silk-road-explainer

New Age. (2013). *China, the world leader in 2030 with the economy*. Retrieved from http://www.yenicaggazetesi.com.tr/cin-ekonomisi-ile-2030da-dunya-lideri-90237h.htm

Pamir, N. (2005). *Çin ve Enerji Güvenliği*. Retrieved from www.asam.org.tr/tr/yuidosyagoster.asp

Qin, S. (1997). *China*. İstanbul: Yeni Yıldız Publication.

Sachs, D. J. (2004). *Welcome To The Asian Century By 2050, China and maybe India will overtake the U.S. economy in size*. Retrieved from: https://money.cnn.com/magazines/fortune/fortune_archive/2004/01/12/357912/index.htm

Statista. (2018). *Top 20 export countries worldwide in 2017*. Retrieved from. https://www.statista.com/statistics/264623/leading-export-countries-worldwide/

The Union of Chambers and Commodity Exchanges of Turkey. (2005). *Çin*. Ankara: Bilgi Tabanlı Yükselen Ekonomi.

Tuncay, N. (2003). Information Administration, Petroleum Supply Weekly And Monthly Status Report. *US Energy*.

Unay, İ. (2005). *Çin Ekonomisinde Rekabet Avantajı Sağlayan Etkenler ve Rekabetin Sürdürülebilirliği*. Bursa.

Varaprasad, S. D. (2015). *Science and Technology in Contemporaray China*. Cambridge University Press.

Visvizi, A. (2018). Policy making for smart cities: innovation and social inclusive economic growth for sustainability. *Journal of Science and Technology Policy Management, 9*(2). Retrieved from: https://www.emeraldinsight.com/doi/full/10.1108/JSTPM-07-2018-079

Wikipedia. (n.d.a). Internalization. *Wikipedia.* Retrieved from: https://en.wikipedia.org/wiki/Internalization

Wikipedia. (n.d.b). China. *Wikipedia.* Retrieved from: https://en.wikipedia.org/wiki/China

Wikipedia. (n.d.c). International trade. *Wikipedia.* Retrieved from: https://en.wikipedia.org/wiki/International_trade

Wikipedia. (n.d.d). Reform. *Wikipedia.* Retrieved from: https://en.wikipedia.org/wiki/Reform

Wikipedia. (n.d.e). Transport. *Wikipedia.* Retrieved from: https://en.wikipedia.org/wiki/Transport

World Bank. (2018). *National Accounts Data, GDP Growth Annual (%).* Retrieved from https://data.worldbank.org/indicator/ny.gdp.mktp.kd.zg?end=2017&locations=cn&start=1961

World Bank. (2015). *National Income in China came to $ 7800.* Retrieved from https://www.haberler.com/cin-de-kisi-basina-milli-gelir-7-bin-800-dolara-7841637-haberi

Worldbank National Accounts Data. (n.d.). *China's Trade % of GDP.* Retrieved from: https://data.worldbank.org/indicator/NE.TRD.GNFS.ZS?locations=CN

Yılmaz, R., & Koyuncu, C. (2005). *Çin:Dragon Ekonomisinin Onlenemeyen Yükselişi.* Bursa Ekin Kitabevi.

Chapter 4
Doing Business in China:
An EU Firm Perspective

Anna Maria Tavanli
Deree – The American College of Greece, Greece

ABSTRACT

This chapter examines how the intersection of economy, politics, law, and culture in contemporary China influences the choices and alternatives of EU businesses seeking to invest in China. Although China recorded a tremendous growth of its trade volume with other countries, the institutional and regulatory frameworks of the Chinese economy have proven to be at least challenging to EU businesses. In fact, several disputes have arisen and many of them have been dealt with in the WTO Dispute Settlement Body. The chapter elaborates on one of them to explain in which ways China may not be the easiest place to conduct business.

DOI: 10.4018/978-1-5225-8980-8.ch004

INTRODUCTION

China has experienced a record high FDI inflow over the past two decades. It has become the largest recipient of FDI among the developing countries as well as a major destination point for multinational companies (Awokuse & Yin, 2010). To a large extent this positive tendency has been the outcome of China's progressive integration in the global trading and investment system (Alexandru & Gabriela, 2008). Over the past decades China has established collaboration various countries in the world. The European Union and the United States remain the key business partners (Hsieh, 2009). China has managed to become one of the European Union's main trading partners since the Chinese economy nowadays is one of the fastest growing economies. For instance, the EU represents more than 19 percent of China's external trade and European companies more specifically, have helped China develop its productive capacity because of the transfer of capital goods, knowledge and technology (Appendix). It is important to note that technology transfer from China to other countries has grown massively over the years (Nayaar, 2016). Due to the country's size and development requirements, the China is one of the biggest importers of technology worldwide. Technology plays a vital role for manufacturing companies when it comes to creating a competitive advantage since technology is part of their organizational knowledge that gives to the company distinctive capabilities in order to compete (Bruun & Bennett, 2002).

Despite the many opportunities for businesses, it is inevitable not to have any challenges. Several authors stress that EU exports in China still face restrictions and tariff barriers such as labelling standards and product certification although the Chinese tariffs have gone down because of China's 2008 accession in the World Trade Organization (Pranee & Hsieh, 2009). Because the Chinese national standards differ from the international ones, this results in high compliance costs affecting directly European firms. Thus, EU companies often face challenges when operating in the Chinese market. Nonetheless, the institutional, political and legal framework of China's has given little incentive for foreign firms to innovate in the specific market let alone establish their companies abroad. Foreign investment regulations have a different regulatory framework than domestic Chinese investments (Liu, 2018). All of the aforementioned, consequently led to trading disputes between China and the European Union which has been in the scenery for several years (Voituriez & Wang, 2015). Both countries have tried over the years to set up constructive and preventive mechanisms in order to stabilize trade and, consequently, strengthen their economic ties. Although the EU's prime objective with China's integration in the WTO was for China to conform to the legal and regulatory framework of the WTO and thus, promote China's growth as 'liberal trade power', China did not comply to such set of rules (Michalski & Pan, 2017). In fact, China acted as a passive actor and lead the EU to admit that China is not always an easy partner (European Commission, 2001, p.7).

There are both opportunities and risks when European companies invest in China. Although China is an attractive destination for multinational firms, and especially, European ones, there is a serious entry risk for the companies since China lacks in terms of its institutional landscape. Hence, there is a need for a meticulous market analysis prior to taking the decision to enter the market. In this context, China's judicial system has to be examined carefully in order to first and foremost comprehend the way of how their legal landscape works and consequently overcome the challenges. There is also a need for drastic measures in the matter of trade disputes as well as additional trade dialogues between the countries in order to resolve the aforementioned. Having said this, the big question is what kind of institutional barriers foreign companies encounter in China when transferring their technology in the specific country? And how foreign companies deal with challenges inherent in China's legal landscape? It is argued that although China seems to be a promising country for investment the reality is more complex than that. This chapter sets on to add to this discussion. The argument in this chapter is organized as follows. Firstly, the chapter will investigate China's institutional landscape. Secondly there will be reference to a trade dispute between China and the EU because of China's poorly institutional landscape. Furthermore, technology transfer in China will be analyzed since the country is one of the biggest importers of technological goods, knowledge and capacity. To continue, suggestions will be presented in order to overcome the aforementioned challenges. Conclusions follow.

CHINA'S BUSINESS LANDSCAPE

Multinational firms experience difficulties when operating in the Chinese market because of its institutional landscape. Hence, five factors of its institutional environment will be analyzed in this chapter. It is with no doubt that multinational companies nowadays come across several opportunities and challenges when operating in a new country which is unfamiliar. Yet, when internationalizing in a country such as China, a competitive strategic plan is needed in order for the firm to conquer the Chinese market (Williamson & Zeng, 2004). According to the authors, in a country such as China everything is possible because of the vast opportunities that the market offers. However, it will be challenging due to the country's competitive environment. In order to exploit the Chinese market and pinpoint some of the opportunities and challenges faced by international companies, this chapter will introduce some key factors that need to be taken into consideration. Specifically, it is important to look at the existing economic, political, legal and cultural framework of the country as well as how EU companies should adjust depending on the different framework. The rapid and sustained improvement of China's economic growth have made the country into the second-largest economy in the world (Zhu, 2012). The inexplicable growth of the Chinese economy has been addressed by economists as the 'Chinese miracle' (Spies, 2011). China's real GDP per capita has grown at an average rate exceeding 8 percent per year. For what is more, in terms of nominal GDP, China has added to its economy, 12.24 trillion USD (Euromonitor International, 2017) making the country therefore, an economic threat for the rest of the world.

Corruption is a highly-debated issue in China since the Maoist era (Nayaar, 2016). China is the largest source of pirated products worldwide (Keupp et al., 2010). This inevitably deters foreign investment since there is no legal protection of the right of EU companies. As far as China's laws are concerned, China had no Intellectual Property Rights (IPR) protection before 1985 making the expansion of foreign companies into the Chinese market even more challenging (Awokuse & Yin, 2010). IPR issues in the context of unprotected patents and trademarks have been in China's scenery for quite long. However, China has undergone a gradual reform of its patent systems with the establishment of its first patent law in 1985 as well as with its membership in the WTO that required Chinese IPR laws that should be in a better alignment with the WTO's Agreement on Trade-Related Aspects of Intellectual Property Rights (Liu, 2008).

The Legal Environment

Many regulations result in decisions favoring the local Chinese operators. For example, in the manufacturing and services sectors, the European investors are not allowed to set up a wholly owned foreign enterprise and are required to use joint ventures with Chinese partners as a mode of entry. As a result, EU companies are competing on unfair terms in the Chinese market (Liu, 2008). For what is more, China has imposed local requirements through direct legislation limiting EU exports. Hence, there is an inadequate legal protection for EU companies since

China's regulatory regime is in favor of local producers. The European Union will continue to press China to protect the rights of EU companies through a transparent legal and judicial systems since the EU represents more than 19 percent of China's external trade. Nevertheless, in order for the Chinese government to encourage foreign investment in China, they offer an appealing tax exemption and deduction for joint venture entities (Baocheng, 2007). Also, what is crucial for companies when forming a joint venture is to discover a partner that brings to the venture valuable government relations and industry knowledge (Pranee, 2009). For what is more, there is an ongoing dialogue between the European Commission and the Chinese Government to improve European business in China since the EU-China trade reflects the overall trade of the EU with emerging markets.

The cultural framework of each country is pivotal for international entries since it has direct impacts on their performance (Brouthers, 2002). According to the author, the national culture of the country includes investment risks associated with the company that chooses to entry a specific country. Focusing on China, the Chinese exercise a diverse standard when they treat people (Lu, 2012). More specifically, this standard is linked to an essential Chinese word named Guanxi which means relationship among people

The cultural framework of each country is pivotal for international entries since it has direct impacts on their performance (Brouthers, 2002). According to the author, the national culture of the country includes investment risks associated with the company that chooses to entry a specific country. Focusing on China, the Chinese exercise a diverse standard when they treat people (Lu, 2012). More specifically, this standard is linked to an essential Chinese word named Guanxi which means relationship among people. The Chinese society can be explained through three circles (Lu, 2012). The inner circle consists of his or her family, the middle circle consists of relatives, neighbors, employees as well as close friends, whereas the outer circle includes strangers. Furthermore, there are three types of rules when individuals in societies exchange or allocate resources. First and foremost, the equity rule which states that people in a society should be rewarded for their contributions. Secondly, the equality rule indicates that all individuals should contribute to benefits and losses in an equal manner without actually consider the amount of the contribution they have given. Finally, the need rule states that the sharing of benefits in a society should include each individual's practical needs no matter his or her contribution to society (Hwang, 1987).

From the business sector perspective, because the Chinese treat individuals according to 'Guanxi', the Chinese will want to get to know the actual person before closing any deal and there is a need for mutual trust and respect (ibid). Moreover, business etiquette for the Chinese is crucial in terms of business interactions. Business etiquette for the Chinese means that a person is sincere about his or her intentions, resources and goals (Vollmer, 2012). In other words, generating goodwill is a sign of true commitment and respect for business transactions.

The DS549 Case

Several cases were brought to the dispute settlement mechanism (DSM) in recent years. This chapter will analyze a case in relation the technology transfer as it was already discussed earlier. Technology transfer in China is one of the biggest importers of technology worldwide.

There was a Dispute Settlement (DS549) between the European Union and China regarding the transfer of foreign technology in China, were the European Union claimed on June 1, 2018, that the Government of the People's Republic of China imposes a different set of rules for the importation of technology through its domestic legislation (WTO, 2018). More specifically, there is reference to the limited protection of foreign Intellectual Property rights as well as allegations for discrimination against foreign firms that are not in compliance with WTO's obligations. Japan as well as the United States requested to join the consultations. This topic is of great importance since it emphasizes on the different institutional environment that China encompasses where there is limited opportunity for firm internationalization. According to the authors (1999), technology transfer can be used as strategic mean for increased collaboration between the EU and the Chinese economies, therefore such barriers are of primary concern (Michalski & Pan, 2017).

Copyright and trademark piracy in China have reached a peak level according to Bird (2006). More specifically, piracy levels have reached ninety percent across all the sectors of copyright and there are at least eighty three manufacturing plants in China with the purpose of manufacturing pirated goods. Although China has enacted a patent law, the increased competition in their domestic market pressures them be more protective of their own domestic intellectual property rather than the foreign one (Behrman et al., 1989). For what is more, despite the new Chinese laws that were introduced in the Supreme Judicial Court of China, there are limited efforts for reducing piracy because the country feels that foreign investments threaten their sovereignty (Behrman et al., 1989).

Western companies cannot enforce their IP rights in China because of its weak legal system (Bieberbach, 2012). More specifically, there is limited protection of foreign IPR in the areas of patents, copyrights and trademarks where they can easily be imitated by local competitors that put their domestic priorities first. According to the developing countries they argue that they achieved their current development levels because there were restricted IP rules (Bird, 2006). For what is more, they respond that if they were to accept strong intellectual property restrictions there would be less opportunities for them to catch up to more advanced nations.

There is a certain way in which WTO law categorizes developing countries. First and foremost, each country has to declare itself a 'developing country' where this status is in compliance with specific provisions arising from part of the agreements of the Uruguay Round which encompasses a special and differential treatment (Sautenet, 2007). Therefore, China declared itself to be a developing country in the Report of the Working Group on the Accession of China to the WTO and thus can enforce policies concerning IP rights protection that favor their domestic economy. Such restrictions on IP rights protection, try to restrict foreign firms to produce products or offer services that are of the same quality and become a monopolist in the market (Wu, 2001). Stricter IP rights protection in china scope in protecting the profits of the country as well as improving China's export quality and terms of trade in the long-run with less adverse income or even unskilled labor (Wu, 2001).

TECHNOLOGY TRANSFER (TT) IN CHINA

The legal framework for the relations between EC-China is the "1985 EC-China Trade and Cooperation Agreement" where EC-China Joint Committee reviews once a year all topics related to trade issues. In the 1998 Communication, the commission identified the importance of promoting foreign investment between Europe and China (Bruun & Bennett, 2002). According to the European Council, China is considered to be a major partner of the EU with the aim of implementing strategic partnerships in the future (Sautenet, 2007). After its accession to the WTO, the country sets out on the path of a global, stable and long-term relationship with the EU and imply that it will act on the basis of WTO rules and fair competition.

The Chinese government has encouraged foreign technology transfer despite China's strong investment laws and regulations that put severe pressure on foreign investors (Andreosso-O'Callaghan & Qian, 1999). The European Union is China's major supplier of advanced technology since it accounts for a large part of China's total imports (ibid). Many European firms had positive outcomes from TT into the specific market. For example, many EU firms have benefited from China's rapid economic growth rates, the size of the market, the abundance of technological resources that the country offers as well as incentives in promoting technology-embodied FDI (ibid). To sum up, there are benefits for EU TT into the Chinese market; nevertheless, in the long run there might be a loss of advantage due to the country's weak legal system (Bruun & Bennett, 2002).

Nonetheless, European companies must weigh also the risks when considering to transfer their technology to the Chinese market. Because of China's eagerness to dominate the technological market, they sometimes discriminate foreign firms that import technologies into the particular market (Jarrett & Wendholt, 2010). This is due to the ineffective legal institution of China's that negatively affects foreign business operations. Ensuring the protection of the technological transfer is of primary concern for foreign firms that target the Chinese market. More specifically, there are numerous risks due to the insufficient legal protection of IPR rights that derives from the different legislation that China has when compared to Western systems (Bruun & Bennett, 2002). Moreover, the inadequacy of IPR protection can make the intellectual property fall into the hands of rivals and ultimately cost the future of the company (Bruun & Bennett, 2002). To reciprocate, there are both benefits and risks that need to be taken into consideration when foreign companies decide to transfer their technology into the Chinese market.

OVERCOMING THE CHALLENGES

In the case of FDI, finding a Chinese partner that will bring valuable government relations and industry knowledge is of great importance (Pranee, 2009). In order to overcome some of the aforementioned challenges that foreign firms face when transferring their technology into the Chinese market, there is a need for a transparent legal system that needs to be critically evaluated prior entry into the market (Baocheng, 2007). More specifically, in 2008 China issued a National IP Strategy with the aim of protecting IP rights for both China and third parties as well as improving IP Law enforcement in general (Bieberbach, 2012). However, according to a new implementation strategy that involved patent issues, problems are still remaining because the patent system has not being yet fully integrated with the ongoing development of China's. Therefore, international companies should take into consideration the ongoing changes related to the IP landscape of China's in order to use the appropriate IP strategy (Bieberbach, 2012).

In the case of patents, they should be published as a 'defensive publication' for example via the internet in order to make them prior art and to prevent Chinese companies to file their own IP rights and modify them (2012). In general, there is a need for experimental evidence and specific data of all actions in order to prove the product's or service authenticity. Last but not least, it is of vital importance for foreign companies choose an IP experienced court in China (Beijing or Shanghai) instead of a local Administration for Industry and Commerce (AIC) in order to avoid local protectionism. Furthermore, Western companies should establish a system or representation such as the chambers of commerce in China in order to communicate with the Chinese authorities and resolve such disputes.

CONCLUSION

The trade between the EU and China has grown substantially over the years since there is a common interest in implementing strategic partnerships that will encourage further economic development for both nations (Sautenet, 2007). Both the European Union and China have made tremendous progress in investing on building a global strategic partnership. In order to be more specific, in the sixth EU-China summit the two parties endorsed the development of creating such a relationship and focus overall on enriching both economies (Sautenet, 2007). Furthermore, technology transfer has being in China's spotlight for decades since it involves financial benefits and incentives for further collaborations with foreign companies (Jarrett & Wendholt, 2010). However, due to the country's weak legal system and more particularly in the context of limited protection when it comes to IPR, European firms hesitate to invest in such markets (Landry et al., 1999). Although China has gradually reformed its patent system with its accession in the WTO, issues still arise concerning the protection of Intellectual Property Rights.

In a changing environment such as that of China's the IP system is not recommended to rely solely on the European IP system even if it is rather similar nowadays. Therefore in order to overcome the legal challenges that China has, there is a need for an internal IP structure that will include all aspects of its protection, clear empirical data in case of a dispute as well as establishing relationships with systems such as the chamber of commerce in China in order to communicate and resolve any future issues that might arise. The Director- General Designate of the WTO, Supachai Panitchpakdi characterizes China's accession into the WTO as a 'wakeup call' with reference to other Asian countries that should accelerate their reforms as well in order to boost their economic performance not only in the rest developing Asia but also in the rest of the world. Therefore, such reforms increase the country's openness for foreign trade as well as pinpointing opportunities for future businesses.

ACKNOWLEDGMENT

This chapter was developed in the framework of B-in-EU, i.e. Jean Monnet Module On European Union And Active EU Citizenship For Business Students: An Interdisciplinary Approach, coordinated by Dr. Anna Visvizi, co-funded by the European Commission under the Erasmus+ Jean Monnet funding scheme [Project Reference: 587632-EPP-1-2017-1-US-EPPJMO-MODULE].

REFERENCES

Alexandru, B., & Gabriela, S. (2008). Opportunities and challenges of the European businesses in China. *Annals of the University of Oradea. Economic Science Series*, *17*(1), 63–66.

Andreosso-O'Callaghan, B., & Qian, W. (1999). Technology Transfer: A Mode of Collaboration Between the European Union and China. *Europe-Asia Studies*, *51*(1), 123–142. doi:10.1080/09668139999155

Awokuse, T., & Yin, H. (2010). Intellectual property rights protection and the surge in FDI in China. *Journal of Comparative Economics*, *38*(2), 217–224. doi:10.1016/j.jce.2009.10.001

Baocheng, L. (2007). Entry Encounters into China Market. *International Management Review*, *3*(3), 97–105.

Behrman, J. N., Fischer, W. A., & Simon, D. F. (1989). Transferring Technology to China. *The International Trade Journal*, *4*(1), 49–67. doi:10.1080/08853908908523683

Bieberbach, A. (2012). IP strategies in business operations with China. *Journal of Business Chemistry*, *9*(3), 161–166. Retrieved from https://acg.idm.oclc.org/login?url=http://search.ebscohost.com/login.aspx?direct=true&db=bth&AN=83388048&scope=site

Bird, R. C. (2006). Defending Intellectual Property Rights in the Bric Economies. *American Business Law Journal*, *43*(2), 317–363. doi:10.1111/j.1744-1714.2006.00019.x

Brouthers, K. D. (2002). Institutional, Cultural and Transaction Cost Influences on Entry Mode Choice and Performance. *Journal of International Business Studies*, *33*(2), 203–221. doi:10.1057/palgrave.jibs.8491013

Bruun, P., & Bennett, D. (2002). Transfer of Technology to China: A Scandinavian and European Perspective. *European Management Journal*, *20*(1), 98–106. doi:10.1016/S0263-2373(01)00118-9

Dai, C. (2010). Corruption and Anti-Corruption in China: Challenges and Countermeasures. *Journal of International Business Ethics*, *3*(2), 58–70.

Holtbrügge, D., & Baron, A. (2013). Market Entry Strategies in Emerging Markets: An Institutional Study in the BRIC Countries. *Thunderbird International Business Review*, *55*(3), 237–252. doi:10.1002/tie.21541

Hsieh, P. (2009). China-United States Trade Negotiations and Disputes: The WTO and Beyond. *Asian Journal of WTO & International Health Law and Policy*, *4*(2), 368–399.

Hwang, K. (1987). Face and Favor: The Chinese Power Game. *American Journal of Sociology*, *92*(4), 944–974. doi:10.1086/228588

Jarrett, K., & Wendholt, A. (2010). Transferring Technology to Transform China--Is It Worth It? *The China Business Review*, *37*(2), 20–24. Retrieved from https://acg.idm.oclc.org/login?url=http://search.ebscohost.com/login.aspx?direct=true&db=bth&AN=48666412&scope=site

Keupp, M. M., Beckenbauer, A., & Gassmann, O. (2010). Enforcing Intellectual Property Rights in Weak Appropriability Regimes. *Management International Review*, *50*(1), 109–130. doi:10.100711575-009-0020-9

Landry, S. P., Wai-Yee Canri, C., & Renner, C. J. (1999). Doing Business with China: How to Steer Clear of Dangerous Legal Pitfalls. *Journal of Corporate Accounting & Finance (Wiley)*, *10*(4), 63–71. doi:10.1002/(SICI)1097-0053(199922)10:4<63::AID-JCAF6>3.0.CO;2-#

Liu, M. (2018). The New Chinese Foreign Investment Law and Its Implication on Foreign Investors. *Northwestern Journal of International Law & Business, 38*(2), 285–306. Retrieved from https://acg.idm.oclc.org/login?url=http://search.ebscohost.com/login.aspx?direct=true&db=bth&AN=128778956&scope=site

Michalski, A., & Pan, Z. (2017). *Role Dynamics in a Structured Relationship: The EU-China Strategic Partnership*. Retrieved from https://acg.idm.oclc.org/login?url=http://search.ebscohost.com/login.aspx?direct=true&db=eoh&AN=EP122343928&scope=site

Nayyar, D. (2016). BRICS, developing countries and global governance. *Third World Quarterly*, *37*(4), 575–591. doi:10.1080/01436597.2015.1116365

Pranee, D. C. (2009). Impact of Chinese Cultural Development and Negotiation Strategies, FDI, Competitiveness, China International Business Growth, and Management Practice. *International Journal of Organizational Innovation*, *2*(1), 13–40.

Sautenet, A. (2007). The Current Status and Prospects of the 'Strategic Partnership' between the EU and China: Towards the Conclusion of a Partnership and Cooperation Agreement. *European Law Journal*, *13*(6), 699–731. doi:10.1111/j.1468-0386.2007.00395.x

Spies, W. T. (2011). The Chinese Miracle & the Fifteen-Year Fuse. *ISM Journal of International Business*, *1*(2), 2–42.

Voituriez, T., & Wang, X. (2015). Real Challenges Behind the EU–China PV Trade Dispute Settlement. *Climate Policy*, 670-677. doi:10.1080/14693062.2015.1009868

Vollmer, S. (2012). Business Etiquette in China. *Journal of Accountancy*, *214*(6), 18.

Williamson, P., & Zeng, M. (2004). Strategies for Competing in a Changed China. *MIT Sloan Management Review*, *45*(4), 85–91.

World Trade Organization. (n.d.). Retrieved October 27, 2018, from https://www.wto.org/english/tratop_e/dispu_e/cases_e/ds549_e.htm

Wu, X. (2001). Foreign direct investment, intellectual property rights, and wage inequality in China. *China Economic Review, 11*, 361-384. doi:10.1016/S1043-951X(01)00035-9

Zhu, X. (2012). Understanding China's Growth: Past, Present, and Future. *The Journal of Economic Perspectives*, *26*(4), 103–124. doi:10.1257/jep.26.4.103

APPENDIX

Figure 1.

Figure 2.

European Commission | Directorate-General for Trade

China

Main Indicators

Indicator Source IMF (World Economic Outlook)	unit	2013	2014	2015	2016	2017
Population	Millions of inhabitants	1,361	1,368	1,375	1,383	1,390
GDP	Billions of euros	7,255	7,930	10,118	10,138	10,635
GDP per capita	Euros	5,332	5,797	7,361	7,332	7,651
Real GDP growth	%	7.8	7.3	6.9	6.7	6.9
Inflation rate	%	2.6	2.0	1.4	2.0	1.6
Current account balance	% of GDP	1.5	2.2	2.7	1.8	1.4

Trade in Goods

China with World (Source IMF) | EU with China (Source Eurostat)

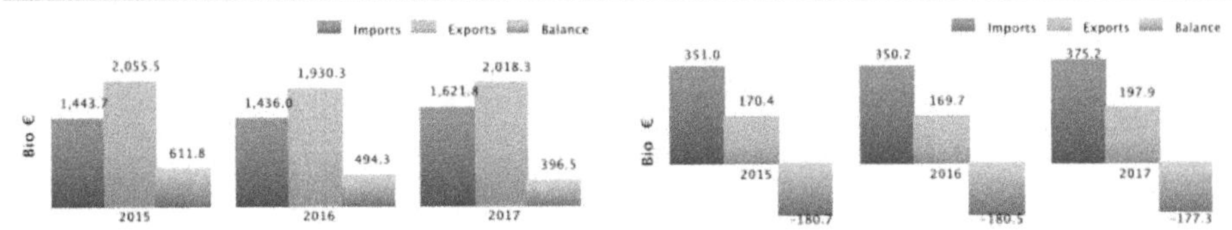

Figure 3.

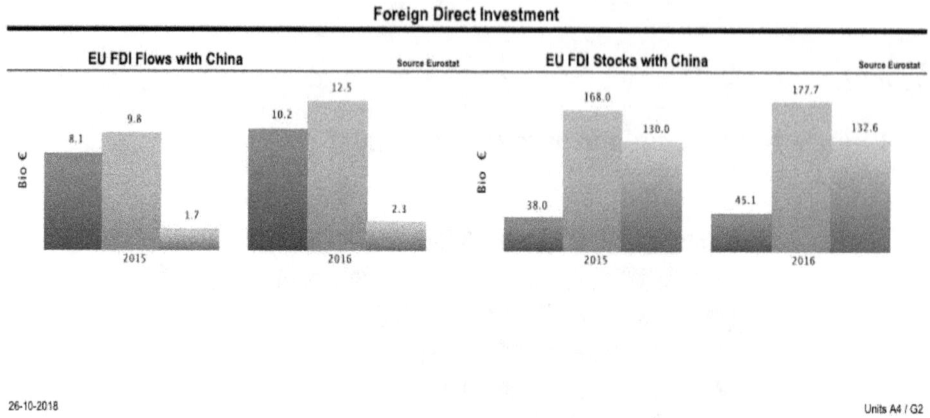
Foreign Direct Investment
EU FDI Flows with China
Source Eurostat
EU FDI Stocks with China
Source Eurostat
Bio €
8.1
9.8
1.7
2015
10.2
12.5
2.1
2016
Bio €
38.0
168.0
130.0
2015
45.1
177.7
132.6
2016
26-10-2018
Units A4 / G2

Chapter 5
Literature Survey on the "Belt and Road" Initiative:
A Bibliometric Analysis

Saleh Shahriar
https://orcid.org/0000-0001-5199-3258
Northwest A&F University, China

ABSTRACT

The purpose of this chapter is to analyze some peer-reviewed publications to find out the key research journals, contents, and emerging issues of the "B&R" Initiative led by China. Based on the tools and techniques of bibliometric approach, a total of 210 research papers were extracted systematically from the Scopus, Science Direct, and the Web of Science databases. The research methods integrated in this chapters are systematic literature review, bibliometric citation, authorships and affiliations, and contents analyses. This chapter argues that there are growing academic interests and attentions in the B&R research across the world. The principal reasons for the increase in research with regard to the B&R Initiative are the appearance of publications in prestigious journals, the global economic rise of China and its model of development, and the policy priorities of the government of China. The results show that a total of 32 peer-reviewed research papers were published in 10 prestigious journals.

DOI: 10.4018/978-1-5225-8980-8.ch005

INTRODUCTION

China is an emerging economic powerhouse in the world. It launched the 'Belt and Road' (B&R afterward) Initiative in 2013. The Initiative consists of two parts, namely, the Silk Road Economic Belt and the 21st Century Maritime Silk Road. There are 65 countries from different continents along the Belt and Road Initiative. According to the China Statistical Yearbook 2016, China's foreign direct investment in Asia, Africa, Europe, Latin America and pacific Islands totaled about $12.6 million. China's stock of capital has grown by an average rate of about 12% per year over the last 20 years, and its capital-output ratio has increased rapidly since the 1990s. China initiated 'going global' policy in 2002 mainly to promote its overseas investment activity. After 2007 global economic crisis, the Chinese government launched a bailout plan of 4 trillion yuan in November 2008 and expressed its desire to move from export-led growth to promoting domestic demand and expand internal markets. Now China is a 'global trade power' (Naughton, 2007). The Chinese economy has undergone a rapid change in the past two decades or so, we need to have a systematic picture of the recent development and the present situations. China has pledged to invest US$ 1.25 trillion worldwide by 2025, exceeding any previous investment record made either by the US or the Soviet Union in their past geopolitical rivalry for global domination(Tracy, Shvarts, Simonov, & Babenko, 2017). Since 2013, the 'B&R' Initiative has emerged as a main feature of China's international economic policy (Julien Chaisse & Mitsuo Matsushita, 2018). The geographical location of the 65 countries along the Belt & Road Initiative are mentioned in the Appendix (See Table 6).

What are the key journals and impactful articles in the B&R research? Which are the current research contents and emerging themes in the B&R studies? What are the underlying research themes? Who has published and what has been written? There is an increasing amount of literature on the B&R Initiative. For example, the Chinese scholars and academics published more than 8400 papers in 2015, as compared to 492 in 2014 (Rolland, 2017). In 2017, the 'B&R' Initiative was declared as a 'project of the century'. This chapter is a sound contribution to the emerging literature on the 'B&R' Initiative, focusing on the state of the topic in the current lines and trends of work. The motivation for this work is explained in the next section.

The remainder of this chapter is structured as follows. Section 2 explains the data sources, database search technique and methodology. The main findings, results and discussions are presented in section 3. This section is also divided into several sub-sections and thematic segments. Finally, section 4 concludes the chapter.

RESEARCH MOTIVATION AND METHODOLOGY

Systematic Literature Search

Ethridge said, 'The central purpose of the literature review is to provide the researcher and the reader with an understanding of the body of literature as it relates to the current or proposed research. The purpose includes an understanding of the strengths and weaknesses of the prior research' (Ethridge, 2004). I have followed the standard procedures of data collection; such as, identification, screening, eligibility, and inclusion of studies (Khan, Kunz, Kleijnen, & Antes, 2003; Xiao & Watson, 2017). This paper attempts to collect, appraise, and synthesize available empirical evidence that meets pre-defined criteria in order to achieve the research purpose. There are different types of literature review techniques; such as, systematic literature review, critical review, content analysis, meta-analysis, bibliometric analysis, citation analysis, word and co-word analysis, co-authors and affiliations analysis etc. The application of systematic literature review is observed in multiple disciplines (Fleary, Joseph, & Pappagianopoulos, 2018; Piccarozzi, Aquilani, & Gatti, 2018; Pisani, Reyes, & García, 2009; Ritz, Brewer, & Neumann, 2016).

The Bibliometric Approach

A bibliometric analysis examines bibliographic materials from an objective and quantitative perspective that proves useful in organizing information within a specific field. The bibliometric methods have already been applied in the areas of business economics (Castillo-Vergara, Alvarez-Marin, & Placencio-Hidalgo, 2018), green supply chain management (Maditati, Munim, Schramm, & Kummer, 2018), public administration (Ni, Sugimoto, & Robbin, 2017), agricultural economics (Q. Chen, Geng, & Zhu, 2018; Luo, Ji, Qiu, & Jia, 2018), markets studies (Cintra, Cassol, Ribeiro, & de Carvalho, 2018), and healthcare research (Musa, Park, Munkhdalai, & Ryu, 2018). There is, however, a dearth of research on the bibliometric analysis of the 'B&R' Initiative. This study is a timely attempt to fill that research gap.

Figure 1 shows the flow diagram of the major steps in the data collection process. The research works under review have been published over a period of 4 years, ranging from 2015 to 2018. The materials used in this chapter are obtained from several data sources, including the Science Direct, Scopus, Google Scholar, China Knowledge Resource Integrated Database (CNKI) and the Web of Science.

Figure 1. Literature review flow diagram
Source: Based on Khan, Kunz, Kleijnen, and Antes (2003)

First Step: Searched Question

What are the institutional features of the Belt and Road Initiative?

↓

Second Step: Research Questions

Q1: What are the key papers and journals in the Belt and Road research?

Q2: What are the underlying research streams?

Q3: Who has published and what has been written on the issue of the B&R Initiative?

↓

Third Step: Primary Searches

- ***Initial search with key words:*** One Belt and One Road Initiative (OBOR), Belt and Road Initiative (BRI), Asian Infrastructure Investment Bank (AIIB), Economic Corridors, Silk Road Fund, Silk Road Economic Belt
- ***Search engine:*** Google scholar, Web of Science, Scopus, Science Direct, Chinese Baidu, and CNKI

↓

Fourth Step: Title and Abstract Review

Reviewed the title and abstract of the studies selected in the primary search process. Only those studies were considered for reviews that were matched with our keywords and objective.

↓

Fifth Step: Full Text Review

In the final step, the studies were included on the basis of the availability of desired information and completeness of reporting.

The analysis presented in this study is selective in a number of ways. First, we only focus on the peer-reviewed journals. As a result, we haven't included any media outlet, judgmental article, or opinion piece. The research papers are the unit of analysis in the bibliometric analysis. There is no doubt that some working papers are potentially good publications in near future, and they can strength our understanding on the 'B&R' Initiative. Second, our article is limited towards the research paper published in English Language Journal. The selection has no implication on our views with regard to the quality of other journals or publications. Our inclusion criterion for systematic review was simple and reliable, because we have picked up the Social Science Citation Index (SSCI) and the Science Citation Index (SCI) papers for the present study (Table 1). It is to be noted here that the majority of our papers are indexed in the SSCI. All the papers, we selected, have been published in peer-reviewed journals. Most of the technical reports, organization-based publications, and online presentations are avoided because of the absence of rigorous peer review process. That doesn't necessarily mean that the remaining works that are beyond our analytical scope lags behind in research quality. The Endnote X8 was used in importing the bibliometric data and citation managements. Also, the Origin 2018b Graphing & Analysis software was used in the analysis of the results.

RESULTS

Results of the Literature Search

With regard to the B&R Initiative, the Web of Science core collection database covers 3,47 documents, as of October 2018. The results were then filtered by document type and research fields. Published research article is here the principal unit of analysis. Out of 3,47 documents, as depicted in Figure 2, 155 research articles were identified

Figure 2. 'B&R' literature in the Web of Science database
Source: Author's own work using the Web of Science (WoS) Database

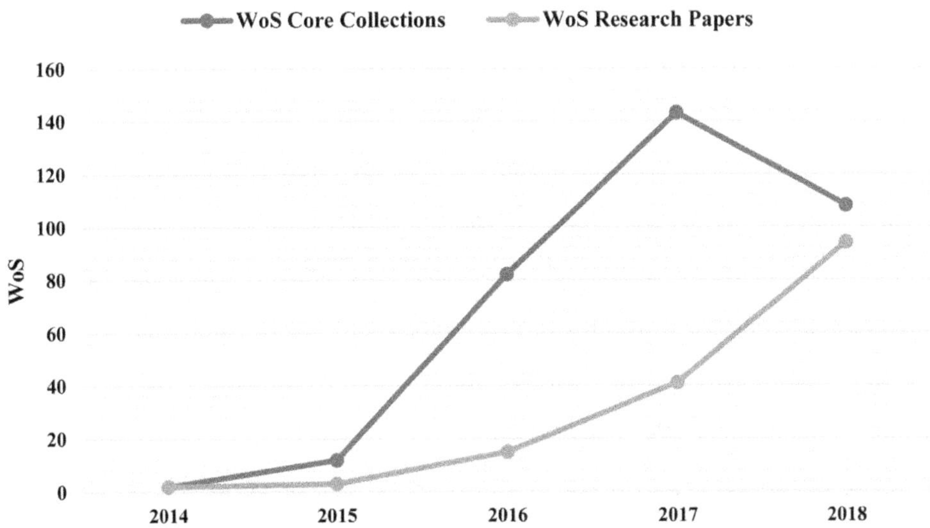

by reviewing their titles, abstracts, key words, journal names, date of publication and research themes. The research field-based distributions of those 155 articles are presented in Figure 3. A total of 33, 32, and 24 articles were published in the fields of economics, international relations and environmental sciences respectively. Also, from the Science Direct database, as shown in Figure 4, we have identified 55 research Papers. The curves in both Figure 2 and Figure 4 show an upward trend of publications. In this way, a total of 210 papers (155+55) are used as sample in this study.

Findings of the Systematic Literature Review

The key findings and main conclusions, derived from the systematic literature review, are summarized in Table 1.

Citation Analysis

Citation analysis is a useful tool to evaluate the performance of the journals. We have found four impactful papers in the broader fields of the 'B&R' studies. The 4 works are regarded as the 'highly cited paper' in the Web of Science database. Table

Figure 3. Research field-wise plotting of 155 papers collected from the WoS database
Source: Author's own construction

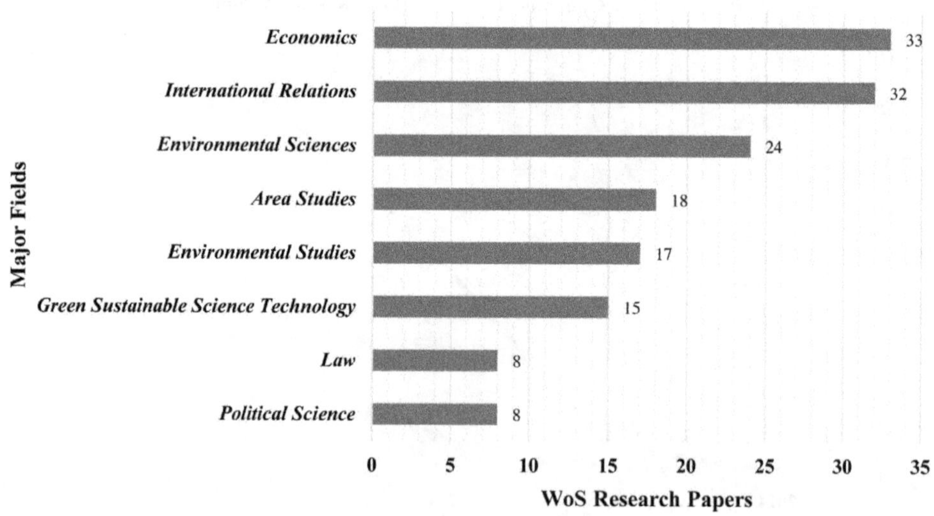

Figure 4. 'B&R' literature in the Science Direct and Scopus Database
Source: Author's own construction

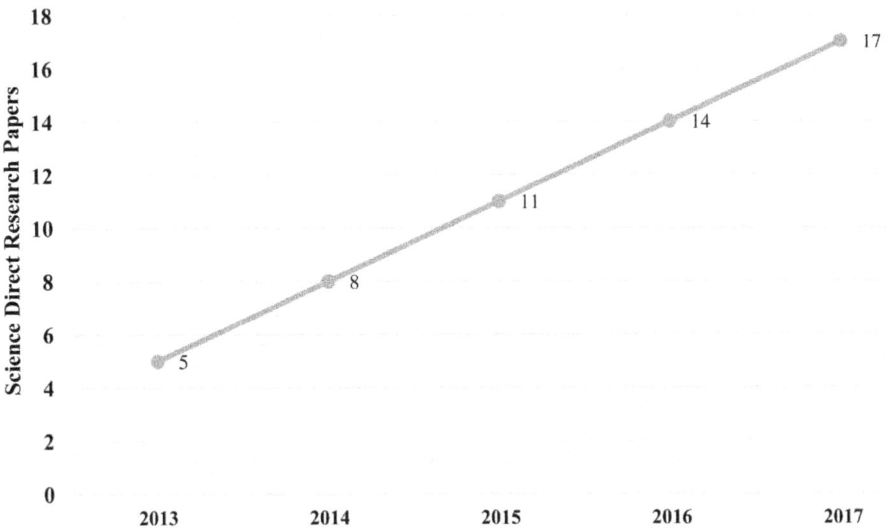

2 presents the details of those 4 papers. The papers were, on an average, cited more than 37 times and published in four impact factor journals. In addition, we attempt to identify the key journals publishing the papers on the issue of the B&R Initiative. Table 3 shows the principal journals, articles, authors and the years of publications. The analysis refers to the ranking of the journals in terms of numbers of papers, authorships and the years of publication. The highest numbers of papers (7) were published in the *China & World Economy*, followed by the *Journal of contemporary China*, an outlet containing 5 papers. The 3rd outlets were the *Geopolitics* (4) and *the Washington Quarterly* (4) altogether. The *China Economic Review* (3) and the *Eurasian Geography and Economics* (3) are together in the 4th position. In essence, a total of 32 research papers with regard to the B&R Initiative were published in 10 leading peer-reviewed journals.

Authorships and Affiliations Analyses

Table 4 presents the analytical results of 32 papers' authorships and their status of institutional affiliations diffused in countries across the globe. Out of 32, 20 papers (62%) were written by a single author whereas the remaining 12 papers (38%) were written by multiple authors (Figure 5). A curious look at the affiliations of the

Table 1. Key findings from the review of the 'B&R' papers (2015-2018)

Authors	Findings and conclusions
Nordin and Weissmann (2018)	The Belt and Road Initiative consists of a network of overland routes and railways, oils and natural gas pipelines and power grids. The researchers argue that China is keen to build a Sino-centric world order based on a networked capitalism.
Zhai (2018)	China is making huge efforts to invest in the countries along the Belt and Road Initiative. This paper explores that China's projected investment under the Initiative ranges from US $ 1.4 trillion to US $ 6 trillion
Garlick (2018)	This paper elucidates the economic and political issues involved in the operation of the China-Pakistan Economic Corridors. It concludes that China's intentions with this economic corridor is more geopolitical than geo-economic.
Cui, Zhang, Wu, and Tseng (2018)	This study examines the issues of agribusiness and stakeholder's theory under the Belt and Road Initiative. It addresses the issues of climate change, green business, sustainable food production, and risks measurements by means of the interpretive structural modeling (ISM). It concludes that agribusiness must serve as an important bridge balancing the interests of people, plants and products.
Tekdal (2018)	The paper highlights the main challenges of the Belt & Road Initiative, and documents how the project is designed to overcome the problems of stagnations in exports, energy dependency, and underdevelopment of Western China. The Initiative is related to increasing China's leverage in its neighborhood, promoting the 'go global', internationalizing the Renminbi (RMB) and reforming global economic governance.
Chung and Voon (2017)	The authors discuss the costs and benefits of participation in the Maritime Silk Road for the South-east Asian countries
Jean-Marc F. Blanchard and Flint (2017)	The Maritime Silk Road Initiative (MSRI) is a geopolitical project with extensive territorial consequences
Jacob (2017)	The paper explains the Indian concerns about the China-Pakistan Economic Corridor. This work argues for the promotion of Sino-Indian engagement on the joint development of the Belt and Road Initiative in South Asia
Ivan Timofeev, Yaroslav Lissovolik, and Liudmila Filippova (2017)	The researchers explain the Russian approach to the Belt and Road Initiative. Russia defines the Initiative as a key priority in its collaboration with China, because it would be 'mutually beneficial projects' for the countries involved
Sidaway and Woon (2017)	This study evaluates the Belt & Road Initiative from the perspective of geopolitics. The paper reviews the Chinese language writings on the topic. The Belt and Road projects are related to China's anti-encirclement struggle. The Initiative reflects the narratives of anti-imperialism and anti-colonialism. It links the harmonious and peaceful developments of China and brings win-win benefits for the global community.
Palit (2017)	The researcher examines the Maritime Silk Road Initiative and argues that it is important for India to appreciate the geopolitical character of this unprecedented infrastructure initiative.
Y. Huang (2016)	This paper provides a preliminary assessment of China's Belt and Road Initiative and explains the motivation behind the Initiative. The work considers the Initiative as one of China's major international initiative along with the AIIB and BRICS New Development Bank. It explains how the high-speed railroads, oil and gas pipelines and telecom and electricity links to the cross-country projects. But the main challenges lie in the economically underdeveloped and politically unstable 'Belt and Road' regions.

continued on following page

Table 1. Continued

Authors	Findings and conclusions
Brewster (2017)	The study analyzes the factors and dynamics of China's growing geo-strategic interest in the Indian Ocean
M. M. Du (2016)	This paper shows statistically that Chinese overseas direct investment has increased significantly after the inaugural of the Belt & Road Initiative
R. Xiao (2016)	The study argues that the Belt and Road Initiative could be seen as an institution-building effort on the part of China. The establishment of the AIIB is an innovative financial institution.
Herrero and Xu (2017)	The study consider trade as a key pillar of the Belt and Road Initiative. It concludes that the Initiative would improve transport infrastructure and would be advantageous for Europe.
Lemoine and Unal (2017)	The paper analyzes the 'new normal' economic growth of China. They reveal that since the financial crisis of 2007-08 China's foreign trade continued to grow faster than international trade. The new normal growth has an impact on the trade patterns of China. Between 2007 and 2015, China's share in global exports increased from 9% to 14%.
L.-H. Chan (2017)	The paper raises the question: was there any strategic rationale for China to initiate a multinational development bank like the AIIB? According to her, China felt threatened by the Obama Administration's rebalance to the Asia Pacific strategy. The 'B&R' Initiative was, as result, China's soft balancing against the US 'pivot to Asia'.
Vangeli (2017)	This paper is about China's relationship with the 16 countries of Central, East and Southeast Europe under the Belt and Road Initiative. The Initiative is about to bring a global political economic paradigm shifts and its spirit will be central in determining the bilateral regional relationship.
Rolland (2017)	The paper analyzes the elements of the Belt and Road Initiative including the economic corridors, AIIB, China Dream and its implications. The Initiative is colored by the Chinese exceptionalism that is an alternative to American hegemony. This contributor draws the attentions of the Western scholars and policy makers to give more attention to the development, underlying motives, and possible strategic implications of China's Belt and Road Initiative.
Fan, Zhang, Liu, and Pan (2016)	The study investigates China's outward FDI efficiency along the countries of the Belt and Initiative by using the stochastic frontier gravity model for the period, 2003 -2013. There are significant differences in FDI performance between Belt countries and Road countries. The study, therefore, concludes that China has large FDI potentials in these countries and needs to remove various trade barriers.
Summers (2016)	The paper argues that China's New Silk Road is developmental in nature. The spatial relations of Silk Road Political economy reflect networks with neighboring countries, known as the 'neighborhood diplomacy'
Y. Huang (2016)	The paper evaluates the benefits and opportunities provided by the opening of the Belt and Road Initiative. According to the study, there are several risk factors, namely, the problems of coordination, political values conflicts, international input prices and anxiety, and sustainability of the cross-border infrastructure projects.
Ferdinand (2016)	Using the published materials from China, the writer in this paper shows the elements of the 'China Dream' campaign of Xi Jinping administration. The Belt and Road Initiative, according to him, is Xi's main foreign policy innovation that attempts to lay the basis for a more active and distinctive long-term foreign policy.

continued on following page

Table 1. Continued

Authors	Findings and conclusions
H. Yu (2016)	The author analyzes the motivation, context and background of China's One Belt and One Road Initiative and the establishment of the AIIB. The study concludes that the Initiative is the reflection of the rise of China as a global power
Karim (2015)	The author has analyzed the challenges and opportunities of the Maritime Silk Road with special reference to the Bay of Bengal region. China proposed to build a Deep Seaport at Chittagong, Bangladesh. The probable fear is that the Bay of Bengal may turn out to be another frontier of great power rivalry.

Source: Based on author's previous paper (Shahriar, Qian, Irshad, Kea, Abdullahi & Sarkar, 2018)

Table 2. Top cited papers and principal authors' affiliated institutions

Papers, journals and citations			JCR*			
HCP*	**Journal**	**TC***	**JCR Category**	**5-year IF**	**Rank in Category**	**QIC**
Ferdinand (2016)	International Affairs	45	International Relations	2.703	8 of 85	Q1
Y. Huang (2016)	China Economic Review	34	Economics	2.397	96 of 353	Q2
Summers (2016)	Third World Quarterly	29	Planning and Development	2.246	25 of 57	Q2
S.-O. Lee, Wainwright, and Glassman (2018)	Environment and Planning A	41	Environmental Studies	2.152	47 of 109	Q2

Source: Author's own work *Note: TC= Total Citation, HCP= Highly Cited Paper, JCR=Journal Citation Reports, IF=Impact Factor, QIC: Quartile in Category.

principal authors reveal the diverse geographical locations and global institutions. The first authors of the 10 papers are found to be affiliated in the Mainland institutions of China; such as, the Peking University, East China Normal University, Fudan University and Wuhan University. Also, interested were those who were affiliated in the institutions that remain outside of China- especially in the USA, Australia, England, Italy, Poland, Russia, India, Netherlands, Iran and Turkey. There are instances of international collaborations among authors. It is my observation that the South-East, South- Asian and African authors elicited less interests in the B&R research.

Table 3. Leading 10 journals in 'B&R' research

No.	Name of the journal	#Articles	Authors and the year of publication
1	China & World Economy	7	Jacob (2017);Vangeli (2017); Herrero and Xu (2017); Gabusi (2017); Ivan Timofeev, Yaroslav Lissovolik, and Liudmila Filippova (2017b); Cinar, Johnson, and Geusz (2016); Shariatinia and Azizi (2017)
2	Journal of Contemporary China	5	H. Yu (2016); Malik (2017); J.-M.F. Blanchard (2018); Garlick (2018),; Reeves (2018)
3	Geopolitics	4	Jean-Marc F. Blanchard and Flint (2017); Brewster (2017); Jean-Marc F. Blanchard (2017); X. Zhang (2017)
4	The Washington Quarterly	4	Rolland (2017); Zongyou (2017); Poh (2017); Xiaotong and Keith (2017)
5	China Economic Review	3	Cheng (2016); Y. Huang (2016); J. Du and Zhang (2018)
6	Eurasian Geography and Economics	3	Hofman (2016); Jackson and Dear (2016); Tracy et al. (2017)
7	International Affairs	2	Ferdinand (2016); Nordin and Weissmann (2018)
8	The Pacific Review	2	Tekdal (2018); R. Xiao (2016)
9	Third World Quarterly	1	Summers (2016)
10	Environment and Planning A	1	S.-O. Lee et al. (2018)
Total	**10**	**32**	

Source: Author's own work (Source: Author's calculation based on the Scopus, WoS, CNKI, and the Google Scholar)

Identification of the Emerging Research Fields and Underlying Trends Through the Content Analysis

Table 5 presents the emerging subject-matters and research trends in the B&R Initiative. The largest numbers of papers were published on the issue of the AIIB (10) and maritime silk road (11) respectively. Topic-wise distribution of the remaining papers were as follows: AIIB (10), maritime silk road (10), the South China Sea (7), OFDI (6), the Silk Road Economic Belt (6). economic integration (6), border issues (6), international trade (6), terrorism and security (5) and others.

Table 4. Authorship status of 32 paper and institutional affiliations

Serial	Authors, Years	Institutions of the first author	Authorship
1	Ferdinand (2016)	University of Warwick, England	Single author
2	Y. Huang (2016)	Peking University, China	Single author
3	Summers (2016)	Chinese University of Hong Kong, China	Single author
4	S.-O. Lee et al. (2018)	Korea Advanced Institute of Science and Technology, South Korea	Coauthors
5	Jacob (2017)	Institute of Chinese Studies, India	Single author
6	Vangeli (2017)	Graduate School for Social Research, Polish Academy of Sciences, Poland	Single author
7	Herrero and Xu (2017)	Beijing Normal University, China	Coauthors
8	Gabusi (2017)	University of Turin, Italy	Single author
9	Timofeev et al. (2017a)	Moscow State Institute of International Relations of the Ministry of Foreign Affairs of Russia, Russia	Coauthors
10	Cinar et al. (2016)	Loyola University Chicago, Chicago, USA	Coauthors
11	Shariatinia and Azizi (2017)	Shahid Beheshti University, Iran	Coauthors
12	H. Yu (2016)	East Asian Institute, National University of Singapore	Single author
13	Malik (2017)	Daniel K. Inouye Asia–Pacific Center for Security Studies in Honolulu, USA	Single author
14	J.-M.F. Blanchard (2018)	School of Advanced International and Area Studies, East China Normal University, China	Single author
15	Garlick (2018)	University of Economics, Prague, Czech Republic	Single author
16	Reeves (2018)	Daniel K. Inouye Asia Pacific Center for Security Studies in Honolulu, Hawaii, USA	Single author
17	Jean-Marc F. Blanchard and Flint (2017)	School of Advanced International Studies, East China Normal University, Shanghai, China	Coauthors
18	Brewster (2017)	Australian National University, Canberra, Australia	Coauthors
19	Jean-Marc F. Blanchard (2017)	School of Advanced International and Area Studies, East China Normal University, Shanghai, China	Single author
20	X. Zhang (2017)	Center for Russian Studies, School of Advanced International and Area Studies, East China Normal, University, Shanghai, China	Single author
21	Rolland (2017)	National Bureau of Asian Research (NBR), USA	Single author
22	Zongyou (2017)	Center for American Studies, Fudan University, Shanghai, China	Single author

continued on following page

Table 4. Continued

Serial	Authors, Years	Institutions of the first author	Authorship
23	Poh (2017)	S. Rajaratnam School of International Studies (RSIS), Nanyang Technological University, Singapore	Single author
24	Xiaotong and Keith (2017)	School of Political Science and Public Administration, Wuhan University, China	Coauthors
25	Cheng (2016)	Lingnan University, Hong Kong	Single author
26	J. Du and Zhang (2018)	Chinese University of Hong Kong, Hong Kong	Coauthors
27	Hofman (2016)	Leiden University Institute for Area Studies (LIAS), Leiden University, Leiden, The Netherlands	Single author
28	Jackson and Dear (2016)	Metropolitan State University of Denver, USA	Coauthors
29	Tracy et al. (2017)	Amur Branch of WWF Russia, Vladivostok, Russia	Coauthors
30	Nordin and Weissmann (2018)	University of Lancaster, Lancaster, England.	Coauthors
31	Tekdal (2018)	Eskisehir Osmangazi University, Eskisehir, Turkey	Single author
32	R. Xiao (2016)	Institute of International Studies, Fudan University, Shanghai, China	Single author

Source: Author's own work

Figure 5. Authorship distributions of 32 papers (Source: Author's own calculation)

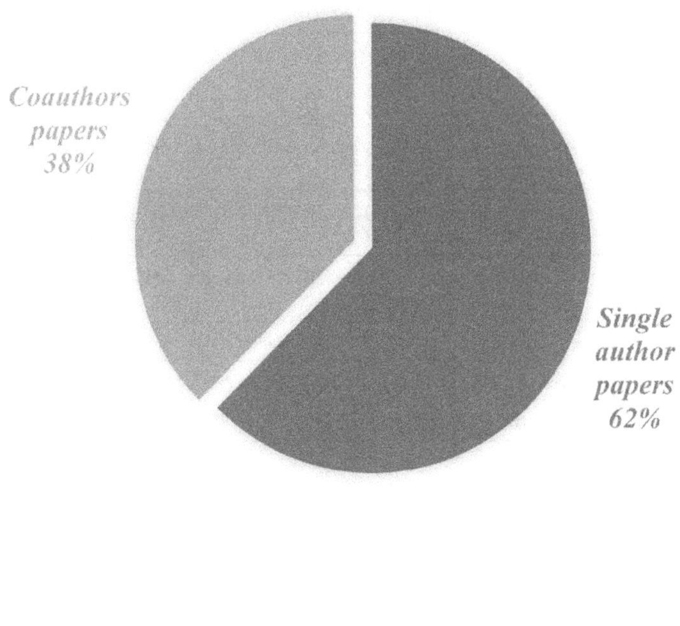

Table 5. Content analysis in B&R studies

Serial	#Studies	Authors and year of publications	Research topic
1	11	Daksueva and Yilmaz (2018) ; Etzioni (2016); L.-H. Chan (2017); Gu (2017); Hameiri and Jones (2018); Mishra (2016); R. Xiao (2016); Peng and Tok (2016); Y. Wang (2018); Peng and Tok (2016); Chin (2016)	Asian Infrastructure Investment Bank (AIIB)
2	11	Kondapalli (2018) ; Palit (2017); Jiang, Li, and Gong (2018); Malik (2017); J.-M.F. Blanchard (2018); Chaziza (2018); Y.-k. Chan (2018); Zongyou (2017); Schinas and Westarp (2017); Shariatinia and Azizi (2017); P. T.-W. Lee, Hu, Lee, Choi, and Shin (2018)	Maritime Silk Road
3	6	Dadwal and Purushothaman (2017); Ptak and Hommel (2016); K. Shi, Yu, Huang, Wu, and Sun (2018); Y. Li and Chang (2015); Sarker, Hossin, Hua, Sarkar, and Kumar (2018); Duan, Jib, Liu, and Fan (2018)	Energy Security
4	8	L. Chen (2016); Fravel (2011); Taffer (2015); Majumdar (2015); TØNnesson (2006); Purbrick (2018); Poh (2017); Uras (2017)	South China Sea
5	6	Schneider (2017); Nguyen, Pham, and Vallée (2016); Soong (2014); Verbiest (2013); S. Huang, Fidrmuc, and Fidrmuc (2015); P. Cai (2016)	Economic Integration
6	7	Fan et al. (2016); H. Liu et al. (2018); Paul and Benito (2017); Ali and Wang (2018); H. Y. Liu, Tang, Chen, and Poznanska (2017); Tuman and Shirali (2017);Chang (2014)	Outward Foreign Direct Investment
7	6	Z. Liu, Wang, Sonn, and Chen (2018); Z. Liu et al. (2018); Jiang et al. (2018); Ye, Binwei, and Starkey (2018); Julien Chaisse and Mitsuo Matsushita (2018); Cinar et al. (2016)	International Trade
8	7	Hofman (2016) ; P. Li, Qian, Howard, and Wu (2015); Howard and Howard (2016); Ostrovskii (2018); Dellios (2017) ;Ye et al. (2018); Clarke (2018)	Silk Road Economic Belt
9	5	Ding (2018); Chaudhuri (2016); Kim (2017); Mackerras (2015); Tschantret (2016)	Terrorism and Security Threats
10	5	Kong (2015); Han (2017); Kurowska-Pysz and Szczepa ́nska-Woszczyna (2017); Agbiboa (2017); Bie, Li, and Zhou (2014)	Border Management
11	4	Johansson and Zhang (2014); C. Zhang (2015); Molero-Simarro (2017); L. Shi (2016)	Income inequality
12	3	Akhtaruzzaman, Berg, and Lien (2017); Busse and Erdogan (2016); Diop and Veeck (2012)	Sino-African relations
13	3	Nie (2016); Chang-Liao (2016); Ferdinand (2016)	Foreign Policy
14	3	Brewster (2017) ; J. Zhang (2016); Khurana (2008)	Indian Ocean
15	2	Shah (2018); Garlick (2018)	Economic Corridors

continued on following page

Table 5. Continued

Serial	#Studies	Authors and year of publications	Research topic
16	2	Feng, Sui, Dong, Jiang, and Chang (2017) ; Brown (2018)	Corruption
17	2	J. Yu and Wu (2018); X. Cai, Che, Zhu, Zhao, and Xie (2018)	Environmental Pollutions
18	3	Cui et al. (2018); J. Yu and Wu (2018), Gong (2018)	Sustainable Agriculture
19	1	Karim (2015)	Bay of Bengal
20	4	Fukase and Martin (2016); J. Huang and Yang (2017); Zhu (2016);X. Yu (2015)	Food Security
21	1	Laborde (2016);	Economic Policy
22	5	H. Liu et al. (2018) ; Hidalgo Martinez and Cartier (2017); Deng, Huang, Rozelle, Zhang, and Li (2015); X. Shi and Yan (2018); Xie et al. (2016)	Urbanization and City Development

Source: Author's own work

Discussion

The aim of this chapter has been to analyze the growth and research trends of peer-reviewed publications in the field of 'B&R' Initiative. As seen above, the analysis shows an increased attention and rise in scientific publications of the B&R Initiative. Several factors could be cited to explain the rise in the number of publications. Of particular importance is the appearance of research publications in the prestigious journals- the *Geopolitics, The Third World Quarterly, International Affairs, China & World Economy, China Economic Review, Eurasian Geography and Economics, International Affairs, and Third World Quarterly* -which encouraged researchers in various disciplines to get involved in this research topic. A potentially second reason is the findings that the B&R Initiative emerged as the top priority project in Xi Jinping's administration. Over 100 countries and international organizations became involved in the Initiative (Jinping, 2017). China is also enthusiastic to advance diplomatically a 'new type of great power relations' with the key international players including the United States of America (Zeng, 2017; Zhao, 2017). As an emerging global power, China has both conflictual and cooperative relations with the USA. Some analysts predicted the negative consequences of the likelihood of a trade war between China and the USA (E. I. Chen, 2014; Hughes, 2005; Stiglitz, 2018; Liu & Woo, 2018).

A third possible reason is the global economic rise of China (Abraham & Van Hove, 2005; Jianwei, 2017; Napoli, 2014; Paul, 2016; Z. Wang, 2017; Y. Xuetong, 2006; L. Zhang, 2010). For instance, the Chinese outward foreign direct investment (OFDI) reached a record high of U.S.$107.84 billion in 2013. This was first time that Chinese OFDI exceeded U.S.$100 billion and represented a 23% rise relative to 2012(Ameer, Xu, & Alotaish, 2017). Again in 2013, China's combined imports and exports rose to USD 4.16 trillion, replacing the US to become the world's largest trading country in merchandise for the first time (Qiu & Xue, 2014). The Chinese scholars put emphasis on the peaceful rise of China (Yan Xuetong, 2014; Yiwei, 2016). Nevertheless, the overall economic investments and activities in countries along the B&R Initiative are on the increase (J. Du & Zhang, 2018; Irshad, Xin, Shahriar, & Arshad, 2018; NBSC, 2011; Tokunaga & Iwasaki, 2017). It was reported that China's Silk Road Fund became active in February 2015, for which China promised $40 billion for 'B&R' Initiative related investment. The Chinese firms are relocating business and operations to the outside world for investment, trade and commerce as part of the 'going out' policy. The New Development Bank, established in July 2014, has allocated $100 billion for supporting infrastructure in BRICS[1] countries (O'Trakoun, 2017). The fourth reason is the development model of China (Maddison, 2005; Stiglitz, 2008). China has success stories in poverty alleviations in the developing world. It has drastically reduced the numbers of poor people (Qin & Chong, 2016). Broadly speaking, the Chinese Initiative is driven towards the following goals: a) to accelerate Chinese economic development, b) to build up China's international image, and c) to lead the world through the combinations and connectedness of trade facilitation, cross-border regional integration and cross-cultural communications. The present low-growth rate of China's economy might be the most significant risk to the B&R Initiative. This slow pace of development is known as 'new normal' growth. China intends to internationalize its currency- renminbi or RMB to create a new financial order, (Ito, 2017; Kwon, 2015; Wei, 2017).

Some analysts are, however, critical of Xi Jinping's B&R Initiative and his nationalistic narrative of the 'Chinese dream' as a tool for centralization of power and sustained crackdowns on freedom of expression (S. Lee, 2017; Qiang, 2019; Zhao, 2016). The B&R Initiative is often criticized as a 'dept trap' for developing countries. But, the Chinese President Xi Jinping emphatically rejects the so-called 'Thucydides Trap' and its analogy that a rising China is destined for war with the United States (Er, 2016). Despite the delivery and prevalence of political rhetorical speeches, the U.S.–China economic relations have expanded significantly over the last 30 years. China is currently the United States' second largest trading partner with

$ 597 billion in total (two ways) goods trade during 2015. U.S. direct investment in China rose up to $65.77 billion in 2014 from $ 59.89 billion in 2013.26 Also, Chinese direct investment in the United States doubled to $14 billion in 2013. Though Chinese direct investment in 2014 slightly decreased to $12 billion, the United States is still is a major destination for Chinese deal flow (Thi Thuy Hang, 2016).

There are risks and uncertainties in the policies adopted by China (F. Zhang, 2016). The rural-urban gap and regional inequality are the long-standing problems in China (Shahriar, 2019; Wu & He, 2018; H. Zhang, 2017). Another major problem for China is to overcome its middle-income trap (Doner & Schneider, 2016; Estrada, Han, Park, & Tian, 2018; Yao, 2015; Zeng & Fang, 2014). Again and again, it is alleged that the B&R Initiative is geared towards ‘creating a China-dominated hegemonic framework’ (Bhattacharya, 2016). Research indicates the conflicts of interests in the implementations of the Chinese projects in several countries. China’s High-Speed Railway projects in Myanmar, for instance, generated local resistance due to the fears of environmental consequences. A section of the people are, therefore, worried about the ‘threat of Chinese dominance’ and high-speed ‘railway imperialism’ (J. J. Wang & Yau, 2018). China could make innovative efforts to work peacefully in the emerging issues of maritime trade, infrastructure, food security, energy, environments & climate change, land border managements, regional developments, agriculture, security and sustainable developments. The ‘B&R’ Initiative has overall five major goals: policy coordination, facilities connectivity, unimpeded trade, financial integration and people-to-people bond (China, 2016). In this regard, China has policies and plans to achieve the stated goals. A noted Chinese scholar has recently reported the progress of the B&R-related works in the following sentences:

China invested more than $70 billion in countries and regions involved in the Belt and Road Initiative (BRI) since its inception in 2013, with commodity trade exceeding $5 trillion. China has set up 75 overseas economic and trade cooperation zones, with an investment exceeding $27 billion and created jobs for more than 200,000 local people. China’s Silk Road Fund has inked 19 projects with committed investment of $7 billion. In the next five years, Chinese outbound investment in BRI countries will reach up to 500 billion USD; Chinese tourists going abroad are expected to reach 700 million. (Yiwei, 2018, p. 2)

The findings are consistent with the general objective and and broad theme of this book. China is creating an internal and external environments for international business and opportunities for technological innovation and sustainable economic development. The 'B&R' could communicate and disseminate knowledge on technology, international business research, and success stories that demonstrate the capacity of China to improve the economic sustainability model in China and to enrich the various value propositions for combined international business innovation. The countries along the 'B&R' have a huge free-trade market (Peyrouse, 2017). As a matter of fact, China could build up an innovative network for emerging markets and sustainable development. Moreover, China has initiated the urbanization programs, and city development is a major objective of the programs. The Chinese cities are turning into the centers of economic growth, productivity, and innovations. So, in accordance with the global experience there is ample research opportunity to develop the smart city innovations and policies in China (A. Visvizi & M. Lytras, 2018; A. Visvizi & M. D. Lytras, 2018; Visvizi, Lytras, Damiani, & Mathkour, 2018).

The present contributor has tried his best to collect all peer-reviewed papers in the domain of B&R studies to endorse research and encourage other researchers to get engaged in this emerging field. However, the author acknowledges the fact that not all publications and journals are indexed in Scopus, Science Direct, Web of Science, and the Google Scholar, and therefore, some publications in the field would perhaps be missing. This is a common limitation in bibliometric studies.

CONCLUSION

The 'B&R' Initiative is one of the most discussed and debated topic in the world. In this chapter, a bibliometric analysis of the 'B&R' research was conducted analyzing 210 articles identified from the Science Direct, Scopus, ISI Web of Science, Google Scholar and CNKI databases. With the help of systematic literature review, bibliometric technique, citation and content analyses, the chapter has identified the key journals, influential papers, and emerging issues in the 'B&R' Initiative. The *China & World Economy, Journal of Contemporary China, Geopolitics, the Washington Quarterly, China Economic Review, International Affairs* are, among other outlets, the leading peer-reviewed journals. In those 10 leading journals, a total of 32 papers were published with regard to the 'B&R' Initiative. Moreover, 4 highly cited influential papers are identified. The institutional affiliations of the first author suggest that they are distributed globally. The authors affiliated in the Chinese universities and research centers were found to be more active in publishing the 'B&R'-related research works than their counterparts. Several mainland universities in China, such as the Peking University, East China Normal University, Fudan University and Wuhan University were the leading institutions in 'B&R'-related publications. This chapter, for the first time, has integrated several research methods and approaches including the systematic literature review, bibliometric, citation, authorships, affiliations and content analyses in the research of China-led B&R Initiative. The central argument made in this chapter is that there are increasing interests and attentions in the 'B&R' research across the world. The principal reasons for the increase in research interests are the appearance of the 'B&R' related publications in several prestigious journals, the global economic emergence of China and its model of development, and the facilitating roles of the government of China.

Last but not least, this study has some important contributions and policy implications. First, the findings generated would help prioritize policies and programs in consistent with the prior research inputs and insights. The implication is that the study would facilitate the informed decision processes, as well as the policy planning resulting in the welfare of a large number of populations along the 'B&R' Initiative. Second, it will guide the future researchers in undertaking more rigorous empirical works. Since the 'B&R' Initiative is still in a nascent stage of development (2013-2018), more studies will facilitate the better understandings of the unexplored issues along the 'B&R' countries. Further research projects could be undertaken to conduct a meta-analysis by using some advanced statistical packages; such as, VOSviewer, SciMAT, HistCite, and R software. Future collaborative studies might focus on the research synthesis and development of a conceptual framework and a theoretical model to better explain the ''B&R' Initiative.

ACKNOWLEDGMENT

I would like to thank the *China Scholarship Council* (CSC) for the financial support. I am grateful to professor Lu Qian for providing valuable suggestions and supervisions. Also, I would like to thank Mr. Sokvibol Kea and Mr. Md Ashraful Islam, Northwest A&F University, Yangling, Shaanxi, for their research assistance. I am grateful to Mrs.Hu Zong-li for her cordial cooperation during my library works and data collection. However, I am responsible for the contents of the paper. I have no conflicts of interest.

REFERENCES

Abraham, F., & Van Hove, J. (2005). The Rise of China: Prospects of Regional Trade Policy. *Review of World Economics*, *141*(3), 486–509. doi:10.100710290-005-0040-x

Agbiboa, D. E. (2017). Borders that Continue to Bother Us: The Politics of Cross-Border Security Cooperation in Africa's Lake Chad Basin. *Commonwealth and Comparative Politics*, *55*(4), 403–425. doi:10.1080/14662043.2017.1312730

Akhtaruzzaman, M., Berg, N., & Lien, D. (2017). Confucius Institutes and FDI Flows from China to Africa. *China Economic Review*, *44*, 241–252. doi:10.1016/j.chieco.2017.02.004

Ali, U., & Wang, J.-J. (2018). Does Outbound Foreign Direct Investment Crowd Out Domestic Investment in China? Evidence from Time Series Analysis. *Global Economic Review*, 1–15. doi:10.1080/1226508x.2018.1492431

Ameer, W., Xu, H., & Alotaish, M. S. M. (2017). Outward Foreign Direct Investment and Domestic Investment: Evidence from China. *Economic Research-Ekonomska Istraživanja*, *30*(1), 777–788. doi:10.1080/1331677X.2017.1314824

Bhattacharya, A. (2016). Conceptualizing the Silk Road Initiative in China's Periphery Policy. *East Asia*, *33*(4), 309–328. doi:10.100712140-016-9263-9

Bie, Q., Li, C., & Zhou, S. (2014). Evaluation of the Effectiveness of Border Policies in Dehong Prefecture of Yunnan, China. *Sustainability*, *6*(8), 5284–5299. doi:10.3390u6085284

Blanchard, J.-M. F. (2017). Probing China's Twenty-First-Century Maritime Silk Road Initiative (MSRI): An Examination of MSRI Narratives. *Geopolitics*, *22*(2), 246–268. doi:10.1080/14650045.2016.1267147

Blanchard, J.-M. F. (2018). China's Maritime Silk Road Initiative (MSRI) and Southeast Asia: A Chinese 'pond' not 'lake' in the Works. *Journal of Contemporary China*, 1–15. doi:10.1080/10670564.2018.1410959

Blanchard, J.-M. F., & Flint, C. (2017). The Geopolitics of China's Maritime Silk Road Initiative. *Geopolitics*, *22*(2), 223–245. doi:10.1080/14650045.2017.1291503

Brewster, D. (2017). Silk Roads and Strings of Pearls: The Strategic Geography of China's New Pathways in the Indian Ocean. *Geopolitics*, *22*(2), 269–291. doi:10.1080/14650045.2016.1223631

Brown, K. (2018). The Anti-Corruption Struggle in Xi Jinping's China: An Alternative Political Narrative. *Asian Affairs*, *49*(1), 1–10. doi:10.1080/03068374.2018.1416008

Busse, M., Erdogan, C. M., & Mühlen, H. (2016). China's Impact on Africa: The Role of Trade, FDI and Aid. *Kyklos*, *69*(2), 228–262. doi:10.1111/kykl.12110

Cai, P. (2016). China's Responses to Mega-Regional FTAs: A Chinese Perspective. *Asian Survey*, *56*(6), 1123–1144. doi:10.1525/as.2016.56.6.1123

Cai, X., Che, X., Zhu, B., Zhao, J., & Xie, R. (2018). Will Developing Countries Become Pollution Havens for Developed Countries? An Empirical Investigation in the Belt and Road. *Journal of Cleaner Production*, *198*, 624–632. doi:10.1016/j.jclepro.2018.06.291

Castillo-Vergara, M., Alvarez-Marin, A., & Placencio-Hidalgo, D. (2018). A Bibliometric Analysis of Creativity in the Field of Business Economics. *Journal of Business Research*, *85*, 1–9. doi:10.1016/j.jbusres.2017.12.011

Chaisse, J., & Matsushita, M. (2018). China's Belt And Road Initiative: Mapping the World Trade Normative and Strategic Implications. *Journal of World Trade*, *52*(1).

Chaisse, J., & Matsushita, M. (2018). China's 'Belt And Road' Initiative: Mapping the World Trade Normative and Strategic implications. *Journal of World Trade*, *52*(1), 163–186.

Chan, L.-H. (2017). Soft Balancing against the US 'Pivot to Asia': China's Geostrategic Rationale for Establishing the Asian Infrastructure Investment Bank. *Australian Journal of International Affairs*, *71*(6), 568–590. doi:10.1080/10357718.2017.1357679

Chan, Y. (2018). Cultural Heritage on China's 21st-century Maritime Silk Road. *China Report (New Delhi, India)*, *54*(2), 159–174. doi:10.1177/0009445518761078

Chang, S.-C. (2014). The Determinants and Motivations of China's Outward Foreign Direct Investment: A Spatial Gravity Model Approach. *Global Economic Review*, *43*(3), 244–268. doi:10.1080/1226508X.2014.930670

Chang-Liao, N. (2016). China's New Foreign Policy under Xi Jinping. *Asian Security*, *12*(2), 82–91. doi:10.1080/14799855.2016.1183195

Chaudhuri, D. (2016). A Survey of the Economic Situation in Xinjiang and its Role in the Twenty-first Century. *China Report (New Delhi, India)*, *41*(1), 1–28. doi:10.1177/000944550504100101

Chaziza, M. (2018). The Chinese Maritime Silk Road Initiative. *Mediterranean Quarterly*, *29*(2), 54–69. doi:10.1215/10474552-6898099

Chen, E. I. (2014). U.S.-China Trade Relations and Economic Distrust. *Chinese Economy*, *47*(3), 57–69. doi:10.2753/CES1097-1475470304

Chen, L. (2016). *Acceleration in Interconnectivity Construction in Southwest China Boosts the Development of the "Belt and Road"*. Academic Press. doi:10.1007/978-981-10-0167-3_5

Chen, Q., Geng, N., & Zhu, K. (2018). Review and Bibliometric Analysis of Chinese Agricultural Economics Research: 2006-2015. *China Agricultural Economic Review*, *10*(1), 152–172. doi:10.1108/CAER-07-2017-0141

Cheng, L. K. (2016). Three Questions on China's "Belt and Road Initiative". *China Economic Review*, *40*, 309–313. doi:10.1016/j.chieco.2016.07.008

Chin, G. T. (2016). Asian Infrastructure Investment Bank: Governance Innovation and Prospects. *Global Governance*, *22*(1), 11–26. doi:10.1163/19426720-02201002

China, P. R. (2016). Appendix: Vision and Proposed Actions Outlined on Jointly Building Silk Road Economic Belt and the 21st-Century Maritime Silk Road. In L. Ji, F. Peng, & D. Jiliang (Eds.), *A Guide to the Belt and Road Initiative* (pp. 369–387). Gansu, China: Gansu Culture Press.

Chung, C.-P., & Voon, T. J. (2017). China's Maritime Silk Road Initiative:Political-Economic Calculations of Southeast Asian States. *Asian Survey*, *57*(3), 416–449.

Cinar, E. M., Johnson, J., & Geusz, K. (2016). Estimating Chinese Trade Relationships with the Silk Road Countries. *China & World Economy*, *24*, 85–103.

Cintra, R. F., Cassol, A., Ribeiro, I., & de Carvalho, A. O. (2018). Corruption and Emerging Markets: Systematic Review of the Most Cited. *Research in International Business and Finance*, *45*, 607–619. doi:10.1016/j.ribaf.2017.07.177

Clarke, M. (2018). The Belt and Road Initiative: Exploring Beijing's Motivations and Challenges for its New Silk Road. *Strategic Analysis*, *42*(2), 84–102. doi:10.1080/09700161.2018.1439326

Cui, L., Zhang, M., Wu, K.-J., & Tseng, M.-L. (2018). Constructing a Hierarchical Agribusiness Framework in Chinese Belt and Road Initiatives under Uncertainty. *Sustainability*, *10*(251), 1–17. doi:10.3390u10010251 PMID:30607262

Dadwal, S. R., & Purushothaman, C. (2017). CPEC in Pakistan's Quest for Energy Security. *Strategic Analysis, 41*(5), 515–524. doi:10.1080/09700161.2017.1343270

Daksueva, O., & Yilmaz, S. (2018). The AIIB and China-ASEAN Relations: Shaping a New North-South Paradigm. *China Quarterly of International Strategic Studies, 04*(01), 95–121. doi:10.1142/S2377740018500021

Dellios, R. (2017). Silk Roads of the Twenty-first Century: The Cultural Dimension. *Asia & the Pacific Policy Studies, 4*(2), 225–236. doi:10.1002/app5.172

Deng, X., Huang, J., Rozelle, S., Zhang, J., & Li, Z. (2015). Impact of Urbanization on Cultivated Land Changes in China. *Land Use Policy, 45*, 1–7. doi:10.1016/j.landusepol.2015.01.007

Ding, M. (2018). Security Matters in Marriage: Uyghurs' Perceptions of Security in Xinjiang, China. *Central Asian Survey, 37*(1), 85–99. doi:10.1080/02634937.2017.1338247

Diop, S. H. A., & Veeck, G. (2012). Chinese Engagement with Africa: The Case of Madagascar. *Eurasian Geography and Economics, 53*(3), 400–418. doi:10.2747/1539-7216.53.3.400

Doner, R. F., & Schneider, B. R. (2016). The Middle-Income Trap: More Politics than Economics. *World Politics, 68*(4), 608–644. doi:10.1017/S0043887116000095

Du, J., & Zhang, Y. (2018). Does One Belt One Road Initiative Promote Chinese Overseas Direct Investment? *China Economic Review, 47*, 189–205. doi:10.1016/j.chieco.2017.05.010

Du, M. M. (2016). China's "One Belt, One Road" Initiative: Context, Focus, Institutions, and Implications. *The Chinese Journal of Global Governance, 2*(1), 30–43. doi:10.1163/23525207-12340014

Duan, F., Jib, Q., Liu, B.-Y., & Fan, Y. (2018). Energy Investment Risk Assessment for Nations along China's Belt & Road Initiative. *Journal of Cleaner Production, 170*, 535–547. doi:10.1016/j.jclepro.2017.09.152

Er, L. P. (2016). China, the United States, Alliances, and War: Avoiding the Thucydides Trap? *Asian Affairs: An American Review, 43*(2), 36–46. doi:10.1080/00927678.2016.1150765

Estrada, G., Han, X., Park, D., & Tian, S. (2018). Asia's Middle-Income Challenge: An Overview. *Emerging Markets Finance & Trade*, *54*(6), 1208–1224. doi:10.1080/1540496X.2017.1421939

Ethridge, D. (2004). *Research Methodology in Applied Economics*. Iowa, USA: Blackwell Publishing.

Etzioni, A. (2016). The Asian Infrastructure Investment Bank: A Case Study of Multifaceted Containment. *Asian Perspective*, *40*(2), 173–196. doi:10.1353/apr.2016.0008

Fan, Z., Zhang, R., Liu, X., & Pan, L. (2016). China's Outward FDI Efficiency Along the Belt and Road: An Application of Stochastic Frontier Gravity Model. *China Agricultural Economic Review*, *8*(3), 455–479. doi:10.1108/CAER-11-2015-0158

Feng, G.-F., Sui, B., Dong, M.-Y., Jiang, C., & Chang, C.-P. (2017). Border is Better than Distance? Contagious Corruption in One Belt One Road Economies. *Quality & Quantity*, *52*(4), 1909–1928. doi:10.100711135-017-0579-3

Ferdinand, P. (2016). Westward ho-the China Dream and 'One Belt, One Road': Chinese Foreign Policy Under Xi Jinping. *International Affairs*, *92*(4), 941–957. doi:10.1111/1468-2346.12660

Fleary, S. A., Joseph, P., & Pappagianopoulos, J. E. (2018). Adolescent Health Literacy and Health Behaviors: A Systematic Review. *Journal of Adolescence*, *62*, 116–127. doi:10.1016/j.adolescence.2017.11.010 PMID:29179126

Fravel, M. T. (2011). China's Strategy in the South China Sea. *Contemporary Southeast Asia*, *33*(3), 292–319. doi:10.1355/cs33-3b

Fukase, E., & Martin, W. (2016). Who Will Feed China in the 21st Century?Income Growth and Food Demand and Supply in China. *Journal of Agricultural Economics*, *67*(1), 3–23. doi:10.1111/1477-9552.12117

Gabusi, G. (2017). "Crossing the River by Feeling the Gold": The Asian Infrastructure Investment Bank and the Financial Support to the Belt and Road Initiative. *China & World Economy*, *25*(5), 23–45. doi:10.1111/cwe.12212

Garlick, J. (2018). Deconstructing the China–Pakistan Economic Corridor: Pipe Dreams Versus Geopolitical Realities. *Journal of Contemporary China*, *27*(112), 519–533. doi:10.1080/10670564.2018.1433483

Gong, B. (2018). Agricultural Reforms and Production in China: Changes in Provincial Production Function and Productivity in 1978–2015. *Journal of Development Economics*, *132*, 18–31. doi:10.1016/j.jdeveco.2017.12.005

Gu, B. (2017). Chinese Multilateralism in the AIIB. *Journal of International Economic Law*, *20*(1), 137–158. doi:10.1093/jiel/jgx006

Hameiri, S., & Jones, L. (2018). China Challenges Global Governance? Chinese International Development Finance and the AIIB. *International Affairs*, *94*(3), 573–593. doi:10.1093/ia/iiy026

Han, E. (2017). Geopolitics, Ethnic Conflicts along the Border, and Chinese Foreign Policy Changes toward Myanmar. *Asian Security*, *13*(1), 59–73. doi:10.1080/14799855.2017.1290988

Herrero, A. G., & Xu, J. (2017). China's Belt and Road Initiative: Can Europe Expect Trade Gains? *China & World Economy*, *25*(6), 84–99. doi:10.1111/cwe.12222

Hidalgo Martinez, M., & Cartier, C. (2017). City as province in China: The Territorial Urbanization of Chongqing. *Eurasian Geography and Economics*, *58*(2), 201–230. doi:10.1080/15387216.2017.1312474

Hofman, I. (2016). Politics or Profits along the "Silk Road": What Drives Chinese Farms in Tajikistan and Helps Them Thrive? *Eurasian Geography and Economics*, *57*(3), 457–481. doi:10.1080/15387216.2016.1238313

Howard, K. W. F., & Howard, K. K. (2016). The New "Silk Road Economic Belt" as a Threat to the Sustainable Management of Central Asia's Transboundary Water Resources. *Environmental Earth Sciences*, *75*(11), 1–12. doi:10.100712665-016-5752-9

Huang, J., & Yang, G. (2017). Understanding Recent Challenges and New Food Policy in China. *Global Food Security*, *12*, 119–126. doi:10.1016/j.gfs.2016.10.002

Huang, S., Fidrmuc, J., & Fidrmuc, J. (2015). Whither China? Reform and Economic Integration among Chinese Regions. *China Economic Review*, *33*, 94–110. doi:10.1016/j.chieco.2014.12.007

Huang, Y. (2016). Understanding China's Belt & Road Initiative: Motivation, Framework and Assessment. *China Economic Review*, *40*, 314–321. doi:10.1016/j.chieco.2016.07.007

Hughes, N. C. (2005). A Trade War with China? *Foreign Affairs*, *84*(4), 94–106. doi:10.2307/20034423

Irshad, M. S., Xin, Q., Shahriar, S., & Arshad, H. (2018). A Panel Data Analysis of China's Trade Pattern with OPEC Members: Gravity Model Approach. *Asian Economic and Financial Review*, *8*(1), 103–116. doi:10.18488/journal.aefr.2018.81.103.116

Ito, T. (2017). A New Financial Order in Asia: Will a RMB Bloc Emerge? *Journal of International Money and Finance*, *74*, 232–257. doi:10.1016/j.jimonfin.2017.02.019

Jackson, S. L., & Dear, D. (2016). Resource Extraction and National Anxieties: China's Economic Presence in Mongolia. *Eurasian Geography and Economics*, *57*(3), 343–373. doi:10.1080/15387216.2016.1243065

Jacob, J. T. (2017). China's Belt and Road Initiative: Perspectives from India. *China & World Economy*, *25*(5), 78–100. doi:10.1111/cwe.12215

Jiang, B., Li, J., & Gong, C. (2018). Maritime Shipping and Export Trade on "Maritime Silk Road". *The Asian Journal of Shipping and Logistics*, *34*(2), 83–90. doi:10.1016/j.ajsl.2018.06.005

Jianwei, W. (2017). The Discourse on China's Rise. *China. International Journal (Toronto, Ont.)*, *15*(1), 24–40.

Jinping, X. (2017). *The Governance of China* (Vol. 2). Beijing, China: Foreign Language Press.

Johansson, A. C., & Zhang, X. (2014). Inequality, Growth and the Middle-Income Trap in China. *China Economic Review*, *31*, 365–366. doi:10.1016/j.chieco.2014.11.007

Karim, M. A. (2015). China's Proposed Maritime Silk Road: Challenges and Opportunities with Special Reference to the Bay of Bengal Region. *Pacific Focus*, *30*(3), 297–319. doi:10.1111/pafo.12059

Khan, K. S., Kunz, R., Kleijnen, J., & Antes, G. (2003). Five Steps to Conducting a Systematic Review. *Journal of the Royal Society of Medicine*, *96*, 118–121.

Khurana, G. S. (2008). China's 'String of Pearls' in the Indian Ocean and Its Security Implications. *Strategic Analysis*, *32*(1), 1–39. doi:10.1080/09700160801886314

Kim, K. (2017). Xinjiang and the Modern Chinese State. *Central Asian Survey*, *37*(1), 176–178. doi:10.1080/02634937.2017.1366468

Kondapalli, S. (2018). The Maritime Silk Road and China–Maldives Relations. In J.-M. F. Blanchard (Ed.), *China's Maritime Silk Road Initiative and South Asia* (pp. 173–201). Palgrave. doi:10.1007/978-981-10-5239-2_7

Kong, L. (2015). The Belt and Road Initiative and China's Foreign Policy Toward Its Territorial and Boundary Disputes. *China Quarterly of International Strategic Studies*, *01*(02), 325–345. doi:10.1142/S2377740015500165

Kurowska-Pysz, J., & Szczepa ´nska-Woszczyna, K. (2017). The Analysis of the Determinants of Sustainable Cross-Border Cooperation and Recommendations on Its Harmonization. *Sustainability*, *9*(12), 2226. doi:10.3390u9122226

Kwon, E. (2015). China's Monetary Power: Internationalization of the Renminbi. *Pacific Focus*, *30*(1), 78–102. doi:10.1111/pafo.12038

Laborde, A. (2016). Chinese Economic Development Policies as an Example for Mexico: The One-Belt-One-Road Program. *Fudan Journal of the Humanities and Social Sciences*, *10*(2), 127–144. doi:10.100740647-016-0157-4

Lee, P. T.-W., Hu, Z.-H., Lee, S.-J., Choi, K.-S., & Shin, S.-H. (2018). Research Trends and Agenda on the Belt and Road (B&R) Initiative with a Focus on Maritime Transport. *Maritime Policy & Management*, *45*(3), 282–300. doi:10.1080/03088839.2017.1400189

Lee, S. (2017). An Institutional Analysis of Xi Jinping's Centralization of Power. *Journal of Contemporary China*, *26*(105), 325–336. doi:10.1080/10670564.2016.1245505

Lee, S.-O., Wainwright, J., & Glassman, J. (2018). Geopolitical Economy and the Production of Territory: The Case of US-China Geopolitical-Economic Competition in Asia. *Environment & Planning A*, *50*(2), 416–436. doi:10.1177/0308518X17701727

Lemoine, F., & Unal, D. (2017). China s Foreign Trade: A "New Normal". *China & World Economy*, *25*(2), 1–21. doi:10.1111/cwe.12191

Li, P., Qian, H., Howard, K. W. F., & Wu, J. (2015). Building a New and Sustainable "Silk Road Economic Belt". *Environmental Earth Sciences*, *74*(10), 7267–7270. doi:10.100712665-015-4739-2

Li, Y., & Chang, Y. (2015). Infrastructure Investments for Power Trade and Transmission in ASEAN+2: Costs, Benefits, Long-Term Contracts and Prioritized Developments. *Energy Economics*, *51*, 484–492. doi:10.1016/j.eneco.2015.08.008

Liu, H., Fang, C., Miao, Y., Ma, H., Zhang, Q., & Zhou, Q. (2018). Spatio-Temporal Evolution of Population and Urbanization in the Countries along the Belt and Road 1950–2050. *Journal of Geographical Sciences*, *28*(7), 919–936. doi:10.100711442-018-1513-x

Liu, H. Y., Tang, Y. K., Chen, X. L., & Poznanska, J. (2017). The Determinants of Chinese Outward FDI in Countries Along "One Belt, One Road". *Emerging Markets Finance & Trade*, *53*(6), 1374–1387. doi:10.1080/1540496X.2017.1295843

Liu, T., & Woo, W. T. (2018). Understanding the U.S.-China Trade War. *China Economic Journal*, *11*(3), 319–340. doi:10.1080/17538963.2018.1516256

Liu, Z., Wang, T., Sonn, J. W., & Chen, W. (2018). The Structure and Evolution of Trade Relations Between Countries along the Belt and Road. *Journal of Geographical Sciences*, *28*(9), 1233–1248. doi:10.100711442-018-1522-9

Luo, J., Ji, C., Qiu, C., & Jia, F. (2018). Agri-Food Supply Chain Management: Bibliometric and Content Analyses. *Sustainability*, *10*(1573), 1–22. doi:10.3390u10051573 PMID:30607262

Mackerras, C. (2015). Xinjiang in China's Foreign Relations: Part of a New Silk Road or Central Asian Zone of Conflict? *East Asia*, *32*(1), 25–42. doi:10.100712140-015-9224-8

Maddison, A. (2005). Measuring and Interpreting World Economic Performance, 1500-2001. *Review of Income and Wealth*, *51*(1), 1–35. doi:10.1111/j.1475-4991.2005.00143.x

Maditati, D. R., Munim, Z. H., Schramm, H.-J., & Kummer, S. (2018). A Review of Green Supply Chain Management: From Bibliometric Analysis to a Conceptual Framework and Future Research Directions. *Resources, Conservation and Recycling*, *139*, 150–162. doi:10.1016/j.resconrec.2018.08.004

Majumdar, M. (2015). The ASEAN Way of Conflict Management in the South China Sea. *Strategic Analysis*, *39*(1), 73–87. doi:10.1080/09700161.2014.980545

Malik, J. M. (2017). Myanmar's Role in China's Maritime Silk Road. *Journal of Contemporary China*. doi:10.1080/10670564.2018.1410969

Mishra, R. (2016). Asian Infrastructure Investment Bank: An Assessment. *India Quarterly*, *72*(2), 163–176. doi:10.1177/0974928416643582

Molero-Simarro, R. (2017). Inequality in China Revisited. The Effect of Functional Distribution of Income on Urban Top Incomes, the Urban-Rural Gap and the Gini Index, 1978–2015. *China Economic Review*, *42*, 101–117. doi:10.1016/j.chieco.2016.11.006

Musa, I., Park, H., Munkhdalai, L., & Ryu, K. (2018). Global Research on Syndromic Surveillance from 1993 to 2017: Bibliometric Analysis and Visualization. *Sustainability*, *10*(10), 3414. doi:10.3390u10103414

Napoli, C. (2014). China's Economic Rise: Implications for ASEAN Trade Flows. *Southeast Asian Economies*, *31*(3), 345-360. doi:10.1355/ae31-3a

Naughton, B. (2007). *The Chinese Economy: Transitions and Growth.* MIT Press.

NBSC. (2011). *The 2010 Statistical Bulletin of China's Outward Foreign Direct Investment*. Retrieved from Beijing: http://www.stats.gov.cn/english/

Nguyen, T. N. A., Pham, T. H. H., & Vallée, T. (2016). Economic Integration in ASEAN+3: A Network Analysis. *Journal of Economic Integration*, *31*(2), 275–325. doi:10.11130/jei.2016.31.2.275

Ni, C., Sugimoto, C. R., & Robbin, A. (2017). Examining the Evolution of the Field of Public Administration through a Bibliometric Analysis of Public Administration Review. *Public Administration Review*, *77*(4), 496–509. doi:10.1111/puar.12737

Nie, W. (2016). Xi Jinping's Foreign Policy Dilemma One Belt, One Road or the South China Sea? *Contemporary Southeast Asia*, *38*(3), 422–444. doi:10.1355/cs38-3c

Nordin, A. H. M., & Weissmann, M. (2018). Will Trump Make China Great Again? The Belt and Road Initiative and International Order. *International Affairs*, *94*(2), 231–249. doi:10.1093/ia/iix242

O'Trakoun, J. (2017). China's Belt and Road Initiative and Regional Perceptions of China. *Business Economics (Cleveland, Ohio)*, *53*(1), 17–24. doi:10.105711369-017-0062-0

Ostrovskii, A. V. (2018). Prospects to interface the silk road economic belt and the Eurasian Economic Union projects. *Herald of the Russian Academy of Sciences*, *87*(6), 480–490. doi:10.1134/S1019331617060041

Palit, A. (2017). India's Economic and Strategic Perceptions of China's Maritime Silk Road Initiative. *Geopolitics*, *22*(2), 292–309. doi:10.1080/14650045.2016.1274305

Paul, J. (2016). The Rise of China: What, When, Where, and Why? *The International Trade Journal*, *30*(3), 207–222. doi:10.1080/08853908.2016.1155513

Paul, J., & Benito, G. R. G. (2017). A Review of Research on Outward Foreign Direct Investment from Emerging Countries, including China: What Do We Know, How Do We Know and Where Should We Be Heading? *Asia Pacific Business Review*, *24*(1), 90–115. doi:10.1080/13602381.2017.1357316

Peng, Z., & Tok, S. K. (2016). The AIIB and China's Normative Power in International Financial Governance Structure. *Chinese Political Science Review*, *1*(4), 736–753. doi:10.100741111-016-0042-y

Peyrouse, S. (2017). The Evolution of Russia's Views on the Belt and Road Initiative. *Asia Policy*, *24*(1), 96–102. doi:10.1353/asp.2017.0026

Piccarozzi, M., Aquilani, B., & Gatti, C. (2018). Industry 4.0 in Management Studies: A Systematic Literature Review. *Sustainability*, *10*(10), 3821. doi:10.3390u10103821

Pisani, M. J., Reyes, J. C., & García, B. G. (2009). Looking Back Twenty-Three Years: An Analysis of Contributors and Contributions to the Journal of Borderlands Studies, 1986 (volume 1, number 1) to 2008 (volume 23, number 2). *Journal of Borderland Studies*, *24*(1), 1–17. doi:10.1080/08865655.2009.9695714

Poh, A. (2017). The Myth of Chinese Sanctions over South China Sea Disputes. *The Washington Quarterly*, *40*(1), 143–165. doi:10.1080/0163660X.2017.1302744

Ptak, T., & Hommel, D. (2016). The Trans-Political Nature of Southwest China's Energy Conduit, Yunnan Province. *Geopolitics*, *21*(3), 556–578. doi:10.1080/14650045.2015.1114471

Purbrick, M. (2018). Pirates of the South China Seas. *Asian Affairs*, *49*(1), 11–26. doi:10.1080/03068374.2018.1416010

Qiang, X. (2019). President XI's Surveillance State. *Journal of Democracy*, *30*(1), 53–67. doi:10.1353/jod.2019.0004

Qin, C., & Chong, T. T. L. (2016). Can Poverty be Alleviated in China? *Review of Income and Wealth*, 1–21. doi:10.1111/roiw.12273

Qiu, L. D., & Xue, Y. (2014). Understanding China's Foreign Trade: A literature Review (I). *China Economic Journal*, *7*(2), 168–186. doi:10.1080/17538963.2014.928967

Reeves, J. (2018). China's Silk Road Economic Belt Initiative: Network and Influence Formation in Central Asia. *Journal of Contemporary China*, *27*(112), 502–518. doi:10.1080/10670564.2018.1433480

Ritz, A., Brewer, G. A., & Neumann, O. (2016). Public Service Motivation: A Systematic Literature Review and Outlook. *Public Administration Review*, *76*(3), 414–426. doi:10.1111/puar.12505

Rolland, N. (2017). China's "Belt and Road Initiative": Underwhelming or Game-Changer? *The Washington Quarterly*, *40*(1), 127–142. doi:10.1080/0163660X.2017.1302743

Sarker, M. N. I., Hossin, M. A., Hua, Y., Sarkar, M. K., & Kumar, N. (2018). Oil, Gas and Energy Business under One Belt One Road Strategic Context. *Open Journal of Social Sciences*, *06*(04), 119–134. doi:10.4236/jss.2018.64011

Schinas, O., & Westarp, A. G. (2017). Assessing the Impact of the Maritime Silk Road. *Journal of Ocean Engineering and Science*, *2*(17), 186–195. doi:10.1016/j.joes.2017.08.002

Schneider, C. J. (2017). The Political Economy of Regional Integration. *Annual Review of Political Science*, *20*(1), 229–248. doi:10.1146/annurev-polisci-051215-023006

Shah, A. R. (2018). How Does China-Pakistan Economic Corridor Show the Limitations of China's 'One Belt One Road' Model. *Asia & the Pacific Policy Studies*, *5*(2), 378–385. doi:10.1002/app5.224

Shahriar, S. (2019). *Understanding China's Belt & Road Initiative: The Institutional Economics Approach*. Beau Bassin, Mauritius: Lambert.

Shahriar, S., Qian, L., Irshad, M. S., Kea, S., Abdullahi, N. M, & Sarkar,, A. (2018). Institutions of the Belt & Road Initiative. *Journal of Law, Policy and Globalization*, *77*, 1–13.

Shariatinia, M., & Azizi, H. (2017). Iran–China Cooperation in the Silk Road Economic Belt: From Strategic Understanding to Operational Understanding. *China & World Economy*, *25*(5), 46–61. doi:10.1111/cwe.12213

Shi, K., Yu, B., Huang, C., Wu, J., & Sun, X. (2018). Exploring spatiotemporal patterns of electric power consumption in countries along the Belt and Road. *Energy*, *150*, 847–859. doi:10.1016/j.energy.2018.03.020

Shi, L. (2016). Income Inequality and Economic Growth in China in the Last Three Decades. *The Round Table*, *105*(6), 641–665. doi:10.1080/00358533.2016.1246858

Shi, X., & Yan, Z. (2018). Urbanization and Risk Preference in China: A Decomposition of Self-Selection and Assimilation Effects. *China Economic Review*, *49*, 210–228. doi:10.1016/j.chieco.2017.04.009

Sidaway, J. D., & Woon, C. Y. (2017). Chinese Narratives on "One Belt, One Road" (一带一路) in Geopolitical and Imperial Contexts. *The Professional Geographer*, 1–13. doi:10.1080/00330124.2017.1288576

Soong, J.-J. (2014). Is China Becoming the Core of Regional Trade and Market Integration in the Asia-Pacific? *Chinese Economy*, *47*(3), 3–7. doi:10.2753/CES1097-1475470300

Stiglitz, J. E. (2008). China: Towards A New Model of Development. *China Economic Journal*, *1*(1), 33–52. doi:10.1080/17538960701564858

Stiglitz, J. E. (2018). Rethinking Globalization in the Trump Era: US-China Relations. *Frontiers of Economics in China*, *13*(2), 133–146. doi:10.3868060-007-018-0010-3

Summers, T. (2016). China's 'New Silk Roads': Sub National Regions and Networks of Global Political Economy. *Third World Quarterly*, *37*(9), 1628–1643. doi:10.1080/01436597.2016.1153415

Taffer, A. (2015). State Strategy in Territorial Conflict: A Conceptual Analysis of China's Strategy in the South China Sea. *Contemporary Southeast Asia*, *37*(1), 85-108. doi:10.1355/cs37-1d

Tekdal, V. (2018). China's Belt and Road Initiative: At the Crossroads of Challenges and Ambitions. *The Pacific Review*, *31*(3), 373–390. doi:10.1080/09512748.2017.1391864

Thi Thuy Hang, N. (2016). The United States and China: Can They Cooperate? *Asian Affairs: An American Review*, *43*(3), 67–77. doi:10.1080/00927678.2016.1200332

Timofeev, I., Lissovolik, Y., & Filippova, L. (2017). Russia's Vision of the Belt and Road Initiative: From the Rivalry of the Great Powers to Forging a New Cooperation Model in Eurasia. *China & World Economy*, *25*(5), 62–77. doi:10.1111/cwe.12214

Tokunaga, M., & Iwasaki, I. (2017). The Determinants of Foreign Direct Investment in Transition Economies: A Meta-analysis. *World Economy*, *40*(12), 2771–2831. doi:10.1111/twec.12477

Tønnesson, S. (2006). The South China Sea in the Age of European Decline. *Modern Asian Studies*, *40*(01), 1-57. doi:10.1017/S0026749X06001727

Tracy, E. F., Shvarts, E., Simonov, E., & Babenko, M. (2017). China's New Eurasian Ambitions: The Environmental Risks of the Silk Road Economic Belt. *Eurasian Geography and Economics*, *58*(1), 56–88. doi:10.1080/15387216.2017.1295876

Tschantret, J. (2016). Repression, Opportunity, and Innovation: The Evolution of Terrorism in Xinjiang, China. *Terrorism and Political Violence*, *30*(4), 569–588. doi:10.1080/09546553.2016.1182911

Tuman, J. P., & Shirali, M. (2017). The Political Economy of Chinese Foreign Direct Investment in Developing Areas. *Foreign Policy Analysis*, *13*(1), 154–167. doi:10.1111/fpa.12092

Uras, A. (2017). The South China Sea and the Building of a National Maritime Culture. *Asian Survey*, *57*(6), 1008–1031. doi:10.1525/as.2017.57.6.1008

Vangeli, A. (2017). China s Engagement with the Sixteen Countries of Central, East and Southeast Europe under the Belt and Road Initiative. *China & World Economy*, *25*(5), 101–124. doi:10.1111/cwe.12216

Verbiest, J.-P. A. (2013). Regional Cooperation and Integration in the Mekong Region. *Asian Economic Policy Review*, *8*(1), 148–164. doi:10.1111/aepr.12015

Visvizi, A., & Lytras, M. (2018). It's Not a Fad: Smart Cities and Smart Villages Research in European and Global Contexts. *Sustainability*, *10*(8), 2727. doi:10.3390u10082727

Visvizi, A., & Lytras, M. D. (2018). Rescaling and Refocusing Smart Cities Research: From Mega Cities to Smart Villages. *Journal of Science and Technology Policy Management*, *9*(2), 134–145. doi:10.1108/JSTPM-02-2018-0020

Visvizi, A., Lytras, M. D., Damiani, E., & Mathkour, H. (2018). Policy Making for Smart Cities: Innovation and Social Inclusive Economic Growth for Sustainability. *Journal of Science and Technology Policy Management*, *9*(2), 126–133. doi:10.1108/JSTPM-07-2018-079

Wang, J. J., & Yau, S. (2018). Case Studies on Transport Infrastructure Projects in Belt and Road Initiative: An Actor Network Theory Perspective. *Journal of Transport Geography*, *71*, 213–223. doi:10.1016/j.jtrangeo.2018.01.007

Wang, Y. (2018). The Political Economy of Joining the AIIB. *The Chinese Journal of International Politics*, *11*(2), 105–130. doi:10.1093/cjip/poy006

Wang, Z. (2017). The Economic Rise of China: Rule-Taker, Rule-Maker, or Rule-Breaker? *Asian Survey*, *57*(4), 595–617. doi:10.1525/as.2017.57.4.595

Wei, L. (2017). Partners, Institutions and International Currencies: The International Political Foundations for the Rise of the Renminbi. *Social Sciences in China*, *38*(2), 114–141. doi:10.1080/02529203.2017.1302236

Wu, J.-X., & He, L.-Y. (2018). Urban–Rural Gap and Poverty Traps in China: A Prefecture Level Analysis. *Applied Economics*, *50*(30), 3300–3314. doi:10.1080/00036846.2017.1420890

Xiao, R. (2016). China as an Institution Builder: The Case of the AIIB. *The Pacific Review*, *29*(3), 435–442. doi:10.1080/09512748.2016.1154678

Xiao, Y., & Watson, M. (2017). Guidance on Conducting a Systematic Literature Review. *Journal of Planning Education and Research*, 1–20. doi:10.1177/0739456x17723971

Xiaotong, Z., & Keith, J. (2017). From Wealth to Power: China's New Economic Statecraft. *The Washington Quarterly*, *40*(1), 185–203. doi:10.1080/0163660X.2017.1302746

Xie, L., Yang, Z., Cai, J., Cheng, Z., Wen, T., & Song, T. (2016). Harbin: A Rust Belt City Revival From Its Strategic Position. *Cities (London, England)*, *58*, 26–38. doi:10.1016/j.cities.2016.05.009

Xuetong, Y. (2006). The Rise of China and its Power Status. *The Chinese Journal of International Politics*, *1*(1), 5–33. doi:10.1093/cjip/pol002

Xuetong, Y. (2014). From Keeping a Low Profile to Striving for Achievement. *The Chinese Journal of International Politics*, *7*(2), 153–184. doi:10.1093/cjip/pou027

Yao, Z. (2015). How Can China Avoid the Middle Income Trap? *China & World Economy*, *23*(5), 26–42. doi:10.1111/cwe.12126

Ye, H., Binwei, L., & Starkey, G. (2018). Economic and Cultural Implications of China's One Belt One Road Initiative for the Film Industry: Cultural Distance and Taste Preference. *Australian Economic Papers*, *57*(3), 250–264. doi:10.1111/1467-8454.12116

Yiwei, W. (2016). *The Belt and Road Initiative: What Will China Offer the World in Its Rise*. Beijing, China: New World Press.

Yiwei, W. (2018). Belt and Road Initiative: Mutual Connectivity of the World. *China and the World*, *01*(04), 1–15. doi:10.11422591729318500232

Yu, H. (2016). Motivation Behind China's 'One Belt, One Road' Initiatives and Establishment of the Asian Infrastructure Investment Bank. *Journal of Contemporary China*, *26*(105), 353–368. doi:10.1080/10670564.2016.1245894

Yu, J., & Wu, J. (2018). The Sustainability of Agricultural Development in China: The Agriculture–Environment Nexus. *Sustainability*, *10*(6), 1776. doi:10.3390u10061776

Yu, X. (2015). Meat Consumption in China and Its impact on international Food Security: Status Quo, Trends, and Policies. *Journal of Integrative Agriculture*, *14*(6), 989–994. doi:10.1016/S2095-3119(14)60983-7

Zeng, J. (2017). Does Europe Matter? The Role of Europe in Chinese Narratives of 'One Belt One Road' and 'New Type of Great Power Relations'. *Journal of Common Market Studies*, *55*(5), 1162–1176. doi:10.1111/jcms.12535

Zeng, J., & Fang, Y. (2014). Between Poverty and Prosperity: China's Dependent Development and the 'Middle-Income Trap'. *Third World Quarterly*, *35*(6), 1014–1031. doi:10.1080/01436597.2014.907725

Zhai, F. (2018). China's Belt and Road Initiative: A Preliminary Quantitative Assessment. *Journal of Asian Economics*, *55*, 84–92. doi:10.1016/j.asieco.2017.12.006

Zhang, C. (2015). Income Inequality And Access To Housing: Evidence From China. *China Economic Review*, *36*, 261–271. doi:10.1016/j.chieco.2015.10.003

Zhang, F. (2016). China as a Global Force. *Asia & the Pacific Policy Studies*, *3*(1), 120–128. doi:10.1002/app5.115

Zhang, H. (2017). Opportunity or New Poverty Trap: Rural-Urban Education Disparity and Internal Migration in China. *China Economic Review*, *44*, 112–124. doi:10.1016/j.chieco.2017.03.011

Zhang, J. (2016). *Maritime Silk Road and China's Indian Ocean Strategy: An Analysis from the Perspective of Cooperative Security*. Academic Press. doi:10.1007/978-981-10-0167-3_4

Zhang, L. (2010). The Rise of China: Media Perception and Implications for International Politics. *Journal of Contemporary China*, *19*(64), 233–254. doi:10.1080/10670560903444199

Zhang, X. (2017). Chinese Capitalism and the Maritime Silk Road: A World-Systems Perspective. *Geopolitics*, *22*(2), 310–331. doi:10.1080/14650045.2017.1289371

Zhao, S. (2016). Xi Jinping's Maoist Revival. *Journal of Democracy*, *27*(3), 83–97. doi:10.1353/jod.2016.0051

Zhao, S. (2017). American Reflections on the Engagement with China and Responses to President Xi's New Model of Major Power Relations. *Journal of Contemporary China*, *26*(106), 489–503. doi:10.1080/10670564.2017.1274814

Zhu, Y. (2016). International Trade and Food Security: Conceptual Discussion, WTO and the Case of China. *China Agricultural Economic Review*, *8*(3), 399–411. doi:10.1108/CAER-09-2015-0127

Zongyou, W. (2017). China's Maritime Trap. *The Washington Quarterly*, *40*(1), 167–184. doi:10.1080/0163660X.2017.1302745

ENDNOTE

1 Brazil, Russia, India, China, and South Africa (BRICS)

APPENDIX: LIST OF COUNTRIES ALONG THE 'B&R' INITIATIVE

Table 6.

Region	No.	Countries
Central Asian countries	5	Kazakhstan, Kyrgyzstan, Tajikistan, Uzbekistan, Turkmenistan
Mongolia and Russia	2	Mongolia and Russia
Southeast Asian countries	11	Vietnam, Laos, Cambodia, Thailand, Malaysia, Singapore, Indonesia, Brunei, the Philippines, Burma, East Timor
South Asian countries	8	Bangladesh, India, Pakistan,, Afghanistan, Nepal, Bhutan, Sri Lanka, the Maldives
Central and East European countries	19	Poland, the Czech Republic, Slovakia, Hungary, Slovenia, Croatia, Romania, Bulgaria, Serbia, Montenegro, Macedonia, Bosnia and Herzegovina, Albania, Estonia, Lithuania, Latvia, Ukraine, Belarus, Moldova
West Asian and Middle East countries	19	Turkey, Iran, Syria, Iraq, the United Arab Emirates, Saudi Arabia, Qatar, Bahrain, Kuwait, Lebanon, Oman, Yemen, Jordan, Israel, Palestine, Armenia, Georgia, Azerbaijan, Egypt

Source: Shahriar (2019).

Section 2
Belt and Road Initiative and International Collaboration

Chapter 6
China's Belt and Road Initiative:
Its Landscape (and Trajectory) in the Islamic World

Muhammad Khalil Khan
Zhejiang University, China

Cornelius B. Pratt
Guangdong University of Foreign Studies, China & Temple University, USA

ABSTRACT

China's multibillion-dollar Belt and Road Initiative (BRI) is a common fixture on the radar of policymakers and researchers because of the massive financial investment it involves and the economic opportunities it provides disadvantaged Eurasian states. BRI promises fast-track infrastructural development, transnational connectivity, and unimpeded trade. It predicates economic growth in developing countries on the shared development model. However, BRI has also engendered sensitive economic and security challenges. The Islamic world embraces BRI even as China's engagement there poses critical challenges to its foreign policy. This chapter highlights key markers on the landscape of BRI projects in the Islamic world and presents their implications for China's foreign policy. It also provides useful policy guidelines for a more effective implementation of BRI-related projects, thereby protecting China from possible conflict with regional and global powers.

DOI: 10.4018/978-1-5225-8980-8.ch006

INTRODUCTION

China's government is changing the trajectory of global and regional discourse on geopolitics, geoeconomics and finance—and on transnational collaboration. It is making a difference in people's well-being, upping the ante on the true meaning of regional and international integration. Its Belt and Road Initiative (BRI), an ambitious, proactive, and globally driven strategic foreign policy venture announced by President Xi Jinping's government in September 2013, is a cornucopia of a large number of international infrastructural development projects and opportunities for economic cooperation for mutual benefit and regional integration. It promises vibrant networks of roads and railways for landlocked economies of Asia, Africa and Europe. It seeks to link China with South Asia, Southeast Asia, the Middle East, East Africa, and Western Europe through the "21st Century Maritime Silk Road" and the South China Sea, Mediterranean Sea, and the Indian Ocean (Figure 1). China is developing six economic corridors: (a) China–Indochina Peninsula Economic Corridor, (b) China–Pakistan Economic Corridor (CPEC), (c) Bangladesh–China–India–Myanmar

Figure 1. Infrastructural network of China's Belt and Road Initiative
Source: Mercator Institute for China Studies, 2015

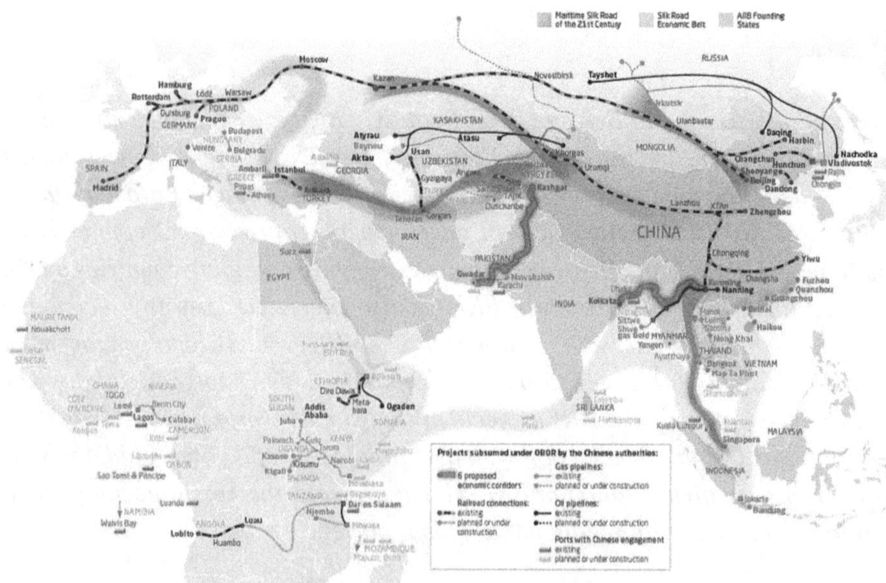

Economic Corridor, (d) China-Central and West Asia Economic Corridor, (e) New Eurasian Land Bridge, and (f) China–Mongolia–Russia Economic Corridor, supplemented by networks of oil and gas pipelines, high-speed fiber optic cables and developing infrastructure geared to enhance regional connectivity, economic activity and transportation among nations. The Chinese government acknowledges that the absence of regional and international economic integration through land hinders the economies of Eurasia; therefore, BRI is a significant step toward building stronger bridges between those economies and China (Rolland, 2017).

In recent years, China has significantly increased its political and economic stature at the global level. Now, it is seeking strategic partners and alliances to promote, through BRI, its strategic interests in the region and beyond. China's unprecedented economic growth, its diplomatic policies and military rise earned it reasonable influence in the Islamic world, which has embraced BRI as a means toward developing its communication and energy infrastructure and toward refurbishing its economies. In addition, the West's, particularly the United States', political meddling in the Islamic world's internal affairs; the favorable policies toward Israel vis-à-vis the plight the Palestinian people; and the military intervention in sovereign Islamic states have all generated concerns among the Muslim Ummah that are seeking an alternative power to provide leverage in helping to settle lingering political disputes. China has often been viewed as a more reliable partner than the United States in the Islamic world. Therefore, BRI provides a strategic opportunity to China to fill the vacuum created by the mistrust of the United States in the Islamic world and to establish strong political and economic relationship with the Islamic world. China's cordial relationship with the Islamic world will not only fulfill China's future energy needs but will also provide strategic and political support to world powers. BRI projects are active in 30 Muslim countries; therefore, the initiative can play a vital role in boosting China's political, economic and social influence in the Islamic world. However, China's engagement in the Islamic world will also engender serious political, economic and cultural challenges.

The purpose of this chapter is to highlight issues immanent on the BRI landscape, which offers mammoth opportunities for international collaboration, even as it is fraught with ground-level uncertainties and occasional tensions. This chapter is organized into three main parts. The first presents disparate views on Sino-Islamic relationship and BRI, the second focuses on opportunities and challenges that emanate from that relationship and that comprise the trajectory of the BRI landscape, and the third makes recommendations for enhancing BRI in an environment associated with apoplectic geopolitical and geoeconomic concerns and religious tensions. Why BRI vis-à-vis China's Islamic relationship? Because the infrastructural program is implemented in 30 Islamic nations whose populations—e.g., those of Indonesia and Pakistan—are among the world's highest and whose economies are historically tied to that of China.

SINO-ISLAMIC RELATIONSHIP

The Sino-Islamic relationships are deeply rooted in the historic Silk Road, which connected two great civilizations under the principles of peace, mutual respect, mutual cooperation for mutual benefits, openness and inclusivity, and learning from each other's experiences to achieve a win-win outcome. Sino-Islamic relationships are based on friendly relations. The historic ties between the two civilizations can be traced to the Silk Road era, as significant contributors of civilized culture to humankind (Zambelis & Gentry, 2008). Silk Road fueled Chinese civilization, paving the way for representatives to spread their dogmas to Europe through Muslim countries in West Asia and Africa, while equally facilitating Islamic civilization, Muslim merchants and Islamic preachers to visit China to spread Islamic culture. The integration of two great civilizations fomented mutual understanding and established strong relationships between China and the Islamic world (Zhu, 2011).

Relations between China and the Islamic world deepened when Chinese Premier Zhou Enlai visited Indonesia to participate in the 1955 Bandung Conference, where he interacted with Islamic leaders from Egypt, Pakistan, Saudi Arabia, Sudan, Libya, Afghanistan, among others, and with representatives form Palestine. The goal was to attenuate the level of misunderstanding of Islamic world regarding China's ideological, social and religious policies. In his speech at the conference, Premier Zhou Enlai emphasized China's diplomatic principle of peaceful co-existence and spirit of "seeking common ground while putting aside differences" to facilitate mutual understanding and friendly relations with Islamic countries. Egyptian President Gamal A. Nasser commended Zhou Enlai on his speech and promised to send a diplomatic mission to Beijing (X. Yu, 2006; Zhan, 2006). Subsequently, a number of Muslim countries, such as Indonesia, Pakistan, Egypt, Syria, and Iraq established diplomatic relations with the People's Republic of China in the early 1950s (Bhola, 1986; Elmagherbi, 2010).

Sino-Islamic diplomatic relationship helped nix Western blockade and containment. Egyptian leadership helped China establish diplomatic relations with

African and Latin American countries and with other Asian nations (Zhu, 2011). Similarly, Pakistan had made significant contributions to China's earning membership of the United Nations and also to its facilitating a congenial relationship between China and the United States during the Cold War era. Islamic countries consistently supported the "One China" principle over China's dispute with Taiwan. Therefore, China had always demonstrated its high regard toward the Islamic world (Bhola, 1986; Elmagherbi, 2010).

The relationship between China and the Islamic world is multifaceted, largely developed from regional and multilateral relations. The Islamic world is concerned about Western meddling in its internal matters. Moreover, perceived perennial distrust in the Islamic world over Western political directives and the West's hegemonic stance on regional issues—for example, the Israeli-Palestinian conflict, the wars in Syria and Afghanistan, and Iran's nuclear program—have fueled resentment toward the United States in the Islamic world. This overarching perception provides an opportunity for China to establish, through BRI, its economic influence and increase its political stature as a reliable and responsible global power in the Islamic world.

DISPARATE VIEWPOINTS ON BRI

Since launching BRI in 2013, China has allocated US$8 trillion to it for developing infrastructure, energy and economic corridors in Eurasia to accomplish five primary goals: (a) free trade, (b) financial integration, (c) regional connectivity, (d) systematic policy coordination, and (e) people-to-people bonds (Bao, 2016; Khan, Sandano, Pratt, & Farid, 2018). BRI promises huge infrastructural development in poor Eurasian countries to foster trust among them by guaranteeing state sovereignty, political choice, shared economic interest and mutual benefits (Mingjiang, 2015; Swaine, 2015; Yi, 2015). President Xi Jinping described BRI as a joint development initiative that will adhere to "the principle of wide consultation, joint contribution, and shared benefits. The programs of development will be open and inclusive, not exclusive. They will be a real chorus comprising all countries along the routes, not a solo for China itself" (Xi, 2015).

Chinese scholars argue that BRI is not restricted to international infrastructural development; rather, it will connect various cultures, regions and nations, encouraging cultural and policy dialogues among them and promoting peaceful coexistence and social harmony (Jia, 2017; Jin, Li, & Wu, 2016; D. Yang, Jiang, & Ng, 2018).

Western scholars, on the other hand, argue that BRI is developed strategically to strengthen China's diplomacy in developing countries, particularly with its neighbors, even as it promises infrastructural development, commercial and economic benefits under the umbrella of "shared development," "win-win outcomes," and "mutual benefits for all" (Ikenberry, 2008; Mogato & Petty, 2017; Shambaugh, 2013; Swaine, 2014). Swaine (2015) argues that BRI will "leverage China's growing economic power and influence [along its periphery] in order to strengthen and expand cooperative interactions, create an integrated web of mutually beneficial economic, social and political ties, and ultimately lower distrust and enhance a sense of common security."

Washington concerns over China's initiatives, such as BRI and the Asian Infrastructure Investment Bank (AIIB) are intertwined strategically with China's interest in dislodging a West-centric economic and political order from China-centered economic and political rules (Yu, 2017). For example, former U.S. President Barack Obama in his State of the Union address to Congress on January 20, 2015, said: "But as we speak, China wants to write the rules for the world's fastest-growing region. That would put our workers and our businesses at a disadvantage. Why would we let that happen? We should write those rules" (Obama, 2015).

China has repeatedly refuted those concerns, arguing that these initiatives were meant to complement and facilitate existing financial and economic governance; and that China has no intention of challenging Western dominance of the economic and political order through BRI, but to facilitate unimpeded trade and connectivity among developing countries through infrastructural development and economic corridors (Bijian, 2012; Huang, 2016; Khan, Sadano, Pratt, & Farid, 2018).

From a security perspective, the United States and the Association of Southeast Asian Nations have also expressed concerns over the New Maritime Silk Road and argue that China will use BRI infrastructure for political and military purposes (e.g., China's military base in Djibouti and the militarization and fortification of the South China Sea). BRI will boost China's naval power and maritime capabilities, positioning it to enhance international maritime security, freedom of navigation and free trade activities on the South China Sea and on the Indian Ocean (Jones & Liu, 2017; Mogato & Petty, 2017). India is concerned about China's growing financial investment in Gwadar port, Pakistan; in Chittagong, Bangladesh; in Hambantota, Sri Lanka; and in Sittwe, Myanmar; it views these strategic facilities as a threat to its national security, arguing that they will provide strategic advantages to China over India and jeopardize Indian strategic interests on the Indian Ocean (Kaya, 2017). China rebuts these claims, as do several Chinese scholars (e.g., Bei, 2017; Bijian, 2017; Lai, Tang, and Yin, 2018).

PROSPECTS AND STUMBLING BLOCKS

BRI's blueprint calls for connecting 65 Eurasian countries through roads, railways, seaports, airports, fiber optic cables, and pipelines; it will also establish six economic corridors in Asia, Africa and Europe. BRI projects in 30 major Islamic countries are part of the official BRI plan (Table 1). Five out of six economic corridors will directly pass through Islamic countries, making the Islamic world a backbone of the BRI (Figure 1). The Islamic world maintains a social, political, economic and cultural system that is different from that of the rest of the world. Therefore, it provides unique advantages and disadvantages to China's BRI.

Political and Strategic Benefits

BRI will create political and strategic capital for both China and the Islamic world.

First, the Islamic world has geostrategic, geopolitical, and geo-economic global significance (Weir, 2003b). It comprises of 49 Muslim-majority countries that

Table 1. Geographical distribution of Muslim and non-Muslim countries associated with the Belt and Road Initiative

Geographical Zones	Muslim Countries (N = 30)	Non-Muslim Countries (N = 35)
East Asia	None	China, Mongolia
Southeast Asia	Brunei, Indonesia, Malaysia,	Cambodia, Laos, Myanmar, Philippines, Singapore, Thailand, Timor-Leste, Vietnam
Central Asia	Kazakhstan, Kyrgyzstan, Tajikistan, Turkmenistan, Uzbekistan	None
Middle East and North Africa	Bahrain, Egypt, Iran, Iraq, Jordan, Kuwait, Lebanon, Oman, Qatar, Saudi Arabia, Palestine, Syria, United Arab Emirates, Yemen	Israel
South Asia	Afghanistan, Bangladesh, Pakistan, Maldives	Bhutan, India, Nepal, Sri-Lanka
Europe	Albania, Azerbaijan, Bosnia and Herzegovina, Turkey	Armenia, Belarus, Bulgaria, Croatia, Czech Republic, Estonia, Georgia, Hungary, Latvia, Lithuania, Macedonia, Moldova, Montenegro, Poland, Romania, Russia, Serbia, Slovakia, Slovenia, Ukraine

account for 21.7 percent of the world's total land mass. About 1.62 billion people or 23.4 percent of the world's population hold the Islamic faith; 62.1 percent of Muslims live in Asia, close to China's geographical location (Li, 2018; Sherani, 2013). And an influential Islamic political bloc of 57 nation-states under the banner of Organization of Islamic Cooperation (OIC) has galvanized its geopolitical and geostrategic importance in global politics as it constitutes the second-largest intergovernmental body, after the United Nations. The Islamic world is also home to natural energy resources, particularly oil and gas. Today, the Middle East contributes 42 percent of oil and 26 percent of natural gas to the world's energy supply chain and it possesses 65.36 percent of the world proven oil reserves and 51 percent of the world total natural gas resources. Saudi Arabia, Iraq, and Iran are the world's largest oil exporters and China's large chunk of oil-related imports come from these Islamic countries.

Second, the steady decline of U.S. global preëminence and emergence of a wider spectrum of threats and conflicts in the Middle East region, and unprecedented changes in global politics have prompted the emerging powers to search for partners and for new alliances aimed at promoting their strategic interests in the region. Even though China has significantly increased its stature in global politics through its unprecedented growth in its economy and military stature, its strategic interests are still threatened. The quadrilateral alliance of China's rivals—India, the United States, Japan and Australia—poses serious challenges to its strategic interest in the region and its future ambition of being the next superpower. U.S. unilateral actions in the Middle East and Central Asia have destabilized the region, threaten China's access to vital energy resources, and hurtled its ability to project itself as a regional force in the Middle East. Therefore, China's cordial relationship with the Islamic world is worth billions as it will not only fulfill China's future energy needs but will also provide strategic and political support in game-playing between major world powers (Malik, 2002). Therefore, BRI can provide a much-needed impetus to fortifying strategic political and economic relationships between China and the Islamic world.

Third, the Islamic world is concerned about U.S. political meddling in its national affairs and state sovereignty; it is searching for an alternative power bring about a settlement of its political disputes. China's engagement with the Islamic world can encourage state sovereignty, noninterference in internal affairs and a peaceful settlement of political disputes in that region. Therefore, China is seen as a best possible substitute of U.S. in the Islamic world (Elmagherbi, 2010; Hayoun, 2013; Zambelis & Gentry, 2008; Zhu, 2011). In addition, China is emerging as a global power and a permanent member of the United Nations Security Council that support the just cause of the Palestinian people and oppose U.S. invasion, occupation and interference in Islamic countries. King Abdullah of Saudi Arabia categorically described China as a close and friendly country that "always stands on the side of truth and justice, always on the side of the just cause of the Palestinian people and the Arab people" (Zhu, 2011, p.8). Therefore, BRI will strengthen a new form of relationship between China and Islamic world, based on a win-win cooperation that will ultimately boost China's political leverage in South Asia, Central Asia, Southeast Asia, and West Asia.

Fourth, China's robust economic performance in global financial markets and its success in lifting more than 800 million of its own people out of poverty within 30 years ("The World Bank," 2018) have earned it a favorable global image. China's standing in the world has grown in recent years and the competitive favorability advantage of the United States over China has declined from 25 to 12 countries in which the United States has a more promising image (Vice, 2017). However, China's favorable image is still largely being challenged in many countries, particularly in nations such as Japan, Vietnam, Turkey, South Korea, Egypt, Sweden, Spain, and the United States, where more than 50 percent of the population hold an unfavorable image of China (*Pew Research Center*, 2014-2017; Xie & Page, 2013). Interestingly, four of these nations—Turkey, Jordan, Lebanon, and Egypt—are in the Islamic world. In addition, China's public perception in Saudi Arabia is also negative and hostile (Al-sudairi, 2013). Therefore, China can parlay BRI-projects into the public-diplomacy arena to enhance its positive image in the Islamic world.

Economic and Energy Interests

The Islamic world is a market of more than 1.8 billion people and of vast (natural) resources of oil, gas, and minerals. But it lacks industrial skills, modern technologies, communication and transportation infrastructure. There is also an acute shortage of electricity in some Islamic countries (e.g., Pakistan) (Galal, 2014; Yang, 2014). China, through BRI, can capture this market by facilitating infrastructural development (e.g., highways, motorways, railways, seaports, airports); investment in the energy sector (e.g., exploration and transportation of natural resources oil, gas and minerals; and generation of electricity) and by fostering industrial development (free economic zones) in the Islamic world. Reciprocally, BRI will advance China's economic growth and fulfill its energy need through vibrant economic and energy corridors between China and the Islamic world. The raison d'être for such outcomes is fourfold.

First, on the heels of its open-market policy, China is pivoting westward (mainly toward Islamic countries) for its energy needs and economic interests even as the Islamic world is tilting eastward, particularly toward China for financial investment and political support (Galal, 2014). Therefore, BRI can fulfill the common aspiration of both China and the Islamic world as it promises significant investment in infrastructure with a focus on transportation (i.e., roads, railways, seaports and airports) to ease free trade, energy generation, transmission and transportation (i.e., oil and gas pipelines) to overcome energy shortage and communication linkages via fiber-optic cables. This has the potential to create an economic and energy corridor between China and the Islamic world for a win-win outcome (Amighini, 2017; Selmier-II, 2018). For example, in the BRI flagship project of US$62 billion, CPEC is playing a central role in developing infrastructure and generating economic activities in Pakistan and it also reduces 9,000 km geographical distance to link China's Xinjiang province with the Middle East and Africa through Gwadar port, facilitating China's access to vital energy resources and easing its exports to maintain its economic growth.

Second, the Islamic financial market has resources that can be invested in BRI-related projects. According to the State of the Global Islamic Economy Report (2018/2019), the Islamic world owns funds worth US$4.9 trillion in the form of US$3.2 trillion OIC sovereign wealth funds and of US$1.7 trillion "dry powder" (unutilized capital) funds that are accessible for future investment. The Islamic world also offers enormous economic opportunities for China's investment in the fast-growing Islamic market, estimated at US$6.6 trillion in 2017 and expected to achieve accumulated wealth of US$8.3 trillion till 2023 (Table 2).

Table 2. An estimated size of Islamic economy market in U.S. billion dollars

	2017	**2023**	**Average**
Islamic Banking and Finance	2,438	3,809	3,124
Halal Food	1,303	1,863	1,583
Travel	177	274	226
Fashion	270	361	316
Media and Recreation	209	288	249
Pharmaceutical	87	131	109
Cosmetics	61	90	76
Total	**6,562**	**8,839**	**7,701**

Source: State of the Global Islamic Economy report, 2018/2019

In recent years, Islamic banking and finance (IBF) has shown steady growth and experts forecast an estimated growth of US$3-US$4.4 trillion in IBF industry through 2020 (Figure 2). The Islamic world is gravitating toward the IBF system and countries such as Qatar, Saudi Arabia, UAE, Kuwait, Bahrain, Malaysia, and Oman have great potential to plug a sizable funding gap in BRI-related projects through IBF. It is predicted that BRI-related projects will face an estimated funding gap of US$49 trillion from 2015 through 2030 (Li, 2018; Townsend, 2018). AIIB can link up with Islamic financial products, using such a setup for risk management in BRI-related projects in the Islamic world (Hayoun, 2013; Li, 2018).

IBF industries are rapidly expanding in Hong Kong and have grown from US$1.1 trillion in 2013 to US$1.6 trillion in 2018. In September 2014, the Hong Kong government made a five-year investment of US$4.7 billion in Sukuk Islamic bonds. Therefore, Hong Kong can play a key role in Islamic financing for BRI-related projects and ultimately become a hub of Islamic finance center in mainland China (Li, 2018).

Third, halal food is another significant part of the growing Islamic economy at the global level. It accounts for about 19 percent of the global food market; it is estimated at US$1.3 trillion and will ultimately reach US$1.9 trillion in 2023 (Table 2). China has more than 23 million Muslims, most of whom live in the underserved regions of Xinjiang, Ningxia, Gansu, and Qinghai. There are also significant numbers of

Figure 2. Size and growth of Islamic banking and finance
Source: The Global Islamic Finance report, 2017

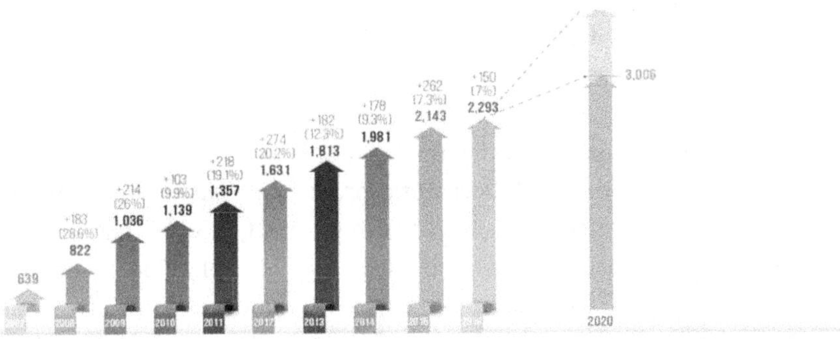

NOTE: All the figures are in US$ billion. For example, at the end of 2016, global size of the Islamic financial services industry was US$2.293 billion, and this was due to an incremental increase of US$150 billion over the previous year. Two estimates, i.e., US$3.006 billion and US$4.362 billion, are presented for the year 2020. The former is based on the assumption that the industry continues to grow at the current growth rate of 7% in the next four years; and the latter assumes that the industry will grow by compound annual growth rate of (CAGR) of 15.27% by 2020.

Islamic enterprises, businesspeople, students and workers in China who use halal food every day, thus, creating a potential for halal trade between China and the Islamic world. China can use BRI to facilitate its Muslim population to optimize on halal trade and benefit from the opportunity to export halal food to Muslim countries. It will improve living and economic standards in China's Muslim areas, strengthening China's economic and political relations with the Islamic world. China has already established China-Malaysia Halal E-commercial Center and International Halal Certificate Service Center in Ningxia to accomplish a win-win outcome. There are several other potential areas for BRI, for example, travel, fashion, media and recreation, pharmaceutical and cosmetics where China can optimize the opportunities to export to Islamic countries (Table 2).

Fourth, as stated in a preceding paragraph, the Islamic world is replete with energy resources. China is the world's largest importer of petroleum products and importing 8.4 million barrels crude oil per day, superseding United States' gross crude oil import of 7.9 million barrels per day (Barron, 2018). Additionally, China's domestic oil resources are shrinking gradually and it will heavily depend on imported oil for its future sustainable economic growth. BRI has a great potential to strengthen energy cooperation between China and the Islamic world. Most Islamic countries lack financial capital, mechanical equipment, technical expertise, and industrial standards in the petroleum engineering sectors, for example, in exploration, extraction, refining and transportation. Beijing can secure its access to rich oil resources by pledging investment cooperation and extending technical support in the field of petroleum and natural gas as a reliable partner to the Islamic world (Kamel, 2018; Li, 2018; Selmier-II, 2018). For example, various BRI projects related to oil and gas pipelines in Azerbaijan, Turkmenistan, Uzbekistan, Kazakhstan, Pakistan, and Malaysia can play a vital role in fulfilling China's future energy needs by providing alternative and competitiveness energy supply routes from Central Asia, Middle East, and African countries.

Chinese state companies have already embraced the opportunity to invest, under BRI, in the much-needed infrastructural projects in Islamic countries. China has already established financial institutions (e.g., AIIB, NSRF) that pledge generous amounts to development in Islamic countries. For example, China will invest US$62 billion through CPEC, a flagship project of BRI to develop infrastructure, energy sectors and to build Gwadar port in Pakistan (Rafiq, 2017). China has pledged financial support of US$50 billion to the Egyptian government for development of its new administrative capital in Cairo. Additionally, China is also collaborating with Egypt to construct a new Suez Canal cooperation zone. Beijing has signed a bilateral agreement of US$65 billion with Saudi Arabia for mutual economic cooperation in the fields of petroleum engineering, space technology and renewable energy. Recently, China Railway Construction Corporation completed the US$16 billion "Haramain high-speed rail project" between the two holy cities of Islam: Makkah and Madinah, in Saudi Arabia. That project, the largest railway project in the Middle East, is economically crucial to the well-being of the Muslim Ummah; it will facilitate the annual Hajj (Islamic pilgrimage) experience of 60 million pilgrims, reducing by two hours the 10-hour road journey between Makkah and Madinah. China is also investing US$10.7 billion in "Sino-Oman Industrial City" to construct an oil refinery capable of handling 235,000 barrels per day (Kliman & Grace, 2018; Lehr, 2018). China has planned to construct 3,200 Km Silk Road high-speed railway between China's northwest province, Xinjiang, and Tehran through Central Asian states—Kazakstan, Kyrgyzstan Uzbekistan, and Turkmenistan. This route will provide an alternative to the ocean freight and will reduce the time and cost of transporting goods between China and the Islamic world (Macauley, 2015). China has also opened a US$10 billion credit line for Iran to support its economic development through the CITIC group. Regardless of U.S. economic sanction on Iran, China's trade with that nation is growing at the rate of 19 percent annually; it exceeded US$37 billion in 2017. War-ridden countries such as Yemen, Syria, Iraq, Libya and Afghanistan need significant investments for restoring their shattered infrastructure. Therefore, BRI under the Xi version of "community with shared future for mankind" can play a significant role in the much-needed development of modern infrastructure in the Islamic world and move Sino-Islamic relationships to new heights of strategic friendship based on mutual interest for mutual benefits and shared development (Kliman & Grace, 2018; Lehr, 2018).

Political Instability and Security Issues

Political instability and security issues are the main obstacles to completing BRI-related projects in the Islamic world. Islamic countries like Iraq, Syria, Libya, Yemen, Sudan, and Afghanistan are under the stresses of continuing wars. Pakistan, Egypt, Turkey and Saudi Arabia have also suffered from terrorism and political instability. Except for a handful of Islamic countries (e.g., Malaysia and United Arab Emirates), the Islamic world faces political and security crises.

The issue of Uighur Muslims in China's Xinjiang province is still a bone of contention between China and the Islamic world, particularly Turkey's agitation against China's alleged suppression of Uighur Muslims of Turkic origins. For example, during ethnic violence in 2009, Turkish President Tayyab Erdogan condemned in strong terms China's crackdown on Uighur Muslims, describing it "a kind of genocide" (BBC News, 2009). Similarly, a Iranian senior religious cleric criticized the Chinese government for its alleged role in ethnic violence during a public sermon. The Iranian public and media have also exhibited discontent over China's support of a U.N. Security Council Resolution that imposed economic sanctions on Iran in 2010 (Chen, 2011). China's alleged use of "reëducation" camps for Uighur Muslims also faces a backlash from the Islamic and Western Press even though Chinese government terms it a deradicalizing effort to contain extremism and radicalism in the region (Dabashi, 2018; Page, Dou, & Shah, 2018). Consequently, there is anger in Islamic countries toward China, of which more than 50 percent of the population in four major Islamic countries (Turkey, Jordan, Lebanon, and Egypt) hold an unfavorable opinion (*Pew Research Center*, 2014-2017; Xie & Page, 2013).

Clash of Interest

China's BRI-related projects are resulting a clash of interests among regional and global players. For example, India has disavowed its partnership with BRI, opposing strongly CPEC, a central project of BRI proposed to connect China with the Middle East and Africa through Gwadar port in Pakistan because it passes through the disputed territory of Kashmir. Similarly, China is expanding gradually its engagement and presence in the Middle East. During the last decade, China's political, economic, security, and diplomatic influence has increased in the Middle East, posing a challenge to U.S. hegemony in the region. Even though, China maintains a low profile and focuses on economic and energy-related activities, regional forces are requiring it to adopt a more proactive and leading role in resolving the political and security situation in the Middle East. Therefore, Middle Eastern countries may use China's economic and energy interest as a leverage to gain China's support for certain political issues (e.g., the long-drawn Arabs-Israel conflict). Arab League Secretary General Amr Musa referred to such options when he said: "If you protect my interests, I will protect yours. If you take a position that does not reflect that will, I will take a similar position"(Chen, 2011, p. 6).

China's continuing support of and economic engagement with Iran are also an irritant to the United States. Iran is China's major trading partner. In 2010, China opposed the UN Security Council resolution demanding strict punitive action against Iran; it supported only the weakest form of such sanction. The United States is convinced that in spite of UN sanctions, China is still engaged with Iran, further undercutting the effectiveness of the economic sanctions. In addition, Saudi Arabia's King Abdullah, despite being an ally and a primary security partner of the United States in the Middle East visited China as his first foreign destination on ascending to the throne in January 2006. These developments indicate the heft of China's influence in the Islamic world, particularly in the Middle East. Therefore, China's engagement through BRI will intersect with the economic and political dynamics of the region, ultimately generating a clash of interests between China and the United States in the Middle East. Sun Bigan, a former Chinese diplomat in the Middle East, argues that the rift between the U.S. and China will deepen over the political influence and oil trade in the Middle East and "Bilateral quarrels and clashes are unavoidable" in the future (*The Daily Star*, 2009).

There is a palpable cleavage based on intrafaith division in the Middle East: the Sunni and Shia blocs. The Sunni bloc is led by Saudi Arabia, the Shia guided by Iran. The strategic and economic interests of both countries collide over Middle East issues such as the outbreak of civil war in Yemen in 2012, Iran's support for the Houthis (Shia anti-government militia) whereas Saudi Arabia firmly stands with President Abdrabbuh Mansur Hadi (Sunni leader). There is also a clash of interest over the Iranian nuclear program, wars in Iraq and Iranian support of Syria's Bashar al-Asad. Therefore, clashes of interests in the region between these two rival blocs can affect the BRI-related projects in the Middle East. In addition, China's close relationship with Israel can be exploited by the Arab countries over political or economic favors (Ferdinand, 2016).

Financial Debt and Local Resentment

According to the Center for Global Development (CGD) report (2017), 23 out of 68 BRI's countries are in "quite high" risk category of debt distress; and eight of them—Pakistan, the Maldives, Kyrgyzstan, Tajikistan, Laos, Djibouti, Montenegro, and Mongolia—could have difficulty meeting their debt payment to China (Ming, 2018).

The fragile economies in many Muslim countries cannot allow investing in modern infrastructure. For example, Malaysia recently abandoned a multibillion dollar high-speed railway project to "avoid being declared bankrupt" (Shukry & Park, 2018). CGD notes that Pakistan will be the largest country at high risk of debt distress, as China finances 80 percent of the US$62 billion CPEC-related projects in loans (Ming, 2018). Therefore, Pakistan's new government is reviewing some major CPEC-related projects, putting some on hold while seeking compelling evidence to move on them in a teetering national economy (Anderlini, Sender, & Bokhari, 2018; Kiani, 2019).

Local producers and merchants consider the influx of cheap Chinese consumer goods a threat to local industries. Some Islamic countries anticipate anti-dumping actions against Chinese commodities (Zhu, 2011). There is concern that China's establishing a free economic zone through BRI will further limit the financial opportunities available to local entrepreneurs and industries and facilitate China's major businesses taking over the fragile local manufacturing sector, constraining local production and a country's export capacity. Besides, in the Islamic world, major issues have been raised in Chinese firms: employment incentives, hiring patterns, workplace practices (Feng & Liang, 2018; Zambelis & Gentry, 2008).

Religious Issues and Cultural Gap

Since the eighth century, the Silk Road has conjoined China with Islamic countries through old land routes from Xinjiang to Turkey and bound them as trade partners to facilitate trade activities between two civilizations. But the economic impetus of BRI in modern Islamic economies should consider historical roots and the Islamic finance system. Islam forbids (*haram*) certain kinds of financial engagements, e.g., *riba* (charging any form of fixed interest) on financial transactions, but encourages fair competition and a profit-and-loss financial engagement (risk sharing). Islam also advocates the general communal aspect of the financial system such as charity (*zakat*, a levied tax imposed on the wealthy and high-income people) and restricts investment in drug trades, alcohol-related business, and other unlawful social and ethical activities. However, these practices vary from country to country and from community to community, e.g., Sunni and Shia Islamic countries both have different Islamic financial systems (Khan, 2015; Rethel, 2011).

There is understandably a wide cultural and religious gap between China and the Islamic world. China is a secular country where people do not practice any dominant religion. But the Islamic world strictly follows the code of conduct stipulated in Islam. There is a lot of cultural and Islamic sensitivity in the Islamic world, which, if confronted, might trigger a devastating response. Therefore, it is logical to expect China to have a strategic plan subsumed under BRI and a pragmatic approach to regional and international integration while securing commercial incentives and availing itself of economic opportunities in the Islamic world. An illustration: the construction of the "Grand Mosque of Algiers" by China State Construction Engineering Corporation triggered resentment in Algiers and raised several questions: (a) "Can we entrust an atheist enterprise from an atheist state that represses its own Uighur minority in Xinjiang [in China's far West province] to construct a mosque here in Algeria?" (b) "What glory and what blessing will we get from this project—constructing a mosque as an act of faith that will reinforce the oppression of our Uighur brothers at the cost of a billion dollars?"(Hayoun, 2013, p. 96). These kinds of sentiments can be associated with BRI, racing through the public mind-set, generating nefarious impressions of BRI in the Islamic world.

THE WAY FORWARD

Tensions in the Islamic world provide ample opportunities for China to establish strong BRI cooperation between it and the Islamic world. However, Beijing may be well served by considering the following suggestions as it implements BRI-related projects in the Islamic world:

1. The Islamic world is in two major cultural blocs: the Sunni and the Shia, led by two rival Islamic countries, Saudi Arabia and Iran, respectively. There is a concerning political tension between the two countries, particularly on political issues related to the Middle East, broadly, that is, to the conflicts in Yemen and Syria. Therefore, it is prudent for China to adhere consistently to its signature principle of non-interference in the internal affairs of sovereign nations. Anything less has the potential to disrupt China's fervent economic and political interest in the Islamic world.
2. China could play a facilitator role to mitigate the tense relationship between Riyadh and Tehran. The United States and Russia have failed to strike a balance between Tehran and Riyadh. But, China maintains a solid economic and political relationship with both Iran and Saudi Arabia while using this opportunity to nurture symmetrical communication between the two capitals. Such a disinterested Chinese posture in that region will be viewed in positive light in all three capitals.
3. China's understanding of Islamic culture and IBF are limited. China can launch strategic people-to-people contacts, e.g., politicians, scholars, journalists, students and business enterprises from the Islamic world could be invited regularly to China—and vice versa. China could hire Islamic IBF experts to explore new opportunity to use Islamic financial resources for BRI-projects. The appointment of a former governor of the Malaysian Central Bank, Dr. Tan Sri Zeti, to AIIB's International Advisory Panel on Islamic Financing was an appropriate decision, which can generate a sizable Islamic capital for BRI projects and reduce significantly the financial risk of Chinese investments in the Islamic world

4. Washington has been the sole hegemonic power in the Middle East for decades and cannot afford to ignore the Arabs' growing interest in China as a potential alternative force in the Middle East. China and the United States have different strategic priorities and interests in the Middle East, even though areas of mutual interest are also palpable. China should keep a balanced, disinterested approach to the political disputes in the Middle East and explore common areas of mutual interests (e.g., counterterrorism) for a more productive engagement with the United States in the Middle East. Beijing's avoiding confronting U.S. strategic, political and economic interest in the Middle East will result in a significant lessening of tensions between China and the United States.

CONCLUSION

Global discourses on geopolitics, geoeconomics, and finance are at a transitional stage—and at an upward trajectory that is pivoting toward a post-U.S. hegemony. China is reconfiguring, at a global scale, its geopolitical, economic, and business stature through BRI. On the one hand, the growing political, economic, and trade tensions between China and the U.S. are nudging China toward looking westward—that is, mainly to Islamic countries for political and economic incentives (e.g., access to vibrant resources of oil and gas and inclusive opportunities for financial investment in infrastructure and industries). On the other, the Islamic world in general is concerned about U.S. and Western nations' meddling in its internal matters, about U.S. support of Israel over the interests of the Palestinian people, and about military intervention in sovereign Islamic countries. There is some resentment toward the United States in the Islamic world that is seeking an alternative power dynamic for the settlement of their lingering disputes, the overhaul their strained economies, and the development of modern infrastructure to boost economic growth and uplift living standards.

China is being viewed in the Islamic world as the best possible option to the United States. Islamic countries tend to view cooperation under BRI as a win-win situation for both China and the Islamic world, fulfilling their common aspiration of shared development by guaranteeing state sovereignty, shared economic interest, political choice and mutual benefits (Mingjiang, 2015; Swaine, 2015; Yi, 2015). BRI has the potential to extend China's economic and political influence in the Islamic world, which will fulfill China's energy needs and enhance its access to new markets for its exports. To the Islamic world, participating fully in BRI translate into a resistance to the (perceived) hegemony of the United States.

There is likelihood of a backlash from China's deep involvement in the Islamic world. The BRI investments in Islamic countries might pose considerable risks for three reasons: massive financial debts, unconscionable export of terrorism, unintended collision of strategic interests. For example, Islamic countries like Pakistan, the Maldives, Kyrgyzstan, Tajikistan and Djibouti are rated under "quite high" risk of debt distress by the CGD. There is a fair chance that these countries will struggle to repay their Chinese loans (Ming, 2018). China's close relationship with the Middle East and African countries might also produce devastating knock-on effects for China because it may import extremist ideologies from the Middle East (e.g., Syria, Iraq, Yemen) and African countries (e.g., Sudan) into China's Muslim communities in Xinjiang province, refueling "East Turkmenistan" issues (Luft, 2016). China's growing political and economic influence in the Middle East, strategic partnership with Pakistan and persistent support of Iran are challenging the strategic interests of India and of the U.S. in Asia. Therefore, BRI-related engagement with these countries might play out as a spoiler for future relationships among the three countries—China, India, the United States—because of the collision of their strategic interests in Asia.

ACKNOWLEDGMENT

This research was supported by the China Postdoctoral Science Foundation (Grant No. 2018T110583).

REFERENCES

Al-sudairi, M. T. (2013, February). China in the eyes of the Saudi media. *Gulf Research Centre*, 1–38.

Amighini, A. (2017). *China's Belt and Road: A game changer?* Alessandria, Italy: Edizioni Epoké.

Anderlini, J., Sender, H., & Bokhari, F. (2018, September 10). Pakistan rethinks its role in Xi's Belt and Road plan. *Financial Times*. Retrieved from https://www.ft.com/content/d4a3e7f8-b282-11e8-99ca-68cf89602132

Barr, M. (2012). Nation branding as nation building: China's image campaign. *East Asia, 29*(1), 81–94. doi:10.100712140-011-9159-7

Barron, J. (2018, February 5). China surpassed the United States as the world's largest crude oil importer in 2017. *The U.S. Energy Information Administration*. Retrieved from https://www.eia.gov/todayinenergy/detail.php?id=34812

Bei, J. (2017). Economic globalization 3. 0 and the concept of interconnection under the. *Chinese Economy, 12*(2), 2–21.

Bhola, P. L. (1986). *Pakistan-China relations: Search for politico-strategic relationship*. RBSA Publishers.

Bijan, Z. (2005). China's peaceful rise to great-power status. *Foreign Affairs, 84*(5), 18. doi:10.2307/20031702

Bijian, Z. (2017). China's One Belt, One Road plan marks the next phase of globalization. *New Perspectives Quarterly, 34*(3), 27–31. doi:10.1111/npqu.12090

Brown, K. (2018). The Belt and Road: Security dimensions. *Asia Europe Journal, 16*(3), 213–222. doi:10.100710308-018-0514-9

Cai, K. G. (2018). The One Belt One Road and the Asian Infrastructure Investment Bank: Beijing's new strategy of geoeconomics and geopolitics. *Journal of Contemporary China, 27*(114), 831–847. doi:10.1080/10670564.2018.1488101

Callahan, W. A. (2016). China's "Asia Dream" The Belt Road Initiative and the new regional order. *Asian Journal of Comparative Politics, 1*(3), 226–243. doi:10.1177/2057891116647806

Chen, J. (2011, December). The emergence of China in the Middle East. In *Strategic Forum* (No. 271, p. 1). National Defense University.

Dabashi, H. (2018, December 22). Muslim cleansing: A global pandemic? *Al-Arabiya English*.

De Bao, X. (2016). One Belt, One Road: China's reconstruction for global communication and international discourse power. *International Institute for Asian Studies, Summer*. Retrieved from http://iias.asia/the-newsletter/article/one-belt-one-road-chinas-reconstruction-global-communication-international

Elmagherbi, F. I. (2010). A case study of China relations with the Arab world. *2010 2nd IEEE International Conference on Information and Financial Engineering*, 646–650. doi:10.1109/ICIFE.2010.5609442

Fair, C. C. (2017, July 3). Argument: Pakistan can't afford China's friendship. *Foreign Policy*. Retrieved from https://foreignpolicy.com/2017/07/03/pakistan-cant-afford-chinas-friendship/

Feng, D. H., & Liang, H. (2018). Understanding the issues surrounding the Belt and Road Initiative (BRI). *China and the World: Ancient and Modern Silk Road, 1*(03).

Ferdinand, P. (2016). Westward ho - the China dream and "one belt, one road": Chinese foreign policy under Xi Jinping. *International Affairs*, *92*(4), 941–957. doi:10.1111/1468-2346.12660

Galal, M. N. (2014). "China-Arab States Cooperation Forum": Achievements, challenges and prospects. *Arab World Studies,* (2).

Hayoun, M. (2013, January). Strange bedfellows: China's Middle Eastern inroads. *World Affairs*, 89–96.

Holslag, J. (2017). How China's New Silk Road threatens European trade. *The International Spectator*, *52*(1), 46–60. doi:10.1080/03932729.2017.1261517

Huang, Y. (2016). Understanding China's Belt & Road Initiative: Motivation, framework and assessment. *China Economic Review*, *40*, 314–321. doi:10.1016/j.chieco.2016.07.007

Ikenberry, G. J. (2008). The rise of China and the future of the West: Can the liberal system survive? *Foreign Affairs*, *87*(1), 23–37.

Jia, W. (2017). Now, globalization with Chinese characteristics. *YaleGlobal Online*. Retrieved from http://yaleglobal.yale.edu/content/now-globalization-chinese-characteristics

Jin, X., Li, D. D., & Wu, S. (2016). How will China shape the world economy? *China Economic Review*, *40*, 272–280. doi:10.1016/j.chieco.2016.07.006

Jones, D. A., & Liu, H. (2017). Management of Chinese Foreign Direct Investment: "One Belt, One Road" across Eurasia to Africa and Europe amidst maritime tensions in the South China Sea region. *International Relations and Diplomacy*, *5*(8), 486–500.

Kamel, M. S. (2018). China's Belt and Road Initiative: Implications for the Middle East. *Cambridge Review of International Affairs*, *7571*, 1–19.

Kaya, T. Ö. (2017). Sino-Indian strategic rivalry in the Indian ocean region. *Insan ve Toplum*, *7*(2), 155.

Khan, F. (2015). *Islamic Banking in Pakistan: Shariah-compliant Finance and the quest to make Pakistan more Islamic*. New York: Routledge. doi:10.4324/9781315670249

Khan, M. K., Sandano, I. A., Pratt, C. B., & Farid, T. (2018). China's Belt and Road Initiative: A global model for an evolving approach to sustainable regional development. *Sustainability*, *10*(11), 4234. doi:10.3390u10114234

Kiani, K. (2019, January 14). Govt puts major CPEC power project on hold. *Dawn*. Retrieved form https://www.dawn.com/news/1457449

Kliman, D., & Grace, A. (2018, June 18). China smells opportunity in the Middle East's crisis. *Foreign Policy*. Retrieved from https://foreignpolicy.com/2018/06/14/china-smells-opportunity-in-the-middle-easts-crisis/

Lai, T. L., Tang, J., & Yin, H. (2018). Spatial Economics in the era of One Belt One Road and counter-globalization. *Modern Economy*, *9*(1), 61–66. doi:10.4236/me.2018.91004

Lehmacher, W. (2016, November 22). Why China could lead the next phase of globalization. *World Economic Forum*. Retrieved from https://www.weforum.org/agenda/2016/11/china-lead-globalization-after-united-states

Lehr, D. (2018, July 21). How China is winning over the Middle East. *The Diplomat*. Retrieved from https://thediplomat.com/2018/07/how-china-is-winning-over-the-middle-east/

Li, F. (2018). The role of Islam in the development of the Belt and Road Initiative. *Asian Journal of Middle Eastern and Islamic Studies*, *12*(1), 35–45. doi:10.1080/25765949.2018.1439617

Luft, G. (2016, January 26). China's new grand strategy for the Middle East. *Foreign Policy*.

Macauley, R. (2015, November 23). China wants to build a high-speed rail link to a newly open Iran. *Quartz*. Retrieved from https://qz.com/557009/chinas-next-big-idea-is-a-high-speed-railway-to-iran/

Malik, M. (2002). Dragon China's on terrorism : Assessing gains tactical and strategic losses after 11 September. *Contemporary Southeast Asia*, *24*(2), 252–293. doi:10.1355/CS24-2D

Ming, C. (2018, March 5). China's mammoth Belt and Road Initiative could increase debt risk for 8 countries. *CNBC*. Retrieved from https://www.cnbc.com/2018/03/05/chinas-belt-and-road-initiative-raises-debt-risks-in-8-nations.html

Mingjiang, L. (2015). *China's "One Belt, One Road" Initiative: New round of opening up? RSIS Commentaries*. Nanyang Technological University.

Mogato, M., & Petty, M. (2017, April 27). Push for South China Sea code stirs ASEAN suspicions about Beijing's endgame. *Reuters*. Retrieved from https://www.reuters.com/article/us-southchinasea-asean-analysis-idUSKBN17T0A5

BBC News. (2009, July 10). Turkey attacks China "genocide." *BBC News*.

Obama, B. (2015, January 20). Remarks by the President in State of the Union Address. *The White House*. Retrieved from https://obamawhitehouse.archives.gov/the-press-office/2015/01/20/remarks-president-state-union-address-January-20-2015

Page, J., Dou, E., & Shah, S. (2018, September 27). China's Muslim detention camps spark protests in Islamic world. *The Wall Street Journal*.

Pew Research Center. (2017). *China Image: Do you have a favorable or unfavorable view of China?* Retrieved from http://www.pewglobal.org/database/indicator/24/survey/17/response/Unfavorable/

Rafiq, A. (2017, October 24). China's $62 billion bet on Pakistan. *Foreign Affairs*.

Rethel, L. (2011). Whose legitimacy? Islamic finance and the global financial order. *Review of International Political Economy*, *18*(1), 75–98. doi:10.1080/09692290902983999

Rolland, N. (2017). China's "Belt and Road Initiative": Underwhelming or game-changer? *The Washington Quarterly*, *40*(1), 127–142. doi:10.1080/0163660X.2017.1302743

Schultz, K. (2017, December). Sri Lanka, struggling with debt, hands a major port to China. *The New York Times*. Retrieved from https://www.nytimes.com/2017/12/12/world/asia/sri-lanka-china-port.html

Selmier-II, W. T. (2018). The Belt and Road Initiative and the influence of Islamic economies. *Economic and Political Studies*, *6*(3), 257–277. doi:10.1080/20954816.2018.1498989

Shambaugh, D. (2013). *China goes global: The partial power*. Oxford University Press.

Sherani, S. (2013, August 12). Economies of the ummah. *Dawn*. Retrieved from https://www.dawn.com/news/1035026

Shukry, A., & Park, K. (2018, May). Malaysia scraps multibillion-dollar high-speed rail project to Singapore. *Bloomberg*.

Sum, N.-L. (2018). The intertwined geopolitics and geoeconomics of hopes/fears: China's triple economic bubbles and the 'One Belt One Road' imaginary. *Territory, Politics, Governance: An International Journal of Policy, Administration and Institutions*, 1–25. doi:10.1080/21622671.2018.1523746

Swaine, M. D. (2014). Chinese views and commentary on periphery diplomacy. *China Leadership Monitor, 44*(1).

Swaine, M. D. (2015). Chinese views and commentary on the "One Belt, One Road" Initiative. *China Leadership Monitor, 47*, 1–24. Retrieved from http://www.hoover.org/sites/default/files/research/docs/clm47ms.pdf

The Daily Star. (2009, October 1). What will China's rising influence mean for the Middle East region? *The Daily Star*. Retrieved from http://www1.dailystar.com.lb/Opinion/Editorial/2009/Oct-01/119578-what-will-chinas-rising-influence-mean-for-the-middle-east-region.ashx

Townsend, S. (2018, October 30). Islamic banking key to financing China's Belt and Road. *The National Business*.

Vice, M. (2017). *In global popularity contest, U.S. and China – not Russia – vie for first*. Retrieved from http://www.pewresearch.org/fact-tank/2017/08/23/in-global-popularity-contest-u-s-and-china-not-russia-vie-for-first/

Xi, J. (2015). Asia's new future: Towards a community of common destiny. In *Boao Forum for Asia Annual Conference 2015*. Hainan: Boao Forum. Retrieved from http://english.boaoforum.org/u/cms/www2/201503/25112018qw3q.pdf

Xie, T., & Page, B. I. (2013). What affects China's national image? A cross-national study of public opinion. *Journal of Contemporary China*, *22*(83), 850–867. doi:10.1080/10670564.2013.782130

Xu, X. (2000). China and the Middle East: Cross-investment in the energy sector. *Middle East Policy*, *7*(3), 122–136. doi:10.1111/j.1475-4967.2000.tb00168.x

Yang, D., Jiang, L., & Ng, A. K. Y. (2018). One Belt one Road, but several routes: A case study of new emerging trade corridors connecting the Far East to Europe. *Transportation Research Part A: Policy and Practice, 117*, 190–204. doi:10.1016/j.tra.2018.08.001

Yang, F. (2014). Invigorating Sino-Arab relations by One Belt and One Road strategy. *Journal of Middle Eastern and Islamic Studies*, *8*(4), 1–26. doi:10.1080/19370679.2014.12023254

Yi, H. (2015, March 20). China's One Belt/One Road' policy is open to all nations. *Executive Intelligence Review*. Retrieved from http://schillerinstitute.org/economy/phys_econ/2015/27-29_EIR12-one_belt_one_road.html

Yu, H. (2017). Motivation behind China's 'One Belt, One Road' initiatives and establishment of the Asian infrastructure investment bank. *Journal of Contemporary China*, *26*(105), 353–368. doi:10.1080/10670564.2016.1245894

Yu, X. (2006). *50 Years of Sino-Egyptian diplomacy, Silk Road Stories: 50 Years of Diplomacy between New China and Arab Countries*. Beijing: World Affairs Press.

Zambelis, C., & Gentry, B. (2008). China through Arab eyes : American influence in the Middle East. *Parameters, 38*(1), 60–73.

Zhan, S. (2006). *Premier Zhou Enlai works for Sino-Egyptian and Sino-Arab friendship. Silk Road stories: 50 years of diplomacy between new China and Arab countries*. Beijing: World Affairs Press.

Zhu, W. (2011). On the strategic relationship between China and Islamic countries in the Middle East. *Journal of Sino-Islamic Communications*, *3*(1), 1–27.

Chapter 7
OBOR:
A New Hope for Future Indonesian or a New Trap? Case Study in Indonesia

Effnu Subiyanto
https://orcid.org/0000-0001-7879-2499
Widya Mandala Surabaya Catholic University, Indonesia

ABSTRACT

One Belt One Road (OBOR) first declared by the China's President is believed by some to be a new hope and a new horizon for a number of developing countries. OBOR has been viewed as a new challenging proposal and as an ice breaking for the decades-long stagnant infrastructure in Indonesia, the largest economic region in Association Southeast Asian Nations (ASEAN). This chapter is an update on OBOR's recent development in Indonesian which also coincidentally was declared as a new maritime-axis when new reform government has taken into power since 2014. Many views have been released, pro-contra has been severely dispatched into two separate blocks of Indonesian experts in two standpoints, one to support and the other to challenge involving Indonesia in the OBOR. This chapter has been thoroughly analyzed by mining information and data from big data sources, combined with semi-structured interviews of various executives and contractors.

DOI: 10.4018/978-1-5225-8980-8.ch007

INTRODUCTION

No one to challenge that China recently has intensely increased their investment in Assocation of Southeast Asian Nations (ASEAN) region, especially in Indonesia. Since then a number of experts of Indonesia and China have frequently published their writings, from the fear of China's rise as a new epicentrum regional power to a balanced view of China to dispelling such a fear. But less have said about few questions: why does Indonesia matter to China? (Bria, 2017). What drives China to put billions of US dollar in Indonesia following various multilateral and bilateral agreements at the ASEAN level, especially between Indonesia and China? (Gourdon, 2015).

One should note that since the early 2000s, China has signed strategic partnership agreements with 47 countries and three international organizations in which ASEAN is one of them. It seeks to expand converging interests and seek common ground on the major issues while shelving differences on the minor ones (Jing, 2016). Along with Indonesia, other ASEAN members who have signed strategic partnerships with China are Vietnam, Cambodia, Laos, Myanmar, Thailand and Malaysia. The strategic partnership is used by China as a diplomatic tool to protect its core interests, which include state sovereignty, national security, territorial integrity and national reunification. These core interests are well reflected in all documents of China's strategic partnerships (Bin, 2015).

Feng Zhongping and Huang Jing (2014) argue that the boom of China's strategic partnerships is a result of China's embrace of globalization and multi-dimensional diplomacy. It is a diplomatic instrument to secure China's core interests and its peaceful rise as a global power. A comprehensive strategic partnership as articulated by the Chinese premier, Wen Jiabao (2004), was an all-dimensional and multilayered, long-term and stable partnership that transcends differences in ideologies and social systems. Energy security for China means the acquisition of sufficient energy supplies to protect China's core objectives (Downs, 2006).

After the signing of the Indonesia-China strategic partnership in 2005 and the upgrade into a comprehensive strategic partnership in 2013, China is now Indonesia's largest trading partner (Sun, 2010). Since 2017, China consistently became always the third largest investor in Indonesia after Japan and Singapore. The question then is, why does Indonesia more broadly deserve a position as China's strategic partner?

ENERGY SCARCITY IN CHINA

Within last few years to come China has emerged as a global importer in the energy sector. This is a result of soaring economic growth, hovered between 9% and 10% per year for three decades since 1980, and since 2012 China still showed impressive growth of 7% to 8%. This is why China's demand for energy is massive and propels the country to undertake energy acquisitions worldwide. Domestic energy reserve in China is scarce except in coal, but with low quality.

China became a net oil importer in 1993, a net gas importer in 2007, a net coal importer in 2008 and the first global oil importer in 2014. It means that in 2014, China has become a consumer of 30% of global oil consumption and 45% of global coal consumption. Given this enormous energy demand, China has no other option but to go overseas to secure energy supply.

Why is ASEAN strategic for China? It is because about 60% of China's oil import is transported through the Strait of Malacca (Bria, 2017). A strategic partnership with ASEAN will help mitigate the risks of disruptions in China's energy transport from piracy, congested traffic, terrorist attacks and especially the naval forces of other major powers like the United States and Japan. One way to mitigate the risk in the Strait of Malacca is the construction of the oil and gas pipeline from Maday Island in Myanmar to Yunan Province in China, which has been operational since 2015. It has cut by 30% the time needed to transport crude oil to China and reduced the risk of piracy and other risks. Since November 2016, China and Malaysia signed deals on defense. The two parties also agreed to resolve the South China Sea's cases on a bilateral basis. This further secures China's energy interest in the Strait of Malacca and South China Sea.

ASEAN countries encompass all of China's energy shipping routes from the Middle East, Africa and Latin America. Therefore, it is in China's core interest to maintain peace and stability in the region and seek closer economic cooperation with ASEAN member countries including Indonesia.

INDONESIA INFRASTRUCTURE'S POLICY

When President Joko Widodo came in to power 2014, He projected Indonesia as one of an influential maritime-axis and this prestigious agenda has become central policy in Indonesia-China relations since 2015. It sits well with China's Maritime

Silk Road ambition (Schinas, 2017). To get benefit between parties, Indonesia's President has been frequently attending many serial high level meetings to strengthen the agenda. Following executive meeting was at the Hangzhou Exhibition Center of G20 Summit in September 2016 in Hangzhou, China. The agenda then further held in the two-day One Belt One Road (OBOR) summit in Beijing in May 15th, 2017. Previously, OBOR initiative was said to process of developing as a blueprint of an interconnected worldwide infrastructure's programs. But everyone is realizing that the ultimate goal of OBOR initiative is designed to boost connectivity between mainland China and 65 countries in Asia and Europe by building infrastructure network in all logistics' moda of rails, roads, airports, and sea ports.

But even though OBOR is expected to help draw the region together by creating infrastructure-related investment opportunities, China needs to nurture better understanding of its intentions and its vision for the OBOR initiative while it tries to flex its economic muscle as a regional and global power to prevent unnecessary suspicions about its geopolitical ambition. It was not surprisingly that China has pledged its money, stating to commit standby loan over than US$200 billion as funding resources through China's state banks. Additional US$100 billion was allocated through the Asian Infrastructure Investment Bank (AIIB), and further US$50 billion through the Silk Road Infrastructure Fund.

Further, China Development Bank by late 2015 started to disburse US$3 billion in a 10-year loans to three Indonesia's state banks, Mandiri, BNI and BRI. The funding has been utilized to finance infrastructure's projects such as power generations, light-rail transportation, highway roads, smelters, and airport expansion. In addition, the Industrial and Commercial Bank of China, one of the world's largest banks, has also locked US$30 billion in loan commitments to financing other infrastructure's projects (Subiyanto, 2018). Since mid of 2015, Indonesia's government received softloan funding Rp 520 trillion (US$35.86 billion) through *China Development Bank* and *Industrial and Commercial Bank of China* (ICBC).

Indeed, such long-term loans came with certain conditions: the loans should be extended to Indonesian state-owned companies, which tie up with China's companies during infrastructure's construction; and about 30% of the total loans should be extended in yuan to strengthen the internationalization of the renminbi.

By the such Indonesia's infrastructure strategy, The Economist Corporate Network (2016) concluded that Indonesia stands to be one of the biggest beneficiaries among ASEAN economies from the geographic point of views. While China, the world's second-largest economy, is vying for getting good images, it has become also the largest trading partner and largest foreign investor in Indonesia, the Southeast Asia's largest economy.

At first, every Indonesian does not see any problems with such loans as long as the engineering, procurement and construction (EPC) contract, all of them are supervised by capable, independent, and qualified engineering consultants. We should not be paranoid about arriving of China's highly trained and skilled workers. Certainly, the construction of many big infrastructure projects funded by Chinese's banks and constructed by Chinese's companies will be accompanied large numbers of workers from China. Here they came as parts of contracts, guaranted prerequisition, besides they were more professional than Indonesia's workers in skill and knowledge. However, they will be going to their homecountries after the completion of their projects.

Insufficient Funding in Indonesia

Here is problems starting as many infrastructure's projects and targets desired while in facts Indonesia's government is facing severely limitation in terms of funding's sources. According to Presidential Decree No. 3/2016 there are 225 infrastructure mandatory project titles have been executed, but only 16 projects completed i.e. highway toll road Pandaan-Gempol for Rp 1.13 trillion (US$77.93 million), The New Sentani Jayapura airport Rp 1.47 trillion (US$101.38 million), expantion of Jakarta Sukarno Hatta airport Rp 4.7 trillion (US$324.14 million). Further completed infrastructures were development Kalibaru's seaport 1st phase Rp 4.7 trillion (US$324.14 million) and Jatigede's dam Rp 980 billion (US$67.58 million).

It had been reported that about 109 project titles were late due to insufficient fundings. It still remains questioning until today; are highway Sumatra's toll road, medium speed train project Jakarta-Bandung, and the light rail transit (LRT) at the Capital Jakarta would be continued as scheduled or to be slightly slowed down by renewing time extention. The appointed main contractor State-owned Hutama Karya (HK) is still in doubt to execute highway Sumatra's toll road. State has participated in National Budget 2018 to HK only Rp 5.6 trillion (US$386.21 million) while prior estimation to execute 8 priority projects to complete into commercial in 2019 was at least Rp 50 trillion (US$3.45 billion). HK further recently has planned to issue a new corporate debt to resolve the insufficient funding.

The highway Sumatra's toll road saga happened also to the medium speed train project Jakarta-Bandung. The problems even more complex as Government Decree of Provincial Spatial Planning were not finished yet, land acquisition was still 85%, and also technical design for bridge and tunnel were not examined by the Bridge and Tunnel Road Security Committee. The Committee was invited regarding unstable land topography due to sliding of Cisomang's bridge and frequently collapse of the Cipali's highway toll road last 2017 (Subiyanto, Logistics and Cisomang's Bridge, 2017). Absence the critical design to anticipate future incidents have increased planned budget previously US$5.5 billion to US$5.9 billion. The State-owned-China consortium which are consisting of Wijaya Karya (WIKA), Indonesia rail way operator (PTKAI), 8rd Plantation Firm (PTPN VIII), Jasa Marga and China Railways seemingly must present more hard works to solve the issues. Meanwhile ceremony and groundbreaking the project had been inaugurated by Indonesia's President on Januari 21st, 2016 to be initially completed into operational latest by first quarter in 2019.

Evenmore a prestigious project LRT in the Capital of Indonesia, Jakarta was also uncertain while completion was set at May 31st, 2019. State-owned contractor Adhi Karya and PTKAI were getting difficulties to get total funding required Rp 27 trillion (US$1.86 billion) as National Budget only allocated Rp 9 trillion (US$620.69 million). Again the State-own would create a number of new form of corporate bonds.

Besides, electricity projects were also found lot of problems. Finding of the Finance and Development Comptroller (BPKP), the State was potentially losing Rp 4.94 trillion (US$340.69 million) due to 34 coal-fired power plants (PLTU) were stalled for 7 years to 8 years. It confirmed that 12 PLTU projects must be stopped, the others 22 projects require additionally funding about Rp 7.25 trillion (US$500 million). In overall, all PLTU projects were unsatisfied due to only getting 9.4% into Commercial on Date (COD) for commercial. Until Augustus 2018, there are 71 project titles from remaining 109 project titles still in planning phase and procurement.

Excessive Seeking Funding for Infrastructure

The things Indonesian the most concerning is skyrocketing amount total debts both foreign and domestics debts as consequence to execute of massif projects. The debts have increased within period 2014 to April 2018 was 92.92% by amount from Rp 2,608.78 trillion (US$179.92 billion) in 2014 to a new amount Rp 5,032.92 trillion (US$347.09 billion) as per April 2018. Debts from foreigns have made the most concerning as they could be source triggering capital outflow, decreasing Indonesia's currency exchange, and potentially be able to take over completed projects gradually. Total foreign debts only as per April 2018 was US$165.296 billion as following Table 1. Its foreign's debt ratio to the Indonesia' GNP is recording of 34.5% (December 2018), the highest ever been since the fall of Suharto's era 1998.

Table 1. Detail Indonesia's foreign debts in various currencies converted in million US$

No	Currency of debts	2013	2014	2015	2016	2017	2018	
							March	April
1	United States (US$)	127,926	148,342	151,954	141,604	153,883	150,473	154,433
2	Japan (Yen)	7,133	6,289	6,073	5,874	5,652	5,852	5,768
3	British Poundsterling (GBP)	5,167	6,407	7,028	6,676	8,165	8,851	869
4	European (EUR)	839	939	707	932	1,506	1,779	1,755
5	Switzerland Franc (CHF)	623	688	848	802	760	721	719
6	India (IDR)	222	245	250	254	498	518	595
7	Singapore (SG$)	188	208	246	260	318	317	317
8	China Renminbi (CNY)	192	212	201	222	271	351	337
9	Malaysia Ringgit (MYR)	203	300	205	307	164	206	174
10	Korea Won (KRW)	98	80	80	88	117	129	92
11	Hong Kong Dollar (HK$)	81	80	82	73	99	88	87
12	Thailand Baht (THB)	25	28	37	41	70	75	75
13	Australia Dollar (AU$)	29	32	32	40	50	50	51
14	Swedia Kroner (SEK)	5	8	10	17	20	13	16
15	Other currency	3	4	5	8	8	8	8
16	Total	142,734	163,862	167,758	157,198	171,581	169,431	165,296

Source: data internet gathered and calculated by Author (2018)

According to the above Table 1 it found constantly increasing amount debt to only from China to Indonesia. It showed that OBOR was intensively campaigned while China seemingly committed to pour their fund to Indonesia as proponent its OBOR's policy.

RESEARCH MODEL

This study has been thoroughly analyzed by mining information and data from big data internet-based sources. It has been combining with semi-structured interviews of various executives and contractors. They have been gathered, selected, and analyzed for five years starting 2013. This study also utilizing mixed study both in quantitative and qualitative analysis to build comprehensive conclusion for preliminary recommendation.

Combining qualitative tools are gathered which are consisting phenomenons, cases studies, hystories, dan grounded theory. Phenomenons have been considered as infrastructure's issues have spread over the nations due to development in advanced technology (James H Watt, 1995). Author considers to lift Indonesia and China cases as Author knows of the countries well and interacting day-to-day with all of them. Historically both countries have long relationship formal and informally.

Based on previous qualitative tools, grounded theory are presented which is influenced direct-indirect with induction, deduction, and verification observations.

ANALYZING DATA

With carefully examination as following Table 2 from exploration Table 1 by percentage basis, it found China's trending amount debts were improving for Indonesia. Correlation between its OBOR's campaigns is significant by perspective of Indonesian. Average debts' growth performed by China within period of 2014 to 2017 rose to 21.49% surpassed following of the US, Japan, European Union, India, Singapore, and Hong Kong.

Comprehensive figure of China committing to finance Indonesia's infrastructure can be seen at following Figure 1. Sweden and Thailand are at the top two, but as their amount are far below than China then its contribution for Indonesia is minor. China's seriousness to all out help Indonesia's projects evenmore can be significantly seen at Figure 2.

DISCUSSION

Despite pros and cons, OBOR and also maritime-axis policy initiated by Indonesia have brought strategic to become important backbone for both countries. China has certain interests to secure their things while Indonesia has targets connecting over

Table 2. Growth of the top lists countries as the biggest creditor to Indonesia up to April 2018

No	Country	2014	2015	2016	2017	2018		Average
						March	April	
1	United States (US$)	15,96%	2,43%	-6,81%	8,67%	-2,22%	2,63%	3,44%
2	Japan (JPY)	-11,83%	-3,43%	-3,28%	-3,78%	3,54%	-1,44%	-3,37%
3	India (IDR)	24,00%	9,69%	-5,01%	22,30%	8,40%	-90,18%	-5,13%
4	European (EUR)	11,92%	-24,71%	31,82%	61,59%	18,13%	-1,35%	16,23%
5	Singapore (SGD)	10,43%	23,26%	-5,42%	-5,24%	-5,13%	-0,28%	2,94%
6	China (CNY)	10,36%	2,04%	1,60%	96,06%	4,02%	14,86%	21,49%
7	Korea (KRW)	10,64%	18,27%	5,69%	22,31%	-0,31%	0,00%	9,43%
8	Malaysia (MYR)	10,42%	-5,19%	10,45%	22,07%	29,52%	-3,99%	10,55%
9	Hong Kong (HKD)	47,78%	-31,67%	49,76%	-46,58%	25,61%	-15,53%	4,89%
10	Switzerland (CHF)	-18,37%	0,00%	10,00%	32,95%	10,26%	-28,68%	1,03%
11	England (GBP)	-1,23%	2,50%	-10,98%	35,62%	-11,11%	-1,14%	2,28%
12	Thailand (THB)	12,00%	32,14%	10,81%	70,73%	7,14%	0,00%	22,14%
13	Australia (AUD)	10,34%	0,00%	25,00%	25,00%	0,00%	2,00%	10,39%
14	Swedia (SEK)	60,00%	25,00%	70,00%	17,65%	-35,00%	23,08%	26,79%
15	Other currency	33,33%	25,00%	60,00%	0,00%	0,00%	0,00%	19,72%

Source: Source: data internet gathered and calculated by Author (2018)

17.000 islands that spreaded throughout Indonesia separated by water and seas. Naturally, every costs to exchange goods and services for Indonesia will be definitely higher than China; as the country does have single mainland. In terms of geographic views, OBOR will be much benefiting for Indonesia than China.

China's the most interest regarding OBOR is requiring security reason for their domestic things. Due the high level economic growth, food security for their 1.38

Figure 1. Indonesia's creditor per April 2018 (%)

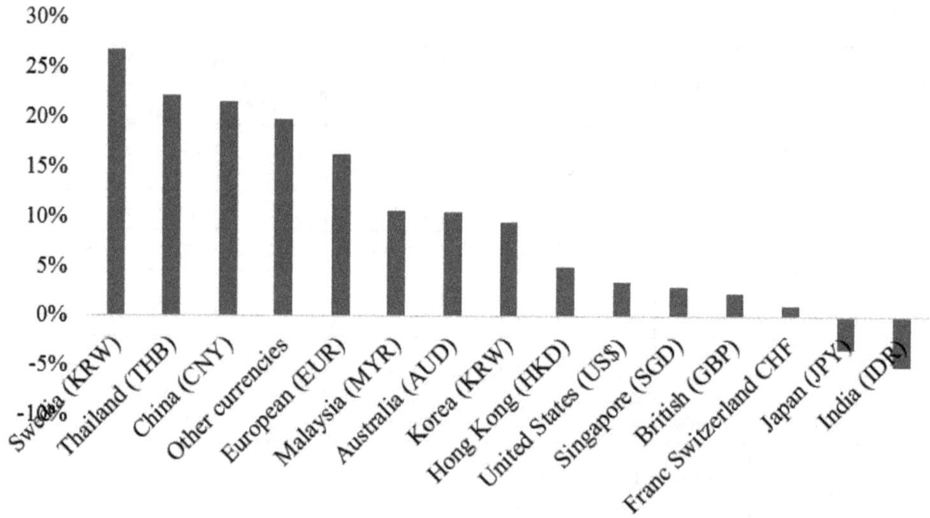

Figure 2. Trend amount credit to Indonesia 2014 to April 2018 (%)

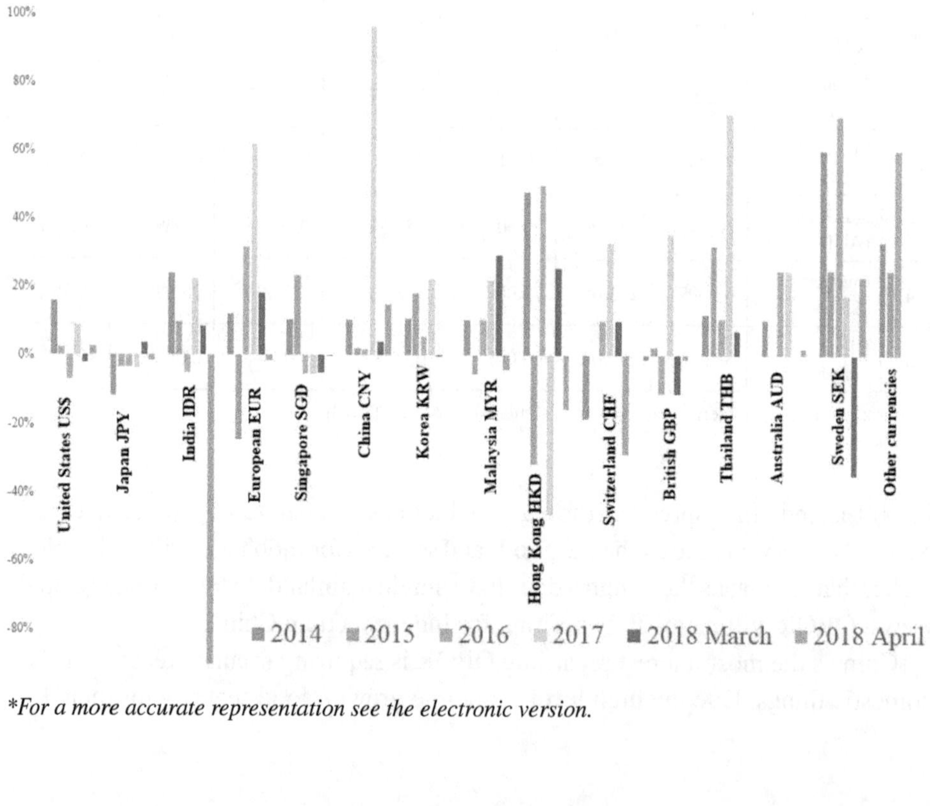

**For a more accurate representation see the electronic version.*

billion China's citizens are at top priority. Further China's concerning is fuel reserves for their industries, following will be requiring the very fast response to secure its natural resources will be urgency. The OBOR is a strategic tools to grab them all in one time. Else, the OBOR is opportunity to meet closer their citizen from Beijing to every corner of the world.

However, eventhough China's OBOR offers much benefit, some concerns came out as number of facts displaying skyrocketing debts (Girault, 2018) to region. From the amount previously dedicated by China of US$5 trillion to support the programs, it was surpassed US$60 billion in early September 2018. The newly elected Malaysia's Prime Minister Mahathir Mohamad had decided to postphone its infrastructure China-backed projects, including a US$20 billion railway. Pakistan's new Prime Minister Imran Khan has vowed more transparency amid fears about the country's ability to repay Chinese loans related to the multi-billion-dollar China-Pakistan Economic Corridor. The exiled leader of the opposition in the Maldives Mohamed Nasheed has said China's actions in the Indian Ocean archipelago amounted to a "land grab" and "colonialism" due over 80% of its debt held by Beijing. Sri Lanka has already paid a heavy price for being highly indebted to China as the island nation had to grant a 99-year lease on a strategic port to Beijing over its inability to repay loans for the US$1.4 billion project in 2017.

The others of 6 countries were also in heavily trapped by China's huge debts recently in 2018. Following countries are Djibouti. Mongolia. Laos. Montenegro. Tajikistan and Kyrgyzstan. The cost of a China-Laos railway project US$6.7 billion represents over than half of the Southeast Asian country's GDP. In Djibouti, the IMF has warned that the Horn of Africa country faces a "high risk of debt distress" as its public debt jumped from 50% of GDP in 2014 to 85% in 2016 (Eno, 2014).

Different facts in Indonesia has occurred indicating mismanagement handling various infrastructure projects. The impact is skyrocketing amount debts as per April 2018 had reached US$165.296 billion accounted for government only. The fundings are for primarily to finance for highway tollroads, seaports, airports, and capital goods including sea vessels. There found mismatched between amount debt to the project completed were indicating mark-up amount project value. The Java highway tolls for example presented 19 lines total length for 847.85 kilometers have required amount debt US$8.7 billion which is simply calculated cost assigned for every kilometer toll road was US$10.26 million. This is one fact that project's transparency is questioning for all.

CONCLUSION

OBOR in a glance is offering opportunity as its strategy to connect separate regions in the world became closer. Only country with huge sources of funding, labor, natural resources, and interests can promote OBOR, and China has the preliminary conditions perfectly. China as a new centrum in Asia's region is entering new phase to become more influencial to legitimate its giant power. However, China is requiring teamworks and Indonesia as the largest economic power in ASEAN region is viewed to meet criterias China to bolster OBOR.

For Indonesian, OBOR has identical meaning with maritime-axis policy which widely campaigned by the new reform government. Indonesia has interested OBOR due to China equipped with abundance resources that support the Jokowi's agenda. The amount national reserve China of US$3.14 trillion per December 2017 will be a top guarantee for Indonesia. China-backed for maritime-axis policy was fueling Indonesia to seek new debts for the periode since 2014 and after.

International trade first campaigned to promote OBOR is to cut high cost in logistics, enabling exchange goods and services worldwide easily. Indonesia has interest also in the term in order to perform export and import to and from other side of worldwide efficiently and effectively. As an archipelagoes country mainly separated by water and sea, OBOR is a new horizon, new paradigm, and at the same time new challenge as huge opportunity offered within.

ACKNOWLEDGMENT

This research received no specific grant from any funding agency in the public, commercial, or not-for-profit sectors.

REFERENCES

Bin, L. (2015). "One Belt and One Road" and China's Geopolitical Strategy. Science and Economic Society, 50-54.

Bria, E. (2017). *Why Do Indonesia*. ASEAN Matter to China.

Eno, M. A. (2014). China-Africa Relations: How Tight are the "Strings" Attached? *The International Journal of Humanities & Social Studies*, 196-203.

Girault, J. (2018). *China's Silk Road project runs into debt jam*. France-Press.

Gourdon, J. (2015). *Trade Policy and Industrial Policy in China: What Motivates Public Authorities to Apply Restrictions on Exports?* CEPII Working Paper.

Gray, K. L. (2017). The Rescaling of the Chinese State and Sino-North Korean Relations: Beyond State-Centrism. *Journal of Contemporary Asia*.

Hongyu, Z. Y. (2016). The Hopes and Challenges of China and Central and Eastern Europe Cooperation under the "One Belt and One Road" Framework. *International Business Studies*, 23-30.

James, H., & Watt, S. A. (1995). *Research Methods for Communication Science*. Boston: Allyn and Bacon.

Jing, F. Z. (2016). One Belt and One Road" Cooperation Motivation and Expectation and Prospects Between China and Europe. *Modern International Relations*, 93–99.

Junxuan, W. (2016). *Geographically Watching the World*. Academic Press.

Li, X., & Zeng, K. (2018). *To Join or Not To Join*. How Chinese Firms View the Belt and Road Initiative.

Limin, H. (2017). "One Belt and One Road" Initiative: A Geopolitical and Economic Analysis. *Journal of Xi 'an University of Finance and Economics*, 85-89.

Schinas, O. W. (2017). Assessing the Impact of the Maritime Silk Road. *Journal of Ocean Engineering and Science*, 186-195.

Shusen, Y. S. (2014). Silk Road Economic Belt: Strategic Conception and Challenges. *Journal of Lanzhou University*, 36-41.

Subiyanto, E. (2017). *Logistics and Cisomang's Bridge*. Jakarta: Koran Jakarta.

Subiyanto, E. (2018). *Infrastructure and 2019's Political Year*. Jakarta: Media Indonesia.

Sun, P. H. (2010). *International Trade and Its Effects on Economic Growth in China*. Discussion Paper.

Victoria, A. (2018). *Bullet Train One Belt One Road OBOR*. Academic Press.

Wei, Z. (2017). Research on the Geographical Strategy of China's "One Belt and One Road" Construction. *Journal of Jilin University*, 77-81.

Wenmu, Z. (2015). The Political Significance of "One Belt and One Road". Asian Infrastructure Investment Bank, 204-224.

Wltz, K. (1979). *Theory of International Politics*. Academic Press.

Xintao, Y. (2014). Analysis of National Strategy for the Construction of "One Belt and One Road". *The Theory of Monthly*, 5-9.

Yanjie, L. (2017). The Risk of "One Belt and One Road" Policy in Central Asia. *Journal of Xinjiang Normal University*, 76-79.

Zhao, W. (2016). The Theoretical Consideration and Practical Significance of the" One Belt and One Road". *Intersection Point*, 68-74.

Section 3

Technology-Driven Innovation in Belt and Road Initiative (BRI)

Chapter 8
Use of Learning Analytics in China:
A Benchmarking Model for Higher Education

Konstantinos Skampagiannis
Deree – The American College of Greece, Greece

Athanasios Pletsas
Deree – The American College of Greece, Greece

ABSTRACT

This chapter per the authors examines the feasibility of a learning analytics tool in the Chinese Higher Institutions educational environment. At first, the general definition of learning analytics is examined. Additionally, the authors shed light on case studies of universities that have already implemented learning analytics. Moreover, the Chinese educational environment is examined through a thorough analysis of the learning analytics necessity. Based on the literature review, a learning analytics tool is proposed. In a technical basis, the tool is a combination of ELLI or Effective Lifelong Learning Inventory, a dispositional learning analytics tool and a recommender system. The ultimate function of the tool is that it links students with a specific educational profile with successful students with similar profiles. Finally, the author identified the key limitations of the prototype and performed a general analysis on the tools goals and expectations in the Chinese Higher Education Institutions.

DOI: 10.4018/978-1-5225-8980-8.ch008

INTRODUCTION

As the Knowledge Era has succeeded the Industrial Era, the investment in the knowledge domain is an immediate consequence. Inevitably a big portion of this investment heads towards higher education. This can be shown by students' increased demand for participation in higher education (Gaševic, Dawson, & Siemens, 2014). This tendency is no different also for China. From early 70s, China has faced a great success in its economic functionality by increasing its GDP more than 9% (Li, Morgan & Ding, 2008). The prosperous economic activity favored workers to assume education as an essential investment (Li, Morgan & Ding, 2008). More precisely, from 1990 to 2004, the number of students attending universities has increased around 160% (Li, Morgan & Ding, 2008). Since then, each year nearly 1 million students enroll to higher education institution ("China: Number Of Students At Universities 2017 | Statistic"). Consequently, the increased amount of student enrollment creates a corresponding increase on the students demand towards a better academic environment, while the academic performance competition between students increases as well (Abugabah, Sanzogni, 2010). China's high population in combination with the introduction of technology-enhanced learning since the 2010, promises a new opportunity in the area for higher education to be digitalized and personalized. The vast amount of Chinese students creates a need for Institutions to adjust to a more personalized environment, since otherwise could hardly recognize students' personal needs (Lynch, 2017). Learning Analytics satisfy this need by personalizing the academic through a digital medium (Ferguson & Schum 2012). Following that guideline, we proposed a custom-made prototype for personalized learning in the Chinese higher institution system that incorporates a learning analytics tool and a recommender system. The proposed concept takes into consideration various aspects of the Chinese Educational system as well as successful case studies of universities that have already integrated learning analytics in the learning arsenal.

RESEARCH METHODOLOGY

This paper bases its research primarily on secondary sources. The main focus is to present and analyze a literature review of contemporary sources that explore not only the socioeconomic background of China but also the current application of learning analytics in higher education institutions. In addition, the research is conducted based on the already established Chinese higher education institutional policies and procedures seeking to enhance the students' learning experience. The collection of those sources will be synthesized in order to present a prototype of a learning analytics tool that can be incorporated in the Chinese educational system. Furthermore, the proposed tool has its foundations on the Chinese government willingness to cover essential need for complex issues in a rather innovative way.

LITERATURE REVIEW

The Concept of Learning Analytics

Analysis of data is a concept extensively discussed in the business sector. In a century where, big data has become a major point of concern in nearly every aspect of the everyday life, the need of tools and applications that process data from various data streams is immense. In such ground, various analytics platforms have been created to collect, analyze and visualize data from a variety of data sources. Generally, analytics cover a broad area of industries. As seen in the below picture, the industry sectors of analytics differ from financial analytics to insurance analytics and educational analytics. In this chapter, the focus will be shifted on the educational analytics and more accurately on the learning analytics concept.

As Siemen highlights, Learning Analytics (LA), are techniques attempting to gather students' data in order to assist them with their academic performance respectively (Gašević, Dawson, & Siemens, 2014). In most cases, LAs provide assistance to weak students, since professors are getting continuously informed about their students' performance (Leeuwen, Janssen, Erkens, & Brekelmans, 2015).

Figure 1. Industry sectors for UCD MSc business analytics projects
Source: Defining business analytics: an empirical approach

Learning Analytics in Higher Education Institutions

Following the digitalization trend of the 21st century, educational institutions nowadays strive to improve the student's learning experience by implementing a plethora of tools and processes such as smart classrooms, online blackboards and even learning analytics. In fact, the case of learning analytics has only been used the past few years by several highly-accredited universities globally. Generally, there has been limited progress in accumulating the extremely rich data that flow through higher education systems for the purpose of acquiring usable information for students, instructors, administrators and the public (Attaran, Stark & Stotler, 2018). However, according to a study conducted by Billy Tak Ming Wong at the University Research Centre of The Open University of Hong Kong, US universities like Harvard and Purdue and non-US such as the University of Sydney and the University of Edinburgh have already been using learning analytics tools to increase their students' problem-solving capability, enhance the student's learning experience and achieve optimization on the utilization of learning resources.

Characteristically, Harvard University has utilized the learning analytics seeking to predict student's performance through collaborative learning since it utterly mines classroom data (Wong, 2017). In fact according to a paper published by the

Figure 2. Percentages of learning analytics use in higher education
Source: The current landscape of learning analytics in higher education

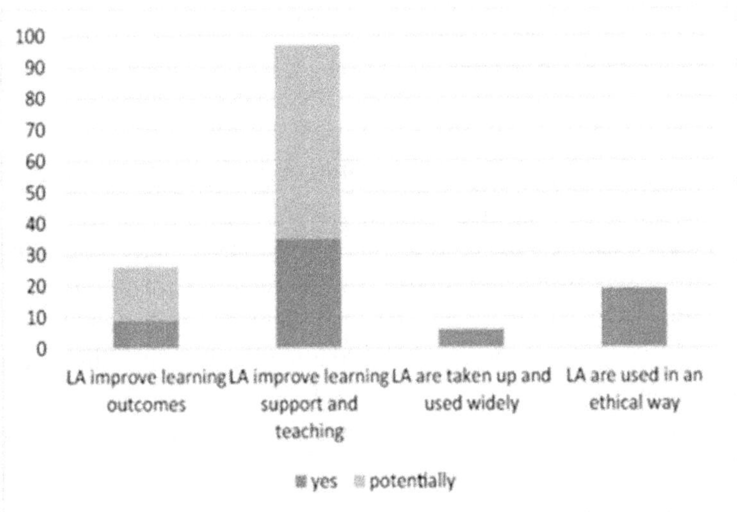

International Council of Open and Distance Education, "[a] basic pattern of learning/ teaching (depending if you are a student or a teacher) is the following: "students log in to their interactive classroom, the professor produces a problem generated on the students' screen for them to answer; the system analyzes the answers and decides how to pair students as study partners; messaging appears on the students' screens indicating who they will work with; and the professor receives a map of information displaying how the students did so the professor can decide who to assist" (Boyer & Bonnin, 2016). Similarly, the Purdue University, which adopted a tool called "Course Signal", aiming to find students in need and help them accordingly. The outcome of that project indicated that 90% of the students that participated marked the effect of this LA tool quite positive (Arnold & Pistilli, 2012). Apart from the high-end universities, learning analytics have already been introduced in institutions with lower reputation. In Spain, the Universidad Internacional de La Rioja has been working on the A4 learning project12 that combines data with information visualization, providing each student with ongoing information that enables them to think critically about their learning and their goals (Wong, 2017). In another case, the City University of London joined the Jisc Effective Learning Analytics project; an application was created that allows students to view "how [their] learning activity compares with others and set targets to do better in their courses" ("Learning Analytics Project (Leap)"). As evident from the above examples, learning analytics tools even in a preliminary stage are operated by the higher education institutions showing limitless potential on optimizing the learning efficiency and effectiveness.

The Need of Learning Analytics in the Chinese Educational System

According to the National Bureau of Statistics of China, in 2017 the number of students in the regular higher education institutions was approximately 27.5 million students, while steadily increasing according to Statista since 2007.

That fact combined with the total population of the Chinese country depicts the necessity for a rather personalized approach on the student. Learning analytics nature seems to be able to satisfy such a special need. Such an implementation though is characterized by high complexity. At first the government is mainly responsible for introducing innovation, even in the educational sector (Chen & Fan, 2018). Therefore, all the local administrative authorities instructed by the government are the ones who have decision making power and can implement any reforming step

Figure 3. Number of students in the Chinese higher education in 2017
Source: National Bureau of Statistics of China

Item	Graduates	Entrants	Enrolment
Higher Education			
Postgraduates	578045	806103	2639561
Doctor's Degree	58032	83878	361997
Master's Degree	520013	722225	2277564
Undergraduate in Regular HEIs	7358287	7614893	27535869
Normal Courses	3841839	4107534	16486320
Short-cycle Courses	3516448	3507359	11049549
Undergraduate in Adult HEIs	2470370	2175302	5441429
Normal Courses	1091226	1023981	2589809
Short-cycle Courses	1379144	1151321	2851620
Web-based Undergraduates	1777905	2861143	7359267
Normal Courses	659559	993253	2587338
Short-cycle Courses	1118346	1867890	4771929

towards education instead of the universities' faculty and the members of academia (Chen & Fan, 2018). In that case, the institutional reform is usually conducted by technocrats and not people with a deep understanding of the student's expectations, needs and goals in the education constituents. Certainly, that creates a bureaucratic obstacle in modernizing the learning environment. In addition to that, the Chinese population is highly unsatisfied with the current examination system, under which students are mainly focused on how to pass the exam without acquiring a deep knowledge (Chen & Fan, 2018). That issue can be giantized in terms of lack of knowledge through the inappropriate utilization of the learning resources. As a general rule, the educational system should be heavily focused on optimizing the students learning experience by utilizing all the available tools without any constraints. Apart from the abovementioned particularities, China's "National Mid-to-Long-term Educational Reform and Development Plan" creates a prosperous environment for learning analytics tools that could eventually improve students learning experience (Reform, Chinese Education, 2010). As studies have shown, China invests a lot in advancing IT infrastructures and integrate them within the educational unit (Chen & Fan, 2018). Based on that fact, the ground for learning analytic tools implantation is extremely prosperous. In fact, such a tool can resolve not the exam problem by providing a more wholistic view of knowledge and increasing metacognition levels of students but also enable the academic society to have a better management view on the students understanding of the learning material.

RESEARCH QUESTIONS

1. How successful it is to convert tacit knowledge into explicit to create digital, personalized student profiles?
2. How LA tools can be implemented and how fast are they going to provide significant results?
3. Can benchmarking help learning analytics further?

RESEARCH HYPOTHESIS AND METHODOLOGY

Tacit vs Explicit Knowledge Challenges

As Nonaka describes, tacit and explicit are two different, almost opposite types of knowledge. Explicit refers to knowledge that is codifiable, like number (Nonaka, 2000). At the same time, tacit knowledge has more abstract features, since it refers to experiences and personal insights a person possesses (Nonaka, 2000). In the case of LA, a transformation of tacit into explicit, from analog to digital is attempted in order to digitalize and codify students' profiles. Nonaka describes this process as "externalization" and as the author explains that the basic requirements for a successful "externalization" are a good analogy and a good model. Misleading analogy can lead to misleading results, like in the case of a study at University of Missouri. The correlation of that LA tool was based on the assumption that the more the students accessed their learning content, the more likely will get a better final grade. However, this assumption in praxis was rejected (Mullan & Sclater & Peasgood, 2016) . The authors highlight that overlying in quantitative results coming from LA tools can lead to misinterpretations (Mullan & Sclater & Peasgood, 2016). However. that, many other LA that have been applied and discussed above showed satisfactory results and high accuracy. For overcoming the barrier of the content accuracy of the designed model of the LA the authors address the need for higher communication from the teaching stuff of the University (Mullan & Sclater & Peasgood, 2016).

Rapid Outcome Research Approach: Room for Innovation

An effective implementation of a learning analytics tool requires a suitable implementation plan that needs to be followed strictly by all the associated stakeholders. SHEILA project, co-funded by Erasmus Programme of EU focuses on how Institutions can implement Learning Analytics (Tsai & Gasevic, 2017). Similarly, Rapid Outcome Research Approach (R.O.M.A) is a model developed by Overseas Development Institution, for the integration of learning analytics in higher education. R.O.M.A analyzes the following six factors when considering LA implementation:

1. **Policy**: The institution needs to find where institutions' benefits coincide with students' and faculties.'
2. **Stakeholders**: The institution should decide whom it is going to extract the data from and how.
3. **Reasons**: The institution needs to estimate the reasons why it should implement LA; what the benefits will be.
4. **Strategy**: The institution needs to specify which academic data wants to collect and what the aim is for collecting them. Moreover, a decision needs to be made concerning the participating parties.
5. **Proactivity**: Various possible technical challenges related with LA need to be discussed before integration. Examples of such challenges can be: 2018 GDPR, technical difficulties using LA etc.
6. **Effectiveness**: The institution is required to have a specific stakeholder constantly measuring the impact of LA on the institution. (Tsai, Moreno-Marcos, Tammets, Kollom, & Gasevic, 2018).

As can be easily understood, the tool implementation should be processed and facilitated in a collaborative space of the government, the universities and even the students. The ROMA model would be applied in the Chinese context by taking into account the need for learning analytics and also the positive attitude towards them by all related stakeholders. A hierarchical approach on the discussed model in necessary though. The government acceptance for that approach is mandatory. In that case, China should follow the European Union's approach on educational technological development and either adopt the model or create another version of it. Consequently, institutions and students should positively embrace the rather beneficial model to them by foreseeing the positive outcomes without disregarding the data policies and guidelines issued by the Chinese government and the international agencies.

PROTOTYPE

Dispositional Learning Analytic Tool

The Effective Lifelong Learning Inventory or ELLI is a dispositional learning analytic tool created to maximize student engagement and personal development. More specifically it is a research-validated system where learners can take stock of their learning strengths, and with supported interventions can build on them. ELLI data can also be used for benchmarking and is fully compatible with SIMS and SPSS. Its measurable statistics can also help identify patterns of learning across the student body. This system interacts directly with the user in question-answer and collects the answers to create a dispositional matrix. It actually creates a "seven-dimensional scheme of dispositions" which presents an overview of learner's experiences, motivation and types of intelligence (Ferguson & Shum, 2012. As it has already been mentioned dispositional learning analytics are quite effective in helping students increase their metacognition levels (Ferguson & Shum, 2012). ELLI is learning analytics dispositional tool that analyzes student's dispositional level. ELLI receives feedback by students by asking them questions concerning their learning experience through a questionnaire format. Then automatically a graph of based on the students' answer is plotted showing learner's dispositions levels (https://www.elli.org.uk/how-elli-works/). The student can see in that way his/her progress over a lifetime period. An added feature of a such tool could be professors' feedback on students' dispositions for a more accurate view.

Recommender System

Recommender System as the title implies are systems that recommend the user resources, other users that match his/her profile activity. In a more general sense, '[r]ecommender Systems (RSs) are software tools and techniques that provide suggestions for items that are most likely of interest to a particular user' (Ricci, Rokach & Shapira, 2017). Recommender Systems are widely used in many domains application, including the Technology Enhanced Learning application (TEL) (Verbert, Manouselis & Ochoa, 2012). Generally, there are two approaches on the design of recommender systems. The first approach is the collaborative filtering approach which suggests that the recommendations are performed by taking as input a vast amount of the user's data, behaviors, activities, preferences and the similarities of those with other users. The second approach is the content filtering approach which suggests that the recommendations are facilitated by using past data such as activities and behaviors. Thus, it is crystal clear that the first approach is a more holistic approach on data gathering and recommendations.

The Proposed System

As seen in the above picture, our model consists of a learning analytics tool, in this case the Effective Lifelong Learning Inventory (ELLI), and a collaborative filtering recommendation system. At first, students are guided by the ELLI learning analytics tool to input their data in the platform. This is facilitated through questionnaires

Figure 4. The proposed prototype for learning analytics
Source: Authors' creation.

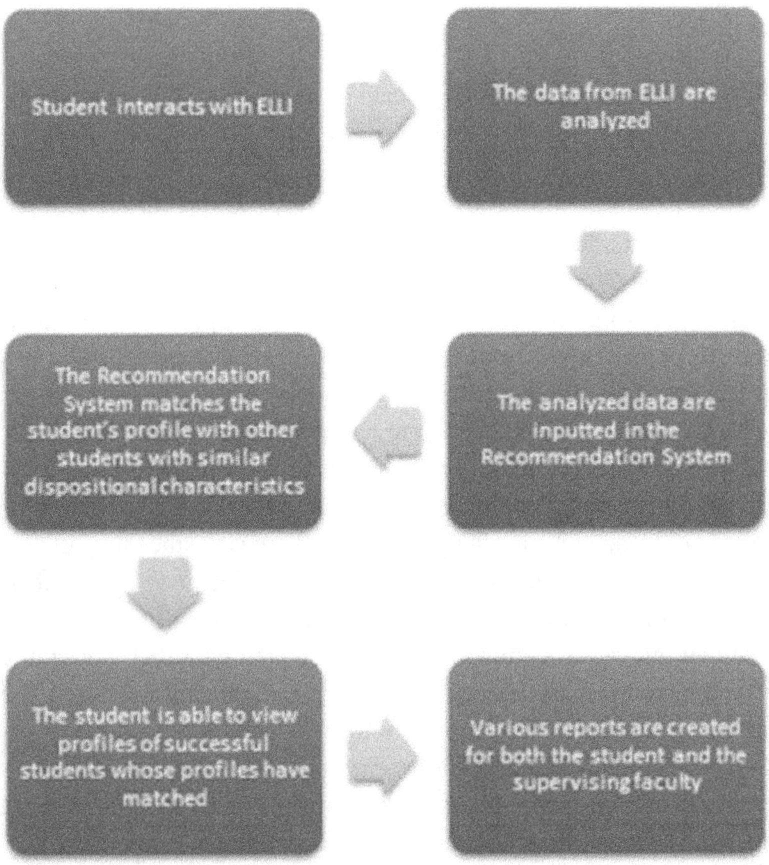

filling, following ELLI's essential input method as mentioned above. Consequently, the learning analytics tool applies data processing and analysis techniques to create the student's dispositional profile. After the data are processed, students are able to view their dispositional profiles and own learning goals. At the subsequent step students are prompted to other students with similar profiles, or similar goals that are high achievers and have succeeded on attaining their own goals. This procedure is generated by a recommender system that matches similar student profiles according to its algorithm. Under that reasoning, students can communicate fellow students with similar dispositional characteristics whose academic performance is high and facilitate peer to peer learning on a collaborative basis sponsored by the high achievers' academic experience and performance. The whole process could be monitored by the faculty and various reports could be generated from the system with respect to student's academic performance fluctuations, learning statistics and overall learning analytics.

DISCUSSION AND LIMITATIONS

Discussion

After an extensive literature review, it becomes evident that the space for a learning analytics tool in the Chinese higher education environment is already set. In fact, the government is promoting smart city projects (Yu & Xu, 2018). As the learning analytics concept generally belongs to the smart city's contextual environment the integration of such tool requires effort and acceptance from all stakeholders. In fact, the integration of smart cities research into modern theories of sustainable economic development and applied-technology-enabled innovative projects requires a holistic approach (Visvizi, Lytras, Damiani & Mathkour, 2018). Unquestionably, a project of that scale could lead to a learning process reengineering since it would be able to transform the way students focus on their own set learning goals and performances. On a broad perspective the discussed transformation would allow the digitalization and consequent analysis of previously unmanipulated data that would absolutely improve the educational background of university students following the smart cities innovation principles. It is important to signify that the proposed protype has the potential to revolutionize the Chinese educational system covering the need for personalization and subsequently enhancing the student learning experience through peer to peer communication. In a chaotic country in terms of population the discussed prototype would establish a connection among successful students with students with the same learning goals without any geographical constraints or age limitations. That would eventually benefit not only the student body but also the academic society. In such terms, the lecturers would be able to monitor their student's performance and customize the learning processes based on their needs and goals, taking into consideration the results of the recommender system. Utterly, the proposed prototypes seek to maximize the benefits of the learning process and allow the students to achieve their potential and succeed in their academic and professional life.

Limitations

As far as the limitations are concerned, the issues of data privacy and tool accuracy need to be highlighted. Before the implementation of learning analytics, China needs to take necessary steps to protect their students. Chinese Association of Educational Technology is responsible for creating necessary policies to be proactive against any privacy dilemmas. Most western educational Institutions in that case provide students, while they are registered a consent form that the student voluntarily signs so that his/her academic data can be used (Gkoumas, Gyftakis, Stamopoulos & Pletsas, 2018). Furthermore, it needs to be considered that learning analytics make quantitative analysis, that many times do not showcase the whole truth about students' performance (Papamitsiou & Economides, 2015). Furthermore, the establishment of learning analytics tool generally requires a faculty training concerning the use of the software as well as patience until learning analytics becomes helpful. Finally, it needs to be taken into account that this paper explores theoretically the implementation of learning analytics based mainly on secondary research. A primary research held in China would be a reasonable solution in order to confirm this papers' assumptions.

CONCLUSION

In this chapter, we presented a prototype system that integrates a learning analytics' tool and a recommender system for students and faculty of the higher education institutions of China. Overall, the proposed system uses the student's data regarding their academic performance, learning goals and expectations and through a recommender system indicates what path students should follow to improve. We conceptualized this tool specifically for the Chinese educational environment since the personalization aspect of the learning process that has been proved to be positively affective to the students' performance does not exist in the Chinese educational system. Stepping on the fact that government spending on IT assets in the learning industry is constantly on the rise and the number of undergraduate and graduate students is increasing significantly year by year, we believe that our tool can become a valuable asset for universities to maximize the learning experience. Despite all the bureaucratical procedures that should be followed such an implementation would utterly achieve the most personalized learning system, China has implemented since the beginning of the Knowledge Era. The key findings of the research indicate that the reengineering of the Chinese learning policies and procedures could be initiated through the integration of a learning analytics system enhancing the already established learning system. In a general setting, this tool could be the pioneer for initiations that could cover a variety of needs for technological development of both the Chinese public and private sectors. Nonetheless, such a ground-breaking idea would highlight the need for strategic redevelopment not only in the high level educational environment but also in the elementary levels of education. In fact, similar, tools and ideas could be applied to all levels of the Chinese learning pyramid upon the effective application in the universities. Based on that more research should be conducted by taking into consideration our model and the requirements and necessities of the Chinese current learning state. Furthermore, future work should be specifically address the key technical characteristics of the tool and focus in depth in the programming requirements of the proposed solutions. At final, such an innovative idea would highlight China's strategic development in the IT and education fields and signify the beginning of an era full of technology driven applications in the educational sector of the country.

REFERENCES

Abugabah & Louis. (2010). *Enterprise Resource Planning (ERP) System in Higher Education: A Literature Review and Implications*. Academic Press.

Arnold, K., & Pistilli, M. (2012). Course Signals At Purdue: Using Learning Analytics To Increase Student Success. *2nd International Conference On Learning Analytics And Knowledge*, 267-270. Retrieved from https://dl.acm.org/citation.cfm?doid=2330601.2330666

Attaran. (2018). Opportunities And Challenges For Big Data Analytics In US Higher Education. *Industry and Higher Education*, *32*(3), 169-182. doi:10.1177/0950422218770937

Boyer, A., & Bonnin, G. (2016). *Higher Education And The Revolution Of Learning Analytics*. Oslo: International Council For Open And Distance Education. Retrieved from https://icde.memberclicks.net/assets/RESOURCES/anne_la_report%20cc%20 licence.pdf

Chen, B., & Fan, Y. (2012). Learning analytics: Perspectives from mainland China. *Include Us All! Directions for Adoption of Learning Analytics in the Global South*, 36.

Ferguson, R., & Buckingham Sham, S. (2012). Social learning analytics: five approaches. *2nd International Conference on Learning Analytics & Knowledge*, 23–33.

Gašević, D., Dawson, S., & Siemens, G. (2014). Let's not forget: Learning analytics are about learning. *TechTrends*, *59*(1), 64–71. doi:10.100711528-014-0822-x

How Elli Works. (n.d.). Retrieved from www.elli.org.uk/how-elli-works/

Leeuwen, A. V., Janssen, J., Erkens, G., & Brekelmans, M. (2015). Teacher regulation of cognitive activities during student collaboration: Effects of learning analytics. *Computers & Education*, *90*, 80–94. doi:10.1016/j.compedu.2015.09.006

Lynch, M. (2017). *Why Are Learning Analytics So Important?* Retrieved from https://www.thetechedvocate.org/learning-analytics-important/

Nonaka, I., Toyama, R., & Konno, N. (2000). SECI, Ba and leadership: A unified model of dynamic knowledge creation. *Long Range Planning*, *33*(1), 5–34. doi:10.1016/S0024-6301(99)00115-6

Papamitsiou, Z., & Economides, A. A. (2014). Learning analytics and educational data mining in practice: A systematic literature review of empirical evidence. *Journal of Educational Technology & Society, 17*(4). Retrieved from https://www.researchgate.net/publication/267510046_Learning_Analytics_and_Educational_Data_Mining_in_Practice_A_Systematic_Literature_Review_of_Empirical_Evidence

Power, D. J. (2018). Defining Business Analytics: An Empirical Approach. *Journal of Business Analytics*, *1*(1), 40-53. doi:10.1080/2573234x.2018.1507605

Ricci, F. (2015). *Recommender Systems Handbook* (2nd ed.). Springer. doi:10.1007/978-1-4899-7637-6

Sclater, Peasgood, & Mullan. (2016). *Learning analytics in higher education.* London: JISC.

Statista. (2017). *China: Number Of Students At Universities 2017*. Retrieved from https://www.statista.com/statistics/227028/number-of-students-at-universities-in-china/

Statista. (2018). China Statistical Yearbook 2018. *National Bureau of Statistics of China*. Retrieved from http://www.stats.gov.cn/tjsj/ndsj/2018/indexeh.htm

Verbert, K., Manouselis, N., Ochoa, X., Wolpers, M., Drachsler, H., Bosnic, I., & Duval, E. (2012). Context-aware recommender systems for learning: A survey and future challenges. *IEEE Transactions on Learning Technologies*, *5*(4), 318–335. doi:10.1109/TLT.2012.11

Viberg, O. (2018). The Current Landscape Of Learning Analytics In Higher Education. *Computers in Human Behavior*, *89*, 98-110. doi:10.1016/j.chb.2018.07.027

Visvizi, A. (2018). Policy Making For Smart Cities: Innovation And Social Inclusive Economic Growth For Sustainability. *Journal Of Science And Technology Policy Management*, *9*(2), 126-133. doi:10.1108/jstpm-07-2018-079

Wong, B. T. M. (2017). Learning Analytics In Higher Education: An Analysis Of Case Studies. *Asian Association of Open Universities Journal, 12*(1), 21-40. doi:10.1108/aaouj-01-2017-0009

Yu & Xu. (2018). Developing Smart Cities In China. *International Journal of Public Administration in the Digital Age, 5*(3), 76-91. doi:10.4018/ijpada.2018070106

Chapter 9
Connecting One Belt One Road Countries via Wireless Sensor Network

Kwok Tai Chui
City University of Hong Kong, Hong Kong

Wadee Alhalabi
King Abdulaziz University, Saudi Arabia & Effat University, Saudi Arabia

Ryan Wen Liu
Wuhan University of Technology, China

Patricia Ordóñez de Pablos
University of Oviedo, Spain

ABSTRACT

The economy of China grows rapidly due to the advent of wireless networks. The networks provide connection between nodes (sensors, gateways, systems, people, etc.) for data transmission and communication seamlessly. This is a crucial element to achieve sustainable economics. It is worth mentioning that wireless communication is the optimal solution compared with wired communication given the fact that China has a huge land area and the largest population in the world. Traditional wireless technologies like 4G, Bluetooth, ZigBee, ISA 100.11a, and WirelessHART have been well addressed in literature. In this chapter, the focus is moved to 5G, LoRa, IEEE 802.11 af, ah, ax, and ay. Selected applications health monitoring, toxic gas monitoring, connected target coverage problem, and mobile crowd sensing are discussed in detail. Geographic routing, wireless charging, and wireless coexistence are challenging issues that need to be addressed in the near future.

DOI: 10.4018/978-1-5225-8980-8.ch009

INTRODUCTION

Everybody and object are interconnected via wireless communications seamlessly. It is crucial element because wired communication has restriction on connectivity. When it comes to China, the massive land mass creates fundamental challenge for wired communication (particularly fiber-optic communication). This is the reason for the largest number of mobile users in the world. The level of digital infrastructure construction of many countries along the Silk Road is relatively low, which provides big chance for mobile communication equipment, fixed-line broadband upgrades, data centre and cloud platform. In addition, the development level of each country's information industry varies so companies can implement a niche market strategy and expand the profit margin. China's telecommunications industry is relatively sound and capable of providing complete solutions and cost-effective products. It has enterprises with international competitiveness which can be a basis for enhancing international communications connectivity.

Every growing of data provides tremendous opportunities for data analytics. In doing so, different types of sensors must be utilized to collect the data continuously and has good streaming rate. The world has changed rapidly and it seems that existing wireless protocols cannot fulfil the entire requirement for desired applications, that's why many new protocols have been released or soon to released and they have been addressed in this chapter. To realize the potential of evolving wireless sensor network technologies and software architectures we need to move away from traditional approaches towards an adaptable service oriented hybrid architecture, which should ideally run on the plate for wireless sensor devices, to minimize redundant protocol stack overhead.

One Belt One Road (OBOR) strategy is a key policy initiated by China. It targets on achieving innovation and social inclusive economic growth for sustainability (Visvizi, Lytras, Damiani, & Mathkour, 2018). A key characteristic in China (and many underdeveloped countries) has numerous villages (rural areas) and are migrating towards main cities. Smart villages and cities services have gained attention not only increase people's quality of life bringing but also facilitating foreign business (Lytras, & Visvizi, 2018; Visvizi, & Lytras, 2018).

The contribution of the chapter is (i) an up-to-date state-of-the-art is presented in the field of emerging wireless standards as the supporting elements of fast and reliable data transmission; (ii) key applications are discussed which are hot research topics; and (iii) challenges are highlighted as future research work to build sustainable OBOR network.

The rest of the chapter is organized as follows and is shown in Figure 1. Section 2 presents six emerging standards for wireless protocols. Four applications have been discussed in Section 3. When it comes to challenges, discussion is made in Section 4. Finally, a conclusion is drawn.

EMERGING STANDARDS

Attributed to the concerns in data rate, bandwidth, internet-of-things and big data support, new protocols have newly proposed and in development. In this chapter, authors would like to address the emerging standards, applications and challenges in wireless networks whereas well-known protocols like 4G, Bluetooth, ZigBee, ISA 100.11a and WirelessHART will not be discussed in-depth in here (alternatively Table 1 summarizes the basic characteristics of the protocols).

Figure 1. Overview of chapter listing emerging standards, key applications and challenges

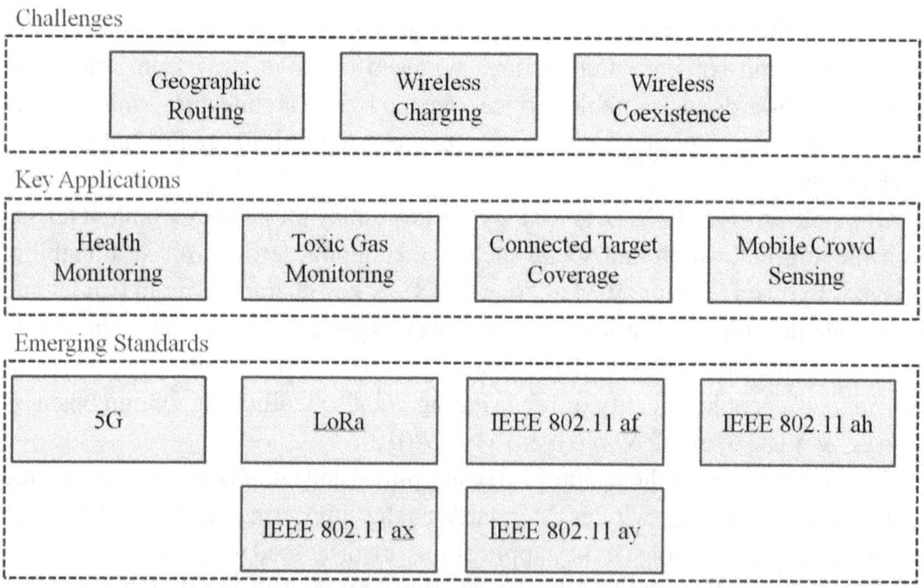

Table 1. Characteristics of traditional industrial wireless protocols

	4G	WiFi	Bluetooth	ZigBee	ISA100.11a	WirelessHART
Family	3GPP	IEEE 802.11	Bluetooth Special Interest Group	IEEE 802.15.4	IEEE 802.15.4	IEEE 802.15.4
Data rate	LTE: 50-100Mbps LTE-advanced: 500-1000Mbps	1-6757 Mbps	Bluetooth 3.0: 1-24 Mbps Bluetooth 4.0: 1-24 Mbps Bluetooth 5: 1-48 Mbps	20-250 kbps	up to 250kbps	up to 250kbps
Bandwidth	100 MHz	20, 22, 40, 80, 160, 2160 MHz	1, 2 MHz	2 MHz	2 MHz	2 MHz
Frequency band(s) (GHz)	Asia: 0.45,0.7, 0.85, 0.9, 1.7, 1.8, 1.9/2.1, 2.3, 2.5 GHz Europe: 0.8, 0.9, 1.8 1.9/2.1, 2.5 GHz US/Canada: 0.7, 0.85, 1.7/2.1, 1.9, 2.5 GHz	0.9, 2.4, 5, 2.4/5, 45/60, 60 GHz	2.4 GHz	0.868, 0.915, 2.4 GHz	2.4 GHz	2.4 GHz
Network topology	Star	Star, tree, mesh	Star, tree, mesh	Star, tree, mesh	Star, tree, mesh	Mesh
Family	3GPP	IEEE 802.11	Bluetooth Special Interest Group	IEEE 802.15.4	IEEE 802.15.4	IEEE 802.15.4

5G

For the wireless protocol, the fifth generation mobile network (5G), is proposed. It aims at higher capacity, density of mobile broadband users, reliability and massive machine communications compared to LTE and LTE-Advanced. It was expected to deploy commercially in 2020 to relieve the 500 exabytes of IP data loading (Yifei, & Longming, 2014). Currently, there is no standard for 5G but the desired requirements will be (i) data rates of 10Mb/s for every 10000 users; (ii) 1 Gb/s simultaneously to multiple users on the same floor; (iii) data rates of 100 Mb/s for metropolitan areas; (iv) at least 100000 simultaneous connections in wireless sensor network; and (v) Latency reduction, spectral efficiency enhancement, coverage improvement and signal efficiency enhancement compared to LTE and LTE-Advanced.

Millimeter wave (mmWave), massive multi-input multi-output (MIMO) and ultra-densification are three most important technologies in 5G (Mahmoud, & Montaser, 2018). Massive MIMO achieves enticing advantages in which it enhances the spectral efficiency without the use of increasing base station densification, smoothes out channel responses, and simple transmit and receive structures.

Challenges of deploying massive MIMO include pilot contamination and overhead reduction, architectural challenges, full-dimension MIMO and elevation beamforming, channel models, and coexistence with existing technologies. In general, researchers have devoted their efforts in concluding the best millimeter wave frequency range for 5G. The analysis of frequency ranges includes 28, 38, 60, 71-76, and 81-86 GHz. The obstacles are path loss, blocking, atmospheric and rain absorption, large arrays and narrow beams, link acquisition, leveraging the legacy 4G networks, and design of transceiver architectures. Thirdly, the ultra-densification leads to challenges, for instance, retaining the cell-splitting gains expectation, determining suitable associations between base stations and users over multiple radio access technologies, and supporting mobility via highly heterogeneous networks.

Readers are highly recommended to read the following review articles on polarization diversity and adaptive beamsteering for 5G reflectarrays (Dahri et al., 2018), physical layer security (Sun, & Du, 2017), wideband reflectarray antennas (Dahri et al., 2017), and receiver architecture (Bronckers, Roc'h, & Smolders, 2017).

LoRa

The digital wireless data communication IoT technology, LoRa seems to be a new concept to many researchers. It is patented and developed by Cycleo of Grenoble, France, and acquired by Semtech in 2012. LoRa uses license-free sub-gigahertz radio frequency bands like 915 MHz (North America), 868 MHz (Europe), 433 MHz and 169 MHz. It supports long range transmission up to 40 km in rural areas and 5 km in urban areas (Centenaro et al., 2016), and it is encouraging to find that LoRa works well in Antarctic which becomes alternative (cheaper) of traditional satellite communication (expensive) (Van Torre et al., 2018). The low power consumption of LoRa extends the lifespan of a battery to more than 10 years which is an important breakthrough which ZigBee and Bluetooth Low Energy can only offer 2-3 years (Patel, & Won, 2017). It is noted that a similar term named low power wide area network (LoRaWAN) refers to the upper layer whereas LoRa is the physical layer.

More and more efforts have devoted in the applications of LoRa. Recent works (academic papers) have demonstrated the adoption of LoRa in various domains, for instance, object tracking (Kim et al., 2017), electric vehicle charging (Ouya et al., 2017), wireless sensor network (Ma, & Chen, 2018), and remote health (Petäjäjärvi et al., 2017). Macroscopically, Semtech has illustrated the possibilities of deploying Lora in supply chain and logistics, metering, environment, cities, home and buildings, industrial control, agriculture and healthcare.

IEEE 802.11af

This wireless local area network-based communication standard (also named White-Fi) defines international specifications for spectrum sharing among licensed services and unlicensed white space devices in the TV white space band. The frequency band coverage in US and Europe are from 54 to 698 MHz (Sun et al., 2014) and from 470 to 790 MHz (Van de Beek et al., 2011) respectively. There are three possible channels, 6, 7 and 8 MHz. The maximum throughput is 26.7 Mbps for 6 and 7 MHz channels and that is 35.6 Mbps for 8 MHz channel.

The rationale of IEEE 802.11af is that broadcast television coverage has to be organised in a way the space is left between the coverage areas of distinct transmitters within the same channels. Therefore, signal interference can be avoided. The design of spacing also depends on the sensitivity to tropospheric propagation which increases the distances over which signals can be received. The drawback can be understood that some spaces need to remain unused, implying spectrum inefficiency.

Recommended reading materials of IEEE 802.11af research are prototype of White-Fi based baseband IC enabling compact device (Matsumura et al., 2017), CMOS transmitter (Cheang et al., 2015), and mobility-compatible database-assisted framework for Dynamic spectrum access (Dai, Wu, & Du, 2018).

IEEE 802.11ah

We can use the name IEEE 802.11ah or Wi-Fi HaLow. It operates in 900 MHz (some scholars refer as sub-1 GHz) as the extension of traditional Wi-Fi at 2.4 GHz and 5 GHz. The maximum throughputs are 13.34 Mbps, 28.9 Mbps, 60 Mbps, 130 Mbps and 234 Mbps using 1 MHz channel, 2 MHz channel, 4 MHz channel, 8 MHz channel and 16 MHz channel respectively.

IEEE 802.11ah can be applied to IoT application owning to the fact that it supports more devices per access point for both outdoor and indoor environments with a much longer transmission range but at a much lower data rate than the use cases and requirements of IEEE 802.11ac (Park, 2015). Technically speaking, the link budget enhancement of IEEE 802.11ah over IEEE 802.11n is 24.5 dB, 3 dB, 3 dB, 18.5 dB, 10 dB and 8.5 dB in total link budget gain, repetition coding, 1 MHz channel width, sub-total link budget gain, noise bandwidth and free space path loss respectively.

For better understanding on the application and current research of IEEE 802.11ah, please refer to the following articles traffic-aware sensor grouping (Chang et al., 2018), digital polar transmitter (Ba et al., 2016), and larm-initiated and regular machine-to-machine traffic (Madueño, Stefanović, & Popovski, 2016).

IEEE 802.11ax

This networking protocol is expected to be officially released in 2019. It is designed to operate in the already existing 5 GHz and 2.4GHz spectrums. Although the nominal data rate is just 37% higher than IEEE 802.11ac, the new amendment is expected to achieve a 4x increase to user throughput—due to more efficient spectrum utilization. The maximum throughput is 143 Mbps, 287 Mbps, 600 Mbps, and 1201 Mbps using 20 MHz, 40 MHz, 80 MHz and 160 MHz channels.

IEEE 802.11ax improves significantly compared to IEEE 802.11ac, in various aspects: symbol duration, guard interval duration, fragmentation, target wake time, network allocation vector, spatial frequency reuse, trigger-based random access multiuser MIMO and orthogonal frequency-division multiple access.

Key readings on intelligent information infrastructure (Deng et al., 2017), uplink and downlink model (Ajami, & Artail, 2017), MAC protocol design (Aijaz, & Kulkarni, 2017), self-scrutinized backoff mechanism (Ali et al., 2018), and throughput comparison between IEEE 802.11ac and ax (Sharon, & Alpert, 2017) are highly recommended.

IEEE 802.11ay

This is another standard that will be released in 2019 (has been delayed by two years). It operates in frequency of 60 GHz (Ghasempour et al., 2017). The link-rate per stream is 44 Gbps, with four streams this goes up to 176 Gbps (MIMO). Backhaul connectivity outside for service providers, and replacement for cables and Ethernet indoor could be achieved via IEEE 802.11 ay.

Signal attenuation is large in millimeter wave spectrum at 60 GHz because oxygen quickly absorbs 60 GHz signals and thus the transmission range is limited (Akyildiz, Han, & Nie, 2018). Moreover, signals at 60 GHz are generally directional, which could be beneficial in some cases. Directional antenna techniques (Yu et al., 2017), channel estimation (Venugopal et al., 2017) are key elements for the successful deployment in reality.

APPLICATIONS

Health Monitoring

Health is always the first element that we must possess before doing anything. Continuous monitoring of body vital signal and behavioural related parameters could improve our quality of life and even prolong our lifespan. It creates limitation and uncomfortableness if we use wired devices for human health monitoring (Tung et al., 2013). As a result, wireless wearable devices are dominated both in industry and academia.

Vital sign monitoring is fundamental and generally clear thresholds are given by medical professionals and alert and notification will be sent if vital sign parameter of the user falls outside the nominal region. Numerous studies have demonstrated the reliability of vital sign monitoring using wireless sensor network (Fajkus et al., 2017; Schires, Georgiou, & Lande, 2018; Villarroel et al., 2014).

Besides, it can be seen that disease diagnosis is a hot topic in health monitoring. It is targeting to all human beings and all of us should experience some kinds of disease. Imagine if we have smart healthcare system that can continuously monitor our health status and analyze if there is potential outbreak of disease via embedding machine learning algorithms (Spruit, & Lytras, 2018). A detailed literature review on innovation, technologies and applications in disease diagnosis can be found in (Chui et al., 2017). Typical health monitoring includes organ inflammation (Chow et al., 2014), drowsiness detection (Chui et al., 2015 July; Chui et al., 2016), diabetes mellitus (Xiong et al., 2018), Alzheimer's disease (Donnelly-Kehoe et al., 2018), glycemic monitoring and prediction (Pang, Chui, & Lytras, 2019) and cardiovascular disease (Chui et al., 2015).

Toxic Gas Monitoring

A continuous toxic gas monitoring is desired because toxic gas is sometimes explosive, corrosive and hazardous. The leakage can wreak havoc on human beings, which may lead to injuries, deaths and equipment destruction and environment poisoning. Compounds such as volatile organic compounds, hydrogen sulfide, carbon monoxide, sulphur dioxide, nitrogen dioxide, bromometance, and bromine represent the typical toxic gases.

A detailed overview of the emerging techniques for continuous toxic gas monitoring can be encountered in (Shu, Mukherjee, & Wu, 2016). Several continuous monitoring algorithms have been discussed in petrochemical plants. Challenges of accurate detection included varying shape, fast movement and invisibility of toxic gas. Current algorithms focused on cluster forming and node density whereas planarization algorithm was applied so that the considered region could be divided into small portions. Authors have proposed two future works. First, a mobile sensor and remote based method can be adopted so that workers can verify the result. Second, in environment of asymmetric radio links, the robustness of proposed DeGas scheme should be studied.

An experiment was carried out in a monitoring area of 200 m2 using 20 wireless hydrocarbon sensors (Chraim, Erol, & Pister, 2016). A phase one change detection algorithm was applied and yielded an accuracy over 90%, average delay of 108s in a testing period of 3 days. The future work is divided into 4-fold (i) network lifetime enhancement via energy reduction; (ii) relationship between nozzle size and flow rate; (iii) reducing response time and signal to noise ratio and also increasing the wake-up time; and (iv) improving the accuracy of the algorithm.

A recent work has focused on prolonging the network lifetime in toxic gas monitoring (Mukherjee, Shu, Hu, Hancke, & Zhu, 2017). The innovation of the sleep scheduling algorithm is to wake-up the sleep nodes if and only if there is a toxic gas leakage. In previous work (Zhu, Leung, Yang, & Shu, 2015), all sleep nodes in the network were awaken. Therefore, it is less energy consumed in (Mukherjee, Shu, Hu, Hancke, & Zhu, 2017) compared to (Zhu, Leung, Yang, & Shu, 2015). Results revealed that the new sleep scheduling algorithm can reduce the number of awake nodes by 11%.

Connected Target Coverage Problem

The connectivity and coverage of IWN are important criteria as ofa successful network. While maintaining the connectivity and coverage, network lifetime and energy-efficient are desired. The problem can be formulated as connected target coverage. Analysis of coverage strategies via four common connected target converge algorithms (Cardei, Wu, Lu, & Pervaiz, 2005; Kim, Han, Mun, Park, & Park, 2010;

Zhao, & Gurusamy, 2008; Zorbas, & Douligeris, 2011) has been extensively discussed (Han, Liu, Jiang, Shu, & Hancke, 2017). Comparisons were made in terms of number of dead nodes, network lifetime, energy consumption, energy balance and time. A structural table has summarized their pros, cons, suitability industrial field and applications. There is no unique algorithm which achieves highest performance in all environments and applications. The future work can be lowered the gap between simulation and experiment as the large-scale IWN remains challenging.

The connected target coverage problem is formulated as a stochastic optimization problem which deals with maximal network scalability and minimal number of sensor nodes, constrained by full coverage (Njoya, Thron, Barry, Abdou, Tonye, Konje, & Dipanda, 2017). The algorithm provides dummy sensors which can merge, move, explode and recombine so that the number of required sensor nodes can be reduced. However, this work has a limitation that the connectivity of the network has not been considered.

Another work (Chand, & Kumar, 2016) has formulated the problem as heuristic maximization of network lifetime. It has focused on determining the critical targets and critical sensors where the former has least covered and the latter covers the critical targets. The rationale is that network becomes exhausted if any critical target is uncovered. For future work, connected or partial coverage can be considered.

Mobile Crowd Sensing

The global number of mobile phone users reaches 4.77 billion in 2017 and is expected to be increased with an annual rate of 3% (Number, 2017). Mobile crowd sensing is an emerging concept due to sensing capabilities of crowd in mobile devices. It has several advantages such as effectiveness, scalability and mobility. A recent review was conducted on the operability and applicability of mobile crowd sensing (Shu, Chen, Huo, Bergmann, & Wang, 2017). The applications can be categorized into daily life and public infrastructure construction. Mobile crowd sensing can contribute to sport experience, healthcare, education, social media and entertainment. On the other hand, public infrastructure construction can be urban planning, geospatial information collection, environment monitoring, smart transportation and predicting and managing crisis. The operability is analyzed in two ways. First, the beneficial effect of mobile crowd sensing in industrial sensing is discussed. Second, it is followed by the evolution of sensing.

In mobile crowd sensing, data collection is one of the most important concern because massive amounts of mobile users keep contributing data. In (Capponi,

Fiandrino, Kliazovich, Bouvry, & Giordano, 2017), a sustainable and distributed framework has been proposed to minimize the cost of sensing and reporting, and maximize the data collection utility. Three directions have been suggested for further research. They are (i) the difficulty of data collection for various network sizes; (ii) data delivery enhancement and (iii) buffering sample via caching policy;

Besides data collection, attention is drawn to quality of service which is determined by service node selection. The problem is formulated as multiobjective optimization problem with objectives related to data transfer rate and opportunistic converge (Ding, He, & Wang, 2017). Future work includes examination of other optimization algorithms and analysis of more types of QoS matrics.

CHALLENGES

Geographic Routing

Geographic routing utilizes information about geographic location. Every node of the network is able to determine its own location. During data transmission, the source node is able to determine the node destination. Compared to traditional topology routing, geographic routing has high scalability and can handle better for highly energy-constraint and dynamic networks. Typical approaches are flooding-based, single-path and multi-path.

The performance of two-phase geographic greedy forwarding based geographic routing in connected K-neighborhood based duty cycled was first analyzed (Shu, Mukherjee, Hu, Bergmann, & Zhu, 2016). The environment setting is an IWSN with radio irregularity. Analysis included shortest routing path length, average routing path length and upper bound for the number of explored routing paths.

Many existing forwarding geographic routing algorithms assume Rician distributed distance estimates and Gaussian distributed location error between sensor nodes. However, in (Popescu, Salman, & Kemp, 2015), the former assumption of Rician property is invalid in both theoretical and simulative ways. Therefore, the previous findings for those assuming Rician property may not reliable.

A three-dimensional space network was considered using geographic routing (Huang, Yin, Luo, Zhang, Min, & Fan, 2016). Different from two-dimensional space, three-dimensional space is still less popular in research. Hence, there are numerous challenges that need to be solved. They are (i) lack of security discussion; (ii) no network distance prediction; (iii) location error is affecting the routing decision; and (iv) limitation of network models.

Wireless Charging

In IWSNs, sensors have limited battery life and it is trivial that it is not practical and time-consuming to use a wire to charge up the battery or to replace the battery by human beings one by one. In recent years, the advancement of wireless technology allows wireless energy transfer so that wireless charging becomes vital for real-world deployment.

A wireless charging vehicle was proposed to charge each sensor node periodically (Qin, Lu, Zhu, Sun, & Shu, 2016). The energy level of each node was studied in initialization cycles which would be charged-up in renewable cycles to its original energy level. A simulation environment of 100 nodes was demonstrated the applicability of proposed method.

Non-deterministic issues like node failures and topological changes increase the difficulty of wireless charging. Maximization of energy efficiency of network and minimization of the number of dead nodes could be optimally achieved via temporal-spatial charging scheduling (Lin, Zhou, Guo, Song, Wu, & Obaidat, 2018). Similar to (Lin, Zhou, Guo, Song, Wu, & Obaidat, 2018), non-deterministic factors have been considered and it was solved by primary and passer-by scheduling algorithm in (Lin, Han, Deng, & Wu, 2017). It had the advantage of interdependency, throughput and survival rate. These two works suggested the introduction of more than one wireless charging vehicles in order to reduce the charging period. The complexity of charging scheduling will be increased and collision avoidance algorithm should be embedded into existing system.

Wireless Coexistence

Multiple heterogeneous wireless systems are said to be coexisted when they can operate the same or adjacent frequency spectrum without affecting others in the transmission and reception of signals.

There are three main factors determine the coexistence: 1) space, 2) frequency, and 3) time. In terms of space, the increase in signal to interference ratio of the intended received signal is equivalent to the increase in the probability of coexistence. For frequency, the increase in frequency separation of channels between networks means the increase in probability of coexistence. For time, the decrease in overall channel occupancy of channel will lead to an increase in the probability of coexistence.

ZigBee, Bluetooth and WiFi are operating in the same ISM frequency band, thus potentially causing interference. Likewise, broadband routers and mobile phones are everywhere. The rising popularity of ZigBee may run the risk of suffering from packet loss with WiFi, Bluetooth, and WLAN technologies (Lee, Chae, Sung, & Kang, 2012; Shin, Park, Choi, & Kwon, 2007; Yi, Iwayemi, & Zhou, 2011). Thus coexistence of wireless signals is an important topic of research.

For the successful employment of ISA100.11a and WirelessHART, it is good if coexistence exists between these technologies and other wireless technologies operating in 2.4GHz radio band. In (Petersen, & Carlsen, 2011), it is suggested that ISA100.11a and WirelessHART can have zero interference in channels 15, 20, 25 and 26.

Channel blacklisting is useful for interference avoidance in selection of the use of channels. A device changes the hop pattern when the channel is blacklisted. For ISA100.11a, it uses adaptive blacklisting which allows each device to blacklist any problematic channel. For WirelessHART, the channel blacklisting is optional, and network administrator is responsible for it.

CONCLUSION

In this chapter, we have presented various emerging standards, applications and challenges in wireless sensor networks. These are crucial elements for OBOR initiative to connect the silk road countries. Fundamentally, the world is believed to have ever growing and infinite alike data that can be collected (sensors are required) and system to manage the data collection (wireless sensor network is desired). It creates many open opportunities but new challenges as future research work that need to be addressed properly. The emerging wireless protocols have demonstrated to be applicable to key applications in wireless sensor network. Particularly, many experts have a strong wish on moving a big step forward via 5G. Ultimately, the wireless systems will be upgraded towards higher data rate. The technology MIMO is believed to be a possible solution which has been proven theoretically. The business between China and foreign countries must be relied on wireless technologies to ensure sustainable economics. Particularly, underdeveloped countries could receive highest benefit as their economies grow significantly in large extent. Overseas markets enable chances for information service providers to become internationalized companies in the internet age.

REFERENCES

Aijaz, A., & Kulkarni, P. (2017). Simultaneous transmit and receive operation in next generation IEEE 802.11 WLANs: A MAC protocol design approach. *IEEE Wireless Communications*, *24*(6), 128–135. doi:10.1109/MWC.2017.1700012

Ajami, A. K., & Artail, H. (2017). On The Modeling and Analysis of Uplink and Downlink IEEE 802.11 ax Wi-Fi With LTE in Unlicensed Spectrum. *IEEE Transactions on Wireless Communications*, *16*(9), 5779–5795. doi:10.1109/TWC.2017.2715834

Akyildiz, I. F., Han, C., & Nie, S. (2018). Combating the Distance Problem in the Millimeter Wave and Terahertz Frequency Bands. *IEEE Communications Magazine*, *56*(6), 102–108. doi:10.1109/MCOM.2018.1700928

Ali, R., Shahin, N., Bajracharya, R., Kim, B. S., & Kim, S. W. (2018). A self-scrutinized backoff mechanism for IEEE 802.11 ax in 5G unlicensed networks. *Sustainability*, *10*(4), 1201. doi:10.3390u10041201

Ba, A., Liu, Y. H., van den Heuvel, J., Mateman, P., Büsze, B., Dijkhuis, J., ... De Groot, H. (2016). A 1.3 nJ/b IEEE 802.11 ah fully-digital polar transmitter for IoT applications. *IEEE Journal of Solid-State Circuits*, *51*(12), 3103–3113. doi:10.1109/JSSC.2016.2596786

Bronckers, S., Roc'h, A., & Smolders, B. (2017). Wireless receiver architectures towards 5G: Where are we? *IEEE Circuits and Systems Magazine*, *17*(3), 6–16. doi:10.1109/MCAS.2017.2713306

Capponi, A., Fiandrino, C., Kliazovich, D., Bouvry, P., & Giordano, S. (2017). A cost-effective distributed framework for data collection in cloud-based mobile crowd sensing architectures. *IEEE Transactions on Sustainable Computing*, *2*(1), 3–16. doi:10.1109/TSUSC.2017.2666043

Cardei, M., Wu, J., Lu, M., & Pervaiz, M. O. (2005, August). Maximum network lifetime in wireless sensor networks with adjustable sensing ranges. In *Wireless and Mobile Computing, Networking and Communications, 2005. (WiMob'2005), IEEE International Conference on* (Vol. 3, pp. 438-445). IEEE. 10.1109/WIMOB.2005.1512935

Centenaro, M., Vangelista, L., Zanella, A., & Zorzi, M. (2016). Long-range communications in unlicensed bands: The rising stars in the IoT and smart city scenarios. *IEEE Wireless Communications*, *23*(5), 60–67. doi:10.1109/MWC.2016.7721743

Chand, S., & Kumar, B. (2016). Maximising network lifetime for target coverage problem in wireless sensor networks. *IET Wireless Sensor Systems*, *6*(6), 192–197. doi:10.1049/iet-wss.2015.0094

Chang, T. C., Lin, C. H., Lin, K. C. J., & Chen, W. T. (2018). Traffic-Aware Sensor Grouping for IEEE 802.11 ah Networks: Regression Based Analysis and Design. *IEEE Transactions on Mobile Computing*.

Cheang, C. F., Un, K. F., Yu, W. H., Mak, P. I., & Martins, R. P. (2015). A combinatorial impairment-compensation digital predistorter for a sub-GHz IEEE 802.11 af-WLAN CMOS transmitter covering a 10x-wide RF bandwidth. *IEEE Transactions on Circuits and Systems. I, Regular Papers*, *62*(4), 1025–1032. doi:10.1109/TCSI.2015.2390561

Chow, W. H., Wu, C. K., Tsang, K. F., Li, B. Y. S., & Chui, K. T. (2014, October). Wrist pulse signal classification for inflammation of appendix, pancreas, and duodenum. In *Industrial Electronics Society, IECON 2014-40th Annual Conference of the IEEE* (pp. 2479-2483). IEEE. 10.1109/IECON.2014.7048853

Chraim, F., Erol, Y. B., & Pister, K. (2016). Wireless gas leak detection and localization. *IEEE Transactions on Industrial Informatics*, *12*(2), 768–779. doi:10.1109/TII.2015.2397879

Chui, K. T., Alhalabi, W., Pang, S. S. H., Pablos, P. O. D., Liu, R. W., & Zhao, M. (2017). Disease Diagnosis in Smart Healthcare: Innovation, Technologies and Applications. *Sustainability*, *9*(12), 2309. doi:10.3390u9122309

Chui, K. T., Tsang, K. F., Chi, H. R., Ling, B. W. K., & Wu, C. K. (2016). An accurate ECG-based transportation safety drowsiness detection scheme. *IEEE Transactions on Industrial Informatics*, *12*(4), 1438–1452. doi:10.1109/TII.2016.2573259

Chui, K. T., Tsang, K. F., Chi, H. R., Wu, C. K., & Ling, B. W. K. (2015, July). Electrocardiogram based classifier for driver drowsiness detection. In *Industrial Informatics (INDIN), 2015 IEEE 13th International Conference on* (pp. 600-603). IEEE. 10.1109/INDIN.2015.7281802

Chui, K. T., Tsang, K. F., Wu, C. K., Hung, F. H., Chi, H. R., Chung, H. S. H., ... Ko, K. T. (2015). Cardiovascular diseases identification using electrocardiogram health identifier based on multiple criteria decision making. *Expert Systems with Applications*, *42*(13), 5684–5695. doi:10.1016/j.eswa.2015.01.059

Dahri, M. H., Jamaluddin, M. H., Abbasi, M. I., & Kamarudin, M. R. (2017). A review of wideband reflectarray antennas for 5G communication systems. *IEEE Access: Practical Innovations, Open Solutions*, *5*, 17803–17815. doi:10.1109/ACCESS.2017.2747844

Dahri, M. H., Jamaluddin, M. H., Khalily, M., Abbasi, M. I., Selvaraju, R., & Kamarudin, M. R. (2018). Polarization Diversity and Adaptive Beamsteering for 5G Reflectarrays: A Review. *IEEE Access: Practical Innovations, Open Solutions*, *6*, 19451–19464. doi:10.1109/ACCESS.2018.2821358

Dai, Y., Wu, J., & Du, X. (2018). *Hierarchical and Hybrid: Mobility-compatible Database-assisted Framework For Dynamic Spectrum Access*. *IEEE Transactions on Network Science and Engineering*.

Deng, D. J., Lin, Y. P., Yang, X., Zhu, J., Li, Y. B., Luo, J., & Chen, K. C. (2017). Ieee 802.11 ax: Highly efficient wlans for intelligent information infrastructure. *IEEE Communications Magazine*, *55*(12), 52–59. doi:10.1109/MCOM.2017.1700285

Ding, S., He, X., & Wang, J. (2017). Multiobjective Optimization Model for Service Node Selection Based on a Tradeoff Between Quality of Service and Resource Consumption in Mobile Crowd Sensing. *IEEE Internet of Things Journal*, *4*(1), 258–268.

Donnelly-Kehoe, P. A., Pascariello, G. O., & Gómez, J. C. (2018). Looking for Alzheimer's Disease morphometric signatures using machine learning techniques. *Journal of Neuroscience Methods*, *302*, 24–34. doi:10.1016/j.jneumeth.2017.11.013 PMID:29174020

Fajkus, M., Nedoma, J., Martinek, R., Vasinek, V., Nazeran, H., & Siska, P. (2017). A non-invasive multichannel hybrid fiber-optic sensor system for vital sign monitoring. *Sensors (Basel)*, *17*(1), 111. doi:10.339017010111 PMID:28075341

Ghasempour, Y., da Silva, C. R., Cordeiro, C., & Knightly, E. W. (2017). IEEE 802.11 ay: Next-generation 60 GHz communication for 100 Gb/s Wi-Fi. *IEEE Communications Magazine*, *55*(12), 186–192. doi:10.1109/MCOM.2017.1700393

Han, G., Liu, L., Jiang, J., Shu, L., & Hancke, G. (2017). Analysis of energy-efficient connected target coverage algorithms for industrial wireless sensor networks. *IEEE Transactions on Industrial Informatics*, *13*(1), 135–143. doi:10.1109/TII.2015.2513767

Huang, H., Yin, H., Luo, Y., Zhang, X., Min, G., & Fan, Q. (2016). Three-dimensional geographic routing in wireless mobile ad hoc and sensor networks. *IEEE Network*, *30*(2), 82–90. doi:10.1109/MNET.2016.7437029

Kim, D. H., Park, J. B., Shin, J. H., & Kim, J. D. (2017, January). Design and implementation of object tracking system based on LoRa. In *Information Networking (ICOIN), 2017 International Conference on* (pp. 463-467). IEEE. 10.1109/ICOIN.2017.7899535

Kim, Y. H., Han, Y. H., Mun, C. M., Park, C. Y., & Park, D. S. (2010, August). Lifetime maximization considering connectivity and overlapped targets in wireless sensor networks. In *Information Technology Convergence and Services (ITCS), 2010 2nd International Conference on* (pp. 1-6). IEEE. 10.1109/ITCS.2010.5581290

Lee, K., Chae, C. B., Sung, T. K., & Kang, J. (2012). Cognitive beamforming based smart metering for coexistence with wireless local area networks. *Journal of Communications and Networks (Seoul)*, *14*(6), 619–628. doi:10.1109/JCN.2012.00028

Lin, C., Han, D., Deng, J., & Wu, G. (2017). P^{2}S: A Primary and Passer-By Scheduling Algorithm for On-Demand Charging Architecture in Wireless Rechargeable Sensor Networks. *IEEE Transactions on Vehicular Technology*, *66*(9), 8047–8058. doi:10.1109/TVT.2017.2683493

Lin, C., Zhou, J., Guo, C., Song, H., Wu, G., & Obaidat, M. S. (2018). TSCA: A temporal-spatial real-time charging scheduling algorithm for on-demand architecture in wireless rechargeable sensor networks. *IEEE Transactions on Mobile Computing*, *17*(1), 211–224. doi:10.1109/TMC.2017.2703094

Lytras, M., & Visvizi, A. (2018). Who uses smart city services and what to make of it: Toward interdisciplinary smart cities research. *Sustainability*, *10*(6), 1998. doi:10.3390u10061998

Ma, Y. W., & Chen, J. L. (2018, April). Toward intelligent agriculture service platform with lora-based wireless sensor network. In *2018 IEEE International Conference on Applied System Invention* (pp. 204-207). IEEE. 10.1109/ICASI.2018.8394568

Madueño, Stefanović, & Popovski. (2016). Reliable and efficient access for alarm-initiated and regular M2M traffic in IEEE 802.11 ah systems. *IEEE Internet of Things Journal, 3*(5), 673-682.

Mahmoud, K. R., & Montaser, A. M. (2018). Synthesis of multi-polarised upside conical frustum array antenna for 5G mm-Wave base station at 28/38 GHz. *IET Microwaves, Antennas & Propagation.*

Matsumura, T., Ibuka, K., Ishizu, K., Murakami, H., Kojima, F., & Harada, H. (2017). Prototype of IEEE 802.11 af-Based Baseband IC Enabling Compact Device for Wireless Local Area Network Systems in TV White-Spaces. *IEEE Transactions on Cognitive Communications and Networking, 3*(3), 450–463. doi:10.1109/TCCN.2017.2750684

Mukherjee, M., Shu, L., Hu, L., Hancke, G. P., & Zhu, C. (2017). Sleep scheduling in industrial wireless sensor networks for toxic gas monitoring. *IEEE Wireless Communications, 24*(4), 106–112. doi:10.1109/MWC.2017.1600072WC

Njoya, A. N., Thron, C., Barry, J., Abdou, W., Tonye, E., Konje, N. S. L., & Dipanda, A. (2017). Efficient scalable sensor node placement algorithm for fixed target coverage applications of wireless sensor networks. *IET Wireless Sensor Systems, 7*(2), 44–54. doi:10.1049/iet-wss.2016.0076

Ouya, A., De Aragon, B. M., Bouette, C., Habault, G., Montavont, N., & Papadopoulos, G. Z. (2017, October). An efficient electric vehicle charging architecture based on LoRa communication. In *Smart Grid Communications (SmartGridComm), 2017 IEEE International Conference on* (pp. 381-386). IEEE. 10.1109/SmartGridComm.2017.8340723

Pang, S. S. H., Chui, K. T., & Lytras, M. D. (Mar. 2019). Glycemic Monitoring and Prediction with Response Improvement via Psyllium. In *Computational methods and algorithms for medicine and optimized clinical practice*. IGI-Global. doi:10.4018/978-1-5225-8244-1.ch009

Park, M. (2015). IEEE 802.11 ah: Sub-1-GHz license-exempt operation for the internet of things. *IEEE Communications Magazine, 53*(9), 145–151. doi:10.1109/MCOM.2015.7263359

Patel, D., & Won, M. (2017, June). Experimental Study on Low Power Wide Area Networks (LPWAN) for Mobile Internet of Things. In *Vehicular Technology Conference (VTC Spring), 2017 IEEE 85th* (pp. 1-5). IEEE.

Petäjäjärvi, J., Mikhaylov, K., Yasmin, R., Hämäläinen, M., & Iinatti, J. (2017). Evaluation of LoRa LPWAN technology for indoor remote health and wellbeing monitoring. *International Journal of Wireless Information Networks*, *24*(2), 153–165. doi:10.100710776-017-0341-8

Petersen, S., & Carlsen, S. (2011). WirelessHART versus ISA100. 11a: The format war hits the factory floor. *IEEE Industrial Electronics Magazine*, *5*(4), 23–34. doi:10.1109/MIE.2011.943023

Popescu, A. M., Salman, N., & Kemp, A. H. (2015). Rician statistical assumptions for geographic routing in wireless sensor networks. *IET Wireless Sensor Systems*, *5*(4), 204–209. doi:10.1049/iet-wss.2014.0023

Qin, Z., Lu, B., Zhu, M., Sun, L., & Shu, L. (2016). Optimized Charging in Large-Scale Deployed WSNs with Mobile Charger. *Transactions on Internet and Information Systems (Seoul)*, *10*(12).

Schires, E., Georgiou, P., & Lande, T. S. (2018). Vital Sign Monitoring Through the Back Using an UWB Impulse Radar With Body Coupled Antennas. *IEEE Transactions on Biomedical Circuits and Systems*, *12*(2), 292–302. doi:10.1109/TBCAS.2018.2799322 PMID:29570057

Sharon, O., & Alpert, Y. (2017). Single User MAC Level Throughput Comparision: IEEE 802.11 ax vs. IEEE 802.11 ac. *Wireless Sensor Network*, *9*(05), 166–177. doi:10.4236/wsn.2017.95009

Shin, S. Y., Park, H. S., Choi, S., & Kwon, W. H. (2007). Packet error rate analysis of ZigBee under WLAN and Bluetooth interferences. *IEEE Transactions on Wireless Communications*, *6*(8), 2825–2830. doi:10.1109/TWC.2007.06112

Shu, L., Chen, Y., Huo, Z., Bergmann, N., & Wang, L. (2017). When mobile crowd sensing meets traditional industry. *IEEE Access: Practical Innovations, Open Solutions*, *5*, 15300–15307. doi:10.1109/ACCESS.2017.2657820

Shu, L., Mukherjee, M., Hu, L., Bergmann, N., & Zhu, C. (2016). Geographic routing in duty-cycled industrial wireless sensor networks with radio irregularity. *IEEE Access: Practical Innovations, Open Solutions*, *4*, 9043–9052. doi:10.1109/ACCESS.2016.2638441

Shu, L., Mukherjee, M., & Wu, X. (2016). Toxic gas boundary area detection in large-scale petrochemical plants with industrial wireless sensor networks. *IEEE Communications Magazine*, *54*(10), 22–28. doi:10.1109/MCOM.2016.7588225

Spruit, M., & Lytras, M. (2018). Applied Data Science in Patient-centric Healthcare. *Telematics and Informatics*, *35*(4), 643–653. doi:10.1016/j.tele.2018.04.002

Sun, L., & Du, Q. (2017). Physical layer security with its applications in 5G networks: A review. *China Communications*, *14*(12), 1–14. doi:10.1109/CC.2017.8246328

Sun, W., Lee, O., Shin, Y., Kim, S., Yang, C., Kim, H., & Choi, S. (2014). Wi-Fi could be much more. *IEEE Communications Magazine*, *52*(11), 22–29. doi:10.1109/MCOM.2014.6957139

Tung, H. Y., Tsang, K. F., Tung, H. C., Chui, K. T., & Chi, H. R. (2013). The design of dual radio ZigBee homecare gateway for remote patient monitoring. *IEEE Transactions on Consumer Electronics*, *59*(4), 756–764. doi:10.1109/TCE.2013.6689686

Van de Beek, J., Riihijarvi, J., Achtzehn, A., & Mahonen, P. (2011, May). UHF white space in Europe—a quantitative study into the potential of the 470–790 MHz band. In *New Frontiers in Dynamic Spectrum Access Networks (DySPAN), 2011 IEEE Symposium on* (pp. 1-9). IEEE.

Van Torre, P., Gaelens, J., Verhaevert, J., & Rogier, H. (2018). Measurement and characterization of dual-band LoRa communication in the Antarctic. In *EUCAP2018, the 12th European Conference on Antennas and Propagation* (pp. 1-5). Academic Press. 10.1049/cp.2018.0469

Venugopal, K., Alkhateeb, A., Prelcic, N. G., & Heath, R. W. (2017). Channel estimation for hybrid architecture-based wideband millimeter wave systems. *IEEE Journal on Selected Areas in Communications*, *35*(9), 1996–2009. doi:10.1109/JSAC.2017.2720856

Villarroel, M., Guazzi, A., Jorge, J., Davis, S., Watkinson, P., Green, G., ... Tarassenko, L. (2014). Continuous non-contact vital sign monitoring in neonatal intensive care unit. *Healthcare Technology Letters, 1*(3), 87-91.

Visvizi, A., & Lytras, M. D. (2018). Rescaling and refocusing smart cities research: From mega cities to smart villages. *Journal of Science and Technology Policy Management*, *9*(2), 134–145. doi:10.1108/JSTPM-02-2018-0020

Visvizi, A., Lytras, M. D., Damiani, E., & Mathkour, H. (2018). Policy making for smart cities: Innovation and social inclusive economic growth for sustainability. *Journal of Science and Technology Policy Management*, *9*(2), 126–133. doi:10.1108/JSTPM-07-2018-079

Xiong, Z., Liu, T., Tse, G., Gong, M., Gladding, P., Smaill, B. H., ... Zhao, J. (2018). A Machine Learning Aided Systematic Review and Meta-Analysis of the Relative Risk of Atrial Fibrillation in Patients With Diabetes Mellitus. *Frontiers in Physiology*, *9*, 835. doi:10.3389/fphys.2018.00835 PMID:30018571

Yi, P., Iwayemi, A., & Zhou, C. (2011). Developing ZigBee deployment guideline under WiFi interference for smart grid applications. *IEEE Transactions on Smart Grid*, *2*(1), 110–120. doi:10.1109/TSG.2010.2091655

Yifei, Y., & Longming, Z. (2014). Application scenarios and enabling technologies of 5G. *China Communications*, *11*(11), 69–79. doi:10.1109/CC.2014.7004525

Yu, X., Zhang, J., Haenggi, M., & Letaief, K. B. (2017). Coverage analysis for millimeter wave networks: The impact of directional antenna arrays. *IEEE Journal on Selected Areas in Communications*, *35*(7), 1498–1512. doi:10.1109/JSAC.2017.2699098

Zhao, Q., & Gurusamy, M. (2008). Lifetime maximization for connected target coverage in wireless sensor networks. *IEEE/ACM Transactions on Networking*, *16*(6), 1378–1391. doi:10.1109/TNET.2007.911432

Zhu, C., Leung, V. C., Yang, L. T., & Shu, L. (2015). Collaborative location-based sleep scheduling for wireless sensor networks integratedwith mobile cloud computing. *IEEE Transactions on Computers*, *64*(7), 1844–1856. doi:10.1109/TC.2014.2349524

Zorbas, D., & Douligeris, C. (2011). Connected coverage in WSNs based on critical targets. *Computer Networks*, *55*(6), 1412–1425. doi:10.1016/j.comnet.2010.12.023

Compilation of References

Abraham, F., & Van Hove, J. (2005). The Rise of China: Prospects of Regional Trade Policy. *Review of World Economics*, *141*(3), 486–509. doi:10.100710290-005-0040-x

Abugabah & Louis. (2010). *Enterprise Resource Planning (ERP) System in Higher Education: A Literature Review and Implications*. Academic Press.

Acemoglu, D., & Verdier, T. (2000, March). The Choice between Market Failures and Corruption. *The American Economic Review*, *90*(1), 194–211. doi:10.1257/aer.90.1.194

Adams, F. G., Gangnes, B., & Shachmurove, Y. (2006). Why is China so Competitive? Measuring and Explaining China's Competitiveness. *World Economy*, *29*(2), 95–122. doi:10.1111/j.1467-9701.2006.00773.x

Agbiboa, D. E. (2017). Borders that Continue to Bother Us: The Politics of Cross-Border Security Cooperation in Africa's Lake Chad Basin. *Commonwealth and Comparative Politics*, *55*(4), 403–425. doi:10.1080/14662043.2017.1312730

Aghion, P., & Howitt, P. (2009). *The economics of growth*. Cambridge, MA: The MIT Press.

Aijaz, A., & Kulkarni, P. (2017). Simultaneous transmit and receive operation in next generation IEEE 802.11 WLANs: A MAC protocol design approach. *IEEE Wireless Communications*, *24*(6), 128–135. doi:10.1109/MWC.2017.1700012

Aiyar, S., Duval, R., Puy, D., Wu, Y., & Zhang, L. (2013). *Growth Slowdowns and the Middle-Income Trap*. International Monetary Fund Working Paper, WP/13/71, Asia and Pacific Department.

Ajami, A. K., & Artail, H. (2017). On The Modeling and Analysis of Uplink and Downlink IEEE 802.11 ax Wi-Fi With LTE in Unlicensed Spectrum. *IEEE Transactions on Wireless Communications*, *16*(9), 5779–5795. doi:10.1109/TWC.2017.2715834

Akhtaruzzaman, M., Berg, N., & Lien, D. (2017). Confucius Institutes and FDI Flows from China to Africa. *China Economic Review*, *44*, 241–252. doi:10.1016/j.chieco.2017.02.004

Akyildiz, I. F., Han, C., & Nie, S. (2018). Combating the Distance Problem in the Millimeter Wave and Terahertz Frequency Bands. *IEEE Communications Magazine*, *56*(6), 102–108. doi:10.1109/MCOM.2018.1700928

Alexandru, B., & Gabriela, S. (2008). Opportunities and challenges of the European businesses in China. *Annals of the University of Oradea. Economic Science Series*, *17*(1), 63–66.

Ali, R., Shahin, N., Bajracharya, R., Kim, B. S., & Kim, S. W. (2018). A self-scrutinized backoff mechanism for IEEE 802.11 ax in 5G unlicensed networks. *Sustainability*, *10*(4), 1201. doi:10.3390u10041201

Ali, U., & Wang, J.-J. (2018). Does Outbound Foreign Direct Investment Crowd Out Domestic Investment in China? Evidence from Time Series Analysis. *Global Economic Review*, 1–15. doi:10.1080/1226508x.2018.1492431

Al-sudairi, M. T. (2013, February). China in the eyes of the Saudi media. *Gulf Research Centre*, 1–38.

Amadeo, K. (2018). *How China Influences the U.S. Dollar.* Retrieved from https://www.thebalance.com/how-does-china-influence-the-u-s-dollar-3970466

Ameer, W., Xu, H., & Alotaish, M. S. M. (2017). Outward Foreign Direct Investment and Domestic Investment: Evidence from China. *Economic Research-Ekonomska Istraživanja*, *30*(1), 777–788. doi:10.1080/1331677X.2017.1314824

Amighini, A. (2017). *China's Belt and Road: A game changer?* Alessandria, Italy: Edizioni Epoké.

Anderlini, J., Sender, H., & Bokhari, F. (2018, September 10). Pakistan rethinks its role in Xi's Belt and Road plan. *Financial Times*. Retrieved from https://www.ft.com/content/d4a3e7f8-b282-11e8-99ca-68cf89602132

Andersen, B., & Wong, D. (2013, February). *The new normal: Competitive advantage in the digital economy*. London: Big Innovation Centre. Retrieved on June 2, 2018, from: http://www.biginnovationcentre.com/Assets/Docs/The%20New%20Normal.pdf

Andreosso-O'Callaghan, B., & Qian, W. (1999). Technology Transfer: A Mode of Collaboration Between the European Union and China. *Europe-Asia Studies*, *51*(1), 123–142. doi:10.1080/09668139999155

Andrews, D., Criscuolo, C., & Gal, P. N. (2016, September). *The Global Productivity Slowdown, Technology Divergence and Public Policy: A Firm Level Pespective*. Hutchins Center Working Paper #24, Brookings Institution.

Arısoy, E., Bayar, G., & Soranlar, B. (2005). *Asya'nın Devi: Çin Halk Cumhuriyeti*. Retrieved from http://www.dtm.gov.tr/ead/DTDERGI/temmuz2004/asyaI.htm

Arnold, K., & Pistilli, M. (2012). Course Signals At Purdue: Using Learning Analytics To Increase Student Success. *2nd International Conference On Learning Analytics And Knowledge*, 267-270. Retrieved from https://dl.acm.org/citation.cfm?doid=2330601.2330666

Asian Development Bank. (2016). *Reducing Income Inequality in the People's Republic of China*. Retrieved on September 15, 2018, from: https://www.adb.org/publications/reducing-income-inequality-prc

Asian Development Bank. (2018). *Poverty in the People's Republic of China*. Retrieved on September 15, 2018, from: https://www.adb.org/countries/prc/poverty

Association for Talent Development. (2018). *2018 Workplace Learning Report*. Retrieved on August 14, 2018, from: https://www.cornerstoneondemand.com/sites/default/files/partner/asset/files/linkedin-learning-workplace-learning-report-2018.pdf

Atlas Media, M. I. T. (2016). *China*. Observation of Economic Complexity. Retrieved from https://atlas.media.mit.edu/en/profile/country/chn/

Attaran. (2018). Opportunities And Challenges For Big Data Analytics In US Higher Education. *Industry and Higher Education*, *32*(3), 169-182. doi:10.1177/0950422218770937

Awokuse, T., & Yin, H. (2010). Intellectual property rights protection and the surge in FDI in China. *Journal of Comparative Economics*, *38*(2), 217–224. doi:10.1016/j.jce.2009.10.001

Ba, A., Liu, Y. H., van den Heuvel, J., Mateman, P., Büsze, B., Dijkhuis, J., ... De Groot, H. (2016). A 1.3 nJ/b IEEE 802.11 ah fully-digital polar transmitter for IoT applications. *IEEE Journal of Solid-State Circuits*, *51*(12), 3103–3113. doi:10.1109/JSSC.2016.2596786

Baocheng, L. (2007). Entry Encounters into China Market. *International Management Review*, *3*(3), 97–105.

Barr, M. (2012). Nation branding as nation building: China's image campaign. *East Asia*, *29*(1), 81–94. doi:10.100712140-011-9159-7

Barron, J. (2018, February 5). China surpassed the United States as the world's largest crude oil importer in 2017. *The U.S. Energy Information Administration*. Retrieved from https://www.eia.gov/todayinenergy/detail.php?id=34812

Bartelsman, E., Haltiwanger, J., & Scarpetta, S. (2013). Cross-country Differences in Productivity: The Role of Allocation and Selection. *The American Economic Review*, *103*(1), 305–334. doi:10.1257/aer.103.1.305

Bartunek, J. M. (2007). Academic-practitioner collaboration need not require joint or relevant research: Toward a relational scholarship of integration. *Academy of Management Journal*, *50*(6), 1323–1333. doi:10.5465/amj.2007.28165912

BBC News. (2009, July 10). Turkey attacks China "genocide." *BBC News*.

Behrman, J. N., Fischer, W. A., & Simon, D. F. (1989). Transferring Technology to China. *The International Trade Journal*, *4*(1), 49–67. doi:10.1080/08853908908523683

Bei, J., Gang, L., & Zhi, C. (2006). *An Empirical Analysis on International Competitiveness of China Manufacturing since WTO Accession*. China Industrial Economy. Retrieved from http://en.cnki.com.cn/Article_en/CJFDTOTAL-GGYY200610000.htm

Bei, J. (2017). Economic globalization 3. 0 and the concept of interconnection under the. *Chinese Economy*, *12*(2), 2–21.

Berman, A., Mudambi, R., & Shoham, A. (2017). Language Structure and Its Effects on Innovation. *Academy of International Business Insights, 17*(4), 14–17.

Bhattacharya, A. (2016). Conceptualizing the Silk Road Initiative in China's Periphery Policy. *East Asia, 33*(4), 309–328. doi:10.100712140-016-9263-9

Bhatt, P. R. (2008). *Trade Competitiveness in ASEAN. Anveshak, 38(2).*

Bhola, P. L. (1986). *Pakistan-China relations: Search for politico-strategic relationship*. RBSA Publishers.

Bieberbach, A. (2012). IP strategies in business operations with China. *Journal of Business Chemistry, 9*(3), 161–166. Retrieved from https://acg.idm.oclc.org/login?url=http://search.ebscohost.com/login.aspx?direct=true&db=bth&AN=83388048&scope=site

Bie, Q., Li, C., & Zhou, S. (2014). Evaluation of the Effectiveness of Border Policies in Dehong Prefecture of Yunnan, China. *Sustainability, 6*(8), 5284–5299. doi:10.3390u6085284

Bijan, Z. (2005). China's peaceful rise to great-power status. *Foreign Affairs, 84*(5), 18. doi:10.2307/20031702

Bijian, Z. (2017). China's One Belt, One Road plan marks the next phase of globalization. *New Perspectives Quarterly, 34*(3), 27–31. doi:10.1111/npqu.12090

Bilim Kültür Yönetim Platformu. (2004). *Çin Gerçeği*. Ankara: Author.

Bin, L. (2015). "One Belt and One Road" and China's Geopolitical Strategy. Science and Economic Society, 50-54.

Bird, R. C. (2006). Defending Intellectual Property Rights in the Bric Economies. *American Business Law Journal, 43*(2), 317–363. doi:10.1111/j.1744-1714.2006.00019.x

Blackburn, K., Bose, N., & Haque, M. E. (2006). The incidence and persistence of corruption in economic development. *Journal of Economic Dynamics & Control, 30*(12), 2447–2467. doi:10.1016/j.jedc.2005.07.007

Blanchard, J.-M. F. (2017). Probing China's Twenty-First-Century Maritime Silk Road Initiative (MSRI): An Examination of MSRI Narratives. *Geopolitics, 22*(2), 246–268. doi:10.1080/14650045.2016.1267147

Blanchard, J.-M. F. (2018). China's Maritime Silk Road Initiative (MSRI) and Southeast Asia: A Chinese 'pond' not 'lake' in the Works. *Journal of Contemporary China*, 1–15. doi:10.1080/10670564.2018.1410959

Blanchard, J.-M. F., & Flint, C. (2017). The Geopolitics of China's Maritime Silk Road Initiative. *Geopolitics*, *22*(2), 223–245. doi:10.1080/14650045.2017.1291503

Boamah, J., Appiah-Kubi, M., & Osei, M. (2018). Network Structure Analysis of Bilateral Investments of One Belt, One Road Initiative countries. *Scholars Bulletin*, 689-699.

Boyer, A., & Bonnin, G. (2016). *Higher Education And The Revolution Of Learning Analytics*. Oslo: International Council For Open And Distance Education. Retrieved from https://icde.memberclicks.net/assets/RESOURCES/anne_la_report%20cc%20licence.pdf

Bradsher, K. (2018, August 23). As Trade War Intensifies, China Moves to Bolster Its Economy. *New York Times*. Retrieved on September 2, 2018, from: https://www.nytimes.com/2018/08/23/business/china-economy-trade.html

Brewster, D. (2017). Silk Roads and Strings of Pearls: The Strategic Geography of China's New Pathways in the Indian Ocean. *Geopolitics*, *22*(2), 269–291. doi:10.1080/14650045.2016.1223631

Bria, E. (2017). *Why Do Indonesia*. ASEAN Matter to China.

Bronckers, S., Roc'h, A., & Smolders, B. (2017). Wireless receiver architectures towards 5G: Where are we? *IEEE Circuits and Systems Magazine*, *17*(3), 6–16. doi:10.1109/MCAS.2017.2713306

Brookings Institution. (2018). *The New Geopolitics of Asia*. Retrieved on September 3, 2018, from: https://www.brookings.edu/series/the-new-geopolitics-of-asia/

Brouthers, K. D. (2002). Institutional, Cultural and Transaction Cost Influences on Entry Mode Choice and Performance. *Journal of International Business Studies*, *33*(2), 203–221. doi:10.1057/palgrave.jibs.8491013

Brown, K. (2018). The Anti-Corruption Struggle in Xi Jinping's China: An Alternative Political Narrative. *Asian Affairs*, *49*(1), 1–10. doi:10.1080/03068374.2018.1416008

Brown, K. (2018). The Belt and Road: Security dimensions. *Asia Europe Journal, 16*(3), 213–222. doi:10.100710308-018-0514-9

Bruun, P., & Bennett, D. (2002). Transfer of Technology to China: A Scandinavian and European Perspective. *European Management Journal, 20*(1), 98–106. doi:10.1016/S0263-2373(01)00118-9

Business Dictionary. (n.d.). Labor. *Business Dictionary.* Retrieved from: http://www.businessdictionary.com/definition/labor.html

Busse, M., Erdogan, C. M., & Mühlen, H. (2016). China's Impact on Africa: The Role of Trade, FDI and Aid. *Kyklos, 69*(2), 228–262. doi:10.1111/kykl.12110

Cai, K. G. (2018). The One Belt One Road and the Asian Infrastructure Investment Bank: Beijing's new strategy of geoeconomics and geopolitics. *Journal of Contemporary China, 27*(114), 831–847. doi:10.1080/10670564.2018.1488101

Cai, P. (2016). China's Responses to Mega-Regional FTAs: A Chinese Perspective. *Asian Survey, 56*(6), 1123–1144. doi:10.1525/as.2016.56.6.1123

Cai, X., Che, X., Zhu, B., Zhao, J., & Xie, R. (2018). Will Developing Countries Become Pollution Havens for Developed Countries? An Empirical Investigation in the Belt and Road. *Journal of Cleaner Production, 198*, 624–632. doi:10.1016/j.jclepro.2018.06.291

Callahan, W. A. (2016). China's "Asia Dream" The Belt Road Initiative and the new regional order. *Asian Journal of Comparative Politics, 1*(3), 226–243. doi:10.1177/2057891116647806

Campbell, B. A., Coff, R., & Kryscynski, D. (2012). Rethinking Sustained Competitive Advantage from Human Capital. *Academy of Management Review, 37*(3), 376–395. doi:10.5465/amr.2010.0276

Capponi, A., Fiandrino, C., Kliazovich, D., Bouvry, P., & Giordano, S. (2017). A cost-effective distributed framework for data collection in cloud-based mobile crowd sensing architectures. *IEEE Transactions on Sustainable Computing, 2*(1), 3–16. doi:10.1109/TSUSC.2017.2666043

Cardei, M., Wu, J., Lu, M., & Pervaiz, M. O. (2005, August). Maximum network lifetime in wireless sensor networks with adjustable sensing ranges. In *Wireless and Mobile Computing, Networking and Communications, 2005. (WiMob'2005), IEEE International Conference on* (Vol. 3, pp. 438-445). IEEE. 10.1109/WIMOB.2005.1512935

Castillo-Vergara, M., Alvarez-Marin, A., & Placencio-Hidalgo, D. (2018). A Bibliometric Analysis of Creativity in the Field of Business Economics. *Journal of Business Research*, *85*, 1–9. doi:10.1016/j.jbusres.2017.12.011

Catalano, M. T., Leise, T. L., & Pfaff, T. J. (2009). Measuring Resource Inequality: The Gini Coefficient. *Numeracy*, *2*(2), 1–22. doi:10.5038/1936-4660.2.2.4

Centenaro, M., Vangelista, L., Zanella, A., & Zorzi, M. (2016). Long-range communications in unlicensed bands: The rising stars in the IoT and smart city scenarios. *IEEE Wireless Communications*, *23*(5), 60–67. doi:10.1109/MWC.2016.7721743

Center for Economic Policy and Strategic Studies. (2018). *Report on China*. Retrieved from http://tesam.org.tr/cin-raporu/

Chaisse, J., & Matsushita, M. (2018). China's 'Belt And Road' Initiative: Mapping the World Trade Normative and Strategic implications. *Journal of World Trade*, *52*(1), 163–186.

Chaisse, J., & Matsushita, M. (2018). China's Belt And Road Initiative: Mapping the World Trade Normative and Strategic Implications. *Journal of World Trade*, *52*(1).

Chand, M., & Tung, R. L. (2014). The Aging of the World's Population and Its Effects on Global Business. *The Academy of Management Perspectives*, *28*(4), 409–429. doi:10.5465/amp.2012.0070

Chand, S., & Kumar, B. (2016). Maximising network lifetime for target coverage problem in wireless sensor networks. *IET Wireless Sensor Systems*, *6*(6), 192–197. doi:10.1049/iet-wss.2015.0094

Chaney, T. (2014). The Network Structure of International Trade. *The American Economic Review*, *104*(11), 3600–3634. doi:10.1257/aer.104.11.3600

Chang-Liao, N. (2016). China's New Foreign Policy under Xi Jinping. *Asian Security*, *12*(2), 82–91. doi:10.1080/14799855.2016.1183195

Chang, S.-C. (2014). The Determinants and Motivations of China's Outward Foreign Direct Investment: A Spatial Gravity Model Approach. *Global Economic Review*, *43*(3), 244–268. doi:10.1080/1226508X.2014.930670

Chang, T. C., Lin, C. H., Lin, K. C. J., & Chen, W. T. (2018). Traffic-Aware Sensor Grouping for IEEE 802.11 ah Networks: Regression Based Analysis and Design. *IEEE Transactions on Mobile Computing*.

Chan, L.-H. (2017). Soft Balancing against the US 'Pivot to Asia': China's Geostrategic Rationale for Establishing the Asian Infrastructure Investment Bank. *Australian Journal of International Affairs*, *71*(6), 568–590. doi:10.1080/10357718.2017.1357679

Chan, Y. (2018). Cultural Heritage on China's 21st-century Maritime Silk Road. *China Report (New Delhi, India)*, *54*(2), 159–174. doi:10.1177/0009445518761078

Chatterji, A., & Patro, A. (2014). Dynamic Capabilities and Managing Human Capital. *The Academy of Management Perspectives*, *28*(4), 395–408. doi:10.5465/amp.2013.0111

Chaudhuri, D. (2016). A Survey of the Economic Situation in Xinjiang and its Role in the Twenty-first Century. *China Report (New Delhi, India)*, *41*(1), 1–28. doi:10.1177/000944550504100101

Chaziza, M. (2018). The Chinese Maritime Silk Road Initiative. *Mediterranean Quarterly*, *29*(2), 54–69. doi:10.1215/10474552-6898099

Cheang, C. F., Un, K. F., Yu, W. H., Mak, P. I., & Martins, R. P. (2015). A combinatorial impairment-compensation digital predistorter for a sub-GHz IEEE 802.11 af-WLAN CMOS transmitter covering a 10x-wide RF bandwidth. *IEEE Transactions on Circuits and Systems. I, Regular Papers*, *62*(4), 1025–1032. doi:10.1109/TCSI.2015.2390561

Chen, B., & Fan, Y. (2012). Learning analytics: Perspectives from mainland China. *Include Us All! Directions for Adoption of Learning Analytics in the Global South*, 36.

Chen, J. (2011, December). The emergence of China in the Middle East. In *Strategic Forum* (No. 271, p. 1). National Defense University.

Chen, L. (2016). *Acceleration in Interconnectivity Construction in Southwest China Boosts the Development of the "Belt and Road"*. Academic Press. doi:10.1007/978-981-10-0167-3_5

Chen, W., Liu, Z., Wang, T., & Jung, W. S. (2018). The structure and evolution of trade relations between countries along the Belt and Road. *Journal of Geographical Sciences*, 1233–1248.

Chen, E. I. (2014). U.S.-China Trade Relations and Economic Distrust. *Chinese Economy*, *47*(3), 57–69. doi:10.2753/CES1097-1475470304

Cheng, L. K. (2016). Three Questions on China's "Belt and Road Initiative". *China Economic Review*, *40*, 309–313. doi:10.1016/j.chieco.2016.07.008

Chen, Q., Geng, N., & Zhu, K. (2018). Review and Bibliometric Analysis of Chinese Agricultural Economics Research: 2006-2015. *China Agricultural Economic Review*, *10*(1), 152–172. doi:10.1108/CAER-07-2017-0141

Chesbrough, H. W. (2003). *Open Innovation: The New Imperative for Creating and Profiting from Technology*. Cambridge, MA: Harvard Business School Press.

China, P. R. (2016). Appendix: Vision and Proposed Actions Outlined on Jointly Building Silk Road Economic Belt and the 21st-Century Maritime Silk Road. In L. Ji, F. Peng, & D. Jiliang (Eds.), *A Guide to the Belt and Road Initiative* (pp. 369–387). Gansu, China: Gansu Culture Press.

Chin, G. T. (2016). Asian Infrastructure Investment Bank: Governance Innovation and Prospects. *Global Governance*, *22*(1), 11–26. doi:10.1163/19426720-02201002

Chow, E. K. (2018, January 8). China's War on Poverty Could Hurt the Poor Most. *Foreign Policy*. Retrieved on September 17, 2018, from: https://foreignpolicy.com/2018/01/08/chinas-war-on-poverty-could-hurt-the-poor-most/

Chow, W. H., Wu, C. K., Tsang, K. F., Li, B. Y. S., & Chui, K. T. (2014, October). Wrist pulse signal classification for inflammation of appendix, pancreas, and duodenum. In *Industrial Electronics Society, IECON 2014-40th Annual Conference of the IEEE* (pp. 2479-2483). IEEE. 10.1109/IECON.2014.7048853

Chraim, F., Erol, Y. B., & Pister, K. (2016). Wireless gas leak detection and localization. *IEEE Transactions on Industrial Informatics*, *12*(2), 768–779. doi:10.1109/TII.2015.2397879

Christiansen, B., & Kasarci, F. (2016). *Corporate Espionage, Geopolitics, and Diplomacy Issues in International Business*. Hershey, PA: IGI Global.

Chui, K. T., Tsang, K. F., Chi, H. R., Wu, C. K., & Ling, B. W. K. (2015, July). Electrocardiogram based classifier for driver drowsiness detection. In *Industrial Informatics (INDIN), 2015 IEEE 13th International Conference on* (pp. 600-603). IEEE. 10.1109/INDIN.2015.7281802

Chui, K. T., Alhalabi, W., Pang, S. S. H., Pablos, P. O. D., Liu, R. W., & Zhao, M. (2017). Disease Diagnosis in Smart Healthcare: Innovation, Technologies and Applications. *Sustainability*, *9*(12), 2309. doi:10.3390u9122309

Chui, K. T., Tsang, K. F., Chi, H. R., Ling, B. W. K., & Wu, C. K. (2016). An accurate ECG-based transportation safety drowsiness detection scheme. *IEEE Transactions on Industrial Informatics*, *12*(4), 1438–1452. doi:10.1109/TII.2016.2573259

Chui, K. T., Tsang, K. F., Wu, C. K., Hung, F. H., Chi, H. R., Chung, H. S. H., ... Ko, K. T. (2015). Cardiovascular diseases identification using electrocardiogram health identifier based on multiple criteria decision making. *Expert Systems with Applications*, *42*(13), 5684–5695. doi:10.1016/j.eswa.2015.01.059

Chung, C.-P., & Voon, T. J. (2017). China's Maritime Silk Road Initiative:Political-Economic Calculations of Southeast Asian States. *Asian Survey*, *57*(3), 416–449.

CIA Factbook. (2018). *China*. Retrieved on August 31, 2018, from: https://www.cia.gov/library/publications/the-world-factbook/geos/ch.html

Cinar, E. M., Johnson, J., & Geusz, K. (2016). Estimating Chinese Trade Relationships with the Silk Road Countries. *China & World Economy*, *24*, 85–103.

Cintra, R. F., Cassol, A., Ribeiro, I., & de Carvalho, A. O. (2018). Corruption and Emerging Markets: Systematic Review of the Most Cited. *Research in International Business and Finance*, *45*, 607–619. doi:10.1016/j.ribaf.2017.07.177

Clarke, M. (2018). The Belt and Road Initiative: Exploring Beijing's Motivations and Challenges for its New Silk Road. *Strategic Analysis*, *42*(2), 84–102. doi:10.1080/09700161.2018.1439326

Cooper, R. N. (2008, Summer). Global Imbalances: Globalization, Demography, and Sustainability. *The Journal of Economic Perspectives*, *22*(3), 93–112. doi:10.1257/jep.22.3.93

Cui, L., Zhang, M., Wu, K.-J., & Tseng, M.-L. (2018). Constructing a Hierarchical Agribusiness Framework in Chinese Belt and Road Initiatives under Uncertainty. *Sustainability*, *10*(251), 1–17. doi:10.3390u10010251 PMID:30607262

Currell, M. J., & Han, D. (2016). The Global Drain: Why China's Water Pollution Problems Should Matter to the Rest of the World. *Environment*, *59*(1), 16–29. doi:10.1080/00139157.2017.1252605

Dabashi, H. (2018, December 22). Muslim cleansing: A global pandemic? *Al-Arabiya English*.

Dadwal, S. R., & Purushothaman, C. (2017). CPEC in Pakistan's Quest for Energy Security. *Strategic Analysis*, *41*(5), 515–524. doi:10.1080/09700161.2017.1343270

Dahri, M. H., Jamaluddin, M. H., Abbasi, M. I., & Kamarudin, M. R. (2017). A review of wideband reflectarray antennas for 5G communication systems. *IEEE Access: Practical Innovations, Open Solutions*, *5*, 17803–17815. doi:10.1109/ACCESS.2017.2747844

Dahri, M. H., Jamaluddin, M. H., Khalily, M., Abbasi, M. I., Selvaraju, R., & Kamarudin, M. R. (2018). Polarization Diversity and Adaptive Beamsteering for 5G Reflectarrays: A Review. *IEEE Access: Practical Innovations, Open Solutions*, *6*, 19451–19464. doi:10.1109/ACCESS.2018.2821358

Dai, C. (2010). Corruption and Anti-Corruption in China: Challenges and Countermeasures. *Journal of International Business Ethics*, *3*(2), 58–70.

Dai, Y., Wu, J., & Du, X. (2018). *Hierarchical and Hybrid: Mobility-compatible Database-assisted Framework For Dynamic Spectrum Access. IEEE Transactions on Network Science and Engineering*.

Daksueva, O., & Yilmaz, S. (2018). The AIIB and China-ASEAN Relations: Shaping a New North-South Paradigm. *China Quarterly of International Strategic Studies*, *04*(01), 95–121. doi:10.1142/S2377740018500021

De Bao, X. (2016). One Belt, One Road: China's reconstruction for global communication and international discourse power. *International Institute for Asian Studies, Summer*. Retrieved from http://iias.asia/the-newsletter/article/one-belt-one-road-chinas-reconstruction-global-communication-international

De Benedictis, L. & Tajoli, L. (2011). The World Trade Network. *The World Economy*, *34*(8), 1417–1454.

De Vaal, A., & Ebben, W. (2011). Institutions and the Relation Between Corruption and Economic Growth. *Review of Development Economics*, *15*(1), 108–123. doi:10.1111/j.1467-9361.2010.00596.x

Dellios, R. (2017). Silk Roads of the Twenty-first Century: The Cultural Dimension. *Asia & the Pacific Policy Studies*, *4*(2), 225–236. doi:10.1002/app5.172

Deng, D. J., Lin, Y. P., Yang, X., Zhu, J., Li, Y. B., Luo, J., & Chen, K. C. (2017). Ieee 802.11 ax: Highly efficient wlans for intelligent information infrastructure. *IEEE Communications Magazine*, *55*(12), 52–59. doi:10.1109/MCOM.2017.1700285

Deng, X., Huang, J., Rozelle, S., Zhang, J., & Li, Z. (2015). Impact of Urbanization on Cultivated Land Changes in China. *Land Use Policy*, *45*, 1–7. doi:10.1016/j.landusepol.2015.01.007

Ding, M. (2018). Security Matters in Marriage: Uyghurs' Perceptions of Security in Xinjiang, China. *Central Asian Survey*, *37*(1), 85–99. doi:10.1080/02634937.2017.1338247

Ding, S., He, X., & Wang, J. (2017). Multiobjective Optimization Model for Service Node Selection Based on a Tradeoff Between Quality of Service and Resource Consumption in Mobile Crowd Sensing. *IEEE Internet of Things Journal*, *4*(1), 258–268.

Diop, S. H. A., & Veeck, G. (2012). Chinese Engagement with Africa: The Case of Madagascar. *Eurasian Geography and Economics*, *53*(3), 400–418. doi:10.2747/1539-7216.53.3.400

Doner, R. F., & Schneider, B. R. (2016). The Middle-Income Trap: More Politics than Economics. *World Politics*, *68*(4), 608–644. doi:10.1017/S0043887116000095

Donnelly-Kehoe, P. A., Pascariello, G. O., & Gómez, J. C. (2018). Looking for Alzheimer's Disease morphometric signatures using machine learning techniques. *Journal of Neuroscience Methods*, *302*, 24–34. doi:10.1016/j.jneumeth.2017.11.013 PMID:29174020

Drucker, P. (2002). *Management Challenges for the 21st Century*. New York: Butterworth-Heinemann.

Duan, F., Jib, Q., Liu, B.-Y., & Fan, Y. (2018). Energy Investment Risk Assessment for Nations along China's Belt & Road Initiative. *Journal of Cleaner Production*, *170*, 535–547. doi:10.1016/j.jclepro.2017.09.152

Du, J., & Zhang, Y. (2018). Does One Belt One Road Initiative promote Chinese overseas direct investment? *China Economic Review*, *47*, 189–205. doi:10.1016/j.chieco.2017.05.010

Du, M. M. (2016). China's "One Belt, One Road" Initiative: Context, Focus, Institutions, and Implications. *The Chinese Journal of Global Governance*, *2*(1), 30–43. doi:10.1163/23525207-12340014

Economics Help. (2012). Factors that determine international competitiveness. *Economics Help*. Retrieved from: https://econ.economicshelp.org/2007/06/what-determines-international.html

Eichengreen, B. (2015). Secular Stagnation: The Long View. *The American Economic Review*, *105*(5), 66–70. doi:10.1257/aer.p20151104

Elmagherbi, F. I. (2010). A case study of China relations with the Arab world. *2010 2nd IEEE International Conference on Information and Financial Engineering*, 646–650. doi:10.1109/ICIFE.2010.5609442

Eno, M. A. (2014). China-Africa Relations: How Tight are the "Strings" Attached? *The International Journal of Humanities & Social Studies*, 196-203.

Er, L. P. (2016). China, the United States, Alliances, and War: Avoiding the Thucydides Trap? *Asian Affairs: An American Review*, *43*(2), 36–46. doi:10.1080/00927678.2016.1150765

Estrada, G., Han, X., Park, D., & Tian, S. (2018). Asia's Middle-Income Challenge: An Overview. *Emerging Markets Finance & Trade*, *54*(6), 1208–1224. doi:10.1080/1540496X.2017.1421939

Ethridge, D. (2004). *Research Methodology in Applied Economics*. Iowa, USA: Blackwell Publishing.

Etzioni, A. (2016). The Asian Infrastructure Investment Bank: A Case Study of Multifaceted Containment. *Asian Perspective*, *40*(2), 173–196. doi:10.1353/apr.2016.0008

Fagiolo, G., Reyes, J., & Schiavo, S. (2007). *International trade and financial integration: a weighted network analysis. Documents de Travail de l'OFCE. 2007-11*. Observatoire Français des Conjonctures Economiques.

Fair, C. C. (2017, July 3). Argument: Pakistan can't afford China's friendship. *Foreign Policy*. Retrieved from https://foreignpolicy.com/2017/07/03/pakistan-cant-afford-chinas-friendship/

Fajkus, M., Nedoma, J., Martinek, R., Vasinek, V., Nazeran, H., & Siska, P. (2017). A non-invasive multichannel hybrid fiber-optic sensor system for vital sign monitoring. *Sensors (Basel)*, *17*(1), 111. doi:10.339017010111 PMID:28075341

Fan, Z., Zhang, R., Liu, X., & Pan, L. (2016). China's Outward FDI Efficiency Along the Belt and Road: An Application of Stochastic Frontier Gravity Model. *China Agricultural Economic Review*, *8*(3), 455–479. doi:10.1108/CAER-11-2015-0158

Farrel, D. (2006). China's Financial Need an Overhaul. *Business Week Online*.

Feng, D. H., & Liang, H. (2018). Understanding the issues surrounding the Belt and Road Initiative (BRI). *China and the World: Ancient and Modern Silk Road, 1*(03).

Feng, G.-F., Sui, B., Dong, M.-Y., Jiang, C., & Chang, C.-P. (2017). Border is Better than Distance? Contagious Corruption in One Belt One Road Economies. *Quality & Quantity*, *52*(4), 1909–1928. doi:10.100711135-017-0579-3

Ferdinand, P. (2016). Westward ho-the China Dream and 'One Belt, One Road': Chinese Foreign Policy Under Xi Jinping. *International Affairs*, *92*(4), 941–957. doi:10.1111/1468-2346.12660

Ferguson, R., & Buckingham Sham, S. (2012). Social learning analytics: five approaches. *2nd International Conference on Learning Analytics & Knowledge*, 23–33.

Fishman, T. C. (2006). *Çin Inc*. İstanbul: Klan Publication.

Fleary, S. A., Joseph, P., & Pappagianopoulos, J. E. (2018). Adolescent Health Literacy and Health Behaviors: A Systematic Review. *Journal of Adolescence*, *62*, 116–127. doi:10.1016/j.adolescence.2017.11.010 PMID:29179126

Foreign Economic Relations Board of Turkey. (2003). *China Economy and Turkey Relations*. İstanbul: Author.

Foreign Economic Relations Board of Turkey. (2006). *China.* Retrieved from ww.deik.org.tr/bultenler/20061 128 1854 ICin_kasim2006.pdf

Fravel, M. T. (2011). China's Strategy in the South China Sea. *Contemporary Southeast Asia*, *33*(3), 292–319. doi:10.1355/cs33-3b

Friedman, G. (2009). *The Next 100 Years: A Forecast for the 21st Century*. New York: Anchor.

Fukase, E., & Martin, W. (2016). Who Will Feed China in the 21st Century?Income Growth and Food Demand and Supply in China. *Journal of Agricultural Economics*, *67*(1), 3–23. doi:10.1111/1477-9552.12117

Fu, X.-M., Chen, H.-X., & Xue, Z.-K. (2018). Construction of the Belt and RoadTrade Cooperation Network from the Multi-Distances Perspective. *Sustainability*, *10*(5), 1439. doi:10.3390u10051439

Gabusi, G. (2017). "Crossing the River by Feeling the Gold": The Asian Infrastructure Investment Bank and the Financial Support to the Belt and Road Initiative. *China & World Economy*, *25*(5), 23–45. doi:10.1111/cwe.12212

Galal, M. N. (2014). "China-Arab States Cooperation Forum": Achievements, challenges and prospects. *Arab World Studies,* (2).

Garlick, J. (2018). Deconstructing the China–Pakistan Economic Corridor: Pipe Dreams Versus Geopolitical Realities. *Journal of Contemporary China*, *27*(112), 519–533. doi:10.1080/10670564.2018.1433483

Gašević, D., Dawson, S., & Siemens, G. (2014). Let's not forget: Learning analytics are about learning. *TechTrends*, *59*(1), 64–71. doi:10.100711528-014-0822-x

Gates, B., & Hemingway, C. (1999). *Business at the speed of thought*. New York: Warner Books. doi:10.1111/1467-8616.00097

Ghasempour, Y., da Silva, C. R., Cordeiro, C., & Knightly, E. W. (2017). IEEE 802.11 ay: Next-generation 60 GHz communication for 100 Gb/s Wi-Fi. *IEEE Communications Magazine*, *55*(12), 186–192. doi:10.1109/MCOM.2017.1700393

Girault, J. (2018). *China's Silk Road project runs into debt jam*. France-Press.

Global Firepower. (2018). *2018 Military Strength Ranking*. Retrieved on June 2, 2018, from: https://www.globalfirepower.com/countries-listing.asp

Gong, B. (2018). Agricultural Reforms and Production in China: Changes in Provincial Production Function and Productivity in 1978–2015. *Journal of Development Economics*, *132*, 18–31. doi:10.1016/j.jdeveco.2017.12.005

Gourdon, J. (2015). *Trade Policy and Industrial Policy in China: What Motivates Public Authorities to Apply Restrictions on Exports?* CEPII Working Paper.

Gray, K. L. (2017). The Rescaling of the Chinese State and Sino-North Korean Relations: Beyond State-Centrism. *Journal of Contemporary Asia*.

Greenstone, M., & Schwarz, P. (2018, March). *Is China Winning its War on Pollution*? Chicago: Energy Policy Institute at the University of Chicago.

Gu, B. (2017). Chinese Multilateralism in the AIIB. *Journal of International Economic Law*, *20*(1), 137–158. doi:10.1093/jiel/jgx006

Güner, B. (2018). *OBOR Girşimininin Coğrafyası*. Marmara Coğrafya Dergisi. Retrieved from: https://tr.wikipedia.org/wiki/Bir_Kuşak,_Bir_Yol

Hameiri, S., & Jones, L. (2018). China Challenges Global Governance? Chinese International Development Finance and the AIIB. *International Affairs*, *94*(3), 573–593. doi:10.1093/ia/iiy026

Han, E. (2017). Geopolitics, Ethnic Conflicts along the Border, and Chinese Foreign Policy Changes toward Myanmar. *Asian Security*, *13*(1), 59–73. doi:10.1080/14799855.2017.1290988

Han, G., Liu, L., Jiang, J., Shu, L., & Hancke, G. (2017). Analysis of energy-efficient connected target coverage algorithms for industrial wireless sensor networks. *IEEE Transactions on Industrial Informatics*, *13*(1), 135–143. doi:10.1109/TII.2015.2513767

Harris, B. (2018, February 7). *China is an innovation superpower. This is why*. Retrieved on September 2, 2018, from: https://www.weforum.org/agenda/2018/02/these-charts-show-how-china-is-becoming-an-innovation-superpower/

Hayoun, M. (2013, January). Strange bedfellows: China's Middle Eastern inroads. *World Affairs*, 89–96.

Hays Global Skills Index. (2017). *Regional Dynamics of the Global Labour Market: Skills in Demand and Tomorrow's Workforce*. London: Hays PLC.

Herrero, A. G., & Xu, J. (2016). *China's Belt and Road Initiative: Can Europe expect trade gain?* Bruegel working paper series. Issue 5.

Herrero, A. G., & Xu, J. (2017). China's Belt and Road Initiative: Can Europe Expect Trade Gains? *China & World Economy*, *25*(6), 84–99. doi:10.1111/cwe.12222

Hidalgo Martinez, M., & Cartier, C. (2017). City as province in China: The Territorial Urbanization of Chongqing. *Eurasian Geography and Economics*, *58*(2), 201–230. doi:10.1080/15387216.2017.1312474

HKTDC. (n.d.). *The belt and road initiative: Country profiles*. HKTDC. Retrieved from: http://china-trade-research.hktdc.com/business-news/article/The-Belt-and-Road-Initiative/The-Belt-and-Road-Initiative-Country-Profiles/obor/en/1/1X000000/1X0A36I0.htm

Hofman, I. (2016). Politics or Profits along the "Silk Road": What Drives Chinese Farms in Tajikistan and Helps Them Thrive? *Eurasian Geography and Economics*, *57*(3), 457–481. doi:10.1080/15387216.2016.1238313

Holcombe, A.N. (2017, June). *Can China Reduce Entrenched Poverty in Remote Ethnic Minority Regions? Lessons from Successful Poverty Alleviation in Tibetan Areas of China During 1998-2016*. Cambridge, MA: Harvard Kennedy School.

Holslag, J. (2017). How China's New Silk Road threatens European trade. *The International Spectator*, *52*(1), 46–60. doi:10.1080/03932729.2017.1261517

Holtbrügge, D., & Baron, A. (2013). Market Entry Strategies in Emerging Markets: An Institutional Study in the BRIC Countries. *Thunderbird International Business Review*, *55*(3), 237–252. doi:10.1002/tie.21541

Hongyu, Z. Y. (2016). The Hopes and Challenges of China and Central and Eastern Europe Cooperation under the "One Belt and One Road" Framework. *International Business Studies*, 23-30.

How Elli Works. (n.d.). Retrieved from www.elli.org.uk/how-elli-works/

Howard, K. W. F., & Howard, K. K. (2016). The New "Silk Road Economic Belt" as a Threat to the Sustainable Management of Central Asia's Transboundary Water Resources. *Environmental Earth Sciences*, *75*(11), 1–12. doi:10.100712665-016-5752-9

Hsieh, P. (2009). China-United States Trade Negotiations and Disputes: The WTO and Beyond. *Asian Journal of WTO & International Health Law and Policy*, *4*(2), 368–399.

Huang, H., Yin, H., Luo, Y., Zhang, X., Min, G., & Fan, Q. (2016). Three-dimensional geographic routing in wireless mobile ad hoc and sensor networks. *IEEE Network*, *30*(2), 82–90. doi:10.1109/MNET.2016.7437029

Huang, J., & Yang, G. (2017). Understanding Recent Challenges and New Food Policy in China. *Global Food Security*, *12*, 119–126. doi:10.1016/j.gfs.2016.10.002

Huang, S., Fidrmuc, J., & Fidrmuc, J. (2015). Whither China? Reform and Economic Integration among Chinese Regions. *China Economic Review*, *33*, 94–110. doi:10.1016/j.chieco.2014.12.007

Huang, Y. (2016). Understanding China's Belt and RoadInitiative: Motivation, framework and assessment. *China Economic Review*, *40*, 314–321. doi:10.1016/j.chieco.2016.07.007

Hughes, N. C. (2005). A Trade War with China? *Foreign Affairs*, *84*(4), 94–106. doi:10.2307/20034423

Hung-Gay Fung. (2006). *The Chinese Economy* (Vol. 39). ME Sharpe.

Hwang, K. (1987). Face and Favor: The Chinese Power Game. *American Journal of Sociology*, *92*(4), 944–974. doi:10.1086/228588

Iapadre, P. L., & Tajoli, L. (2014). Emerging countries and trade regionalization. A network analysis. *Journal of Policy Modeling*, *36*, 89–110. doi:10.1016/j.jpolmod.2013.10.010

Ikenberry, G. J. (2008). The rise of China and the future of the West: Can the liberal system survive? *Foreign Affairs*, *87*(1), 23–37.

Innovation Cities Program. (2018). *Innovation Cities Index*. Retrieved on September 25, 2018, from: https://www.innovation-cities.com/innovation-cities-index-2018-global/13935/

International Institute of Strategic Studies (IISS). (2018). *The Military Balance 2018*. Retrieved on September 1, 2018, from: https://www.iiss.org/publications/the-military-balance/the-military-balance-2018

International Maritime Organization. (2018). *IMO Profile*. Retrieved on September 17, 2018, from: https://business.un.org/en/entities/13

International Monetary Fund (IMF). (2018). *IMF DataMapper.* Retrieved on September 10, 2018, from: https://www.imf.org/external/datamapper/NGDP_RPCH@WEO/OEMDC/ADVEC/WEOWORLD

Investopedia. (2018). Infrastructure. *Investopedia.* Retrieved from: https://www.investopedia.com/terms/i/infrastructure.asp

Irshad, M. S., Xin, Q., Shahriar, S., & Arshad, H. (2018). A Panel Data Analysis of China's Trade Pattern with OPEC Members: Gravity Model Approach. *Asian Economic and Financial Review*, *8*(1), 103–116. doi:10.18488/journal.aefr.2018.81.103.116

Ito, T. (2017). A New Financial Order in Asia: Will a RMB Bloc Emerge? *Journal of International Money and Finance*, *74*, 232–257. doi:10.1016/j.jimonfin.2017.02.019

Jackson, S. L., & Dear, D. (2016). Resource Extraction and National Anxieties: China's Economic Presence in Mongolia. *Eurasian Geography and Economics*, *57*(3), 343–373. doi:10.1080/15387216.2016.1243065

Jacob, J. T. (2017). China's Belt and Road Initiative: Perspectives from India. *China & World Economy*, *25*(5), 78–100. doi:10.1111/cwe.12215

Jaffe, K. (2014). The Relevance of Science in Development: Scientific Development Favors Economic Prosperity, But Not Necessarily through its Effect on Technological Knowledge in Middle Income Countries. In B. Christiansen & M. Basilgan (Eds.), *Economic Behavior, Game Theory, and Technology in Emerging Markets* (pp. 1–17). Hershey, PA: IGI Global. doi:10.4018/978-1-4666-4745-9.ch001

James, H. (2017, June). *Deglobalization as a Global Challenge*. Ontario, Canada: Center for International Governance Innovation.

James, H., & Watt, S. A. (1995). *Research Methods for Communication Science*. Boston: Allyn and Bacon.

Jarrett, K., & Wendholt, A. (2010). Transferring Technology to Transform China--Is It Worth It? *The China Business Review*, *37*(2), 20–24. Retrieved from https://acg.idm.oclc.org/login?url=http://search.ebscohost.com/login.aspx?direct=true&db=bth&AN=48666412&scope=site

Jia, W. (2017). Now, globalization with Chinese characteristics. *YaleGlobal Online*. Retrieved from http://yaleglobal.yale.edu/content/now-globalization-chinese-characteristics

Jiang, B., Li, J., & Gong, C. (2018). Maritime Shipping and Export Trade on "Maritime Silk Road". *The Asian Journal of Shipping and Logistics*, *34*(2), 83–90. doi:10.1016/j.ajsl.2018.06.005

Jianwei, W. (2017). The Discourse on China's Rise. *China. International Journal (Toronto, Ont.)*, *15*(1), 24–40.

Jiao, K., Xu, M., & Liu, M. (2018). Health status and air pollution-related socioeconomic concerns in urban China. *International Journal for Equity in Health*, *17*(18), 1–11. PMID:29402280

Jing, F. Z. (2016). One Belt and One Road" Cooperation Motivation and Expectation and Prospects Between China and Europe. *Modern International Relations*, 93–99.

Jinping, X. (2017). *The Governance of China* (Vol. 2). Beijing, China: Foreign Language Press.

Jin, X., Li, D. D., & Wu, S. (2016). How will China shape the world economy? *China Economic Review*, *40*, 272–280. doi:10.1016/j.chieco.2016.07.006

Johansson, A. C., & Zhang, X. (2014). Inequality, Growth and the Middle-Income Trap in China. *China Economic Review*, *31*, 365–366. doi:10.1016/j.chieco.2014.11.007

Jones, D. A., & Liu, H. (2017). Management of Chinese Foreign Direct Investment: "One Belt, One Road" across Eurasia to Africa and Europe amidst maritime tensions in the South China Sea region. *International Relations and Diplomacy*, *5*(8), 486–500.

Junxuan, W. (2016). *Geographically Watching the World.* Academic Press.

Kali, R., & Reyes, J. (2007). The architecture of globalization: A network approach to international economic integration. *Journal of International Business Studies*, *38*(4), 595–620. doi:10.1057/palgrave.jibs.8400286

Kamel, M. S. (2018). China's Belt and Road Initiative: Implications for the Middle East. *Cambridge Review of International Affairs*, *7571*, 1–19.

Karim, M. A. (2015). China's Proposed Maritime Silk Road: Challenges and Opportunities with Special Reference to the Bay of Bengal Region. *Pacific Focus*, *30*(3), 297–319. doi:10.1111/pafo.12059

Kaya, T. Ö. (2017). Sino-Indian strategic rivalry in the Indian ocean region. *Insan ve Toplum*, *7*(2), 155.

Keupp, M. M., Beckenbauer, A., & Gassmann, O. (2010). Enforcing Intellectual Property Rights in Weak Appropriability Regimes. *Management International Review*, *50*(1), 109–130. doi:10.100711575-009-0020-9

Khan, F. (2015). *Islamic Banking in Pakistan: Shariah-compliant Finance and the quest to make Pakistan more Islamic*. New York: Routledge. doi:10.4324/9781315670249

Khan, K. S., Kunz, R., Kleijnen, J., & Antes, G. (2003). Five Steps to Conducting a Systematic Review. *Journal of the Royal Society of Medicine*, *96*, 118–121.

Khan, M. K., Sandano, I. A., Pratt, C. B., & Farid, T. (2018). China's Belt and Road Initiative: A global model for an evolving approach to sustainable regional development. *Sustainability*, *10*(11), 4234. doi:10.3390u10114234

Khurana, G. S. (2008). China's 'String of Pearls' in the Indian Ocean and Its Security Implications. *Strategic Analysis*, *32*(1), 1–39. doi:10.1080/09700160801886314

Kiani, K. (2019, January 14). Govt puts major CPEC power project on hold. *Dawn*. Retrieved form https://www.dawn.com/news/1457449

Kim, D. H., Park, J. B., Shin, J. H., & Kim, J. D. (2017, January). Design and implementation of object tracking system based on LoRa. In *Information Networking (ICOIN), 2017 International Conference on* (pp. 463-467). IEEE. 10.1109/ICOIN.2017.7899535

Kim, Y. H., Han, Y. H., Mun, C. M., Park, C. Y., & Park, D. S. (2010, August). Lifetime maximization considering connectivity and overlapped targets in wireless sensor networks. In *Information Technology Convergence and Services (ITCS), 2010 2nd International Conference on* (pp. 1-6). IEEE. 10.1109/ITCS.2010.5581290

Kim, K. (2017). Xinjiang and the Modern Chinese State. *Central Asian Survey*, *37*(1), 176–178. doi:10.1080/02634937.2017.1366468

Kliman, D., & Grace, A. (2018, June 18). China smells opportunity in the Middle East's crisis. *Foreign Policy*. Retrieved from https://foreignpolicy.com/2018/06/14/china-smells-opportunity-in-the-middle-easts-crisis/

Kobrin, S. J. (2017). Bricks and Mortar in a Borderless World: Globalization, the Backlash, and the Multinational Enterprise. *Global Strategy Journal*, *7*(2), 159–171. doi:10.1002/gsj.1158

Kondapalli, S. (2018). The Maritime Silk Road and China–Maldives Relations. In J.-M. F. Blanchard (Ed.), *China's Maritime Silk Road Initiative and South Asia* (pp. 173–201). Palgrave. doi:10.1007/978-981-10-5239-2_7

Kong, L. (2015). The Belt and Road Initiative and China's Foreign Policy Toward Its Territorial and Boundary Disputes. *China Quarterly of International Strategic Studies*, *01*(02), 325–345. doi:10.1142/S2377740015500165

Krugman, P. (2009). *The Return of Depression Economics and the Crisis of 2008*. New York: W.W. Norton & Company.

Küçük, E. (2017). *China is losing the 'labor' advantage*. Retrieved from https://www.dunya.com/dunya/cin-iscilik-avantajini-kaptiriyor-haberi-351690

Kurowska-Pysz, J., & Szczepa ́nska-Woszczyna, K. (2017). The Analysis of the Determinants of Sustainable Cross-Border Cooperation and Recommendations on Its Harmonization. *Sustainability*, *9*(12), 2226. doi:10.3390u9122226

Kuznets, S. (1955). Economic Growth and Income Inequality. *The American Economic Review*, *45*(1), 1–28.

Kwon, E. (2015). China's Monetary Power: Internationalization of the Renminbi. *Pacific Focus*, *30*(1), 78–102. doi:10.1111/pafo.12038

Laborde, A. (2016). Chinese Economic Development Policies as an Example for Mexico: The One-Belt-One-Road Program. *Fudan Journal of the Humanities and Social Sciences*, *10*(2), 127–144. doi:10.100740647-016-0157-4

Lai, T. L., Tang, J., & Yin, H. (2018). Spatial Economics in the era of One Belt One Road and counter-globalization. *Modern Economy*, *9*(1), 61–66. doi:10.4236/me.2018.91004

Landry, S. P., Wai-Yee Canri, C., & Renner, C. J. (1999). Doing Business with China: How to Steer Clear of Dangerous Legal Pitfalls. *Journal of Corporate Accounting & Finance (Wiley)*, *10*(4), 63–71. doi:10.1002/(SICI)1097-0053(199922)10:4<63::AID-JCAF6>3.0.CO;2-#

Lechner, F. J., & Boli, J. (2015). *The Globalization Reader* (5th ed.). New York: Wiley-Blackwell.

Lee, K., Chae, C. B., Sung, T. K., & Kang, J. (2012). Cognitive beamforming based smart metering for coexistence with wireless local area networks. *Journal of Communications and Networks (Seoul)*, *14*(6), 619–628. doi:10.1109/JCN.2012.00028

Lee, P. T.-W., Hu, Z.-H., Lee, S.-J., Choi, K.-S., & Shin, S.-H. (2018). Research Trends and Agenda on the Belt and Road (B&R) Initiative with a Focus on Maritime Transport. *Maritime Policy & Management*, *45*(3), 282–300. doi:10.1080/03088839.2017.1400189

Lee, S. (2017). An Institutional Analysis of Xi Jinping's Centralization of Power. *Journal of Contemporary China*, *26*(105), 325–336. doi:10.1080/10670564.2016.1245505

Lee, S.-O., Wainwright, J., & Glassman, J. (2018). Geopolitical Economy and the Production of Territory: The Case of US-China Geopolitical-Economic Competition in Asia. *Environment & Planning A*, *50*(2), 416–436. doi:10.1177/0308518X17701727

Leeuwen, A. V., Janssen, J., Erkens, G., & Brekelmans, M. (2015). Teacher regulation of cognitive activities during student collaboration: Effects of learning analytics. *Computers & Education*, *90*, 80–94. doi:10.1016/j.compedu.2015.09.006

Lehmacher, W. (2016, November 22). Why China could lead the next phase of globalization. *World Economic Forum*. Retrieved from https://www.weforum.org/agenda/2016/11/china-lead-globalization-after-united-states

Lehr, D. (2018, July 21). How China is winning over the Middle East. *The Diplomat*. Retrieved from https://thediplomat.com/2018/07/how-china-is-winning-over-the-middle-east/

Lein, D.-H. D. (1990). Corruption and allocation efficiency. *Journal of Development Economics*, *33*(1), 153–164. doi:10.1016/0304-3878(90)90013-2

Lemoine, F., & Unal, D. (2017). China s Foreign Trade: A "New Normal". *China & World Economy*, *25*(2), 1–21. doi:10.1111/cwe.12191

Li, F. (2018). The role of Islam in the development of the Belt and Road Initiative. *Asian Journal of Middle Eastern and Islamic Studies*, *12*(1), 35–45. doi:10.1080/25765949.2018.1439617

Lily, K. (n.d.). *What is China's Belt and Road Initiative?* Retrieved from: https://www.theguardian.com/cities/ng-interactive/2018/jul/30/what-china-belt-road-initiative-silk-road-explainer

Limin, H. (2017). "One Belt and One Road" Initiative: A Geopolitical and Economic Analysis. *Journal of Xi 'an University of Finance and Economics*, 85-89.

Lin, C., Han, D., Deng, J., & Wu, G. (2017). P^{2}S: A Primary and Passer-By Scheduling Algorithm for On-Demand Charging Architecture in Wireless Rechargeable Sensor Networks. *IEEE Transactions on Vehicular Technology*, *66*(9), 8047–8058. doi:10.1109/TVT.2017.2683493

Lin, C., Zhou, J., Guo, C., Song, H., Wu, G., & Obaidat, M. S. (2018). TSCA: A temporal-spatial real-time charging scheduling algorithm for on-demand architecture in wireless rechargeable sensor networks. *IEEE Transactions on Mobile Computing*, *17*(1), 211–224. doi:10.1109/TMC.2017.2703094

Li, P., Qian, H., Howard, K. W. F., & Wu, J. (2015). Building a New and Sustainable "Silk Road Economic Belt". *Environmental Earth Sciences*, *74*(10), 7267–7270. doi:10.100712665-015-4739-2

Liu, M. (2018). The New Chinese Foreign Investment Law and Its Implication on Foreign Investors. *Northwestern Journal of International Law & Business, 38*(2), 285–306. Retrieved from https://acg.idm.oclc.org/login?url=http://search.ebscohost.com/login.aspx?direct=true&db=bth&AN=128778956&scope=site

Liu, H. Y., Tang, Y. K., Chen, X. L., & Poznanska, J. (2017). The Determinants of Chinese Outward FDI in Countries Along "One Belt, One Road". *Emerging Markets Finance & Trade*, *53*(6), 1374–1387. doi:10.1080/1540496X.2017.1295843

Liu, H., Fang, C., Miao, Y., Ma, H., Zhang, Q., & Zhou, Q. (2018). Spatio-Temporal Evolution of Population and Urbanization in the Countries along the Belt and Road 1950–2050. *Journal of Geographical Sciences*, *28*(7), 919–936. doi:10.100711442-018-1513-x

Liu, T., & Woo, W. T. (2018). Understanding the U.S.-China Trade War. *China Economic Journal*, *11*(3), 319–340. doi:10.1080/17538963.2018.1516256

Liu, Z., Wang, T., Sonn, J. W., & Chen, W. (2018). The Structure and Evolution of Trade Relations Between Countries along the Belt and Road. *Journal of Geographical Sciences*, *28*(9), 1233–1248. doi:10.100711442-018-1522-9

Li, X., & Zeng, K. (2018). *To Join or Not To Join.* How Chinese Firms View the Belt and Road Initiative.

Li, Y., & Chang, Y. (2015). Infrastructure Investments for Power Trade and Transmission in ASEAN+2: Costs, Benefits, Long-Term Contracts and Prioritized Developments. *Energy Economics*, *51*, 484–492. doi:10.1016/j.eneco.2015.08.008

Li, Y., Su, B., & Liu, Y. (2016). Realizing targeted poverty alleviation in China. *China Agricultural Economic Review*, *8*(3), 443–454. doi:10.1108/CAER-11-2015-0157

Lopes de Andrade, R., & Rêgo, L. C. (2018). The use of nodes attributes in social network analysis with an application to an international trade network. *Physica A*.

Luft, G. (2016, January 26). China's new grand strategy for the Middle East. *Foreign Policy*.

Luo, J., Ji, C., Qiu, C., & Jia, F. (2018). Agri-Food Supply Chain Management: Bibliometric and Content Analyses. *Sustainability*, *10*(1573), 1–22. doi:10.3390u10051573 PMID:30607262

Luo, Y., & Han, B. (2008). Graft and businesses in emerging economies: An ecological perspective. *Journal of World Business*, *44*(3), 225–237. doi:10.1016/j.jwb.2008.08.006

Lynch, M. (2017). *Why Are Learning Analytics So Important?* Retrieved from https://www.thetechedvocate.org/learning-analytics-important/

Lytras, M., & Visvizi, A. (2018). Who uses smart city services and what to make of it: Toward interdisciplinary smart cities research. *Sustainability*, *10*(6), 1998. doi:10.3390u10061998

Macauley, R. (2015, November 23). China wants to build a high-speed rail link to a newly open Iran. *Quartz*. Retrieved from https://qz.com/557009/chinas-next-big-idea-is-a-high-speed-railway-to-iran/

Mackerras, C. (2015). Xinjiang in China's Foreign Relations: Part of a New Silk Road or Central Asian Zone of Conflict? *East Asia*, *32*(1), 25–42. doi:10.100712140-015-9224-8

Maddison, A. (2005). Measuring and Interpreting World Economic Performance, 1500-2001. *Review of Income and Wealth*, *51*(1), 1–35. doi:10.1111/j.1475-4991.2005.00143.x

Maditati, D. R., Munim, Z. H., Schramm, H.-J., & Kummer, S. (2018). A Review of Green Supply Chain Management: From Bibliometric Analysis to a Conceptual Framework and Future Research Directions. *Resources, Conservation and Recycling*, *139*, 150–162. doi:10.1016/j.resconrec.2018.08.004

Madueño, Stefanović, & Popovski. (2016). Reliable and efficient access for alarm-initiated and regular M2M traffic in IEEE 802.11 ah systems. *IEEE Internet of Things Journal*, *3*(5), 673-682.

Mahmoud, K. R., & Montaser, A. M. (2018). Synthesis of multi-polarised upside conical frustum array antenna for 5G mm-Wave base station at 28/38 GHz. *IET Microwaves, Antennas & Propagation*.

Majumdar, M. (2015). The ASEAN Way of Conflict Management in the South China Sea. *Strategic Analysis*, *39*(1), 73–87. doi:10.1080/09700161.2014.980545

Malik, J. M. (2017). Myanmar's Role in China's Maritime Silk Road. *Journal of Contemporary China*. doi:10.1080/10670564.2018.1410969

Malik, M. (2002). Dragon China's on terrorism : Assessing gains tactical and strategic losses after 11 September. *Contemporary Southeast Asia*, *24*(2), 252–293. doi:10.1355/CS24-2D

Maswood, S. J. (2018). *Revisiting Globalization and the Rise of Global Production Networks*. New York: Palgrave Macmillan. doi:10.1007/978-3-319-60294-3

Matsumura, T., Ibuka, K., Ishizu, K., Murakami, H., Kojima, F., & Harada, H. (2017). Prototype of IEEE 802.11 af-Based Baseband IC Enabling Compact Device for Wireless Local Area Network Systems in TV White-Spaces. *IEEE Transactions on Cognitive Communications and Networking*, *3*(3), 450–463. doi:10.1109/TCCN.2017.2750684

Mauro, P. (1995). Corruption and growth. *The Quarterly Journal of Economics*, *110*(3), 681–712. doi:10.2307/2946696

Ma, Y. W., & Chen, J. L. (2018, April). Toward intelligent agriculture service platform with lora-based wireless sensor network. In *2018 IEEE International Conference on Applied System Invention* (pp. 204-207). IEEE. 10.1109/ICASI.2018.8394568

McKinsey & Company. (2017, December). *What can we expect in China in 2018?* Retrieved on September 15, 2018, from: https://www.mckinsey.com/featured-insights/china/what-can-we-expect-in-china-in-2018

McKinsey Global Institute (2015, January). *Global Growth: Can Productivity Save the Day in An Aging World?* New York: McKinsey & Company.

McKinsey Global Institute. (2012, March). *Help wanted: The future of work in advanced economies*. Retrieved on June 1, 2017, from: https://www.mckinsey.com/~/media/McKinsey/Featured%20Insights/Employment%20an d%20Growth/Future%20of%20work%20in%20advanced%20economies/Help_wanted_future_of_work_full_report.ashx

Melikhova, O., & Čížek, J. (2014). Kuznets Inverted U-Curve Hypothesis Examined on Up-to-Date Observations for 145 Countries. *Prague Economic Papers*, *3*(3), 388–410. doi:10.18267/j.pep.490

Michalski, A., & Pan, Z. (2017). *Role Dynamics in a Structured Relationship: The EU-China Strategic Partnership*. Retrieved from https://acg.idm.oclc.org/login?url=http://search.ebscohost.com/login.aspx?direct=true&db=eoh&AN=EP122343928&scope=site

Ming, C. (2018, March 5). China's mammoth Belt and Road Initiative could increase debt risk for 8 countries. *CNBC*. Retrieved from https://www.cnbc.com/2018/03/05/chinas-belt-and-road-initiative-raises-debt-risks-in-8-nations.html

Mingjiang, L. (2015). *China's "One Belt, One Road" Initiative: New round of opening up? RSIS Commentaries*. Nanyang Technological University.

Mishra, R. (2016). Asian Infrastructure Investment Bank: An Assessment. *India Quarterly*, *72*(2), 163–176. doi:10.1177/0974928416643582

Mogato, M., & Petty, M. (2017, April 27). Push for South China Sea code stirs ASEAN suspicions about Beijing's endgame. *Reuters*. Retrieved from https://www.reuters.com/article/us-southchinasea-asean-analysis-idUSKBN17T0A5

Mohrman, S. A., & Lawler, E. E. III. (2012, February). Generating Knowledge that Drives Change. *The Academy of Management Perspectives*, *26*(1), 41–51. doi:10.5465/amp.2011.0141

Molero-Simarro, R. (2017). Inequality in China Revisited. The Effect of Functional Distribution of Income on Urban Top Incomes, the Urban-Rural Gap and the Gini Index, 1978–2015. *China Economic Review*, *42*, 101–117. doi:10.1016/j.chieco.2016.11.006

Morrison, W.M. (2018, February 5). *China's Economic Rise: History, Trends, Challenges, and Implications for the United States*. Washington, DC: Congressional Research Service.

Moussa, B. & Varsakelis, N. C. (2017). International patenting: An application of network analysis. *The Journal of Economic Assymetries.*

Muggah, R., & Tiberghien, Y. (2018, January 30). *5 facts you need to understand the new global order*. Retrieved on August 19, 2018, from: https://www.weforum.org/agenda/2018/01/five-facts-you-need-to-understand-the-new-global-order

Mukherjee, M., Shu, L., Hu, L., Hancke, G. P., & Zhu, C. (2017). Sleep scheduling in industrial wireless sensor networks for toxic gas monitoring. *IEEE Wireless Communications*, *24*(4), 106–112. doi:10.1109/MWC.2017.1600072WC

Musa, I., Park, H., Munkhdalai, L., & Ryu, K. (2018). Global Research on Syndromic Surveillance from 1993 to 2017: Bibliometric Analysis and Visualization. *Sustainability*, *10*(10), 3414. doi:10.3390u10103414

Napoli, C. (2014). China's Economic Rise: Implications for ASEAN Trade Flows. *Southeast Asian Economies*, *31*(3), 345-360. doi:10.1355/ae31-3a

Naughton, B. (2007). *The Chinese Economy: Transitions and Growth.* MIT Press.

Nayyar, D. (2016). BRICS, developing countries and global governance. *Third World Quarterly*, *37*(4), 575–591. doi:10.1080/01436597.2015.1116365

NBSC. (2011). *The 2010 Statistical Bulletin of China's Outward Foreign Direct Investment*. Retrieved from Beijing: http://www.stats.gov.cn/english/

New Age. (2013). *China, the world leader in 2030 with the economy*. Retrieved from http://www.yenicaggazetesi.com.tr/cin-ekonomisi-ile-2030da-dunya-lideri-90237h.htm

Nguyen, T., Pham, T., & Vallee, T. (2016). Economic Integration in ASEAN+3: A Network Analysis. *Journal ofEconomic Integration.*, *31*(2), 275–325. doi:10.11130/jei.2016.31.2.275

Ni, C., Sugimoto, C. R., & Robbin, A. (2017). Examining the Evolution of the Field of Public Administration through a Bibliometric Analysis of Public Administration Review. *Public Administration Review*, *77*(4), 496–509. doi:10.1111/puar.12737

Nie, P., & Sousa-Poza, A. (2017, August). *What Chinese Workers Value: An Analysis of Job Satisfaction, Job Expectations, and Labor Turnover in China*. IZA Institute of Labor Economics, Discussion Paper Series No. 10963, Bonn, Germany.

Nie, W. (2016). Xi Jinping's Foreign Policy Dilemma One Belt, One Road or the South China Sea? *Contemporary Southeast Asia*, *38*(3), 422–444. doi:10.1355/cs38-3c

Njoya, A. N., Thron, C., Barry, J., Abdou, W., Tonye, E., Konje, N. S. L., & Dipanda, A. (2017). Efficient scalable sensor node placement algorithm for fixed target coverage applications of wireless sensor networks. *IET Wireless Sensor Systems*, 7(2), 44–54. doi:10.1049/iet-wss.2016.0076

Nonaka, I., Toyama, R., & Konno, N. (2000). SECI, Ba and leadership: A unified model of dynamic knowledge creation. *Long Range Planning*, *33*(1), 5–34. doi:10.1016/S0024-6301(99)00115-6

Nordin, A. H. M., & Weissmann, M. (2018). Will Trump Make China Great Again? The Belt and Road Initiative and International Order. *International Affairs*, *94*(2), 231–249. doi:10.1093/ia/iix242

Nye, J. S. (2003). *The Paradox of American Power: Why the World's Only Superpower Can't Go It Alone*. Oxford, UK: Oxford University Press. doi:10.1093/0195161106.001.0001

O'Rourke, R. (2018, August 1). *China Naval Modernization: Implications for U.S. Navy Capabilities—Background and Issues for Congress*. Washington, DC: Congressional Research Service.

O'Trakoun, J. (2017). China's Belt and Road Initiative and Regional Perceptions of China. *Business Economics (Cleveland, Ohio)*, *53*(1), 17–24. doi:10.105711369-017-0062-0

Obama, B. (2015, January 20). Remarks by the President in State of the Union Address. *The White House*. Retrieved from https://obamawhitehouse.archives.gov/the-press-office/2015/01/20/remarks-president-state-union-address-January-20-2015

OECD (2015, March). *China in a changing global environment*. Paris: OECD.

OECD. (2016). *OECD Science, Technology, and Innovation Outlook 2016*. Paris: OECD.

Ostrovskii, A. V. (2018). Prospects to interface the silk road economic belt and the Eurasian Economic Union projects. *Herald of the Russian Academy of Sciences*, *87*(6), 480–490. doi:10.1134/S1019331617060041

Otusanya, O. J. (2011). Corruption as an obstacle to development in developing countries: A review of literature. *Journal of Money Laundering Control*, *4*(4), 387–422. doi:10.1108/13685201111173857

Ouya, A., De Aragon, B. M., Bouette, C., Habault, G., Montavont, N., & Papadopoulos, G. Z. (2017, October). An efficient electric vehicle charging architecture based on LoRa communication. In *Smart Grid Communications (SmartGridComm), 2017 IEEE International Conference on* (pp. 381-386). IEEE. 10.1109/SmartGridComm.2017.8340723

Page, J., Dou, E., & Shah, S. (2018, September 27). China's Muslim detention camps spark protests in Islamic world. *The Wall Street Journal.*

Palit, A. (2017). India's Economic and Strategic Perceptions of China's Maritime Silk Road Initiative. *Geopolitics, 22*(2), 292–309. doi:10.1080/14650045.2016.1274305

Pamir, N. (2005). *Çin ve Enerji Güvenliği.* Retrieved from www.asam.org.tr/tr/yuidosyagoster.asp

Pang, S. S. H., Chui, K. T., & Lytras, M. D. (Mar. 2019). Glycemic Monitoring and Prediction with Response Improvement via Psyllium. In *Computational methods and algorithms for medicine and optimized clinical practice*. IGI-Global. doi:10.4018/978-1-5225-8244-1.ch009

Papamitsiou, Z., & Economides, A. A. (2014). Learning analytics and educational data mining in practice: A systematic literature review of empirical evidence. *Journal of Educational Technology & Society, 17*(4). Retrieved from https://www.researchgate.net/publication/267510046_Learning_Analytics_and_Educational_Data_Mining_in_Practice_A_Systematic_Literature_Review_of_Empirical_Evidence

Park, M. (2015). IEEE 802.11 ah: Sub-1-GHz license-exempt operation for the internet of things. *IEEE Communications Magazine, 53*(9), 145–151. doi:10.1109/MCOM.2015.7263359

Patel, D., & Won, M. (2017, June). Experimental Study on Low Power Wide Area Networks (LPWAN) for Mobile Internet of Things. In *Vehicular Technology Conference (VTC Spring), 2017 IEEE 85th* (pp. 1-5). IEEE.

Paul, J. (2016). The Rise of China: What, When, Where, and Why? *The International Trade Journal, 30*(3), 207–222. doi:10.1080/08853908.2016.1155513

Paul, J., & Benito, G. R. G. (2017). A Review of Research on Outward Foreign Direct Investment from Emerging Countries, including China: What Do We Know, How Do We Know and Where Should We Be Heading? *Asia Pacific Business Review, 24*(1), 90–115. doi:10.1080/13602381.2017.1357316

Pells, R. (2018, March 1). *China's Brain Drain is Ending*. Retrieved on September 14, 2018, from: https://www.insidehighered.com/news/2018/03/01/experts-see-end-sight-chinas-brain-drain

Peng, Z., & Tok, S. K. (2016). The AIIB and China's Normative Power in International Financial Governance Structure. *Chinese Political Science Review, 1*(4), 736–753. doi:10.100741111-016-0042-y

Petäjäjärvi, J., Mikhaylov, K., Yasmin, R., Hämäläinen, M., & Iinatti, J. (2017). Evaluation of LoRa LPWAN technology for indoor remote health and wellbeing monitoring. *International Journal of Wireless Information Networks*, *24*(2), 153–165. doi:10.100710776-017-0341-8

Petersen, S., & Carlsen, S. (2011). WirelessHART versus ISA100. 11a: The format war hits the factory floor. *IEEE Industrial Electronics Magazine*, *5*(4), 23–34. doi:10.1109/MIE.2011.943023

Pew Research Center. (2017). *China Image: Do you have a favorable or unfavorable view of China?* Retrieved from http://www.pewglobal.org/database/indicator/24/survey/17/response/Unfavorable/

Pew Research Center. (2018, February 28). *Origins and Destinations of the World's Migrants, 1990-2017.* Retrieved on September 14, 2018, from: http://www.pewglobal.org/2018/02/28/global-migrant-stocks/?country=US&date=2017

Peyrouse, S. (2017). The Evolution of Russia's Views on the Belt and Road Initiative. *Asia Policy*, *24*(1), 96–102. doi:10.1353/asp.2017.0026

Piccarozzi, M., Aquilani, B., & Gatti, C. (2018). Industry 4.0 in Management Studies: A Systematic Literature Review. *Sustainability*, *10*(10), 3821. doi:10.3390u10103821

Pisani, M. J., Reyes, J. C., & García, B. G. (2009). Looking Back Twenty-Three Years: An Analysis of Contributors and Contributions to the Journal of Borderlands Studies, 1986 (volume 1, number 1) to 2008 (volume 23, number 2). *Journal of Borderland Studies*, *24*(1), 1–17. doi:10.1080/08865655.2009.9695714

Poh, A. (2017). The Myth of Chinese Sanctions over South China Sea Disputes. *The Washington Quarterly*, *40*(1), 143–165. doi:10.1080/0163660X.2017.1302744

Popescu, A. M., Salman, N., & Kemp, A. H. (2015). Rician statistical assumptions for geographic routing in wireless sensor networks. *IET Wireless Sensor Systems*, *5*(4), 204–209. doi:10.1049/iet-wss.2014.0023

Porter, M. E. (1998). *Competitive Advantage: Creating and Sustaining Superior Performance*. New York: Free Press. doi:10.1007/978-1-349-14865-3

Power, D. J. (2018). Defining Business Analytics: An Empirical Approach. *Journal of Business Analytics*, *1*(1), 40-53. doi:10.1080/2573234x.2018.1507605

Pranee, D. C. (2009). Impact of Chinese Cultural Development and Negotiation Strategies, FDI, Competitiveness, China International Business Growth, and Management Practice. *International Journal of Organizational Innovation*, *2*(1), 13–40.

PriceWaterhouseCoopers (PwC). (2017, February). *The Long View: How will the global economic order change by 2050?* Retrieved on June 21, 2018, from: https://www.pwc.com/gx/en/world-2050/assets/pwc-world-in-2050-summary-report-feb-2017.pdf

Ptak, T., & Hommel, D. (2016). The Trans-Political Nature of Southwest China's Energy Conduit, Yunnan Province. *Geopolitics*, *21*(3), 556–578. doi:10.1080/14650045.2015.1114471

Purbrick, M. (2018). Pirates of the South China Seas. *Asian Affairs*, *49*(1), 11–26. doi:10.1080/03068374.2018.1416010

Qiang, X. (2019). President XI's Surveillance State. *Journal of Democracy*, *30*(1), 53–67. doi:10.1353/jod.2019.0004

Qin, C., & Chong, T. T. L. (2016). Can Poverty be Alleviated in China? *Review of Income and Wealth*, 1–21. doi:10.1111/roiw.12273

Qin, S. (1997). *China*. İstanbul: Yeni Yıldız Publication.

Qin, Z., Lu, B., Zhu, M., Sun, L., & Shu, L. (2016). Optimized Charging in Large-Scale Deployed WSNs with Mobile Charger. *Transactions on Internet and Information Systems (Seoul)*, *10*(12).

Qiu, L. D., & Xue, Y. (2014). Understanding China's Foreign Trade: A literature Review (I). *China Economic Journal*, *7*(2), 168–186. doi:10.1080/17538963.2014.928967

Rafiq, A. (2017, October 24). China's $62 billion bet on Pakistan. *Foreign Affairs*.

RAND Corporation. (2018). *Corporate Website*. Retrieved on August 2, 2017, from: https://www.rand.org/

Reeves, J. (2018). China's Silk Road Economic Belt Initiative: Network and Influence Formation in Central Asia. *Journal of Contemporary China*, *27*(112), 502–518. doi:10.1080/10670564.2018.1433480

Ren, H. (2016). *Narratives of Worker's Resistance*. Chicago: Haymarket Books.

Rethel, L. (2011). Whose legitimacy? Islamic finance and the global financial order. *Review of International Political Economy*, *18*(1), 75–98. doi:10.1080/09692290902983999

Ricci, F. (2015). *Recommender Systems Handbook* (2nd ed.). Springer. doi:10.1007/978-1-4899-7637-6

Ritz, A., Brewer, G. A., & Neumann, O. (2016). Public Service Motivation: A Systematic Literature Review and Outlook. *Public Administration Review*, *76*(3), 414–426. doi:10.1111/puar.12505

Ritzer, G., & Dean, P. (2015). *Globalization: A Basic Text* (2nd ed.). Malden, MA: Wiley Blackwell.

Roberts, J. T., Hite, A. B., & Chorev, N. (2015). *The Globalization and Development Reader: Perspectives on Development and Global Change* (2nd ed.). Chicester, UK: John Wiley & Sons.

Rolland, N. (2017). China's "Belt and Road Initiative": Underwhelming or Game-Changer? *The Washington Quarterly*, *40*(1), 127–142. doi:10.1080/0163660X.2017.1302743

Ross, R. S. (2018). Nationalism, Geopolitics, and Naval Expansionism: From the Nineteenth Century to the Rise of China. *Naval War College Review*, *71*(4), 17–50.

Roth, M. S., & Dakhli, M. (2000). Regional trade agreements as structural networks: Implications for foreign direct investment decisions. *Connections*, *23*(1), 60–71.

Roth, M. S., & Dakhli, M. (2015). *Regional Trade Agreements as Structural Networks:Implications for Foreign Direct Investment Decisions*. The Dana Moore School of Business.

Sachs, D. J. (2004). *Welcome To The Asian Century By 2050, China and maybe India will overtake the U.S. economy in size.* Retrieved from: https://money.cnn.com/magazines/fortune/fortune_archive/2004/01/12/357912/index.htm

Sarker, M. N. I., Hossin, M. A., Hua, Y., Sarkar, M. K., & Kumar, N. (2018). Oil, Gas and Energy Business under One Belt One Road Strategic Context. *Open Journal of Social Sciences*, *06*(04), 119–134. doi:10.4236/jss.2018.64011

Sautenet, A. (2007). The Current Status and Prospects of the 'Strategic Partnership' between the EU and China: Towards the Conclusion of a Partnership and Cooperation Agreement. *European Law Journal*, *13*(6), 699–731. doi:10.1111/j.1468-0386.2007.00395.x

Scheltema, C. (2017, September 18). China Employment and Labor Disputes: Anticipate the Unexpected, Act to Prevent Disruption. *China Briefing*. Retrieved on September 17, 2018, from: http://www.china-briefing.com/news/2017/09/18/china-employment-and-labor-disputes-anticipate-the-unexpected-act-to-prevent-disruption.html

Schiavo, S., Reyes, J., & Fagiolo, G. (2010). International trade and financial integration: A weighted network analysis. *Quantitative Finance*, *10*(4), 389–399. doi:10.1080/14697680902882420

Schinas, O. W. (2017). Assessing the Impact of the Maritime Silk Road. *Journal of Ocean Engineering and Science*, 186-195.

Schinas, O., & Westarp, A. G. (2017). Assessing the Impact of the Maritime Silk Road. *Journal of Ocean Engineering and Science*, *2*(17), 186–195. doi:10.1016/j.joes.2017.08.002

Schires, E., Georgiou, P., & Lande, T. S. (2018). Vital Sign Monitoring Through the Back Using an UWB Impulse Radar With Body Coupled Antennas. *IEEE Transactions on Biomedical Circuits and Systems*, *12*(2), 292–302. doi:10.1109/TBCAS.2018.2799322 PMID:29570057

Schneider, C. J. (2017). The Political Economy of Regional Integration. *Annual Review of Political Science*, *20*(1), 229–248. doi:10.1146/annurev-polisci-051215-023006

Schultz, K. (2017, December). Sri Lanka, struggling with debt, hands a major port to China. *The New York Times*. Retrieved from https://www.nytimes.com/2017/12/12/world/asia/sri-lanka-china-port.html

Schwab, K. (2017). *The Global Competitiveness Report 2017-2018*. Geneva: World Economic Forum.

Sclater, Peasgood, & Mullan. (2016). *Learning analytics in higher education.* London: JISC.

Selmier-II, W. T. (2018). The Belt and Road Initiative and the influence of Islamic economies. *Economic and Political Studies*, *6*(3), 257–277. doi:10.1080/20954816.2018.1498989

Shah, A. R. (2018). How Does China-Pakistan Economic Corridor Show the Limitations of China's 'One Belt One Road' Model. *Asia & the Pacific Policy Studies*, *5*(2), 378–385. doi:10.1002/app5.224

Shahriar, S. (2019). *Understanding China's Belt & Road Initiative: The Institutional Economics Approach*. Beau Bassin, Mauritius: Lambert.

Shahriar, S., Qian, L., Irshad, M. S., Kea, S., Abdullahi, N. M, & Sarkar,, A. (2018). Institutions of the Belt & Road Initiative. *Journal of Law, Policy and Globalization*, *77*, 1–13.

Shambaugh, D. (2013). *China goes global: The partial power*. Oxford University Press.

Shariatinia, M., & Azizi, H. (2017). Iran–China Cooperation in the Silk Road Economic Belt: From Strategic Understanding to Operational Understanding. *China & World Economy*, *25*(5), 46–61. doi:10.1111/cwe.12213

Sharon, O., & Alpert, Y. (2017). Single User MAC Level Throughput Comparision: IEEE 802.11 ax vs. IEEE 802.11 ac. *Wireless Sensor Network*, *9*(05), 166–177. doi:10.4236/wsn.2017.95009

Sheffield, J., Korotayev, A., & Grinin, L. (2013). *Globalization: Yesterday, Today, and Tomorrow*. Litchfield Park, AZ: Emergent Publications.

Shellekens, P. (2013, May). *A Changing China: Implications for Developing Countries*. New York: The World Bank.

Sherani, S. (2013, August 12). Economies of the ummah. *Dawn*. Retrieved from https://www.dawn.com/news/1035026

Shi, K., Yu, B., Huang, C., Wu, J., & Sun, X. (2018). Exploring spatiotemporal patterns of electric power consumption in countries along the Belt and Road. *Energy*, *150*, 847–859. doi:10.1016/j.energy.2018.03.020

Shi, L. (2016). Income Inequality and Economic Growth in China in the Last Three Decades. *The Round Table*, *105*(6), 641–665. doi:10.1080/00358533.2016.1246858

Shin, S. Y., Park, H. S., Choi, S., & Kwon, W. H. (2007). Packet error rate analysis of ZigBee under WLAN and Bluetooth interferences. *IEEE Transactions on Wireless Communications*, *6*(8), 2825–2830. doi:10.1109/TWC.2007.06112

Shi, X., & Yan, Z. (2018). Urbanization and Risk Preference in China: A Decomposition of Self-Selection and Assimilation Effects. *China Economic Review*, *49*, 210–228. doi:10.1016/j.chieco.2017.04.009

Shliefer, A., & Vishny, R. W. (1993). Corruption. *The Quarterly Journal of Economics*, *108*(3), 599–617. doi:10.2307/2118402

Shukry, A., & Park, K. (2018, May). Malaysia scraps multibillion-dollar high-speed rail project to Singapore. *Bloomberg*.

Shu, L., Chen, Y., Huo, Z., Bergmann, N., & Wang, L. (2017). When mobile crowd sensing meets traditional industry. *IEEE Access: Practical Innovations, Open Solutions*, *5*, 15300–15307. doi:10.1109/ACCESS.2017.2657820

Shu, L., Mukherjee, M., Hu, L., Bergmann, N., & Zhu, C. (2016). Geographic routing in duty-cycled industrial wireless sensor networks with radio irregularity. *IEEE Access: Practical Innovations, Open Solutions*, *4*, 9043–9052. doi:10.1109/ACCESS.2016.2638441

Shu, L., Mukherjee, M., & Wu, X. (2016). Toxic gas boundary area detection in large-scale petrochemical plants with industrial wireless sensor networks. *IEEE Communications Magazine*, *54*(10), 22–28. doi:10.1109/MCOM.2016.7588225

Shusen, Y. S. (2014). Silk Road Economic Belt: Strategic Conception and Challenges. *Journal of Lanzhou University*, 36-41.

Sidaway, J. D., & Woon, C. Y. (2017). Chinese Narratives on "One Belt, One Road" (一带一路) in Geopolitical and Imperial Contexts. *The Professional Geographer*, 1–13. doi:10.1080/00330124.2017.1288576

Soong, J.-J. (2014). Is China Becoming the Core of Regional Trade and Market Integration in the Asia-Pacific? *Chinese Economy*, *47*(3), 3–7. doi:10.2753/CES1097-1475470300

Spies, W. T. (2011). The Chinese Miracle & the Fifteen-Year Fuse. *ISM Journal of International Business*, *1*(2), 2–42.

Spruit, M., & Lytras, M. (2018). Applied Data Science in Patient-centric Healthcare. *Telematics and Informatics*, *35*(4), 643–653. doi:10.1016/j.tele.2018.04.002

Statista. (2017). *China: Number Of Students At Universities 2017*. Retrieved from https://www.statista.com/statistics/227028/number-of-students-at-universities-in-china/

Statista. (2018). China Statistical Yearbook 2018. *National Bureau of Statistics of China*. Retrieved from http://www.stats.gov.cn/tjsj/ndsj/2018/indexeh.htm

Statista. (2018). *Top 20 export countries worldwide in 2017*. Retrieved from. https://www.statista.com/statistics/264623/leading-export-countries-worldwide/

Statista. (2018a). *Employment in China – Statistics and Facts*. Retrieved on September 8, 2018, from: https://www.statista.com/topics/1317/employment-in-china/

Statista. (2018b). *China: Gross domestic product (GDP) per capita in current prices from 2013 to 2023 (in US dollars)*. Retrieved on September 23, 2018, from: https://www.statista.com/statistics/263775/gross-domestic-product-gdp-per-capita-in-china/

Stiglitz, J. E. (2008). China: Towards A New Model of Development. *China Economic Journal*, *1*(1), 33–52. doi:10.1080/17538960701564858

Stiglitz, J. E. (2015). *Globalization and its discontents*. New York: Penguin.

Stiglitz, J. E. (2018). Rethinking Globalization in the Trump Era: US-China Relations. *Frontiers of Economics in China*, *13*(2), 133–146. doi:10.3868060-007-018-0010-3

Strategic Investment Conference (SIC). (2017). *Paradigm Shift: A Destabilizing World*. Omni Orlando Resort.

Stuart, E. (2015, August 19). China has almost wiped out urban poverty. Now it must tackle inequality. *The Guardian*. Retrieved on September 3, 2018, from: https://www.theguardian.com/business/economics-blog/2015/aug/19/china-poverty-inequality-development-goals

Subiyanto, E. (2017). *Logistics and Cisomang's Bridge*. Jakarta: Koran Jakarta.

Subiyanto, E. (2018). *Infrastructure and 2019's Political Year*. Jakarta: Media Indonesia.

Summers, T. (2016). China's 'New Silk Roads': Sub National Regions and Networks of Global Political Economy. *Third World Quarterly*, *37*(9), 1628–1643. doi:10.1080/01436597.2016.1153415

Sum, N.-L. (2018). The intertwined geopolitics and geoeconomics of hopes/fears: China's triple economic bubbles and the 'One Belt One Road' imaginary. *Territory, Politics, Governance: An International Journal of Policy, Administration and Institutions*, 1–25. doi:10.1080/21622671.2018.1523746

Sun, P. H. (2010). *International Trade and Its Effects on Economic Growth in China.* Discussion Paper.

Sun, L., & Du, Q. (2017). Physical layer security with its applications in 5G networks: A review. *China Communications*, *14*(12), 1–14. doi:10.1109/CC.2017.8246328

Sun, W., Lee, O., Shin, Y., Kim, S., Yang, C., Kim, H., & Choi, S. (2014). Wi-Fi could be much more. *IEEE Communications Magazine*, *52*(11), 22–29. doi:10.1109/MCOM.2014.6957139

Swaine, M. D. (2014). Chinese views and commentary on periphery diplomacy. *China Leadership Monitor, 44*(1).

Swaine, M. D. (2015). Chinese views and commentary on the "One Belt One Road" Initiative. *China Leadership Monitor, no. 47.* United nations Conference on Trade and Development. Bilateral FDI Statistics. Retrieved from http://unctad.org/en/Pages/DIAE/FDI%20Statistics/FDI-Statistics-Bilateral.aspx

Swaine, M. D. (2015). Chinese views and commentary on the "One Belt, One Road" Initiative. *China Leadership Monitor, 47*, 1–24. Retrieved from http://www.hoover.org/sites/default/files/research/docs/clm47ms.pdf

Taffer, A. (2015). State Strategy in Territorial Conflict: A Conceptual Analysis of China's Strategy in the South China Sea. *Contemporary Southeast Asia*, *37*(1), 85-108. doi:10.1355/cs37-1d

Teece, D. J. (2014). The Foundations of Enterprise Performance: Dynamic and Ordinary Capabilities in an (Economic) Theory of Firms. *The Academy of Management Perspectives*, *28*(4), 328–352. doi:10.5465/amp.2013.0116

Tekdal, V. (2018). China's Belt and Road Initiative: At the Crossroads of Challenges and Ambitions. *The Pacific Review*, *31*(3), 373–390. doi:10.1080/09512748.2017.1391864

The Daily Star. (2009, October 1). What will China's rising influence mean for the Middle East region? *The Daily Star*. Retrieved from http://www1.dailystar.com.lb/Opinion/Editorial/2009/Oct-01/119578-what-will-chinas-rising-influence-mean-for-the-middle-east-region.ashx

The Union of Chambers and Commodity Exchanges of Turkey. (2005). *Çin*. Ankara: Bilgi Tabanlı Yükselen Ekonomi.

The World Bank. (2014). *South Asia's $2.5 trillion infrastructure gap*. The World Bank. Retrieved from: http://www.worldbank.org/en/news/feature/2014/04/02/south-asia-trillion-infrastructure-gap

Thi Thuy Hang, N. (2016). The United States and China: Can They Cooperate? *Asian Affairs: An American Review*, *43*(3), 67–77. doi:10.1080/00927678.2016.1200332

Thomassen, D. (2016, November). Russian Blue-Water Navy is a Pipe Dream. *U.S. Naval Institute Proceedings*, *142*(11). Retrieved on September 17, 2018, from: https://www.usni.org/magazines/proceedings/2016-11/russian-blue-water-navy-pipe-dream

Timofeev, I., Lissovolik, Y., & Filippova, L. (2017). Russia's Vision of the Belt and Road Initiative: From the Rivalry of the Great Powers to Forging a New Cooperation Model in Eurasia. *China & World Economy*, *25*(5), 62–77. doi:10.1111/cwe.12214

Tokunaga, M., & Iwasaki, I. (2017). The Determinants of Foreign Direct Investment in Transition Economies: A Meta-analysis. *World Economy*, *40*(12), 2771–2831. doi:10.1111/twec.12477

Tønnesson, S. (2006). The South China Sea in the Age of European Decline. *Modern Asian Studies*, *40*(01), 1-57. doi:10.1017/S0026749X06001727

Townsend, S. (2018, October 30). Islamic banking key to financing China's Belt and Road. *The National Business*.

Tracy, E. F., Shvarts, E., Simonov, E., & Babenko, M. (2017). China's New Eurasian Ambitions: The Environmental Risks of the Silk Road Economic Belt. *Eurasian Geography and Economics*, *58*(1), 56–88. doi:10.1080/15387216.2017.1295876

Trading Economics. (2018). *China Employed Persons*. Retrieved on September 10, 2018, from: https://tradingeconomics.com/china/employed-persons

Transparency International (TI). (2017). *Corruption Perceptions Index 2016*. Retrieved on July 27, 2018, from: https://www.transparency.org/news/feature/corruption_perceptions_index_2017

Tschantret, J. (2016). Repression, Opportunity, and Innovation: The Evolution of Terrorism in Xinjiang, China. *Terrorism and Political Violence*, *30*(4), 569–588. doi:10.1080/09546553.2016.1182911

Tuman, J. P., & Shirali, M. (2017). The Political Economy of Chinese Foreign Direct Investment in Developing Areas. *Foreign Policy Analysis, 13*(1), 154–167. doi:10.1111/fpa.12092

Tuncay, N. (2003). Information Administration, Petroleum Supply Weekly And Monthly Status Report. *US Energy.*

Tung, H. Y., Tsang, K. F., Tung, H. C., Chui, K. T., & Chi, H. R. (2013). The design of dual radio ZigBee homecare gateway for remote patient monitoring. *IEEE Transactions on Consumer Electronics, 59*(4), 756–764. doi:10.1109/TCE.2013.6689686

Unay, İ. (2005). *Çin Ekonomisinde Rekabet Avantajı Sağlayan Etkenler ve Rekabetin Sürdürülebilirliği.* Bursa.

UNESCO. (2018). *Poverty.* Retrieved on September 17, 2018, from: http://www.unesco.org/new/en/social-and-human-sciences/themes/international-migration/glossary/poverty/

United Nations (UN). (2018). *World Economic Situation and Prospects.* Retrieved on September 11, 2018, from: https://www.un.org/development/desa/dpad/wp-content/uploads/sites/45/publication/WESP2018_Full_Web-1.pdf

United Nations Conference on Trade and Development (UNCTAD). (2017). *Review of Maritime Transport, 2017.* Geneva: United Nations. Retrieved on August 13, 2018, from: http://unctad.org/en/pages/PublicationWebflyer.aspx?publicationid=1890

University of Cambridge Institute for Manufacturing. (2009). *How to implement open innovation. Lessons from studying large multinational companies.* Cambridge, UK: Institute for Manufacturing.

Uras, A. (2017). The South China Sea and the Building of a National Maritime Culture. *Asian Survey, 57*(6), 1008–1031. doi:10.1525/as.2017.57.6.1008

Van de Beek, J., Riihijarvi, J., Achtzehn, A., & Mahonen, P. (2011, May). UHF white space in Europe—a quantitative study into the potential of the 470–790 MHz band. In *New Frontiers in Dynamic Spectrum Access Networks (DySPAN), 2011 IEEE Symposium on* (pp. 1-9). IEEE.

Van Torre, P., Gaelens, J., Verhaevert, J., & Rogier, H. (2018). Measurement and characterization of dual-band LoRa communication in the Antarctic. In *EUCAP2018, the 12th European Conference on Antennas and Propagation* (pp. 1-5). Academic Press. 10.1049/cp.2018.0469

Vangeli, A. (2017). China s Engagement with the Sixteen Countries of Central, East and Southeast Europe under the Belt and Road Initiative. *China & World Economy*, *25*(5), 101–124. doi:10.1111/cwe.12216

Varaprasad, S. D. (2015). *Science and Technology in Contemporaray China*. Cambridge University Press.

Venugopal, K., Alkhateeb, A., Prelcic, N. G., & Heath, R. W. (2017). Channel estimation for hybrid architecture-based wideband millimeter wave systems. *IEEE Journal on Selected Areas in Communications*, *35*(9), 1996–2009. doi:10.1109/JSAC.2017.2720856

Verbert, K., Manouselis, N., Ochoa, X., Wolpers, M., Drachsler, H., Bosnic, I., & Duval, E. (2012). Context-aware recommender systems for learning: A survey and future challenges. *IEEE Transactions on Learning Technologies*, *5*(4), 318–335. doi:10.1109/TLT.2012.11

Verbiest, J.-P. A. (2013). Regional Cooperation and Integration in the Mekong Region. *Asian Economic Policy Review*, *8*(1), 148–164. doi:10.1111/aepr.12015

Viberg, O. (2018). The Current Landscape Of Learning Analytics In Higher Education. *Computers in Human Behavior*, *89*, 98-110. doi:10.1016/j.chb.2018.07.027

Vice, M. (2017). *In global popularity contest, U.S. and China – not Russia – vie for first*. Retrieved from http://www.pewresearch.org/fact-tank/2017/08/23/in-global-popularity-contest-u-s-and-china-not-russia-vie-for-first/

Victoria, A. (2018). *Bullet Train One Belt One Road OBOR*. Academic Press.

Villafuerte, J., Corong, E., & Zhuang, J. (2016). *The one belt, one road Initiative: Impact on trade and growth*. Paper presented at the 19th annual conference on global economic analysis.

Villarroel, M., Guazzi, A., Jorge, J., Davis, S., Watkinson, P., Green, G., ... Tarassenko, L. (2014). Continuous non-contact vital sign monitoring in neonatal intensive care unit. *Healthcare Technology Letters, 1*(3), 87-91.

Visvizi, A. (2018). Policy Making For Smart Cities: Innovation And Social Inclusive Economic Growth For Sustainability. *Journal Of Science And Technology Policy Management*, *9*(2), 126-133. doi:10.1108/jstpm-07-2018-079

Visvizi, A., & Lytras, M. (2018). It's Not a Fad: Smart Cities and Smart Villages Research in European and Global Contexts. *Sustainability*, *10*(8), 2727. doi:10.3390u10082727

Visvizi, A., & Lytras, M. D. (2018). Rescaling and Refocusing Smart Cities Research: From Mega Cities to Smart Villages. *Journal of Science and Technology Policy Management*, *9*(2), 134–145. doi:10.1108/JSTPM-02-2018-0020

Visvizi, A., Lytras, M. D., Damiani, E., & Mathkour, H. (2018). Policy Making for Smart Cities: Innovation and Social Inclusive Economic Growth for Sustainability. *Journal of Science and Technology Policy Management*, *9*(2), 126–133. doi:10.1108/JSTPM-07-2018-079

Voituriez, T., & Wang, X. (2015). Real Challenges Behind the EU–China PV Trade Dispute Settlement. *Climate Policy*, 670-677. doi:10.1080/14693062.2015.1009868

Vollmer, S. (2012). Business Etiquette in China. *Journal of Accountancy*, *214*(6), 18.

Wan, C.-C. (1998). International Diversification, Industrial Diversification and Firm Performance of Hong Kong MNCs. *Asia Pacific Journal of Management*, *15*(2), 205–217. doi:10.1023/A:1015489514744

Wang, J. J., & Yau, S. (2018). Case Studies on Transport Infrastructure Projects in Belt and Road Initiative: An Actor Network Theory Perspective. *Journal of Transport Geography*, *71*, 213–223. doi:10.1016/j.jtrangeo.2018.01.007

Wang, Y. (2018). The Political Economy of Joining the AIIB. *The Chinese Journal of International Politics*, *11*(2), 105–130. doi:10.1093/cjip/poy006

Wang, Y., Roijakkers, N., Vanhaverbeke, W., & Chen, J. (2012). How Chinese firms employ open innovation to strengthen their innovative performance. *International Journal of Technology Management*, *59*(3/4), 235–354. doi:10.1504/IJTM.2012.047245

Wang, Z. (2017). The Economic Rise of China: Rule-Taker, Rule-Maker, or Rule-Breaker? *Asian Survey*, *57*(4), 595–617. doi:10.1525/as.2017.57.4.595

Wei, Z. (2017). Research on the Geographical Strategy of China's "One Belt and One Road" Construction. *Journal of Jilin University*, 77-81.

Wei, L. (2017). Partners, Institutions and International Currencies: The International Political Foundations for the Rise of the Renminbi. *Social Sciences in China*, *38*(2), 114–141. doi:10.1080/02529203.2017.1302236

Wenmu, Z. (2015). The Political Significance of "One Belt and One Road". Asian Infrastructure Investment Bank, 204-224.

Wikipedia. (n.d.a). Internalization. *Wikipedia.* Retrieved from: https://en.wikipedia.org/wiki/Internalization

Wikipedia. (n.d.b). China. *Wikipedia.* Retrieved from: https://en.wikipedia.org/wiki/China

Wikipedia. (n.d.c). International trade. *Wikipedia.* Retrieved from: https://en.wikipedia.org/wiki/International_trade

Wikipedia. (n.d.d). Reform. *Wikipedia.* Retrieved from: https://en.wikipedia.org/wiki/Reform

Wikipedia. (n.d.e). Transport. *Wikipedia.* Retrieved from: https://en.wikipedia.org/wiki/Transport

Williamson, P., & Zeng, M. (2004). Strategies for Competing in a Changed China. *MIT Sloan Management Review*, *45*(4), 85–91.

Wltz, K. (1979). *Theory of International Politics.* Academic Press.

Wong, B. T. M. (2017). Learning Analytics In Higher Education: An Analysis Of Case Studies. *Asian Association of Open Universities Journal*, *12*(1), 21-40. doi:10.1108/aaouj-01-2017-0009

World Bank Group. (2018). *The World Bank in China*. Retrieved on September 22, 2018, from: http://www.worldbank.org/en/country/china/overview

World Bank. (2015). *National Income in China came to $ 7800.* Retrieved from https://www.haberler.com/cin-de-kisi-basina-milli-gelir-7-bin-800-dolara-7841637-haberi

World Bank. (2018). *National Accounts Data, GDP Growth Annual (%).* Retrieved from https://data.worldbank.org/indicator/ny.gdp.mktp.kd.zg?end=2017&locations=cn&start=1961

World Bank. (2018a). *Where is global growth happening*? Retrieved on September 4, 2018, from: http://www.visualcapitalist.com/chart-global-growth-happening/

World Economic Forum (WEF). (2015). *How does corruption affect economic growth*? Retrieved on June 18, 2017, from: https://www.weforum.org/agenda/2015/05/how-does-corruption-affect-economic-growth/

World Economic Forum (WEF). (2017a). *Global Competitive Index 2017-2018.* Retrieved on July 3, 2018, from: http://www3.weforum.org/docs/GCR2017-2018/04Backmatter/TheGlobalCompetitivenessReport2017%E2%80%932018AppendixB.pdf

World Economic Forum (WEF). (2017b). *5 things you need to know about the global pension crisis.* Retrieved on August 3, 2018, from: https://www.weforum.org/agenda/2017/05/5-things-you-need-to-know-about-the-global-pension-crisis/

World Economic Forum (WEF). (2017c). *Global Pension Timebomb: Funding Gap Set to Dwarf World GDP*. Retrieved on August 31, 2018, from: https://www.weforum.org/press/2017/05/global-pension-timebomb-funding-gap-set-to-dwarf-world-gdp/

World Economic Forum (WEF). (2018). *The World's Biggest Economies in 2018.* Retrieved on July 30, 2018, from: https://www.weforum.org/agenda/2018/04/the-worlds-biggest-economies-in-2018/

World Trade Organization. (n.d.). Retrieved October 27, 2018, from https://www.wto.org/english/tratop_e/dispu_e/cases_e/ds549_e.htm

Worldbank National Accounts Data. (n.d.). *China's Trade % of GDP.* Retrieved from: https://data.worldbank.org/indicator/NE.TRD.GNFS.ZS?locations=CN

Wu, X. (2001). Foreign direct investment, intellectual property rights, and wage inequality in China. *China Economic Review, 11*, 361-384. doi:10.1016/S1043-951X(01)00035-9

Wu, J.-X., & He, L.-Y. (2018). Urban–Rural Gap and Poverty Traps in China: A Prefecture Level Analysis. *Applied Economics*, *50*(30), 3300–3314. doi:10.1080/00036846.2017.1420890

Xiao, R. (2016). China as an Institution Builder: The Case of the AIIB. *The Pacific Review*, *29*(3), 435–442. doi:10.1080/09512748.2016.1154678

Xiaotong, Z., & Keith, J. (2017). From Wealth to Power: China's New Economic Statecraft. *The Washington Quarterly*, *40*(1), 185–203. doi:10.1080/016366 0X.2017.1302746

Xiao, Y., & Watson, M. (2017). Guidance on Conducting a Systematic Literature Review. *Journal of Planning Education and Research*, 1–20. doi:10.1177/0739456x17723971

Xiaoyan, Y. (2015). One belt, one road" can boost China's GDP growth by 0.25 percentage points in 2015. *Jieman*. Retrieved from: http://china-trade-research.hktdc.com/business-news/article/The-Belt-and-Road-Initiative/The-Belt-and-Road-Initiative-Country-Profiles/obor/en/1/1X000000/1X0A36I0.htm

Xie, L., Yang, Z., Cai, J., Cheng, Z., Wen, T., & Song, T. (2016). Harbin: A Rust Belt City Revival From Its Strategic Position. *Cities (London, England)*, *58*, 26–38. doi:10.1016/j.cities.2016.05.009

Xie, T., & Page, B. I. (2013). What affects China's national image? A cross-national study of public opinion. *Journal of Contemporary China*, *22*(83), 850–867. doi:1 0.1080/10670564.2013.782130

Xi, J. (2015). Asia's new future: Towards a community of common destiny. In *Boao Forum for Asia Annual Conference 2015*. Hainan: Boao Forum. Retrieved from http://english.boaoforum.org/u/cms/www2/201503/25112018qw3q.pdf

Xintao, Y. (2014). Analysis of National Strategy for the Construction of "One Belt and One Road". *The Theory of Monthly*, 5-9.

Xiong, Z., Liu, T., Tse, G., Gong, M., Gladding, P., Smaill, B. H., ... Zhao, J. (2018). A Machine Learning Aided Systematic Review and Meta-Analysis of the Relative Risk of Atrial Fibrillation in Patients With Diabetes Mellitus. *Frontiers in Physiology*, *9*, 835. doi:10.3389/fphys.2018.00835 PMID:30018571

Xuetong, Y. (2006). The Rise of China and its Power Status. *The Chinese Journal of International Politics*, *1*(1), 5–33. doi:10.1093/cjip/pol002

Xuetong, Y. (2014). From Keeping a Low Profile to Striving for Achievement. *The Chinese Journal of International Politics*, *7*(2), 153–184. doi:10.1093/cjip/pou027

Xu, X. (2000). China and the Middle East: Cross-investment in the energy sector. *Middle East Policy*, *7*(3), 122–136. doi:10.1111/j.1475-4967.2000.tb00168.x

Yang, D., Jiang, L., & Ng, A. K. Y. (2018). One Belt one Road, but several routes: A case study of new emerging trade corridors connecting the Far East to Europe. *Transportation Research Part A: Policy and Practice, 117*, 190–204. doi:10.1016/j.tra.2018.08.001

Yang, F. (2014). Invigorating Sino-Arab relations by One Belt and One Road strategy. *Journal of Middle Eastern and Islamic Studies*, *8*(4), 1–26. doi:10.1080/19370679.2014.12023254

Yanjie, L. (2017). The Risk of "One Belt and One Road" Policy in Central Asia. *Journal of Xinjiang Normal University*, 76-79.

Yao, Z. (2015). How Can China Avoid the Middle Income Trap? *China & World Economy*, *23*(5), 26–42. doi:10.1111/cwe.12126

Ye, H., Binwei, L., & Starkey, G. (2018). Economic and Cultural Implications of China's One Belt One Road Initiative for the Film Industry: Cultural Distance and Taste Preference. *Australian Economic Papers*, *57*(3), 250–264. doi:10.1111/1467-8454.12116

Yi, H. (2015, March 20). China's One Belt/One Road' policy is open to all nations. *Executive Intelligence Review*. Retrieved from http://schillerinstitute.org/economy/phys_econ/2015/27-29_EIR12-one_belt_one_road.html

Yifei, Y., & Longming, Z. (2014). Application scenarios and enabling technologies of 5G. *China Communications*, *11*(11), 69–79. doi:10.1109/CC.2014.7004525

Yılmaz, R., & Koyuncu, C. (2005). *Çin:Dragon Ekonomisinin Onlenemeyen Yükselişi*. Bursa Ekin Kitabevi.

Yi, P., Iwayemi, A., & Zhou, C. (2011). Developing ZigBee deployment guideline under WiFi interference for smart grid applications. *IEEE Transactions on Smart Grid*, *2*(1), 110–120. doi:10.1109/TSG.2010.2091655

Yiping, H., Qin, G., & Xun, W. (2014). Financial liberalization and the middle-income trap: What can China learn from the cross-country experience? *China Economic Review*, *31*, 426–440. doi:10.1016/j.chieco.2014.04.009

Yiwei, W. (2016). *The Belt and Road Initiative: What Will China Offer the World in Its Rise*. Beijing, China: New World Press.

Yiwei, W. (2018). Belt and Road Initiative: Mutual Connectivity of the World. *China and the World*, *01*(04), 1–15. doi:10.11422591729318500232

Yu & Xu. (2018). Developing Smart Cities In China. *International Journal of Public Administration in the Digital Age*, *5*(3), 76-91. doi:10.4018/ijpada.2018070106

Yue, J. (2018). *China's Rise in the Age of Globalization*. New York: Palgrave Macmillan. doi:10.1007/978-3-319-63997-0

Yu, H. (2016). Motivation Behind China's 'One Belt, One Road' Initiatives and Establishment of the Asian Infrastructure Investment Bank. *Journal of Contemporary China*, *26*(105), 353–368. doi:10.1080/10670564.2016.1245894

Yu, J., & Wu, J. (2018). The Sustainability of Agricultural Development in China: The Agriculture–Environment Nexus. *Sustainability*, *10*(6), 1776. doi:10.3390u10061776

Yu, X. (2006). *50 Years of Sino-Egyptian diplomacy, Silk Road Stories: 50 Years of Diplomacy between New China and Arab Countries*. Beijing: World Affairs Press.

Yu, X. (2015). Meat Consumption in China and Its impact on international Food Security: Status Quo, Trends, and Policies. *Journal of Integrative Agriculture*, *14*(6), 989–994. doi:10.1016/S2095-3119(14)60983-7

Yu, X., Zhang, J., Haenggi, M., & Letaief, K. B. (2017). Coverage analysis for millimeter wave networks: The impact of directional antenna arrays. *IEEE Journal on Selected Areas in Communications*, *35*(7), 1498–1512. doi:10.1109/JSAC.2017.2699098

Zambelis, C., & Gentry, B. (2008). China through Arab eyes : American influence in the Middle East. *Parameters, 38*(1), 60–73.

Zeng, J. (2017). Does Europe Matter? The Role of Europe in Chinese Narratives of 'One Belt One Road' and 'New Type of Great Power Relations'. *Journal of Common Market Studies*, *55*(5), 1162–1176. doi:10.1111/jcms.12535

Zeng, J., & Fang, Y. (2014). Between Poverty and Prosperity: China's Dependent Development and the 'Middle-Income Trap'. *Third World Quarterly*, *35*(6), 1014–1031. doi:10.1080/01436597.2014.907725

Zhai, F. (2018). China's Belt and Road Initiative: A preliminary quantitative assessment. *Journal of Asian Economics*, *55*, 84–92. doi:10.1016/j.asieco.2017.12.006

Zhai, Q., Willis, M., O'Shea, B., Zhai, Y., & Yang, Y. (2013). Big Five personality traits, job satisfaction and subjective wellbeing in China. *International Journal of Psychology,48*(6), 1099–1108. doi:10.1080/00207594.2012.732700 PMID:23075216

Zhang, J. (2016). *Maritime Silk Road and China's Indian Ocean Strategy: An Analysis from the Perspective of Cooperative Security*. Academic Press. doi:10.1007/978-981-10-0167-3_4

Zhang, C. (2015). Income Inequality And Access To Housing: Evidence From China. *China Economic Review, 36*, 261–271. doi:10.1016/j.chieco.2015.10.003

Zhang, F. (2016). China as a Global Force. *Asia & the Pacific Policy Studies, 3*(1), 120–128. doi:10.1002/app5.115

Zhang, H. (2017). Opportunity or New Poverty Trap: Rural-Urban Education Disparity and Internal Migration in China. *China Economic Review, 44*, 112–124. doi:10.1016/j.chieco.2017.03.011

Zhang, L. (2010). The Rise of China: Media Perception and Implications for International Politics. *Journal of Contemporary China, 19*(64), 233–254. doi:10.1080/10670560903444199

Zhang, S., Yang, D., Qiu, S., Bao, X., & Li, J. (2018). Open innovation and firm performance: Evidence from the Chinese mechanical manufacturing industry. *Journal of Engineering and Technology Management, 48*, 76–86. doi:10.1016/j.jengtecman.2018.04.004

Zhang, X. (2017). Chinese Capitalism and the Maritime Silk Road: A World-Systems Perspective. *Geopolitics, 22*(2), 310–331. doi:10.1080/14650045.2017.1289371

Zhan, S. (2006). *Premier Zhou Enlai works for Sino-Egyptian and Sino-Arab friendship. Silk Road stories: 50 years of diplomacy between new China and Arab countries*. Beijing: World Affairs Press.

Zhao, W. (2016). The Theoretical Consideration and Practical Significance of the" One Belt and One Road". *Intersection Point*, 68-74.

Zhao, Q., & Gurusamy, M. (2008). Lifetime maximization for connected target coverage in wireless sensor networks. *IEEE/ACM Transactions on Networking, 16*(6), 1378–1391. doi:10.1109/TNET.2007.911432

Zhao, S. (2016). Xi Jinping's Maoist Revival. *Journal of Democracy*, *27*(3), 83–97. doi:10.1353/jod.2016.0051

Zhao, S. (2017). American Reflections on the Engagement with China and Responses to President Xi's New Model of Major Power Relations. *Journal of Contemporary China*, *26*(106), 489–503. doi:10.1080/10670564.2017.1274814

Zhuang, J., & Shi, L. (2016, July). *Understanding recent trends in income inequality in the People's Republic of China* (ADB Economics Working Paper Series No. 489). Mandaluyong City, Philippines: Asian Development Bank.

Zhu, C., Leung, V. C., Yang, L. T., & Shu, L. (2015). Collaborative location-based sleep scheduling for wireless sensor networks integratedwith mobile cloud computing. *IEEE Transactions on Computers*, *64*(7), 1844–1856. doi:10.1109/TC.2014.2349524

Zhu, W. (2011). On the strategic relationship between China and Islamic countries in the Middle East. *Journal of Sino-Islamic Communications*, *3*(1), 1–27.

Zhu, X. (2012). Understanding China's Growth: Past, Present, and Future. *The Journal of Economic Perspectives*, *26*(4), 103–124. doi:10.1257/jep.26.4.103

Zhu, Y. (2016). International Trade and Food Security: Conceptual Discussion, WTO and the Case of China. *China Agricultural Economic Review*, *8*(3), 399–411. doi:10.1108/CAER-09-2015-0127

Zongyou, W. (2017). China's Maritime Trap. *The Washington Quarterly*, *40*(1), 167–184. doi:10.1080/0163660X.2017.1302745

Zorbas, D., & Douligeris, C. (2011). Connected coverage in WSNs based on critical targets. *Computer Networks*, *55*(6), 1412–1425. doi:10.1016/j.comnet.2010.12.023

Related References

To continue our tradition of advancing information science and technology research, we have compiled a list of recommended IGI Global readings. These references will provide additional information and guidance to further enrich your knowledge and assist you with your own research and future publications.

Abtahi, M. S., Behboudi, L., & Hasanabad, H. M. (2017). Factors Affecting Internet Advertising Adoption in Ad Agencies. *International Journal of Innovation in the Digital Economy*, *8*(4), 18–29. doi:10.4018/IJIDE.2017100102

Agrawal, S. (2017). The Impact of Emerging Technologies and Social Media on Different Business(es): Marketing and Management. In O. Rishi & A. Sharma (Eds.), *Maximizing Business Performance and Efficiency Through Intelligent Systems* (pp. 37–49). Hershey, PA: IGI Global. doi:10.4018/978-1-5225-2234-8.ch002

Alnoukari, M., Razouk, R., & Hanano, A. (2016). BSC-SI: A Framework for Integrating Strategic Intelligence in Corporate Strategic Management. *International Journal of Social and Organizational Dynamics in IT*, *5*(2), 1–14. doi:10.4018/IJSODIT.2016070101

Alnoukari, M., Razouk, R., & Hanano, A. (2016). BSC-SI, A Framework for Integrating Strategic Intelligence in Corporate Strategic Management. *International Journal of Strategic Information Technology and Applications*, *7*(1), 32–44. doi:10.4018/IJSITA.2016010103

Altındağ, E. (2016). Current Approaches in Change Management. In A. Goksoy (Ed.), *Organizational Change Management Strategies in Modern Business* (pp. 24–51). Hershey, PA: IGI Global. doi:10.4018/978-1-4666-9533-7.ch002

Alvarez-Dionisi, L. E., Turner, R., & Mittra, M. (2016). Global Project Management Trends. *International Journal of Information Technology Project Management, 7*(3), 54–73. doi:10.4018/IJITPM.2016070104

Anantharaman, R. N., Rajeswari, K. S., Angusamy, A., & Kuppusamy, J. (2017). Role of Self-Efficacy and Collective Efficacy as Moderators of Occupational Stress Among Software Development Professionals. *International Journal of Human Capital and Information Technology Professionals, 8*(2), 45–58. doi:10.4018/IJHCITP.2017040103

Aninze, F., El-Gohary, H., & Hussain, J. (2018). The Role of Microfinance to Empower Women: The Case of Developing Countries. *International Journal of Customer Relationship Marketing and Management, 9*(1), 54–78. doi:10.4018/IJCRMM.2018010104

Arsenijević, O. M., Orčić, D., & Kastratović, E. (2017). Development of an Optimization Tool for Intangibles in SMEs: A Case Study from Serbia with a Pilot Research in the Prestige by Milka Company. In M. Vemić (Ed.), *Optimal Management Strategies in Small and Medium Enterprises* (pp. 320–347). Hershey, PA: IGI Global. doi:10.4018/978-1-5225-1949-2.ch015

Aryanto, V. D., Wismantoro, Y., & Widyatmoko, K. (2018). Implementing Eco-Innovation by Utilizing the Internet to Enhance Firm's Marketing Performance: Study of Green Batik Small and Medium Enterprises in Indonesia. *International Journal of E-Business Research, 14*(1), 21–36. doi:10.4018/IJEBR.2018010102

Atiku, S. O., & Fields, Z. (2017). Multicultural Orientations for 21st Century Global Leadership. In N. Baporikar (Ed.), *Management Education for Global Leadership* (pp. 28–51). Hershey, PA: IGI Global. doi:10.4018/978-1-5225-1013-0.ch002

Atiku, S. O., & Fields, Z. (2018). Organisational Learning Dimensions and Talent Retention Strategies for the Service Industries. In N. Baporikar (Ed.), *Global Practices in Knowledge Management for Societal and Organizational Development* (pp. 358–381). Hershey, PA: IGI Global. doi:10.4018/978-1-5225-3009-1.ch017

Ávila, L., & Teixeira, L. (2018). The Main Concepts Behind the Dematerialization of Business Processes. In M. Khosrow-Pour, D.B.A. (Ed.), Encyclopedia of Information Science and Technology, Fourth Edition (pp. 888-898). Hershey, PA: IGI Global. doi:10.4018/978-1-5225-2255-3.ch076

Bartens, Y., Chunpir, H. I., Schulte, F., & Voß, S. (2017). Business/IT Alignment in Two-Sided Markets: A COBIT 5 Analysis for Media Streaming Business Models. In S. De Haes & W. Van Grembergen (Eds.), *Strategic IT Governance and Alignment in Business Settings* (pp. 82–111). Hershey, PA: IGI Global. doi:10.4018/978-1-5225-0861-8.ch004

Bashayreh, A. M. (2018). Organizational Culture and Organizational Performance. In W. Lee & F. Sabetzadeh (Eds.), *Contemporary Knowledge and Systems Science* (pp. 50–69). Hershey, PA: IGI Global. doi:10.4018/978-1-5225-5655-8.ch003

Bedford, D. A. (2018). Sustainable Knowledge Management Strategies: Aligning Business Capabilities and Knowledge Management Goals. In N. Baporikar (Ed.), *Global Practices in Knowledge Management for Societal and Organizational Development* (pp. 46–73). Hershey, PA: IGI Global. doi:10.4018/978-1-5225-3009-1.ch003

Benmoussa, F., Nakara, W. A., & Jaouen, A. (2016). The Use of Social Media by SMEs in the Tourism Industry. In I. Lee (Ed.), *Encyclopedia of E-Commerce Development, Implementation, and Management* (pp. 2159–2170). Hershey, PA: IGI Global. doi:10.4018/978-1-4666-9787-4.ch155

Berger, R. (2016). Indigenous Management and Bottom of Pyramid Countries: The Role of National Institutions. In U. Aung & P. Ordoñez de Pablos (Eds.), *Managerial Strategies and Practice in the Asian Business Sector* (pp. 107–123). Hershey, PA: IGI Global. doi:10.4018/978-1-4666-9758-4.ch007

Bharwani, S., & Musunuri, D. (2018). Reflection as a Process From Theory to Practice. In M. Khosrow-Pour, D.B.A. (Ed.), Encyclopedia of Information Science and Technology, Fourth Edition (pp. 1529-1539). Hershey, PA: IGI Global. doi:10.4018/978-1-5225-2255-3.ch132

Bhatt, G. D., Wang, Z., & Rodger, J. A. (2017). Information Systems Capabilities and Their Effects on Competitive Advantages: A Study of Chinese Companies. *Information Resources Management Journal*, *30*(3), 41–57. doi:10.4018/IRMJ.2017070103

Bhushan, M., & Yadav, A. (2017). Concept of Cloud Computing in ESB. In R. Bhadoria, N. Chaudhari, G. Tomar, & S. Singh (Eds.), *Exploring Enterprise Service Bus in the Service-Oriented Architecture Paradigm* (pp. 116–127). Hershey, PA: IGI Global. doi:10.4018/978-1-5225-2157-0.ch008

Bhushan, S. (2017). System Dynamics Base-Model of Humanitarian Supply Chain (HSCM) in Disaster Prone Eco-Communities of India: A Discussion on Simulation and Scenario Results. *International Journal of System Dynamics Applications*, *6*(3), 20–37. doi:10.4018/IJSDA.2017070102

Biswas, A., & De, A. K. (2017). On Development of a Fuzzy Stochastic Programming Model with Its Application to Business Management. In S. Trivedi, S. Dey, A. Kumar, & T. Panda (Eds.), *Handbook of Research on Advanced Data Mining Techniques and Applications for Business Intelligence* (pp. 353–378). Hershey, PA: IGI Global. doi:10.4018/978-1-5225-2031-3.ch021

Bücker, J., & Ernste, K. (2018). Use of Brand Heroes in Strategic Reputation Management: The Case of Bacardi, Adidas, and Daimler. In A. Erdemir (Ed.), *Reputation Management Techniques in Public Relations* (pp. 126–150). Hershey, PA: IGI Global. doi:10.4018/978-1-5225-3619-2.ch007

Bureš, V. (2018). Industry 4.0 From the Systems Engineering Perspective: Alternative Holistic Framework Development. In R. Brunet-Thornton & F. Martinez (Eds.), *Analyzing the Impacts of Industry 4.0 in Modern Business Environments* (pp. 199–223). Hershey, PA: IGI Global. doi:10.4018/978-1-5225-3468-6.ch011

Buzady, Z. (2017). Resolving the Magic Cube of Effective Case Teaching: Benchmarking Case Teaching Practices in Emerging Markets – Insights from the Central European University Business School, Hungary. In D. Latusek (Ed.), *Case Studies as a Teaching Tool in Management Education* (pp. 79–103). Hershey, PA: IGI Global. doi:10.4018/978-1-5225-0770-3.ch005

Campatelli, G., Richter, A., & Stocker, A. (2016). Participative Knowledge Management to Empower Manufacturing Workers. *International Journal of Knowledge Management*, *12*(4), 37–50. doi:10.4018/IJKM.2016100103

Căpusneanu, S., & Topor, D. I. (2018). Business Ethics and Cost Management in SMEs: Theories of Business Ethics and Cost Management Ethos. In I. Oncioiu (Ed.), *Ethics and Decision-Making for Sustainable Business Practices* (pp. 109–127). Hershey, PA: IGI Global. doi:10.4018/978-1-5225-3773-1.ch007

Carneiro, A. (2016). Maturity in Health Organization Information Systems: Metrics and Privacy Perspectives. *International Journal of Privacy and Health Information Management*, *4*(2), 1–18. doi:10.4018/IJPHIM.2016070101

Chan, R. L., Mo, P. L., & Moon, K. K. (2018). Strategic and Tactical Measures in Managing Enterprise Risks: A Study of the Textile and Apparel Industry. In K. Strang, M. Korstanje, & N. Vajjhala (Eds.), *Research, Practices, and Innovations in Global Risk and Contingency Management* (pp. 1–19). Hershey, PA: IGI Global. doi:10.4018/978-1-5225-4754-9.ch001

Chandan, H. C. (2016). Motivations and Challenges of Female Entrepreneurship in Developed and Developing Economies. In N. Baporikar (Ed.), *Handbook of Research on Entrepreneurship in the Contemporary Knowledge-Based Global Economy* (pp. 260–286). Hershey, PA: IGI Global. doi:10.4018/978-1-4666-8798-1.ch012

Charlier, S. D., Burke-Smalley, L. A., & Fisher, S. L. (2018). Undergraduate Programs in the U.S: A Contextual and Content-Based Analysis. In J. Mendy (Ed.), *Teaching Human Resources and Organizational Behavior at the College Level* (pp. 26–57). Hershey, PA: IGI Global. doi:10.4018/978-1-5225-2820-3.ch002

Chaudhuri, S. (2016). Application of Web-Based Geographical Information System (GIS) in E-Business. In U. Panwar, R. Kumar, & N. Ray (Eds.), *Handbook of Research on Promotional Strategies and Consumer Influence in the Service Sector* (pp. 389–405). Hershey, PA: IGI Global. doi:10.4018/978-1-5225-0143-5.ch023

Choudhuri, P. S. (2016). An Empirical Study on the Quality of Services Offered by the Private Life Insurers in Burdwan. In U. Panwar, R. Kumar, & N. Ray (Eds.), *Handbook of Research on Promotional Strategies and Consumer Influence in the Service Sector* (pp. 31–55). Hershey, PA: IGI Global. doi:10.4018/978-1-5225-0143-5.ch002

Dahlberg, T., Kivijärvi, H., & Saarinen, T. (2017). IT Investment Consistency and Other Factors Influencing the Success of IT Performance. In S. De Haes & W. Van Grembergen (Eds.), *Strategic IT Governance and Alignment in Business Settings* (pp. 176–208). Hershey, PA: IGI Global. doi:10.4018/978-1-5225-0861-8.ch007

Damnjanović, A. M. (2017). Knowledge Management Optimization through IT and E-Business Utilization: A Qualitative Study on Serbian SMEs. In M. Vemić (Ed.), *Optimal Management Strategies in Small and Medium Enterprises* (pp. 249–267). Hershey, PA: IGI Global. doi:10.4018/978-1-5225-1949-2.ch012

Daneshpour, H. (2017). Integrating Sustainable Development into Project Portfolio Management through Application of Open Innovation. In M. Vemić (Ed.), *Optimal Management Strategies in Small and Medium Enterprises* (pp. 370–387). Hershey, PA: IGI Global. doi:10.4018/978-1-5225-1949-2.ch017

Daniel, A. D., & Reis de Castro, V. (2018). Entrepreneurship Education: How to Measure the Impact on Nascent Entrepreneurs. In A. Carrizo Moreira, J. Guilherme Leitão Dantas, & F. Manuel Valente (Eds.), *Nascent Entrepreneurship and Successful New Venture Creation* (pp. 85–110). Hershey, PA: IGI Global. doi:10.4018/978-1-5225-2936-1.ch004

David, F., van der Sijde, P., & van den Besselaar, P. (2016). Enterpreneurial Incentives, Obstacles, and Management in University-Business Co-Operation: The Case of Indonesia. In J. Saiz-Álvarez (Ed.), *Handbook of Research on Social Entrepreneurship and Solidarity Economics* (pp. 499–518). Hershey, PA: IGI Global. doi:10.4018/978-1-5225-0097-1.ch024

David, R., Swami, B. N., & Tangirala, S. (2018). Ethics Impact on Knowledge Management in Organizational Development: A Case Study. In N. Baporikar (Ed.), *Global Practices in Knowledge Management for Societal and Organizational Development* (pp. 19–45). Hershey, PA: IGI Global. doi:10.4018/978-1-5225-3009-1.ch002

Delias, P., & Lakiotaki, K. (2018). Discovering Process Horizontal Boundaries to Facilitate Process Comprehension. *International Journal of Operations Research and Information Systems*, *9*(2), 1–31. doi:10.4018/IJORIS.2018040101

Denholm, J., & Lee-Davies, L. (2018). Success Factors for Games in Business and Project Management. In *Enhancing Education and Training Initiatives Through Serious Games* (pp. 34–68). Hershey, PA: IGI Global. doi:10.4018/978-1-5225-3689-5.ch002

Deshpande, M. (2017). Best Practices in Management Institutions for Global Leadership: Policy Aspects. In N. Baporikar (Ed.), *Management Education for Global Leadership* (pp. 1–27). Hershey, PA: IGI Global. doi:10.4018/978-1-5225-1013-0.ch001

Deshpande, M. (2018). Policy Perspectives for SMEs Knowledge Management. In N. Baporikar (Ed.), *Knowledge Integration Strategies for Entrepreneurship and Sustainability* (pp. 23–46). Hershey, PA: IGI Global. doi:10.4018/978-1-5225-5115-7.ch002

Dezdar, S. (2017). ERP Implementation Projects in Asian Countries: A Comparative Study on Iran and China. *International Journal of Information Technology Project Management*, *8*(3), 52–68. doi:10.4018/IJITPM.2017070104

Domingos, D., Martinho, R., & Varajão, J. (2016). Controlled Flexibility in Healthcare Processes: A BPMN-Extension Approach. In M. Cruz-Cunha, I. Miranda, R. Martinho, & R. Rijo (Eds.), *Encyclopedia of E-Health and Telemedicine* (pp. 521–535). Hershey, PA: IGI Global. doi:10.4018/978-1-4666-9978-6.ch040

Domingos, D., Respício, A., & Martinho, R. (2017). Reliability of IoT-Aware BPMN Healthcare Processes. In C. Reis & M. Maximiano (Eds.), *Internet of Things and Advanced Application in Healthcare* (pp. 214–248). Hershey, PA: IGI Global. doi:10.4018/978-1-5225-1820-4.ch008

Dosumu, O., Hussain, J., & El-Gohary, H. (2017). An Exploratory Study of the Impact of Government Policies on the Development of Small and Medium Enterprises in Developing Countries: The Case of Nigeria. *International Journal of Customer Relationship Marketing and Management*, *8*(4), 51–62. doi:10.4018/IJCRMM.2017100104

Durst, S., Bruns, G., & Edvardsson, I. R. (2017). Retaining Knowledge in Smaller Building and Construction Firms. *International Journal of Knowledge and Systems Science*, *8*(3), 1–12. doi:10.4018/IJKSS.2017070101

Edvardsson, I. R., & Durst, S. (2017). Outsourcing, Knowledge, and Learning: A Critical Review. *International Journal of Knowledge-Based Organizations*, *7*(2), 13–26. doi:10.4018/IJKBO.2017040102

Edwards, J. S. (2018). Integrating Knowledge Management and Business Processes. In M. Khosrow-Pour, D.B.A. (Ed.), Encyclopedia of Information Science and Technology, Fourth Edition (pp. 5046-5055). Hershey, PA: IGI Global. doi:10.4018/978-1-5225-2255-3.ch437

Ejiogu, A. O. (2018). Economics of Farm Management. In *Agricultural Finance and Opportunities for Investment and Expansion* (pp. 56–72). Hershey, PA: IGI Global. doi:10.4018/978-1-5225-3059-6.ch003

Ekanem, I., & Abiade, G. E. (2018). Factors Influencing the Use of E-Commerce by Small Enterprises in Nigeria. *International Journal of ICT Research in Africa and the Middle East*, *7*(1), 37–53. doi:10.4018/IJICTRAME.2018010103

Ekanem, I., & Alrossais, L. A. (2017). Succession Challenges Facing Family Businesses in Saudi Arabia. In P. Zgheib (Ed.), *Entrepreneurship and Business Innovation in the Middle East* (pp. 122–146). Hershey, PA: IGI Global. doi:10.4018/978-1-5225-2066-5.ch007

El Faquih, L., & Fredj, M. (2017). Ontology-Based Framework for Quality in Configurable Process Models. *Journal of Electronic Commerce in Organizations, 15*(2), 48–60. doi:10.4018/JECO.2017040104

El-Gohary, H., & El-Gohary, Z. (2016). An Attempt to Explore Electronic Marketing Adoption and Implementation Aspects in Developing Countries: The Case of Egypt. *International Journal of Customer Relationship Marketing and Management, 7*(4), 1–26. doi:10.4018/IJCRMM.2016100101

Entico, G. J. (2016). Knowledge Management and the Medical Health Librarians: A Perception Study. In J. Yap, M. Perez, M. Ayson, & G. Entico (Eds.), *Special Library Administration, Standardization and Technological Integration* (pp. 52–77). Hershey, PA: IGI Global. doi:10.4018/978-1-4666-9542-9.ch003

Faisal, M. N., & Talib, F. (2017). Building Ambidextrous Supply Chains in SMEs: How to Tackle the Barriers? *International Journal of Information Systems and Supply Chain Management, 10*(4), 80–100. doi:10.4018/IJISSCM.2017100105

Fernandes, T. M., Gomes, J., & Romão, M. (2017). Investments in E-Government: A Benefit Management Case Study. *International Journal of Electronic Government Research, 13*(3), 1–17. doi:10.4018/IJEGR.2017070101

Fouda, F. A. (2016). A Suggested Curriculum in Career Education to Develop Business Secondary Schools Students' Career Knowledge Management Domains and Professional Thinking. *International Journal of Technology Diffusion, 7*(2), 42–62. doi:10.4018/IJTD.2016040103

Gallardo-Vázquez, D., & Pajuelo-Moreno, M. L. (2016). How Spanish Universities are Promoting Entrepreneurship through Your Own Lines of Teaching and Research? In L. Carvalho (Ed.), *Handbook of Research on Entrepreneurial Success and its Impact on Regional Development* (pp. 431–454). Hershey, PA: IGI Global. doi:10.4018/978-1-4666-9567-2.ch019

Gao, S. S., Oreal, S., & Zhang, J. (2018). Contemporary Financial Risk Management Perceptions and Practices of Small-Sized Chinese Businesses. In I. Management Association (Ed.), Global Business Expansion: Concepts, Methodologies, Tools, and Applications (pp. 917-931). Hershey, PA: IGI Global. doi:10.4018/978-1-5225-5481-3.ch041

Garg, R., & Berning, S. C. (2017). Indigenous Chinese Management Philosophies: Key Concepts and Relevance for Modern Chinese Firms. In B. Christiansen & G. Koc (Eds.), *Transcontinental Strategies for Industrial Development and Economic Growth* (pp. 43–57). Hershey, PA: IGI Global. doi:10.4018/978-1-5225-2160-0.ch003

Gencer, Y. G. (2017). Supply Chain Management in Retailing Business. In U. Akkucuk (Ed.), *Ethics and Sustainability in Global Supply Chain Management* (pp. 197–210). Hershey, PA: IGI Global. doi:10.4018/978-1-5225-2036-8.ch011

Giacosa, E. (2016). Innovation in Luxury Fashion Businesses as a Means for the Regional Development. In L. Carvalho (Ed.), *Handbook of Research on Entrepreneurial Success and its Impact on Regional Development* (pp. 206–222). Hershey, PA: IGI Global. doi:10.4018/978-1-4666-9567-2.ch010

Giacosa, E. (2018). The Increasing of the Regional Development Thanks to the Luxury Business Innovation. In L. Carvalho (Ed.), *Handbook of Research on Entrepreneurial Ecosystems and Social Dynamics in a Globalized World* (pp. 260–273). Hershey, PA: IGI Global. doi:10.4018/978-1-5225-3525-6.ch011

Gianni, M., & Gotzamani, K. (2016). Integrated Management Systems and Information Management Systems: Common Threads. In P. Papajorgji, F. Pinet, A. Guimarães, & J. Papathanasiou (Eds.), *Automated Enterprise Systems for Maximizing Business Performance* (pp. 195–214). Hershey, PA: IGI Global. doi:10.4018/978-1-4666-8841-4.ch011

Gianni, M., Gotzamani, K., & Linden, I. (2016). How a BI-wise Responsible Integrated Management System May Support Food Traceability. *International Journal of Decision Support System Technology*, *8*(2), 1–17. doi:10.4018/IJDSST.2016040101

Glykas, M., & George, J. (2017). Quality and Process Management Systems in the UAE Maritime Industry. *International Journal of Productivity Management and Assessment Technologies*, *5*(1), 20–39. doi:10.4018/IJPMAT.2017010102

Glykas, M., Valiris, G., Kokkinaki, A., & Koutsoukou, Z. (2018). Banking Business Process Management Implementation. *International Journal of Productivity Management and Assessment Technologies*, *6*(1), 50–69. doi:10.4018/IJPMAT.2018010104

Gomes, J., & Romão, M. (2017). The Balanced Scorecard: Keeping Updated and Aligned with Today's Business Trends. *International Journal of Productivity Management and Assessment Technologies*, *5*(2), 1–15. doi:10.4018/IJPMAT.2017070101

Gomes, J., & Romão, M. (2017). Aligning Information Systems and Technology with Benefit Management and Balanced Scorecard. In S. De Haes & W. Van Grembergen (Eds.), *Strategic IT Governance and Alignment in Business Settings* (pp. 112–131). Hershey, PA: IGI Global. doi:10.4018/978-1-5225-0861-8.ch005

Grefen, P., & Turetken, O. (2017). Advanced Business Process Management in Networked E-Business Scenarios. *International Journal of E-Business Research*, *13*(4), 70–104. doi:10.4018/IJEBR.2017100105

Haider, A., & Saetang, S. (2017). Strategic IT Alignment in Service Sector. In S. Rozenes & Y. Cohen (Eds.), *Handbook of Research on Strategic Alliances and Value Co-Creation in the Service Industry* (pp. 231–258). Hershey, PA: IGI Global. doi:10.4018/978-1-5225-2084-9.ch012

Haider, A., & Tang, S. S. (2016). Maximising Value Through IT and Business Alignment: A Case of IT Governance Institutionalisation at a Thai Bank. *International Journal of Technology Diffusion*, *7*(3), 33–58. doi:10.4018/IJTD.2016070104

Hajilari, A. B., Ghadaksaz, M., & Fasghandis, G. S. (2017). Assessing Organizational Readiness for Implementing ERP System Using Fuzzy Expert System Approach. *International Journal of Enterprise Information Systems*, *13*(1), 67–85. doi:10.4018/IJEIS.2017010105

Haldorai, A., Ramu, A., & Murugan, S. (2018). Social Aware Cognitive Radio Networks: Effectiveness of Social Networks as a Strategic Tool for Organizational Business Management. In H. Bansal, G. Shrivastava, G. Nguyen, & L. Stanciu (Eds.), *Social Network Analytics for Contemporary Business Organizations* (pp. 188–202). Hershey, PA: IGI Global. doi:10.4018/978-1-5225-5097-6.ch010

Hall, O. P. Jr. (2017). Social Media Driven Management Education. *International Journal of Knowledge-Based Organizations*, *7*(2), 43–59. doi:10.4018/IJKBO.2017040104

Hanifah, H., Halim, H. A., Ahmad, N. H., & Vafaei-Zadeh, A. (2017). Innovation Culture as a Mediator Between Specific Human Capital and Innovation Performance Among Bumiputera SMEs in Malaysia. In N. Ahmad, T. Ramayah, H. Halim, & S. Rahman (Eds.), *Handbook of Research on Small and Medium Enterprises in Developing Countries* (pp. 261–279). Hershey, PA: IGI Global. doi:10.4018/978-1-5225-2165-5.ch012

Hartlieb, S., & Silvius, G. (2017). Handling Uncertainty in Project Management and Business Development: Similarities and Differences. In Y. Raydugin (Ed.), *Handbook of Research on Leveraging Risk and Uncertainties for Effective Project Management* (pp. 337–362). Hershey, PA: IGI Global. doi:10.4018/978-1-5225-1790-0.ch016

Hass, K. B. (2017). Living on the Edge: Managing Project Complexity. In Y. Raydugin (Ed.), *Handbook of Research on Leveraging Risk and Uncertainties for Effective Project Management* (pp. 177–201). Hershey, PA: IGI Global. doi:10.4018/978-1-5225-1790-0.ch009

Hassan, A., & Privitera, D. S. (2016). Google AdSense as a Mobile Technology in Education. In J. Holland (Ed.), *Wearable Technology and Mobile Innovations for Next-Generation Education* (pp. 200–223). Hershey, PA: IGI Global. doi:10.4018/978-1-5225-0069-8.ch011

Hassan, A., & Rahimi, R. (2016). Consuming "Innovation" in Tourism: Augmented Reality as an Innovation Tool in Digital Tourism Marketing. In N. Pappas & I. Bregoli (Eds.), *Global Dynamics in Travel, Tourism, and Hospitality* (pp. 130–147). Hershey, PA: IGI Global. doi:10.4018/978-1-5225-0201-2.ch008

Hawking, P., & Carmine Sellitto, C. (2017). Developing an Effective Strategy for Organizational Business Intelligence. In M. Tavana (Ed.), *Enterprise Information Systems and the Digitalization of Business Functions* (pp. 222–237). Hershey, PA: IGI Global. doi:10.4018/978-1-5225-2382-6.ch010

Hawking, P., & Sellitto, C. (2017). A Fast-Moving Consumer Goods Company and Business Intelligence Strategy Development. *International Journal of Enterprise Information Systems, 13*(2), 22–33. doi:10.4018/IJEIS.2017040102

Hawking, P., & Sellitto, C. (2017). Business Intelligence Strategy: Two Case Studies. *International Journal of Business Intelligence Research, 8*(2), 17–30. doi:10.4018/IJBIR.2017070102

Haynes, J. D., Arockiasamy, S., Al Rashdi, M., & Al Rashdi, S. (2016). Business and E Business Strategies for Coopetition and Thematic Management as a Sustained Basis for Ethics and Social Responsibility in Emerging Markets. In M. Al-Shammari & H. Masri (Eds.), *Ethical and Social Perspectives on Global Business Interaction in Emerging Markets* (pp. 25–39). Hershey, PA: IGI Global. doi:10.4018/978-1-4666-9864-2.ch002

Hee, W. J., Jalleh, G., Lai, H., & Lin, C. (2017). E-Commerce and IT Projects: Evaluation and Management Issues in Australian and Taiwanese Hospitals. *International Journal of Public Health Management and Ethics*, *2*(1), 69–90. doi:10.4018/IJPHME.2017010104

Hernandez, A. A. (2018). Exploring the Factors to Green IT Adoption of SMEs in the Philippines. *Journal of Cases on Information Technology*, *20*(2), 49–66. doi:10.4018/JCIT.2018040104

Hernandez, A. A., & Ona, S. E. (2016). Green IT Adoption: Lessons from the Philippines Business Process Outsourcing Industry. *International Journal of Social Ecology and Sustainable Development*, *7*(1), 1–34. doi:10.4018/IJSESD.2016010101

Hollman, A., Bickford, S., & Hollman, T. (2017). Cyber InSecurity: A Post-Mortem Attempt to Assess Cyber Problems from IT and Business Management Perspectives. *Journal of Cases on Information Technology*, *19*(3), 42–70. doi:10.4018/JCIT.2017070104

Igbinakhase, I. (2017). Responsible and Sustainable Management Practices in Developing and Developed Business Environments. In Z. Fields (Ed.), *Collective Creativity for Responsible and Sustainable Business Practice* (pp. 180–207). Hershey, PA: IGI Global. doi:10.4018/978-1-5225-1823-5.ch010

Ilahi, L., Ghannouchi, S. A., & Martinho, R. (2016). A Business Process Management Approach to Home Healthcare Processes: On the Gap between Intention and Reality. In M. Cruz-Cunha, I. Miranda, R. Martinho, & R. Rijo (Eds.), *Encyclopedia of E-Health and Telemedicine* (pp. 439–457). Hershey, PA: IGI Global. doi:10.4018/978-1-4666-9978-6.ch035

Iwata, J. J., & Hoskins, R. G. (2017). Managing Indigenous Knowledge in Tanzania: A Business Perspective. In P. Jain & N. Mnjama (Eds.), *Managing Knowledge Resources and Records in Modern Organizations* (pp. 198–214). Hershey, PA: IGI Global. doi:10.4018/978-1-5225-1965-2.ch012

Jabeen, F., Ahmad, S. Z., & Alkaabi, S. (2016). The Internationalization Decision-Making of United Arab Emirates Family Businesses. In N. Zakaria, A. Abdul-Talib, & N. Osman (Eds.), *Handbook of Research on Impacts of International Business and Political Affairs on the Global Economy* (pp. 1–22). Hershey, PA: IGI Global. doi:10.4018/978-1-4666-9806-2.ch001

Jain, P. (2017). Ethical and Legal Issues in Knowledge Management Life-Cycle in Business. In P. Jain & N. Mnjama (Eds.), *Managing Knowledge Resources and Records in Modern Organizations* (pp. 82–101). Hershey, PA: IGI Global. doi:10.4018/978-1-5225-1965-2.ch006

Jamali, D., Abdallah, H., & Matar, F. (2016). Opportunities and Challenges for CSR Mainstreaming in Business Schools. *International Journal of Technology and Educational Marketing*, *6*(2), 1–29. doi:10.4018/IJTEM.2016070101

James, S., & Hauli, E. (2017). Holistic Management Education at Tanzanian Rural Development Planning Institute. In N. Baporikar (Ed.), *Management Education for Global Leadership* (pp. 112–136). Hershey, PA: IGI Global. doi:10.4018/978-1-5225-1013-0.ch006

Janošková, M., Csikósová, A., & Čulková, K. (2018). Measurement of Company Performance as Part of Its Strategic Management. In R. Leon (Ed.), *Managerial Strategies for Business Sustainability During Turbulent Times* (pp. 309–335). Hershey, PA: IGI Global. doi:10.4018/978-1-5225-2716-9.ch017

Jean-Vasile, A., & Alecu, A. (2017). Theoretical and Practical Approaches in Understanding the Influences of Cost-Productivity-Profit Trinomial in Contemporary Enterprises. In A. Jean Vasile & D. Nicolò (Eds.), *Sustainable Entrepreneurship and Investments in the Green Economy* (pp. 28–62). Hershey, PA: IGI Global. doi:10.4018/978-1-5225-2075-7.ch002

Jha, D. G. (2016). Preparing for Information Technology Driven Changes. In S. Tiwari & L. Nafees (Eds.), *Innovative Management Education Pedagogies for Preparing Next-Generation Leaders* (pp. 258–274). Hershey, PA: IGI Global. doi:10.4018/978-1-4666-9691-4.ch015

Joia, L. A., & Correia, J. C. (2018). CIO Competencies From the IT Professional Perspective: Insights From Brazil. *Journal of Global Information Management*, *26*(2), 74–103. doi:10.4018/JGIM.2018040104

Juma, A., & Mzera, N. (2017). Knowledge Management and Records Management and Competitive Advantage in Business. In P. Jain & N. Mnjama (Eds.), *Managing Knowledge Resources and Records in Modern Organizations* (pp. 15–28). Hershey, PA: IGI Global. doi:10.4018/978-1-5225-1965-2.ch002

K., I., & A, V. (2018). Monitoring and Auditing in the Cloud. In K. Munir (Ed.), *Cloud Computing Technologies for Green Enterprises* (pp. 318-350). Hershey, PA: IGI Global. doi:10.4018/978-1-5225-3038-1.ch013

Kabra, G., Ghosh, V., & Ramesh, A. (2018). Enterprise Integrated Business Process Management and Business Intelligence Framework for Business Process Sustainability. In A. Paul, D. Bhattacharyya, & S. Anand (Eds.), *Green Initiatives for Business Sustainability and Value Creation* (pp. 228–238). Hershey, PA: IGI Global. doi:10.4018/978-1-5225-2662-9.ch010

Kaoud, M. (2017). Investigation of Customer Knowledge Management: A Case Study Research. *International Journal of Service Science, Management, Engineering, and Technology*, *8*(2), 12–22. doi:10.4018/IJSSMET.2017040102

Kara, M. E., & Fırat, S. Ü. (2016). Sustainability, Risk, and Business Intelligence in Supply Chains. In M. Erdoğdu, T. Arun, & I. Ahmad (Eds.), *Handbook of Research on Green Economic Development Initiatives and Strategies* (pp. 501–538). Hershey, PA: IGI Global. doi:10.4018/978-1-5225-0440-5.ch022

Katuu, S. (2018). A Comparative Assessment of Enterprise Content Management Maturity Models. In N. Gwangwava & M. Mutingi (Eds.), *E-Manufacturing and E-Service Strategies in Contemporary Organizations* (pp. 93–118). Hershey, PA: IGI Global. doi:10.4018/978-1-5225-3628-4.ch005

Khan, M. A. (2016). MNEs Management Strategies in Developing Countries: Establishing the Context. In M. Khan (Ed.), *Multinational Enterprise Management Strategies in Developing Countries* (pp. 1–33). Hershey, PA: IGI Global. doi:10.4018/978-1-5225-0276-0.ch001

Khan, M. A. (2016). Operational Approaches in Organizational Structure: A Case for MNEs in Developing Countries. In M. Khan (Ed.), *Multinational Enterprise Management Strategies in Developing Countries* (pp. 129–151). Hershey, PA: IGI Global. doi:10.4018/978-1-5225-0276-0.ch007

Kinnunen, S., Ylä-Kujala, A., Marttonen-Arola, S., Kärri, T., & Baglee, D. (2018). Internet of Things in Asset Management: Insights from Industrial Professionals and Academia. *International Journal of Service Science, Management, Engineering, and Technology, 9*(2), 104–119. doi:10.4018/IJSSMET.2018040105

Klein, A. Z., Sabino de Freitas, A., Machado, L., Freitas, J. C. Jr, Graziola, P. G. Jr, & Schlemmer, E. (2017). Virtual Worlds Applications for Management Education. In L. Tomei (Ed.), *Exploring the New Era of Technology-Infused Education* (pp. 279–299). Hershey, PA: IGI Global. doi:10.4018/978-1-5225-1709-2.ch017

Kożuch, B., & Jabłoński, A. (2017). Adopting the Concept of Business Models in Public Management. In M. Lewandowski & B. Kożuch (Eds.), *Public Sector Entrepreneurship and the Integration of Innovative Business Models* (pp. 10–46). Hershey, PA: IGI Global. doi:10.4018/978-1-5225-2215-7.ch002

Kumar, J., Adhikary, A., & Jha, A. (2017). Small Active Investors' Perceptions and Preferences Towards Tax Saving Mutual Fund Schemes in Eastern India: An Empirical Note. *International Journal of Asian Business and Information Management, 8*(2), 35–45. doi:10.4018/IJABIM.2017040103

Lassoued, Y., Bouzguenda, L., & Mahmoud, T. (2016). Context-Aware Business Process Versions Management. *International Journal of e-Collaboration, 12*(3), 7–33. doi:10.4018/IJeC.2016070102

Lavassani, K. M., & Movahedi, B. (2017). Applications Driven Information Systems: Beyond Networks toward Business Ecosystems. *International Journal of Innovation in the Digital Economy, 8*(1), 61–75. doi:10.4018/IJIDE.2017010104

Lazzareschi, V. H., & Brito, M. S. (2017). Strategic Information Management: Proposal of Business Project Model. In G. Jamil, A. Soares, & C. Pessoa (Eds.), *Handbook of Research on Information Management for Effective Logistics and Supply Chains* (pp. 59–88). Hershey, PA: IGI Global. doi:10.4018/978-1-5225-0973-8.ch004

Lederer, M., Kurz, M., & Lazarov, P. (2017). Usage and Suitability of Methods for Strategic Business Process Initiatives: A Multi Case Study Research. *International Journal of Productivity Management and Assessment Technologies, 5*(1), 40–51. doi:10.4018/IJPMAT.2017010103

Lee, I. (2017). A Social Enterprise Business Model and a Case Study of Pacific Community Ventures (PCV). In V. Potocan, M. Üngan, & Z. Nedelko (Eds.), *Handbook of Research on Managerial Solutions in Non-Profit Organizations* (pp. 182–204). Hershey, PA: IGI Global. doi:10.4018/978-1-5225-0731-4.ch009

Lee, L. J., & Leu, J. (2016). Exploring the Effectiveness of IT Application and Value Method in the Innovation Performance of Enterprise. *International Journal of Enterprise Information Systems*, *12*(2), 47–65. doi:10.4018/IJEIS.2016040104

Lee, Y. (2016). Alignment Effect of Entrepreneurial Orientation and Marketing Orientation on Firm Performance. *International Journal of Customer Relationship Marketing and Management*, *7*(4), 58–69. doi:10.4018/IJCRMM.2016100104

Leon, L. A., Seal, K. C., Przasnyski, Z. H., & Wiedenman, I. (2017). Skills and Competencies Required for Jobs in Business Analytics: A Content Analysis of Job Advertisements Using Text Mining. *International Journal of Business Intelligence Research*, *8*(1), 1–25. doi:10.4018/IJBIR.2017010101

Leu, J., Lee, L. J., & Krischke, A. (2016). Value Engineering-Based Method for Implementing the ISO14001 System in the Green Supply Chains. *International Journal of Strategic Decision Sciences*, *7*(4), 1–20. doi:10.4018/IJSDS.2016100101

Levy, C. L., & Elias, N. I. (2017). SOHO Users' Perceptions of Reliability and Continuity of Cloud-Based Services. In M. Moore (Ed.), *Cybersecurity Breaches and Issues Surrounding Online Threat Protection* (pp. 248–287). Hershey, PA: IGI Global. doi:10.4018/978-1-5225-1941-6.ch011

Levy, M. (2018). Change Management Serving Knowledge Management and Organizational Development: Reflections and Review. In N. Baporikar (Ed.), *Global Practices in Knowledge Management for Societal and Organizational Development* (pp. 256–270). Hershey, PA: IGI Global. doi:10.4018/978-1-5225-3009-1.ch012

Lewandowski, M. (2017). Public Organizations and Business Model Innovation: The Role of Public Service Design. In M. Lewandowski & B. Kożuch (Eds.), *Public Sector Entrepreneurship and the Integration of Innovative Business Models* (pp. 47–72). Hershey, PA: IGI Global. doi:10.4018/978-1-5225-2215-7.ch003

Lhannaoui, H., Kabbaj, M. I., & Bakkoury, Z. (2017). A Survey of Risk-Aware Business Process Modelling. *International Journal of Risk and Contingency Management*, *6*(3), 14–26. doi:10.4018/IJRCM.2017070102

Li, J., Sun, W., Jiang, W., Yang, H., & Zhang, L. (2017). How the Nature of Exogenous Shocks and Crises Impact Company Performance?: The Effects of Industry Characteristics. *International Journal of Risk and Contingency Management*, *6*(4), 40–55. doi:10.4018/IJRCM.2017100103

Lu, C., & Liu, S. (2016). Cultural Tourism O2O Business Model Innovation-A Case Study of CTrip. *Journal of Electronic Commerce in Organizations*, *14*(2), 16–31. doi:10.4018/JECO.2016040102

Machen, B., Hosseini, M. R., Wood, A., & Bakhshi, J. (2016). An Investigation into using SAP-PS as a Multidimensional Project Control System (MPCS). *International Journal of Enterprise Information Systems*, *12*(2), 66–81. doi:10.4018/IJEIS.2016040105

Malega, P. (2017). Small and Medium Enterprises in the Slovak Republic: Status and Competitiveness of SMEs in the Global Markets and Possibilities of Optimization. In M. Vemić (Ed.), *Optimal Management Strategies in Small and Medium Enterprises* (pp. 102–124). Hershey, PA: IGI Global. doi:10.4018/978-1-5225-1949-2.ch006

Malewska, K. M. (2017). Intuition in Decision-Making on the Example of a Non-Profit Organization. In V. Potocan, M. Ünğan, & Z. Nedelko (Eds.), *Handbook of Research on Managerial Solutions in Non-Profit Organizations* (pp. 378–399). Hershey, PA: IGI Global. doi:10.4018/978-1-5225-0731-4.ch018

Maroofi, F. (2017). Entrepreneurial Orientation and Organizational Learning Ability Analysis for Innovation and Firm Performance. In N. Baporikar (Ed.), *Innovation and Shifting Perspectives in Management Education* (pp. 144–165). Hershey, PA: IGI Global. doi:10.4018/978-1-5225-1019-2.ch007

Martins, P. V., & Zacarias, M. (2017). A Web-based Tool for Business Process Improvement. *International Journal of Web Portals*, *9*(2), 68–84. doi:10.4018/IJWP.2017070104

Matthies, B., & Coners, A. (2017). Exploring the Conceptual Nature of e-Business Projects. *Journal of Electronic Commerce in Organizations*, *15*(3), 33–63. doi:10.4018/JECO.2017070103

McKee, J. (2018). Architecture as a Tool to Solve Business Planning Problems. In M. Khosrow-Pour, D.B.A. (Ed.), Encyclopedia of Information Science and Technology, Fourth Edition (pp. 573-586). Hershey, PA: IGI Global. doi:10.4018/978-1-5225-2255-3.ch050

McMurray, A. J., Cross, J., & Caponecchia, C. (2018). The Risk Management Profession in Australia: Business Continuity Plan Practices. In N. Bajgoric (Ed.), *Always-On Enterprise Information Systems for Modern Organizations* (pp. 112–129). Hershey, PA: IGI Global. doi:10.4018/978-1-5225-3704-5.ch006

Meddah, I. H., & Belkadi, K. (2018). Mining Patterns Using Business Process Management. In R. Hamou (Ed.), *Handbook of Research on Biomimicry in Information Retrieval and Knowledge Management* (pp. 78–89). Hershey, PA: IGI Global. doi:10.4018/978-1-5225-3004-6.ch005

Mendes, L. (2017). TQM and Knowledge Management: An Integrated Approach Towards Tacit Knowledge Management. In D. Jaziri-Bouagina & G. Jamil (Eds.), *Handbook of Research on Tacit Knowledge Management for Organizational Success* (pp. 236–263). Hershey, PA: IGI Global. doi:10.4018/978-1-5225-2394-9.ch009

Mnjama, N. M. (2017). Preservation of Recorded Information in Public and Private Sector Organizations. In P. Jain & N. Mnjama (Eds.), *Managing Knowledge Resources and Records in Modern Organizations* (pp. 149–167). Hershey, PA: IGI Global. doi:10.4018/978-1-5225-1965-2.ch009

Mokoqama, M., & Fields, Z. (2017). Principles of Responsible Management Education (PRME): Call for Responsible Management Education. In Z. Fields (Ed.), *Collective Creativity for Responsible and Sustainable Business Practice* (pp. 229–241). Hershey, PA: IGI Global. doi:10.4018/978-1-5225-1823-5.ch012

Muniapan, B. (2017). Philosophy and Management: The Relevance of Vedanta in Management. In P. Ordóñez de Pablos (Ed.), *Managerial Strategies and Solutions for Business Success in Asia* (pp. 124–139). Hershey, PA: IGI Global. doi:10.4018/978-1-5225-1886-0.ch007

Muniapan, B., Gregory, M. L., & Ling, L. A. (2016). Marketing Education in Sarawak: Looking at It from the Employers' Viewpoint. In B. Smith & A. Porath (Eds.), *Global Perspectives on Contemporary Marketing Education* (pp. 112–130). Hershey, PA: IGI Global. doi:10.4018/978-1-4666-9784-3.ch008

Murad, S. E., & Dowaji, S. (2017). Using Value-Based Approach for Managing Cloud-Based Services. In A. Turuk, B. Sahoo, & S. Addya (Eds.), *Resource Management and Efficiency in Cloud Computing Environments* (pp. 33–60). Hershey, PA: IGI Global. doi:10.4018/978-1-5225-1721-4.ch002

Mutahar, A. M., Daud, N. M., Thurasamy, R., Isaac, O., & Abdulsalam, R. (2018). The Mediating of Perceived Usefulness and Perceived Ease of Use: The Case of Mobile Banking in Yemen. *International Journal of Technology Diffusion*, *9*(2), 21–40. doi:10.4018/IJTD.2018040102

Naidoo, V. (2017). E-Learning and Management Education at African Universities. In N. Baporikar (Ed.), *Management Education for Global Leadership* (pp. 181–201). Hershey, PA: IGI Global. doi:10.4018/978-1-5225-1013-0.ch009

Naidoo, V., & Igbinakhase, I. (2018). Opportunities and Challenges of Knowledge Retention in SMEs. In N. Baporikar (Ed.), *Knowledge Integration Strategies for Entrepreneurship and Sustainability* (pp. 70–94). Hershey, PA: IGI Global. doi:10.4018/978-1-5225-5115-7.ch004

Nayak, S., & Prabhu, N. (2017). Paradigm Shift in Management Education: Need for a Cross Functional Perspective. In N. Baporikar (Ed.), *Management Education for Global Leadership* (pp. 241–255). Hershey, PA: IGI Global. doi:10.4018/978-1-5225-1013-0.ch012

Ndede-Amadi, A. A. (2016). Student Interest in the IS Specialization as Predictor of the Success Potential of New Information Systems Programmes within the Schools of Business in Kenyan Public Universities. *International Journal of Information Systems and Social Change*, *7*(2), 63–79. doi:10.4018/IJISSC.2016040104

Nedelko, Z., & Potocan, V. (2016). Management Practices for Processes Optimization: Case of Slovenia. In G. Alor-Hernández, C. Sánchez-Ramírez, & J. García-Alcaraz (Eds.), *Handbook of Research on Managerial Strategies for Achieving Optimal Performance in Industrial Processes* (pp. 545–561). Hershey, PA: IGI Global. doi:10.4018/978-1-5225-0130-5.ch025

Nedelko, Z., & Potocan, V. (2017). Management Solutions in Non-Profit Organizations: Case of Slovenia. In V. Potocan, M. Üngan, & Z. Nedelko (Eds.), *Handbook of Research on Managerial Solutions in Non-Profit Organizations* (pp. 1–22). Hershey, PA: IGI Global. doi:10.4018/978-1-5225-0731-4.ch001

Nedelko, Z., & Potocan, V. (2017). Priority of Management Tools Utilization among Managers: International Comparison. In V. Wang (Ed.), *Encyclopedia of Strategic Leadership and Management* (pp. 1083–1094). Hershey, PA: IGI Global. doi:10.4018/978-1-5225-1049-9.ch075

Nedelko, Z., Raudeliūnienė, J., & Črešnar, R. (2018). Knowledge Dynamics in Supply Chain Management. In N. Baporikar (Ed.), *Knowledge Integration Strategies for Entrepreneurship and Sustainability* (pp. 150–166). Hershey, PA: IGI Global. doi:10.4018/978-1-5225-5115-7.ch008

Nguyen, H. T., & Hipsher, S. A. (2018). Innovation and Creativity Used by Private Sector Firms in a Resources-Constrained Environment. In S. Hipsher (Ed.), *Examining the Private Sector's Role in Wealth Creation and Poverty Reduction* (pp. 219–238). Hershey, PA: IGI Global. doi:10.4018/978-1-5225-3117-3.ch010

Nycz, M., & Pólkowski, Z. (2016). Business Intelligence as a Modern IT Supporting Management of Local Government Units in Poland. *International Journal of Knowledge and Systems Science*, *7*(4), 1–18. doi:10.4018/IJKSS.2016100101

Obaji, N. O., Senin, A. A., & Olugu, M. U. (2016). Supportive Government Policy as a Mechanism for Business Incubation Performance in Nigeria. *International Journal of Information Systems and Social Change*, *7*(4), 52–66. doi:10.4018/IJISSC.2016100103

Obicci, P. A. (2017). Risk Sharing in a Partnership. In *Risk Management Strategies in Public-Private Partnerships* (pp. 115–152). Hershey, PA: IGI Global. doi:10.4018/978-1-5225-2503-5.ch004

Obidallah, W. J., & Raahemi, B. (2017). Managing Changes in Service Oriented Virtual Organizations: A Structural and Procedural Framework to Facilitate the Process of Change. *Journal of Electronic Commerce in Organizations*, *15*(1), 59–83. doi:10.4018/JECO.2017010104

Ojasalo, J., & Ojasalo, K. (2016). Service Logic Business Model Canvas for Lean Development of SMEs and Start-Ups. In N. Baporikar (Ed.), *Handbook of Research on Entrepreneurship in the Contemporary Knowledge-Based Global Economy* (pp. 217–243). Hershey, PA: IGI Global. doi:10.4018/978-1-4666-8798-1.ch010

Ojo, O. (2017). Impact of Innovation on the Entrepreneurial Success in Selected Business Enterprises in South-West Nigeria. *International Journal of Innovation in the Digital Economy*, *8*(2), 29–38. doi:10.4018/IJIDE.2017040103

Okdinawati, L., Simatupang, T. M., & Sunitiyoso, Y. (2017). Multi-Agent Reinforcement Learning for Value Co-Creation of Collaborative Transportation Management (CTM). *International Journal of Information Systems and Supply Chain Management*, *10*(3), 84–95. doi:10.4018/IJISSCM.2017070105

Ortner, E., Mevius, M., Wiedmann, P., & Kurz, F. (2016). Design of Interactional Decision Support Applications for E-Participation in Smart Cities. *International Journal of Electronic Government Research, 12*(2), 18–38. doi:10.4018/IJEGR.2016040102

Pal, K. (2018). Building High Quality Big Data-Based Applications in Supply Chains. In A. Kumar & S. Saurav (Eds.), *Supply Chain Management Strategies and Risk Assessment in Retail Environments* (pp. 1–24). Hershey, PA: IGI Global. doi:10.4018/978-1-5225-3056-5.ch001

Palos-Sanchez, P. R., & Correia, M. B. (2018). Perspectives of the Adoption of Cloud Computing in the Tourism Sector. In J. Rodrigues, C. Ramos, P. Cardoso, & C. Henriques (Eds.), *Handbook of Research on Technological Developments for Cultural Heritage and eTourism Applications* (pp. 377–400). Hershey, PA: IGI Global. doi:10.4018/978-1-5225-2927-9.ch018

Parry, V. K., & Lind, M. L. (2016). Alignment of Business Strategy and Information Technology Considering Information Technology Governance, Project Portfolio Control, and Risk Management. *International Journal of Information Technology Project Management, 7*(4), 21–37. doi:10.4018/IJITPM.2016100102

Pashkova, N., Trujillo-Barrera, A., Apostolakis, G., Van Dijk, G., Drakos, P. D., & Baourakis, G. (2016). Business Management Models of Microfinance Institutions (MFIs) in Africa: A Study into Their Enabling Environments. *International Journal of Food and Beverage Manufacturing and Business Models, 1*(2), 63–82. doi:10.4018/IJFBMBM.2016070105

Patiño, B. E. (2017). New Generation Management by Convergence and Individual Identity: A Systemic and Human-Oriented Approach. In N. Baporikar (Ed.), *Innovation and Shifting Perspectives in Management Education* (pp. 119–143). Hershey, PA: IGI Global. doi:10.4018/978-1-5225-1019-2.ch006

Pawliczek, A., & Rössler, M. (2017). Knowledge of Management Tools and Systems in SMEs: Knowledge Transfer in Management. In A. Bencsik (Ed.), *Knowledge Management Initiatives and Strategies in Small and Medium Enterprises* (pp. 180–203). Hershey, PA: IGI Global. doi:10.4018/978-1-5225-1642-2.ch009

Pejic-Bach, M., Omazic, M. A., Aleksic, A., & Zoroja, J. (2018). Knowledge-Based Decision Making: A Multi-Case Analysis. In R. Leon (Ed.), *Managerial Strategies for Business Sustainability During Turbulent Times* (pp. 160–184). Hershey, PA: IGI Global. doi:10.4018/978-1-5225-2716-9.ch009

Perano, M., Hysa, X., & Calabrese, M. (2018). Strategic Planning, Cultural Context, and Business Continuity Management: Business Cases in the City of Shkoder. In A. Presenza & L. Sheehan (Eds.), *Geopolitics and Strategic Management in the Global Economy* (pp. 57–77). Hershey, PA: IGI Global. doi:10.4018/978-1-5225-2673-5.ch004

Pereira, R., Mira da Silva, M., & Lapão, L. V. (2017). IT Governance Maturity Patterns in Portuguese Healthcare. In S. De Haes & W. Van Grembergen (Eds.), *Strategic IT Governance and Alignment in Business Settings* (pp. 24–52). Hershey, PA: IGI Global. doi:10.4018/978-1-5225-0861-8.ch002

Perez-Uribe, R., & Ocampo-Guzman, D. (2016). Conflict within Colombian Family Owned SMEs: An Explosive Blend between Feelings and Business. In J. Saiz-Álvarez (Ed.), *Handbook of Research on Social Entrepreneurship and Solidarity Economics* (pp. 329–354). Hershey, PA: IGI Global. doi:10.4018/978-1-5225-0097-1.ch017

Pérez-Uribe, R. I., Torres, D. A., Jurado, S. P., & Prada, D. M. (2018). Cloud Tools for the Development of Project Management in SMEs. In R. Perez-Uribe, C. Salcedo-Perez, & D. Ocampo-Guzman (Eds.), *Handbook of Research on Intrapreneurship and Organizational Sustainability in SMEs* (pp. 95–120). Hershey, PA: IGI Global. doi:10.4018/978-1-5225-3543-0.ch005

Petrisor, I., & Cozmiuc, D. (2017). Global Supply Chain Management Organization at Siemens in the Advent of Industry 4.0. In L. Saglietto & C. Cezanne (Eds.), *Global Intermediation and Logistics Service Providers* (pp. 123–142). Hershey, PA: IGI Global. doi:10.4018/978-1-5225-2133-4.ch007

Pierce, J. M., Velliaris, D. M., & Edwards, J. (2017). A Living Case Study: A Journey Not a Destination. In N. Silton (Ed.), *Exploring the Benefits of Creativity in Education, Media, and the Arts* (pp. 158–178). Hershey, PA: IGI Global. doi:10.4018/978-1-5225-0504-4.ch008

Radosavljevic, M., & Andjelkovic, A. (2017). Multi-Criteria Decision Making Approach for Choosing Business Process for the Improvement: Upgrading of the Six Sigma Methodology. In J. Stanković, P. Delias, S. Marinković, & S. Rochhia (Eds.), *Tools and Techniques for Economic Decision Analysis* (pp. 225–247). Hershey, PA: IGI Global. doi:10.4018/978-1-5225-0959-2.ch011

Radovic, V. M. (2017). Corporate Sustainability and Responsibility and Disaster Risk Reduction: A Serbian Overview. In M. Camilleri (Ed.), *CSR 2.0 and the New Era of Corporate Citizenship* (pp. 147–164). Hershey, PA: IGI Global. doi:10.4018/978-1-5225-1842-6.ch008

Raghunath, K. M., Devi, S. L., & Patro, C. S. (2018). Impact of Risk Assessment Models on Risk Factors: A Holistic Outlook. In K. Strang, M. Korstanje, & N. Vajjhala (Eds.), *Research, Practices, and Innovations in Global Risk and Contingency Management* (pp. 134–153). Hershey, PA: IGI Global. doi:10.4018/978-1-5225-4754-9.ch008

Raman, A., & Goyal, D. P. (2017). Extending IMPLEMENT Framework for Enterprise Information Systems Implementation to Information System Innovation. In M. Tavana (Ed.), *Enterprise Information Systems and the Digitalization of Business Functions* (pp. 137–177). Hershey, PA: IGI Global. doi:10.4018/978-1-5225-2382-6.ch007

Rao, Y., & Zhang, Y. (2017). The Construction and Development of Academic Library Digital Special Subject Databases. In L. Ruan, Q. Zhu, & Y. Ye (Eds.), *Academic Library Development and Administration in China* (pp. 163–183). Hershey, PA: IGI Global. doi:10.4018/978-1-5225-0550-1.ch010

Ravasan, A. Z., Mohammadi, M. M., & Hamidi, H. (2018). An Investigation Into the Critical Success Factors of Implementing Information Technology Service Management Frameworks. In K. Jakobs (Ed.), *Corporate and Global Standardization Initiatives in Contemporary Society* (pp. 200–218). Hershey, PA: IGI Global. doi:10.4018/978-1-5225-5320-5.ch009

Renna, P., Izzo, C., & Romaniello, T. (2016). The Business Process Management Systems to Support Continuous Improvements. In W. Nuninger & J. Châtelet (Eds.), *Handbook of Research on Quality Assurance and Value Management in Higher Education* (pp. 237–256). Hershey, PA: IGI Global. doi:10.4018/978-1-5225-0024-7.ch009

Rezaie, S., Mirabedini, S. J., & Abtahi, A. (2018). Designing a Model for Implementation of Business Intelligence in the Banking Industry. *International Journal of Enterprise Information Systems*, *14*(1), 77–103. doi:10.4018/IJEIS.2018010105

Riccò, R. (2016). Diversity Management: Bringing Equality, Equity, and Inclusion in the Workplace. In J. Prescott (Ed.), *Handbook of Research on Race, Gender, and the Fight for Equality* (pp. 335–359). Hershey, PA: IGI Global. doi:10.4018/978-1-5225-0047-6.ch015

Romano, L., Grimaldi, R., & Colasuonno, F. S. (2017). Demand Management as a Success Factor in Project Portfolio Management. In L. Romano (Ed.), *Project Portfolio Management Strategies for Effective Organizational Operations* (pp. 202–219). Hershey, PA: IGI Global. doi:10.4018/978-1-5225-2151-8.ch008

Rostek, K. B. (2016). Risk Management: Role and Importance in Business Organization. In D. Jakóbczak (Ed.), *Analyzing Risk through Probabilistic Modeling in Operations Research* (pp. 149–178). Hershey, PA: IGI Global. doi:10.4018/978-1-4666-9458-3.ch007

Rouhani, S., & Savoji, S. R. (2016). A Success Assessment Model for BI Tools Implementation: An Empirical Study of Banking Industry. *International Journal of Business Intelligence Research, 7*(1), 25–44. doi:10.4018/IJBIR.2016010103

Ruan, Z. (2016). A Corpus-Based Functional Analysis of Complex Nominal Groups in Written Business Discourse: The Case of "Business". *International Journal of Computer-Assisted Language Learning and Teaching, 6*(2), 74–90. doi:10.4018/IJCALLT.2016040105

Ruhi, U. (2018). Towards an Interdisciplinary Socio-Technical Definition of Virtual Communities. In M. Khosrow-Pour, D.B.A. (Ed.), Encyclopedia of Information Science and Technology, Fourth Edition (pp. 4278-4295). Hershey, PA: IGI Global. doi:10.4018/978-1-5225-2255-3.ch371

Ryan, J., Doster, B., Daily, S., & Lewis, C. (2016). A Case Study Perspective for Balanced Perioperative Workflow Achievement through Data-Driven Process Improvement. *International Journal of Healthcare Information Systems and Informatics, 11*(3), 19–41. doi:10.4018/IJHISI.2016070102

Safari, M. R., & Jiang, Q. (2018). The Theory and Practice of IT Governance Maturity and Strategies Alignment: Evidence From Banking Industry. *Journal of Global Information Management, 26*(2), 127–146. doi:10.4018/JGIM.2018040106

Sahoo, J., Pati, B., & Mohanty, B. (2017). Knowledge Management as an Academic Discipline: An Assessment. In B. Gunjal (Ed.), *Managing Knowledge and Scholarly Assets in Academic Libraries* (pp. 99–126). Hershey, PA: IGI Global. doi:10.4018/978-1-5225-1741-2.ch005

Saini, D. (2017). Relevance of Teaching Values and Ethics in Management Education. In N. Baporikar (Ed.), *Management Education for Global Leadership* (pp. 90–111). Hershey, PA: IGI Global. doi:10.4018/978-1-5225-1013-0.ch005

Sambhanthan, A. (2017). Assessing and Benchmarking Sustainability in Organisations: An Integrated Conceptual Model. *International Journal of Systems and Service-Oriented Engineering*, *7*(4), 22–43. doi:10.4018/IJSSOE.2017100102

Sambhanthan, A., & Potdar, V. (2017). A Study of the Parameters Impacting Sustainability in Information Technology Organizations. *International Journal of Knowledge-Based Organizations*, *7*(3), 27–39. doi:10.4018/IJKBO.2017070103

Sánchez-Fernández, M. D., & Manríquez, M. R. (2018). The Entrepreneurial Spirit Based on Social Values: The Digital Generation. In P. Isaias & L. Carvalho (Eds.), *User Innovation and the Entrepreneurship Phenomenon in the Digital Economy* (pp. 173–193). Hershey, PA: IGI Global. doi:10.4018/978-1-5225-2826-5.ch009

Sanchez-Ruiz, L., & Blanco, B. (2017). Process Management for SMEs: Barriers, Enablers, and Benefits. In M. Vemić (Ed.), *Optimal Management Strategies in Small and Medium Enterprises* (pp. 293–319). Hershey, PA: IGI Global. doi:10.4018/978-1-5225-1949-2.ch014

Sanz, L. F., Gómez-Pérez, J., & Castillo-Martinez, A. (2018). Analysis of the European ICT Competence Frameworks. In V. Ahuja & S. Rathore (Eds.), *Multidisciplinary Perspectives on Human Capital and Information Technology Professionals* (pp. 225–245). Hershey, PA: IGI Global. doi:10.4018/978-1-5225-5297-0.ch012

Sarvepalli, A., & Godin, J. (2017). Business Process Management in the Classroom. *Journal of Cases on Information Technology*, *19*(2), 17–28. doi:10.4018/JCIT.2017040102

Satpathy, B., & Muniapan, B. (2016). Ancient Wisdom for Transformational Leadership and Its Insights from the Bhagavad-Gita. In U. Aung & P. Ordoñez de Pablos (Eds.), *Managerial Strategies and Practice in the Asian Business Sector* (pp. 1–10). Hershey, PA: IGI Global. doi:10.4018/978-1-4666-9758-4.ch001

Saygili, E. E., Ozturkoglu, Y., & Kocakulah, M. C. (2017). End Users' Perceptions of Critical Success Factors in ERP Applications. *International Journal of Enterprise Information Systems, 13*(4), 58–75. doi:10.4018/IJEIS.2017100104

Saygili, E. E., & Saygili, A. T. (2017). Contemporary Issues in Enterprise Information Systems: A Critical Review of CSFs in ERP Implementations. In M. Tavana (Ed.), *Enterprise Information Systems and the Digitalization of Business Functions* (pp. 120–136). Hershey, PA: IGI Global. doi:10.4018/978-1-5225-2382-6.ch006

Seidenstricker, S., & Antonino, A. (2018). Business Model Innovation-Oriented Technology Management for Emergent Technologies. In M. Khosrow-Pour, D.B.A. (Ed.), Encyclopedia of Information Science and Technology, Fourth Edition (pp. 4560-4569). Hershey, PA: IGI Global. doi:10.4018/978-1-5225-2255-3.ch396

Senaratne, S., & Gunarathne, A. D. (2017). Excellence Perspective for Management Education from a Global Accountants' Hub in Asia. In N. Baporikar (Ed.), *Management Education for Global Leadership* (pp. 158–180). Hershey, PA: IGI Global. doi:10.4018/978-1-5225-1013-0.ch008

Sensuse, D. I., & Cahyaningsih, E. (2018). Knowledge Management Models: A Summative Review. *International Journal of Information Systems in the Service Sector, 10*(1), 71–100. doi:10.4018/IJISSS.2018010105

Sensuse, D. I., Wibowo, W. C., & Cahyaningsih, E. (2016). Indonesian Government Knowledge Management Model: A Theoretical Model. *Information Resources Management Journal, 29*(1), 91–108. doi:10.4018/irmj.2016010106

Seth, M., Goyal, D., & Kiran, R. (2017). Diminution of Impediments in Implementation of Supply Chain Management Information System for Enhancing its Effectiveness in Indian Automobile Industry. *Journal of Global Information Management, 25*(3), 1–20. doi:10.4018/JGIM.2017070101

Seyal, A. H., & Rahman, M. N. (2017). Investigating Impact of Inter-Organizational Factors in Measuring ERP Systems Success: Bruneian Perspectives. In M. Tavana (Ed.), *Enterprise Information Systems and the Digitalization of Business Functions* (pp. 178–204). Hershey, PA: IGI Global. doi:10.4018/978-1-5225-2382-6.ch008

Shaikh, A. A., & Karjaluoto, H. (2016). On Some Misconceptions Concerning Digital Banking and Alternative Delivery Channels. *International Journal of E-Business Research, 12*(3), 1–16. doi:10.4018/IJEBR.2016070101

Shams, S. M. (2016). Stakeholder Relationship Management in Online Business and Competitive Value Propositions: Evidence from the Sports Industry. *International Journal of Online Marketing*, *6*(2), 1–17. doi:10.4018/IJOM.2016040101

Shamsuzzoha, A. (2016). Management of Risk and Resilience within Collaborative Business Network. In R. Addo-Tenkorang, J. Kantola, P. Helo, & A. Shamsuzzoha (Eds.), *Supply Chain Strategies and the Engineer-to-Order Approach* (pp. 143–159). Hershey, PA: IGI Global. doi:10.4018/978-1-5225-0021-6.ch008

Shaqrah, A. A. (2018). Analyzing Business Intelligence Systems Based on 7s Model of McKinsey. *International Journal of Business Intelligence Research*, *9*(1), 53–63. doi:10.4018/IJBIR.2018010104

Sharma, A. J. (2017). Enhancing Sustainability through Experiential Learning in Management Education. In N. Baporikar (Ed.), *Management Education for Global Leadership* (pp. 256–274). Hershey, PA: IGI Global. doi:10.4018/978-1-5225-1013-0.ch013

Shetty, K. P. (2017). Responsible Global Leadership: Ethical Challenges in Management Education. In N. Baporikar (Ed.), *Innovation and Shifting Perspectives in Management Education* (pp. 194–223). Hershey, PA: IGI Global. doi:10.4018/978-1-5225-1019-2.ch009

Sinthupundaja, J., & Kohda, Y. (2017). Effects of Corporate Social Responsibility and Creating Shared Value on Sustainability. *International Journal of Sustainable Entrepreneurship and Corporate Social Responsibility*, *2*(1), 27–38. doi:10.4018/IJSECSR.2017010103

Škarica, I., & Hrgović, A. V. (2018). Implementation of Total Quality Management Principles in Public Health Institutes in the Republic of Croatia. *International Journal of Productivity Management and Assessment Technologies*, *6*(1), 1–16. doi:10.4018/IJPMAT.2018010101

Smuts, H., Kotzé, P., Van der Merwe, A., & Loock, M. (2017). Framework for Managing Shared Knowledge in an Information Systems Outsourcing Context. *International Journal of Knowledge Management*, *13*(4), 1–30. doi:10.4018/IJKM.2017100101

Soares, E. R., & Zaidan, F. H. (2016). Information Architecture and Business Modeling in Modern Organizations of Information Technology: Professional Career Plan in Organizations IT. In G. Jamil, J. Poças Rascão, F. Ribeiro, & A. Malheiro da Silva (Eds.), *Handbook of Research on Information Architecture and Management in Modern Organizations* (pp. 439–457). Hershey, PA: IGI Global. doi:10.4018/978-1-4666-8637-3.ch020

Sousa, M. J., Cruz, R., Dias, I., & Caracol, C. (2017). Information Management Systems in the Supply Chain. In G. Jamil, A. Soares, & C. Pessoa (Eds.), *Handbook of Research on Information Management for Effective Logistics and Supply Chains* (pp. 469–485). Hershey, PA: IGI Global. doi:10.4018/978-1-5225-0973-8.ch025

Spremic, M., Turulja, L., & Bajgoric, N. (2018). Two Approaches in Assessing Business Continuity Management Attitudes in the Organizational Context. In N. Bajgoric (Ed.), *Always-On Enterprise Information Systems for Modern Organizations* (pp. 159–183). Hershey, PA: IGI Global. doi:10.4018/978-1-5225-3704-5.ch008

Steenkamp, A. L. (2018). Some Insights in Computer Science and Information Technology. In *Examining the Changing Role of Supervision in Doctoral Research Projects: Emerging Research and Opportunities* (pp. 113–133). Hershey, PA: IGI Global. doi:10.4018/978-1-5225-2610-0.ch005

Studdard, N., Dawson, M., Burton, S. L., Jackson, N., Leonard, B., Quisenberry, W., & Rahim, E. (2016). Nurturing Social Entrepreneurship and Building Social Entrepreneurial Self-Efficacy: Focusing on Primary and Secondary Schooling to Develop Future Social Entrepreneurs. In Z. Fields (Ed.), *Incorporating Business Models and Strategies into Social Entrepreneurship* (pp. 154–175). Hershey, PA: IGI Global. doi:10.4018/978-1-4666-8748-6.ch010

Sun, Z. (2016). A Framework for Developing Management Intelligent Systems. *International Journal of Systems and Service-Oriented Engineering*, *6*(1), 37–53. doi:10.4018/IJSSOE.2016010103

Swami, B., & Mphele, G. T. (2016). Problems Preventing Growth of Small Entrepreneurs: A Case Study of a Few Small Entrepreneurs in Botswana Sub-Urban Areas. In N. Baporikar (Ed.), *Handbook of Research on Entrepreneurship in the Contemporary Knowledge-Based Global Economy* (pp. 479–508). Hershey, PA: IGI Global. doi:10.4018/978-1-4666-8798-1.ch020

Tabach, A., & Croteau, A. (2017). Configurations of Information Technology Governance Practices and Business Unit Performance. *International Journal of IT/Business Alignment and Governance*, *8*(2), 1–27. doi:10.4018/IJITBAG.2017070101

Talaue, G. M., & Iqbal, T. (2017). Assessment of e-Business Mode of Selected Private Universities in the Philippines and Pakistan. *International Journal of Online Marketing*, *7*(4), 63–77. doi:10.4018/IJOM.2017100105

Tam, G. C. (2017). Project Manager Sustainability Competence. In *Managerial Strategies and Green Solutions for Project Sustainability* (pp. 178–207). Hershey, PA: IGI Global. doi:10.4018/978-1-5225-2371-0.ch008

Tambo, T. (2018). Fashion Retail Innovation: About Context, Antecedents, and Outcome in Technological Change Projects. In I. Management Association (Ed.), Fashion and Textiles: Breakthroughs in Research and Practice (pp. 233-260). Hershey, PA: IGI Global. doi:10.4018/978-1-5225-3432-7.ch010

Tambo, T., & Mikkelsen, O. E. (2016). Fashion Supply Chain Optimization: Linking Make-to-Order Purchasing and B2B E-Commerce. In S. Joshi & R. Joshi (Eds.), *Designing and Implementing Global Supply Chain Management* (pp. 1–21). Hershey, PA: IGI Global. doi:10.4018/978-1-4666-9720-1.ch001

Tandon, K. (2016). Innovative Andragogy: The Paradigm Shift to Heutagogy. In S. Tiwari & L. Nafees (Eds.), *Innovative Management Education Pedagogies for Preparing Next-Generation Leaders* (pp. 238–257). Hershey, PA: IGI Global. doi:10.4018/978-1-4666-9691-4.ch014

Tantau, A. D., & Frăţilă, L. C. (2018). Information and Management System for Renewable Energy Business. In *Entrepreneurship and Business Development in the Renewable Energy Sector* (pp. 200–244). Hershey, PA: IGI Global. doi:10.4018/978-1-5225-3625-3.ch006

Teixeira, N., Pardal, P. N., & Rafael, B. G. (2018). Internationalization, Financial Performance, and Organizational Challenges: A Success Case in Portugal. In L. Carvalho (Ed.), *Handbook of Research on Entrepreneurial Ecosystems and Social Dynamics in a Globalized World* (pp. 379–423). Hershey, PA: IGI Global. doi:10.4018/978-1-5225-3525-6.ch017

Trad, A., & Kalpić, D. (2016). The E-Business Transformation Framework for E-Commerce Architecture-Modeling Projects. In I. Lee (Ed.), *Encyclopedia of E-Commerce Development, Implementation, and Management* (pp. 733–753). Hershey, PA: IGI Global. doi:10.4018/978-1-4666-9787-4.ch052

Trad, A., & Kalpić, D. (2016). The E-Business Transformation Framework for E-Commerce Control and Monitoring Pattern. In I. Lee (Ed.), *Encyclopedia of E-Commerce Development, Implementation, and Management* (pp. 754–777). Hershey, PA: IGI Global. doi:10.4018/978-1-4666-9787-4.ch053

Trad, A., & Kalpić, D. (2018). The Business Transformation Framework, Agile Project and Change Management. In M. Khosrow-Pour, D.B.A. (Ed.), Encyclopedia of Information Science and Technology, Fourth Edition (pp. 620-635). Hershey, PA: IGI Global. doi:10.4018/978-1-5225-2255-3.ch054

Trad, A., & Kalpić, D. (2018). The Business Transformation and Enterprise Architecture Framework: The Financial Engineering E-Risk Management and E-Law Integration. In B. Sergi, F. Fidanoski, M. Ziolo, & V. Naumovski (Eds.), *Regaining Global Stability After the Financial Crisis* (pp. 46–65). Hershey, PA: IGI Global. doi:10.4018/978-1-5225-4026-7.ch003

Turulja, L., & Bajgoric, N. (2018). Business Continuity and Information Systems: A Systematic Literature Review. In N. Bajgoric (Ed.), *Always-On Enterprise Information Systems for Modern Organizations* (pp. 60–87). Hershey, PA: IGI Global. doi:10.4018/978-1-5225-3704-5.ch004

van Wessel, R. M., de Vries, H. J., & Ribbers, P. M. (2016). Business Benefits through Company IT Standardization. In K. Jakobs (Ed.), *Effective Standardization Management in Corporate Settings* (pp. 34–53). Hershey, PA: IGI Global. doi:10.4018/978-1-4666-9737-9.ch003

Vargas-Hernández, J. G. (2017). Professional Integrity in Business Management Education. In N. Baporikar (Ed.), *Management Education for Global Leadership* (pp. 70–89). Hershey, PA: IGI Global. doi:10.4018/978-1-5225-1013-0.ch004

Vasista, T. G., & AlAbdullatif, A. M. (2017). Role of Electronic Customer Relationship Management in Demand Chain Management: A Predictive Analytic Approach. *International Journal of Information Systems and Supply Chain Management, 10*(1), 53–67. doi:10.4018/IJISSCM.2017010104

Vergidis, K. (2016). Rediscovering Business Processes: Definitions, Patterns, and Modelling Approaches. In P. Papajorgji, F. Pinet, A. Guimarães, & J. Papathanasiou (Eds.), *Automated Enterprise Systems for Maximizing Business Performance* (pp. 97–122). Hershey, PA: IGI Global. doi:10.4018/978-1-4666-8841-4.ch007

Vieru, D., & Bourdeau, S. (2017). Survival in the Digital Era: A Digital Competence-Based Multi-Case Study in the Canadian SME Clothing Industry. *International Journal of Social and Organizational Dynamics in IT*, *6*(1), 17–34. doi:10.4018/IJSODIT.2017010102

Vijayan, G., & Kamarulzaman, N. H. (2017). An Introduction to Sustainable Supply Chain Management and Business Implications. In M. Khan, M. Hussain, & M. Ajmal (Eds.), *Green Supply Chain Management for Sustainable Business Practice* (pp. 27–50). Hershey, PA: IGI Global. doi:10.4018/978-1-5225-0635-5.ch002

Vlachvei, A., & Notta, O. (2017). Firm Competitiveness: Theories, Evidence, and Measurement. In A. Vlachvei, O. Notta, K. Karantininis, & N. Tsounis (Eds.), *Factors Affecting Firm Competitiveness and Performance in the Modern Business World* (pp. 1–42). Hershey, PA: IGI Global. doi:10.4018/978-1-5225-0843-4.ch001

von Rosing, M., Fullington, N., & Walker, J. (2016). Using the Business Ontology and Enterprise Standards to Transform Three Leading Organizations. *International Journal of Conceptual Structures and Smart Applications*, *4*(1), 71–99. doi:10.4018/IJCSSA.2016010104

von Rosing, M., & von Scheel, H. (2016). Using the Business Ontology to Develop Enterprise Standards. *International Journal of Conceptual Structures and Smart Applications*, *4*(1), 48–70. doi:10.4018/IJCSSA.2016010103

Walczak, S. (2016). Artificial Neural Networks and other AI Applications for Business Management Decision Support. *International Journal of Sociotechnology and Knowledge Development*, *8*(4), 1–20. doi:10.4018/IJSKD.2016100101

Wamba, S. F., Akter, S., Kang, H., Bhattacharya, M., & Upal, M. (2016). The Primer of Social Media Analytics. *Journal of Organizational and End User Computing*, *28*(2), 1–12. doi:10.4018/JOEUC.2016040101

Wang, C., Schofield, M., Li, X., & Ou, X. (2017). Do Chinese Students in Public and Private Higher Education Institutes Perform at Different Level in One of the Leadership Skills: Critical Thinking?: An Exploratory Comparison. In V. Wang (Ed.), *Encyclopedia of Strategic Leadership and Management* (pp. 160–181). Hershey, PA: IGI Global. doi:10.4018/978-1-5225-1049-9.ch013

Wang, F., Raisinghani, M. S., Mora, M., & Wang, X. (2016). Strategic E-Business Management through a Balanced Scored Card Approach. In I. Lee (Ed.), *Encyclopedia of E-Commerce Development, Implementation, and Management* (pp. 361–386). Hershey, PA: IGI Global. doi:10.4018/978-1-4666-9787-4.ch027

Wang, J. (2017). Multi-Agent based Production Management Decision System Modelling for the Textile Enterprise. *Journal of Global Information Management, 25*(4), 1–15. doi:10.4018/JGIM.2017100101

Wiedemann, A., & Gewald, H. (2017). Examining Cross-Domain Alignment: The Correlation of Business Strategy, IT Management, and IT Business Value. *International Journal of IT/Business Alignment and Governance, 8*(1), 17–31. doi:10.4018/IJITBAG.2017010102

Wolf, R., & Thiel, M. (2018). Advancing Global Business Ethics in China: Reducing Poverty Through Human and Social Welfare. In S. Hipsher (Ed.), *Examining the Private Sector's Role in Wealth Creation and Poverty Reduction* (pp. 67–84). Hershey, PA: IGI Global. doi:10.4018/978-1-5225-3117-3.ch004

Wu, J., Ding, F., Xu, M., Mo, Z., & Jin, A. (2016). Investigating the Determinants of Decision-Making on Adoption of Public Cloud Computing in E-government. *Journal of Global Information Management, 24*(3), 71–89. doi:10.4018/JGIM.2016070104

Xu, L., & de Vrieze, P. (2016). Building Situational Applications for Virtual Enterprises. In I. Lee (Ed.), *Encyclopedia of E-Commerce Development, Implementation, and Management* (pp. 715–724). Hershey, PA: IGI Global. doi:10.4018/978-1-4666-9787-4.ch050

Yablonsky, S. (2018). Innovation Platforms: Data and Analytics Platforms. In *Multi-Sided Platforms (MSPs) and Sharing Strategies in the Digital Economy: Emerging Research and Opportunities* (pp. 72–95). Hershey, PA: IGI Global. doi:10.4018/978-1-5225-5457-8.ch003

Yusoff, A., Ahmad, N. H., & Halim, H. A. (2017). Agropreneurship among Gen Y in Malaysia: The Role of Academic Institutions. In N. Ahmad, T. Ramayah, H. Halim, & S. Rahman (Eds.), *Handbook of Research on Small and Medium Enterprises in Developing Countries* (pp. 23–47). Hershey, PA: IGI Global. doi:10.4018/978-1-5225-2165-5.ch002

Zanin, F., Comuzzi, E., & Costantini, A. (2018). The Effect of Business Strategy and Stock Market Listing on the Use of Risk Assessment Tools. In *Management Control Systems in Complex Settings: Emerging Research and Opportunities* (pp. 145–168). Hershey, PA: IGI Global. doi:10.4018/978-1-5225-3987-2.ch007

Zgheib, P. W. (2017). Corporate Innovation and Intrapreneurship in the Middle East. In P. Zgheib (Ed.), *Entrepreneurship and Business Innovation in the Middle East* (pp. 37–56). Hershey, PA: IGI Global. doi:10.4018/978-1-5225-2066-5.ch003

About the Contributors

Anna Visvizi is Associate Professor at Deree – The American College of Greece and Visiting Researcher at Effat University, Jeddah, Saudi Arabia. A political scientist and economist, editor and research consultant, with an extensive experience in academia and the think-tank sector, Dr. Visvizi presented her work in many forums across Europe and the US, including Capitol Hill. A practiced team-worker, researcher, analyst and lecturer, Dr. Visvizi's expertise spans the following interrelated areas of research: political economy; migration; smart cities; innovation, competitiveness and policy-making, with the geographical focus of her research defined by the EU, China, and the Arab World.

Miltiadis D. Lytras is Associate Professor at Deree – The American College of Greece, with a research focus on semantic web, knowledge management and e-learning, with more than 100 publications. He has co-edited more than 45 special issues in International Journals (IEEE Transaction on Knowledge and Data Engineering, IEEE Internet Computing, IEEE Transactions on Education, Computers in Human Behaviour, Interactive Learning Environments, Journal of Knowledge Management, Journal of Computer Assisted Learning) and has authored/[co-]edited 42 books [e.g. Open Source for Knowledge and Learning Management, Ubiquitous and Pervasive Knowledge Management, Intelligent Learning Infrastructures for Knowledge Intensive Organizations, Semantic Web Based Information Systems, China Information Technology Handbook, Real World Applications of Semantic Web and Ontologies, Web 2.0: The Business Model, etc]. He (has) serves(ed) as the (Co) Editor in Chief of 8 international journals [e.g. International Journal on Semantic Web and Information Systems, International Journal of Knowledge Society Research, International Journal of Knowledge and Learning, International Journal of Technology Enhanced Learning].

***

Wadee Alhalabi received the Ph.D. degree in electrical and computer engineering from the University of Miami, Coral Gables, FL, in 2008. He joined the Department of Computer Science, King Abdulaziz University, in 2010, as an Assistant Professor where he is now Associate Professor. In 2010, he became an Active Researcher with Effat University. He has authored over 50 journal and conference articles. His research interests include image processing, machine learning, data analytics and the application of virtual reality in the medical field.

Bryan Christiansen is the Chief Executive Officer of Global Research Society, LLC in Michigan, USA. A former business lecturer at universities in Russia, Turkey, and the USA, he has traveled to 41 countries where he has conducted international business since 1985 in multiple languages and various industries with Global 500 firms and smaller. Christiansen received his Bachelor of Science degree in Marketing at the University of the State of New York in 1996 and his MBA degree at Capella University in 2003. The author of 26 Scopus-indexed Reference books on business, cultural studies, economics, and psychology, he is fluent in Chinese, Japanese, Spanish, and Turkish. Christiansen is currently working with a Russian theoretical mathematician on a new economic model for developing nations.

Kwok Tai Chui received the B.Eng. degree in electronic and communication engineering - Business Intelligence Minor from and Ph.D. degree from City University of Hong Kong in 2013 and 2017 respectively. His research interests include artificial intelligence, data analytics, wireless communication, pattern recognition, healthcare, machine learning algorithms and optimization. He was the recipient of 2nd Prize Award (Postgraduate Category) of 2014 IEEE Region 10 Student Paper Contest. Also, he received Best Paper Award in IEEE The International Conference on Consumer Electronics-China, in both 2014 and 2015. He has more than 40 research publications including edited books, book chapters, journal papers and conference papers. He has served as various editorial positions and guest editors in referred international journals and conferences.

Ahu Coşkun Özer was born in Istanbul in 1981, graduated from Marmara University with a bachelor's degree in 2004, graduated from Marmara University with a master's degree in theory of economics in 2007. In 2012, Dr. Özer graduated from Ph.D. in Istanbul University, started to work as a research assistant in 2011, has been working as an assistant professor for 5 years at the Marmara University Vocational School of Social Sciences in Foreign Trade Program. Her research areas are international economics, foreign trade, international political economy, economics, business, and entrepreneurship.

Muhammad Khalil Khan is a Postdoctoral Research Fellow in the College of Media and International Culture, Zhejiang University, Hangzhou, China. He earned his Ph.D. in journalism and communication from Zhejiang University and was awarded the honorary credential of "Outstanding International Graduate" of Zhejiang University in 2017. His research has been published in high-impact-factor SSCI journals (e.g., Journalism and Mass Communication Quarterly) and has also been presented at academic conferences in the United States, Czech Republic, Turkey, Hong Kong, and China. His research interest focuses on China's Belt and Road Initiative, social media effects, strategic communication, and international communication.

Ryan Wen Liu received the B.Sc. degree from the Department of Mathematics, Wuhan University of Technology, Wuhan, China, in 2009, and the Ph.D. degree from The Chinese University of Hong Kong, Hong Kong, in 2015. He is currently an Associate Professor with the School of Navigation, Wuhan University of Technology. His research interests mainly include computational transportation science, image processing, computer vision, and machine learning. He was the Session Chair of the IEEE International Conference on Systems, Man, and Cybernetics in 2015.

Patricia Ordóñez de Pablos is a Professor in the Department of Business Administration in the Faculty of Economics and Business at the University of Oviedo, Spain. Her teaching and research interests focus on the areas of strategic management, knowledge management, intellectual capital, organizational learning, human resources management, information technologies, semantic web, Asia (Bhutan, China, Myanmar), higher education and mobile and distance education. She serves as the Editor-in-Chief of International Journal of Asian Business and Information and Journal of Science and Technology Policy Management.

Cornelius B. Pratt is a professor in the Lew Klein College of Media and Communication at Temple University, USA. He is also a professor in the School of Journalism and Communication at Guangdong University of Foreign Studies, Guangzhou, China. His research focuses on communication for national and regional development, particularly in emerging economies; on international and strategic communication; and on crisis communication. He holds a Ph.D. from the University of Minnesota—Twin Cities, USA.

Saleh Shahriar is a researcher at the College of Economics and Management, Northwest A&F University, Yangling, China. He is a recipient of the prestigious Chinese Government Scholarship to carry out his PhD research program. His research interests include, but are not limited to, the Belt and Road Initiative, International trade, comparative border studies, and good governance. He is the author of a research book, entitled, Understanding China's Belt & Road Initiative: The Institutional Economics Approach (2019). He contributed to a number of peer reviewed international journals, and presented papers in the international conferences. His recent 2019 paper has appeared in the Emerging Market Finance and Trade (SSCI), and forthcoming papers are in production stage for the Territory, Politics, Governance (SSCI); and the Asian Journal of Political Science (ESCI).

Konstantinos Skampagiannis is a Junior year student at Deree – The American College of Greece, studying in the field of Management Information Systems. At the same time he is a certified SAP Business Process Integration Associate Consultant in SAP S/4 HANA applications currently working as a SAP Security Junior Engineer in TITAN Cement Company SA. Additionally, he is the President of the Management Information Systems Society. Lastly, he is a junior academic researched having presented a paper in the 4th International Conference on Data Processing and Applications titled "Data Mining Emotions for Targeted Advertising" at the age of 20.

Effnu Subiyanto is a professional in PT Semen Indonesia (Persero) Tbk, once of the biggest State-owned cement companies in Indonesia for over than 25 years. He earned a bachelor in electrical engineering, master's degree in business strategic from Gadjah Mada University, and doctoral degree in economics from Airlangga University and graduated in 2016. He is especially expert and productive as opinion maker in Indonesia with about over than 600 articles published since 2008. This chapter is his first contribution as he recently has joined academia and is interested in becoming a researcher. He has proposed to hold a research on transports and logistics, economics, and various subjects relating with infrastructure projects. He is now serving as a post-graduate lecturer at the Widya Mandala Surabaya Catholic University in Indonesia.

Anna Maria Tavanli is a senior student at Deree College – The American College of Greece. Ms Tavanli pursues her BA degree in International Business. Her research was conducted in the framework of B-in-EU, i.e. Jean Monnet Module On European Union And Active EU Citizenship For Business Students: An Interdisciplinary Approach, coordinated by Dr. Anna Visvizi, co-funded by the European Commission under the Erasmus+ Jean Monnet funding scheme [Project Reference: 587632-EPP-1-2017-1-US-EPPJMO-MODULE].

Index

J

K

L

M

N

O

P

R

S

T

W

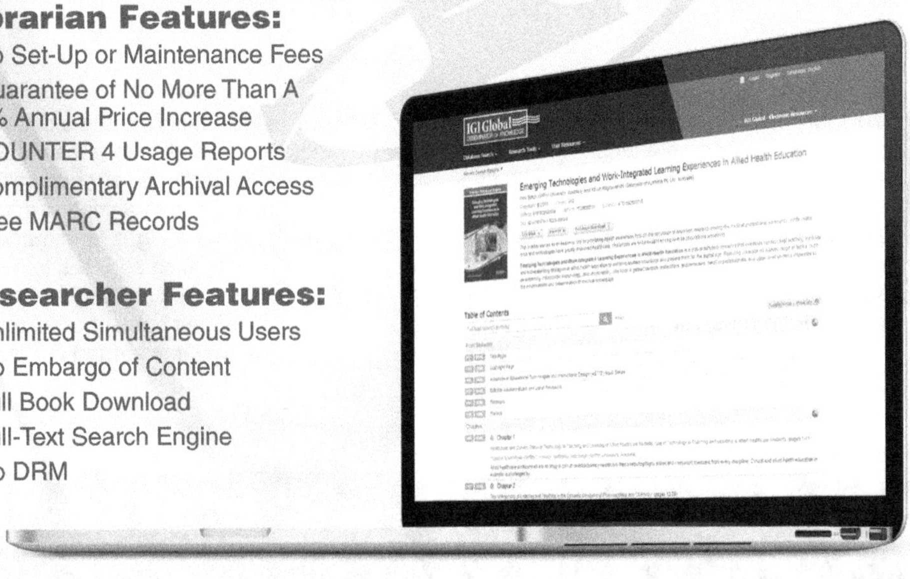

www.ingramcontent.com/pod-product-compliance
Lightning Source LLC
LaVergne TN
LVHW081331021026
849161LV00008BA/1933